W9-AUV-577

The Consumer and Corporate Accountability

edited by Ralph Nader

The Consumer and Corporate Accountability

HARCOURT BRACE JOVANOVICH, INC.

New York / Chicago / San Francisco / Atlanta

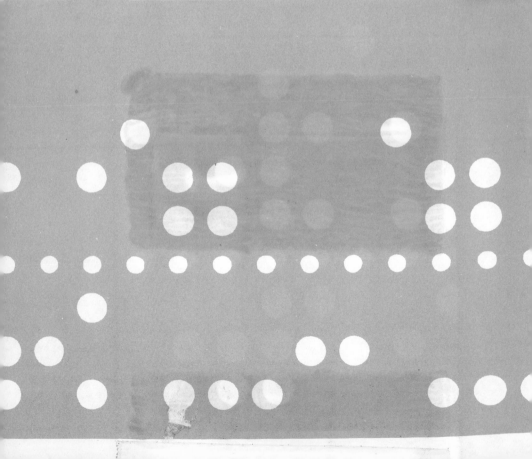

The Consumer and Corporate Accountability

edited by Ralph Nader

Center for the Study of Responsive Law, Washington, D.C.
with the assistance of Jean Carper

PHOTOGRAPH ACKNOWLEDGMENTS

   1 Harbrace by Erik Arnesen
 50 Harbrace by Erik Arnesen
 86 Harbrace
126 Harbrace
176 Magnum by Burt Glinn
214 Harbrace by Erik Arnesen
254 Harbrace by Erik Arnesen
290 Harbrace by Erik Arnesen
310 Harbrace by Erik Arnesen

ISBN: 0-15-513461-2

Library of Congress Catalog Card Number: 72-94552

Printed in the United States of America

PREFACE

Corporate irresponsibility is a compelling subject for study on today's campus. The complex and pervasive nature of corporate behavior affects every citizen in countless ways. And as the pieces in this book suggest, much corporate behavior is harmful and unjust; clearly we cannot yet relegate the dusty maxim *caveat emptor* to the history books.

The issues and problems touched on in this book do not constitute a complete nor even comprehensive survey of consumer ills. But all these problems possess a common denominator—they can no longer be ignored. Moreover, intelligent and just solutions must emanate from students of business, economics, political science, sociology, and law, among others. Although our concern with pollution, unsafe products, false advertising, and the myriad other socio-economic problems of our time seems to be increasing, the debate over their remedy is still too often uninformed, the plans for their correction still too often compromised at the expense of the consumer.

One of the best stimulants to creative solutions for some of our problems is to ask automatically how injustice can be remedied and conditions improved. It is hoped that the readings here will contribute to the kind of critical awareness required of any intelligent consumer who must cope—as we all must—with the day-to-day business of preserving and improving the quality of our society.

I would like to thank Jean Carper for her able editorial assistance in preparing this book.

Ralph Nader

v

CONTENTS

INTRODUCTION

We are seldom judged by our consumer expertise. In fact, most of us would not know where to begin in forming such a judgment. But why not? Most people spend many hours each week earning a salary so they will have the means to purchase goods and services in the marketplace. If that is a major reason for working, then it should also be a major reason for thinking about how to make the fruits of such labor return a higher quality of living.

In this age of big business, camouflaged services, pre-packaged goods, and impersonal distribution and billing systems, knowing what you buy and what you pay for is not easy. But that is not the only problem confronting the consumer. Many Congressional hearings, court cases, investigative reports, and industry whistleblowers have revealed to a dismayed public that hazardous products, monopolistic practices, endlessly clever frauds, overpricing, and swindles run rampant through the economy with very little law enforcement to deter them. The costs in diminished health, safety, and consumer income are massive, as the articles in this volume document so well. And too, unscrupulous business practices give an unfair economic advantage to the unethical businessman and make honest practices unprofitable.

After years of detailed hearings on corporate crime and other mistreatment of the consumer, Senator Philip Hart, Chairman of the Senate Subcommittee on Antitrust and Monopoly, estimated in 1969 that about 25 percent of the consumer dollar receives no value. That totals approximately $200 billion a year! When this waste and fraud are added to the preventable fatalities and injuries which occur because of dangerous automobiles, drugs, household products, flammable fabrics, medical malpractice, and a score of other consumer hazards, it becomes clear that a social and economic emergency prevails. We are not warned of this state of emergency because it is a profitable climate for its sponsors in the business community. When the polluting byproducts of producing goods and services—the lethal chemicals, gases and particulates—result, as they do, in massive compulsory consumption which leads to diseases such as cancer, emphysema, and other ailments, the situation becomes even more precarious. But all this, serious as it is and has been, pales before the prospect for the next generation as the risk levels of consumer and environmental technology (e.g., nuclear power plants and their wastes) threaten the very foundation of organized society. The tender balance between human beings and their environment can be destroyed by the chemical, radioactive, and biological devastations of a tunnel-visioned industrial juggernaut. And the gross national product of our economy can continue to grow without reducing or preventing many of our domestic problems such as unemployment, housing, hunger, poverty, discrimination, mass transit inadequacies, medical needs, crime, and waste.

The examples, case studies, and other material in the following pages will make concrete what these conditions mean for peoples' everyday lives. These experiences may relate to similar ones which you have undergone in one form or another. But empathy does not lead necessarily to incisive thinking about these problems. That is the quest of this book: to make thinking about consumer problems a way of developing analytic skills which connect seemingly separate phenomena into an integrated understanding so as to help prepare you to live wisely and to use more fully your democratic rights as a citizen.

Consumer education, then, can help to develop a variety of life skills and steadfast personal traits through a daily relating of knowing and doing. Many common experiences become relevant material for studies in consumer education: for example, watching television advertisements, purchasing auto insurance, having your automobile repaired, going to your dentist or doctor, buying books at the bookstore and food at the cafeteria, selecting clothes and cosmetics, dealing with your landlord, or obtaining a loan. How rare it is for most people to reflect on these incidents, and to perfect their critical capacities for evaluating any imperfections and consequences. Analyzing real-life problems in classroom and field work exercises is not only practical in saving money and anguish; it is likely to stimulate you to make such judgment part of your normal reactions to future problems long after the final examination.

One educator used to apply his "Five Year Out Test" to the subjects he taught. He would ask himself before each class "Of what benefit will this material be to the student five years hence?" He did not speak of trade schools or training in the manual arts. He referred to that challenge to the student which conquers boredom, compels attention, enhances the desire as well as the ability to make distinctions and connections between facts, events and principles, and cultivates a sense of justice in the context of real problems and solutions to life's little and big dilemmas. What makes consumer education so fulfilling is how it can bring the world to the classroom and the classroom to the world. One useful technique is to become involved in an experience which starts with perception, moves to awareness, evolves into abstraction, and matures toward judgment.

Take, for instance, a commonplace observation—the front bumper of an automobile. Nearly everyday most people casually or unconsciously look at car bumpers. Their view usually stops there. A few moments of consumer education would open the following sequence: Bumpers are supposed to protect automobiles from minor property damage in minor collisions. For many years, however, bumper design has been largely ornamental: bumpers have been recessed and of different heights for different models. Much needless property damage has resulted when cars bumped or crashed at two, three, five, or eight miles per hour. Such damage costs U.S. motorists over one billion dollars a year. Insurance premiums rise as a consequence. More replacement parts, such as fender sectors, grille segments, and headlights have to be produced. More coal, steel, glass, plastic, and other raw materials must be used, and more electricity and fuel expended. Prices of these commodities mount. Pollution of the air and water increases. What consumers spend on bumper repair, they do not spend on other goods and services which they might otherwise have purchased, and so reduce their standard of living as they would have it. Why did the auto companies design such bumpers? It is obvious that they knew how to do better, judging from the models of some fifty years ago, if not from the last generation's advances in technology. Could it be that the companies profited by faulty design and covered their actions by promoting the aesthetics of egg-shell bumpers? Why not write and ask these companies? Why did the auto insurance companies take so long to expose the facts and criticize the auto industry? Why not write and ask insurance companies, government auto safety agencies, university research institutes, and other sources for facts and viewpoints? Why do auto companies now promise to build more protective bumpers in future vehicles? How did this process of change get underway?

A sequential analysis of this kind can be made on literally hundreds of ordinary experiences and observations. Actual projects can be undertaken such as sampling different supermarkets to determine whether different prices are charged for exactly the same food items, as has been found to be the case.* Watching television for a few

---

*For examples of such consumer projects, see Action for a Change, Second Edition, by Ralph Nader and Donald Ross (New York: Grossman, 1972).

evenings to record a variety of advertisements describing consumer products and service lines can be followed by an analysis of the emotional appeals, factual claims, and other devices employed to imprint the desirability of the products on the viewer's mind. Attempts at verification by writing to the presidents of the companies sponsoring the ads can provide additional information and increase your awareness about the nature of the economy, the quality of competition, and the susceptibilities of people. The breakfast cereal, soft drink, cosmetic, pain reliever, auto, tire, detergent, and insurance ads spring from a knowledge of applied social science that deserves study and evaluation from many sides.

Once the zest and skill for acquiring hard-to-get information is developed, the very process of seeking generates an understanding of citizen rights, remedies, and participation in decisions that affect everyone. Institutions, from government agencies to corporations, become household names—as indeed they and their leaders should be. Hearing the names of companies such as General Motors, Standard Oil, Dupont, Citibank, and Prudential should stimulate more than images of products and brand names; it should stimulate us to an awareness of the obligations these companies have to their customers, to their workers, and to the government agencies which regulate them. These obligations are part of the relationships of fairness and justice which we must understand if we are to understand the respective obligations of citizenship in a democratic society. The same should hold true for such agencies as the Department of Transportation, the Interstate Commerce Commission, the Federal Power Commission, state public utilities, insurance and banking agencies, and so forth. Their purpose is to serve the public interest. How they actually operate is a subject for consumer education involvement. I stress the word "involvement," rather than "study," for such closeness to the operations of government exposes the reality, the diversity, the strengths, and weaknesses of both government and student-citizens. This process has worked very well in several courses in Washington, D.C. law schools where students petition federal agencies to remedy abuses, investigate problems, or be more fair to ordinary consumers. They learn the law by using it to win or lose important cases in consumer protection.

On a less specialized scale, students in consumer education courses can learn about consumer rights and remedies and how to use them. The law must be demystified so that it will relate to our understanding of citizenship in a democratic legal order. The average citizen frequently encounters the law—on the highway, at street signs, with loans, warranties, taxes, buying, selling, and employment. It is time to take the mumbo jumbo out of the law and make the law a part of liberal education starting at least at the high school level. If we expect strong citizen effort to defend or advance people's rights and promote justice, then general knowledge of the law and how citizens can activate the law is necessary.

For example, with the intensity and velocity of interrelationships affecting people in our society, there is a grossly inadequate system of resolving complaints at the community, state, and federal levels. Whether it is the pollution from a nearby factory, the unfair enforcement of property tax, the fraudulent door-to-door salesman, the auto or television repair abuses, the evasive practices of banks or finance companies, or the various government agencies which are supposed to protect or serve the consumer but do not, the ordinary citizen hardly knows how and where to complain—and with good reason. Most of the time there is no one who will listen to complaints and act on them. So, in reading the articles in this volume, you may begin to ask: Who *can* use the legal system? Is it an overpriced system when most Americans with consumer complaints about damages under $1,000 cannot resort to it without great sacrifice? Are most Americans who suffer from innumerable small and large injustices effectively shut out of the courts and the agencies which hear and resolve disputes with the companies which manufacture or sell goods and services?

There are, indeed, other questions to ask as you read these articles and statements about consumer injustice and its serious erosion of people's health, safety, income, and general pursuit of happiness:

1. Who were the movers in the action or condition described?
2. What were their powers and advantages?
3. What was the nature of the adverse impact on the aggrieved consumers? Was this impact channeled openly and directly, or secretly and indirectly?
4. How long did the abuse seem to go undetected and why? Who or what made the difference in achieving disclosure?
5. How would you apportion responsibility for what happened? Is it happening between individuals within institutions, or between institutions themselves, or in the interaction of the two?
6. How relevant are the following factors: nefarious intent, indifference, negligence, greed, pressure of one measure of achievement or performance over another?
7. How would you have changed matters if you were in charge? Suppose you weren't in charge, how would you mobilize consumer concern and what would you recommend to prevent such abuses in the future?
8. What is ethical whistleblowing and how can it be justified by religious, ethical, professional, or law-abiding principles? How important is it to preserve and defend the freedom of employees at all levels of government and corporate institutions so

they may use ethical whistleblowing as a last resort to protect the innocent and expose rooted injustice? What are the costs to society and individual conscience if ethical whistleblowing is *not* possible?

9. What would you have done if you were one party or the other in the various events described?

You should be able to think of dozens more insightful inquiries after reading each section. The diversity of subjects which consumer education touches—economics, health, politics, psychology, sociology, regulation, marketing, advertising, finance, engineering, science, et cetera—should draw a diversity of reactions from those specializing or hoping to specialize in these areas. The unity of knowledge stimulated by consumer study and the exposure to such diverse contributions should reduce the overspecialization and academic pigeonholing that too often prevails.

Any process of education which relates intimately to our daily experiences will provide an exciting bridge between knowing and doing. If this process spurs you to think about the human relationships which center around the quality of life and to interconnect abstract principles with concrete facts, you are likely to become a freer person: one who has learned the sweet secret of self-education through citizen engagement. If consumer education has a common theme, it is to assist the student in appreciating that consumer issues are not just individual issues, but social issues as well. A more just society is at stake here. The legal philosopher, Edmund Cahn, wrote that to have a sense of justice, one must develop a sense of injustice. The selections in this book should provide you with ample material to refine your own sensitivity to injustice.

Ralph Nader

1

CHALLENGE TO POWER

Art Buchwald, syndicated newspaper columnist and well-known satirist, once put the problem precisely, if in exaggerated form. It was 1978 and, according to Buchwald's prescience, corporate power had become so concentrated in the United States that, after numerous mergers, only two corporations remained: Samson Securities west of the Mississippi and the Delilah Company east of the Mississippi. Still, in the "public interest," these two giants desired to merge leaving but a single corporation in the entire country. After lengthy discussions the Antitrust Division in the Department of Justice approved the merger. Buchwald's piece ends with this announcement from the attorney general:

While we find drawbacks to only one company being left in the United States, we feel the advantages to the public far outweigh the disadvantages.

Therefore, we're making an exception in this case and allowing Samson and Delilah to merge.

I would like to announce that the Samson and Delilah Company is now negotiating at the White House with the President to buy the United States. The Justice Department will naturally study this merger to see if it violates any of our strong antitrust laws.

When Buchwald wrote that in 1966, the consumer movement still belonged to a few "radicals," the word "consumerism" was openly ridiculed in the circles of corporate power, and it is probable that few of his readers reflected seriously on the fact that the country already was so dominated by corporate power, be it by two hundred corporations instead of Buchwald's fictional one, that substantial control over people's lives already had passed into corporate hands. Even further from most people's minds at that time was the understanding that the new consumer revolution then starting was inextricably connected to the irresponsible use of that corporate power.

The consumer movement, which is now acknowledged as one of the most significant social movements in this century, was deceptively modest in its origins. It began on many fronts, but always concerned itself with the manifestations of corporate power which daily touched people's lives: unsafe automobiles, dangerously adulterated and filthy food, overpriced drugs, hidden credit charges, and the reckless use of pesticides. These issues, taken separately, were not generally perceived to be a concerted attack against a common opponent, the nearly limitless power of big business. Even so, it was a novel approach. The previous targets of consumer protectors had been the "bad apples in the barrel," the fly-by-nights, the few who polluted the honest business atmosphere and spoiled it for legitimate businessmen. This was a myth that business, through such organizations as the Better Business Bureau, cultivated assiduously. It was, therefore, a monumental shock to the business guardians of this myth when they were exposed as the rottenest apples of all. Consumer advocates began to document that consumers were defrauded, injured, and manipulated not by the corner gyp market but by the largest business entities in the world: the U.S. blue-chip business firms such as General Motors, Ford, Union Carbide, General Foods, and the mammoth pharmaceutical firms. It was a new concept, a new emphasis which, as business knew, could only lead to more alarming exposures and more probing questions. It was a strike at the heart of business criminality, and irresponsibility, it was an unprecedented challenge to corporate power.

t is at this stage we find ourselves today. The consumer revolt has matured with the realization that consumer reforms cannot be separated from corporate reforms; they are two sides of the same coin. Consumer discontent and abuses flow from the unbridled power corporations have over the marketplace and the government.

What is the extent of that corporate power, the scope of its impact on life, death, and the pocketbook, and precisely what are the abuses to which it subjects us? The first two selections in this book lay a foundation for understanding how far-reaching and penetrating our challenge to corporate power must be. For the November 21, 1968 issue of the *New York Review of Books,* I wrote an article titled "The Great American Gyp" that analyzed the status of the consumer movement at the time and outlined ten needed reforms. The introductory piece to this book, "A Citizen's Guide to the American Economy," is a fresh and up-dated look at the evolution of the consumer movement. It expands the concept of consumer justice and contends that consumers are obviously cheated by overpriced, shoddy, worthless and sometimes harmful goods, but also that they are victimized by more subtle forces in the corporate economy such as price-fixing, lack of effective competition, corporate tax privileges, and compulsory consumption of air pollution: problems which until recently have rarely been examined or considered front-line issues in the conflict between corporations and consumers.

n the second selection, the Prologue to their book *America, Inc.,* an exciting and damning indictment of arbitrary corporate power, Morton Mintz, a reporter for the *Washington Post,* and Jerry S. Cohen, former chief counsel of the Senate Anti-Trust and Monopoly Subcommittee, warn us of the extent of the danger we suffer from corporations by documenting the pervasive corporate influence. The authors characterize Big Business as a form of government unto itself, without elected representatives, but which, like a government, can impose the equivalent of taxes, destroy or limit livelihoods, adversely affect the quality of life and the environment, and dominate the constitutional governments it resembles. Much of what is called big government today derives from or services large industries and business. In other words, Mintz and Cohen contend, as Buchwald only fictionalized, that the large corporations already essentially "own and operate the United States."

The challenge to that corporate state must be then, as it is with other authoritarian institutions, to devise the economic and political machinery necessary to regain control of our individual and collective futures.

A CITIZEN'S GUIDE TO THE AMERICAN ECONOMY

Ralph Nader

This year the gross national product of the United States will exceed one trillion dollars, while the economy will fail to meet a great many urgent human needs. This contrast between the statistics of growth and the fact of economic deprivation in America has become more and more evident to the public during the past decade—especially in such dramatic cases as that of the medical care industry, which has received vastly higher payments from both the government and patients, while the quality of medical care itself remains unchanged or has become worse. Indeed, the quality of life is deteriorating in so many ways that the traditional statistical measurements of the "standard of living" according to personal income, housing, ownership of cars and appliances, etc., have come to sound increasingly phony.

Nevertheless the methods used to understand the economic system have remained rigid ones. The current analyses of and arguments about "national income levels," "inflation," and "government spending" do little to trace the precise ways in which the operations of the economy affect the life of the consumer. Nor do such analyses

From *The New York Review of Books*, 2 September 1971. Reprinted with permission from *The New York Review of Books*. Copyright © 1971 The New York Review Inc.

make political judgments or assign responsibilities so as to effectively change the consumer's situation. We have all heard arguments about the need to change national priorities in allocating public funds for defense, health, education, welfare, pollution control, etc. But such proposals have so far failed to take account of the ways in which portions of reallocated public funds may be siphoned off or misused before any are used for the purposes originally intended.

The impact on our lives of the largest economic force of all, the corporate economy, has been badly neglected. Most formal inquiries into a more just and efficient use of national wealth have failed to measure how the citizen's dollars are being wasted and depreciated in the market place and his taxes converted into corporate property and income. Instead these studies focus mainly on "aggregate consumer spending" without asking specifically what consumers receive in return.

What are needed now are analyses of the corporate economy that will do what economists for the most part have failed to do: show how corporations, by their control of both the market and government, have been able to divert scarce resources to uses that have little human benefit or are positively harmful. Such studies will have to take account of facts that economists now tend to ignore because they find them untidy or because they cannot fit them into prevailing economic theory. But as they are carried out, they will show the folly of pouring more dollars into the sieve of an irresponsible corporate system.

To encourage more inquiry into the institutionalized abuses of unchecked corporate power, I would like to outline some of the major categories in which the abuses fall and to give a few of the many possible examples of how they work. I call these categories "sub-economies." In each case, the consumer's dollars are inexcusably wasted or his taxes misused.

1. *The involuntary sub-economy.* By this I mean the billions that consumers would not have paid if they knew or could control what they were getting, or if corporations observed elementary standards of honesty, safety, and utility in producing and selling the things that are bought. Consumers are now spending billions of dollars for products sold under false pretenses: meat and poultry that are adulterated with fat and water; patent medicines, mouthwashes, and "aids" to beauty and diet that do far less than they are said to do or nothing at all. Both the Food and Drug Administration and the National Academy of Sciences have compiled lists of drugs, patent medicines,

and mouthwashes that are valueless for the purposes they advertise and often harmful as well, as in the case of certain antibiotics.

Worthless drugs alone cost consumers one billion dollars a year. The Federal Trade Commission estimates that another billion is wasted on fraudulently sold home improvements or repairs. Last February, Senator Philip Hart of Michigan had this to say about worthless auto repairs:

> American consumers spend 25 to 30 billion dollars a year on auto repair. Various studies on the quality of the work were presented to us. They rated the poor, unneeded, or not done work at amounts ranging from 36 per cent to 99 per cent. Even taking the low figure, that means consumers are wasting 8 to 10 billion dollars that they lay out for auto repair yearly.

Equally flagrant is the short-weighting, short-counting, and short-measuring of consumer purchases that were the subject of a report in the *Wall Street Journal* last month. "The pennies add up fast enough," the *Journal* said, "that estimates by state officials of the total US loss from short-weighting start at $1.5 billion a year and rise to as high as $10 billion a year."

All these expenses—and I could list many more—were clearly involuntary: the consumers did not get what they thought they were paying for.

Quite as serious are what might be called "secondary consumer expenditures": the consumer may get something he wants, such as a car, but its defects are such as to force him to incur more costs. The fragile recessed bumpers of most automobiles are a case in point. Collisions at under ten miles per hour have been costing $2 billion a year for damages that could easily have been avoided if these cars had had effective bumpers.

What might be called the "accident-injury industry," composed of companies and professionals providing insurance and medical, legal, and repair services, is now being paid about $12 billion a year. When emergencies occur these services are of course needed; but in fact many of them would not have to be paid for at all if cars were sensibly and safely designed, as could be done without increasing the over-all cost of making cars. Nor would a large proportion of auto repair costs be as expensive or even necessary if key parts were not so inaccessible and fragile, or so constructed that a small defect requires replacement of an entire large unit of the car.

By now some of these involuntary expenditures imposed by the auto industry have become fairly familiar. Less well understood is the way in which many different products, including packaged food, soft drinks, and gasoline, are sold through incredibly expensive advertising of their brand names for which the consumer must bear the cost, but for which he receives nothing of additional value. The staff of Senator Hart's anti-trust committee estimates, moreover, that deceptive packaging and promotion in the food industry alone are causing consumers to lose $14 billion a year, for example, by pushing the large "economy" sized boxes of food that in fact cost more per unit than medium sized boxes. Of course such expenses would not be involuntary for consumers who could set up their own experimental kitchens and prowl the supermarkets with scales and slide rules. But most families are simply duped.

Until recently the involuntary sub-economy I have been describing has been the main concern of the consumer movement. The movement has had some limited success in improving regulatory action against deceptive sales practices and the safety standards of some products, notably cars, and in encouraging private litigation. Its main achievement has been to create an awareness among consumers that they are being gypped and endangered. But it has yet to devise the economic and political machinery that will counterbalance or deplete the power of corporations to impose involuntary expenditures. Meanwhile, however, the drive for consumer justice is extending its emphasis to less visible parts of the corporate economy where political influence, corporate backscratching, and the structure of industry itself all work to victimize the public, as we shall see by examining other sub-economies.

2. It is in the *transfer sub-economy,* for example, that the prices for goods and services may rise unconscionably as they move from the supplier of raw materials to the manufacturer, and then to the wholesaler, the retailer, and the consumer. The announcement of a price increase by the steel, aluminum, and copper industries concerns the White House economists far more than would a sudden increase in retail prices. It is not simply that a rise in the price of steel will cause a rise in the price of steel products. The economists know that such increases will escalate sharply as they pass from one shared monopoly or oligopoly of steel buyers and sellers to another, until they reach the consumer who may well have to buy his car or stove from an "exclusive dealer." To the extent that such price rises are unchecked by effective competition, consumer bargaining, public exposure, or government anti-trust standards at each stage of the economic process, it becomes easier to transfer costs all along the line.

At the moment, to take another example, air, rail and truck cargo thefts are rising to epidemic proportions, causing losses of hundreds of millions of dollars each year. Most of these losses are being passed on to consumers who do not realize that they are paying for the cost of such pilferage and yet would be unable to challenge it in the courts or anywhere else if they did. Thus there is little pressure on the corporations to increase efforts to stop pilferage, instead of transferring the costs to the consumer.

Sometimes pressures can be mounted to stop transfers of costs to the consumer. For years the insurance industry failed to encourage programs for fire and auto safety, preventive medicine, and pollution control, which would have helped to prevent huge losses from taking place. It preferred to pass on these costs to its unorganized and generally uncomplaining policy holders in the form of higher premiums.

Recently, however, premiums for car insurance have become so high that many people cannot pay them, and those who can are becoming angry. At the same time, the public generally has been made more aware of auto safety. The insurance companies, more eager now to lower the damage claims for minor crashes, have decided at last to change their policies. They have lately been sharply critical of the auto industry for making overpowered engines and useless bumpers—and the auto manufacturers are beginning to respond. It now looks as if more functional bumpers may soon be replacing the ones I mentioned earlier; and by adding a surcharge to the insurance rates for high-powered "muscle cars," the insurance companies are driving down the sales of these absurd machines.

The lesson of this story is that we can no longer depend, as classical market theory held, on consumer response alone to encourage efficiency and competition that will result in higher quality. In a complex multilayered economy it is necessary that countervailing economic power be brought to bear at each level of the buying and selling process, however remote from the consumer. This is the only way to prevent excessive transfers of costs and to encourage efficiency and innovation.

We are very far from such a situation now. When railroad and trucking groups obtain rate increases from the all too compliant ICC, the large supermarkets and other retail chains rarely say a word; they calmly transfer the new costs on to the consumer. Since most of the railroads and truckers raise their rates uniformly, the supermarkets have no choice among competing transport services; and so the consumer is forced to pay the bill.

3. Both sub-economies I have mentioned so far are facilitated by the *controlled market sub-economy*. By this I mean the thousands

of arrangements that make it possible for corporations to avoid competition over the price, quantity, and quality of things made and sold, so that the value of what buyers receive is often outrageously distorted, by comparison with what the value would be if the market was not controlled.

Many of the practices in this sub-economy are violations of the anti-trust laws that have become both familiar and tolerated: price fixing, product fixing—for example the auto industry's entrenchment of the internal combustion engine—shared monopolies, etc. They also include other barriers to entry into the market such as excessive restrictions on occupational licenses, oil import quotas, the tying up of patents, and other devices that blatantly serve special economic interests while causing consumers and workers to suffer losses.

How much do they lose? The Federal Trade Commission has estimated that if highly concentrated industries were broken up by the anti-trust laws into more competitive companies so that the four largest firms in any industry would not control more than 40 percent of that industry's sales, prices would fall *by 25 percent or more.* This estimate applies to such major industries as autos, steel, copper, aluminum, containers, chemicals, detergents, canned soups, cereals. Nevertheless the figure reperesents only a small proportion of the unjustifiable costs to the consumer that result from the controlled market.

It is not just a question of price fixing. Concentrated industries can for years resist the innovations that would make them more efficient. The basic oxygen furnace was not used by the big steel firms until 1963, thirteen years after it was developed by a small Austrian steel company. The controlled market, moreover, blocks the individual or small business inventors who are still the source of so many of the really new techniques in our society.

Such inventors find that their chances of entering the market or selling their work to established companies are dim when their ideas would not only serve the consumer but also disturb existing capital commitments or ways of doing business: thus we cannot have a humane and efficient transportation system, nor can we buy engines that cause less pollution, can openers that prevent tiny metal fragments from falling into the can's contents, safer power lawn mowers, and countless other inventions that exist but are not produced. Think of the benefits to the consumer if the computer industry vigorously developed a computerized consumer information system to make more intelligent choices possible in the market place. Or of the uses to which Comsat might be put if it were freed from the heavy hands of the AT&T monopoly complex that controls it.

But the major corporations will go to fantastic lengths to avoid competition over value. The merchandising in the supermarkets attempts to substitute elaborate games of chance, trading stamps, coupons, and other gimmicks—for all of which the consumer finally pays—for decisions based on the price and quality of the goods themselves.

The price and quality of goods and services are also distorted by what might be called "mini-monopolies." Millions of consumers throughout the country have little choice except to use the only bank or finance company or pharmacy in their town. In company towns they must use the company store. Many specialty markets, such as hospital equipment or drugs, are monopolized by one or a few firms, making competition all the more impossible. Even the legally sanctioned monopolies, such as public utilities, usually manage to regulate the public agencies that are supposed to regulate them. The effect on the consumer is the same as if these businesses were private monopolies illegally controlling the market.

Another example of the controlled economy that we all live with—and for the most part tolerate—is the manipulation of zoning by corporations so as to control the use of land. Zoning boards were originally supposed to bring the exploitation of land under democratic control. In most cases, in fact, large corporations and other powerful real estate interests are able to pressure zoning authorities into granting land restrictions, or obtaining "variances" from existing regulations, that are profitable to them. One frequent result is "snob" zoning designed to exclude people who would depress land values or inhibit speculation.

4. Such an example brings us to the *corporate socialism subeconomy* which includes both a) corporate pressure on government to unjustifiably transfer public funds and privileges to corporate control and b) withholding of proper payments and other obligations from the government by the corporations that owe them.

The tax system has become, to a disgraceful degree, an indirect subsidy to corporations and other privileged groups. Many of the glaring tax loopholes that slip through Congress each year are in effect huge payments by the government of money it would otherwise have received: for example the depletion allowances for oil and minerals, the tax dodges allowed to the real estate, timber, and cattle industries, the uses of the capital gains tax that favor the very rich. Thanks to the oil depletion allowance, among other loopholes, the Atlantic Richfield Oil Company, to take an extreme example, had a net income of $797 million, while paying no federal tax whatever, from 1962 until 1968, when it paid at the rate of 1.2 percent.

These "tax expenditures" by the federal government have their local counterparts in the gross underpayment of property taxes by mineral companies, real estate developers, and commercial and industrial property owners. A preliminary estimate shows that local taxpayers are paying a subsidy of at least $7 billion a year to such interests when they allow them to evade property taxes. Of course municipal and county services such as schools, roads, hospitals, and garbage disposal also suffer as a result.

As we might expect, Texas provides excellent examples of such underpayment of property taxes. A recent survey by University of Texas Law School students shows that under-assessment of the value of oil and gas properties belonging to Texaco, Shell, and Atlantic Richfield in one part of west Texas caused county taxes for homeowners and small businessmen to be 33 percent higher than they should have been. Over a period of seven years, a county school board in the region lost $7 million in taxes that it should have collected. Another inquiry by law students showed that in Houston, Texas, industrial and commercial properties are assessed at about 13 percent of fair market value, while residential property is assessed at 31.94 percent.

In Gary, Indiana, the tax situation is shocking. Mayor Hatcher, in an attempt to meet the city's financial crisis, has ordered all city agencies to cut their budgets, including the budget for education. The big company in Gary is US Steel. Between 1961 and 1971 its property assessment only rose from $107 million to $117 million, although during that period the company installed $1.2 billion worth of capital improvements. US Steel refuses to allow the city authorities to examine its books and it refuses to apply for building permits, as required by city law, because this would reveal the size of its taxable investment.

US Steel is able to get away with all this because it exerts raw corporate power in a company town. It is not in any way unusual. Timber companies in Maine, mine owners in Appalachia, paper mills and chemical plants in cities and towns that depend on them for employment—all flagrantly evade the constitutional provisions in their states for equal treatment under property taxes.

Before national priorities can even be determined, it is crucial that Congress and the public know how much money is being spent by the government through the tax system. Tax expenditures now amount to roughly $45 billion a year but there is no systematic way of knowing precisely how much is being spent for what purposes. Some tax expenditures have worthy aims, such as the deduction for contribution to pensions, but it is rarely considered whether such deductions are the most desirable or easy ways to achieve these aims. Others, such as deductions for medical expenses, seem useful but are in fact regressive, allowing the same percentage of deduction to rich and poor alike. Others, as we have seen, are merely subsidies for the rich, particularly the capital gains tax and the allowances for accelerated depreciation of property.

What is needed, first of all, is an annual federal tax expenditure budget which will show exactly how much money the government loses for each tax privilege that is granted and just where that money goes instead. Recently there has been bipartisan support for such an analysis. Senators Javits and Percy have sponsored a bill to include a tax expenditure analysis in the annual budget report. Senator Chiles has introduced a similar bill. The Joint Economic Committee is now making its own analysis of tax expenditures and is publishing its findings. There is some hope that an annual tax expenditure budget may become a reality during this session of Congress.

But a tax expenditure budget will be only a beginning of a reform of the tax system, for the pressures from private interests and from the executive itself to increase tax subsidies are bound to continue. Under the Constitution Congress supposedly has the power to control priorities through the tax system, but this power is being eroded. Recently, for example, the Treasury Department without any Congressional authorization issued its new proposals—the "ADR system"—for allowing depreciations for tax purposes. This system would allow fast write-offs of business equipment without any relation to the useful life of such equipment—the traditionally accepted measure of depreciation for tax purposes.

ADR would mean a tax subsidy to business of over $3 billion a year—more than Nixon's welfare reform proposals (which would cost $2.1 billion). More than a dozen tax authorities, including the former Commissioner of Internal Revenue and experts from the Harvard, Yale, and Pennsylvania law schools, have stated that this multi-billion-dollar tax break is an illegal use of Presidential power. It remains to be seen whether the Congress or the courts will declare it invalid.

The direct subsidies paid for agriculture, shipping, business promotion, and "research" are quite as important—and as much neglected by Congress—as the indirect subsidies paid by the tax system. The Department of Agriculture, for example, is now spending over $4 billion each year for its subsidy programs. Who evaluates these payments and the reasons for making them? As it happens, big corporate farms receive the lion's share and Congress does not question the inequities that result.

Agriculture is only one sector of this sub-economy where hard questions must be asked if the public usefulness of *existing* tax dollars is to be improved. The inflated contract and procurement practices of the government are another. Thanks to Senator Proxmire and others, the public has at least begun to learn of the waste and mismanagement in defense contracting, and the consequent multibillion-dollar "cost-overruns" that have become commonplace—e.g., the $2 billion overrun paid Lockheed for the C5A. But who is looking into the waste in other government contracting—from the leasing of buildings at inordinate cost to the billions of dollars paid for research in "think tanks" and advice from private consulting firms such as A. D. Little, Booze Allen, and hundreds of lesser known outfits, not to mention the hundreds of studies done for HUD, HEW, DOT? Many of these studies are worthless, expensive, used mainly to delay policy decisions and to get the agencies who commission them off the hook. Others are wholly ignored.

If only the grossest forms of waste and corruption in federal, state, and local procurement practices were investigated and eliminated many billions of dollars would be saved and political life itself would get a badly needed shake-up, especially in local politics where procurement procedures are generally antiquated and enmeshed in the spoils system. Over a decade ago the Blatnik Subcommittee of Congress uncovered extensive corruption in highway building programs in states throughout the country; during the last two years officials in New Jersey were arrested for receiving kickbacks from construction contracts and the purchase of supplies. It would be hard to find a state in which similar (if sometimes less egregious) procurement practices involving bribery, campaign contributions, wasteful patronage, and corruption of officials are not costing millions to the taxpayers.

Some idea of how much money is being wasted in local procurement can be gained from a recommendation made to the states two years ago by the General Services Administration, the purchasing and housekeeping agency of the federal government. The GSA suggested that state and local governments cooperate in setting up systems of centralized purchasing direct from manufacturers, thus bypassing the

20 to 30 percent mark-up of the wholesalers. If they did this, they would save between $6 and $7 billion a year.

This recommendation was not followed, nor did the GSA pursue it. The wholesalers' trade association immediately launched a campaign against it in Congress, and the Bureau of the Budget suppressed this somewhat unexpected display of good sense by the GSA. The wholesalers' association has plenty of political muscle and uses it on all levels of government.

The great illusion of the public is that it is protected by the conscience of public officials, when in fact aggressive monitoring of these officials and those they deal with is constantly needed. Even tax funds used directly for medical care are funneled unscrupulously to prosperous doctors and drug companies, or to hospitals that use them for unauthorized purposes. Herbert S. Dennenberg, the Insurance Commissioner of Pennsylvania, stated recently that the "Medicare Program is resulting in the American people being overcharged billions of dollars a year"—a conclusion that has been confirmed by Congressional inquiries and independent studies.

5.   Unlike the other aspects of the economy that have been discussed here, the *compulsory consumption sub-economy* is not part of any recognized system of economic exchange—but it has grave economic effects. I am referring to the compulsory consumption of environmental pollution and compulsory exposure to occupational health and safety hazards. These reduce the *quality* of the gross national product and thus diminish the value of the citizen's dollar, even when they do not directly compel people to pay for medical treatment, for example. We are just beginning to calculate the billions of dollars that pollution costs in damages to health, in cleaning costs, and in damage to property, resources, and agricultural crops. Air and water pollution are each costing at least $14 billion a year. (The yearly damage to California crops alone from air pollution runs to $45 million a year.) The costs to the unborn, or to the environment in the future, have not even been estimated.

Safety and health hazards on jobs in factories, foundries, mines, and other work places are also a form of compulsory consumption. They now cause three times as many injuries as street crime: 15,000 sudden deaths last year, uncounted thousands of deaths resulting from occupational disease, 2.5 million disabling injuries, several million cases of less serious injuries and illness. (These figures are necessarily inadequate—how does one estimate when a case of black lung disease becomes bad enough to be included in the statistics of a given year?)

Clearly the forced consumption of pollution—gases, chemicals, coal and cotton dust—is a silent and sometimes invisible form of violence which compels people to pay insurance, medical, and other costs, including the loss of wages. The polluting corporations inflict these burdens on workers when, for only a fraction of the money they force others to pay, they could have prevented much of the pollution in the first place. (This is patently true in the case of dust control in coal mines, textile mills, and foundries, for example, where a small investment would prevent brutal physical damage to workers.)

The power of corporations to pollute, in short, is far too great for them to exercise responsibly. General Motors, by virtue of the engines it designs and the plants it operates, has been responsible for over 30 percent of the estimated tonnage of US air pollution. Is there any city street where the citizen can escape the pollution of GM engineering when he breathes? Between 1967 and 1969 GM spent $250 million to change its slogan on billboards, dealers' signs, and other promotional material to read "GM Mark of Excellence." With the same funds it could have easily developed a workable nonpolluting engine.

We may expect two developments to occur if certain industries in both the compulsory and the controlled sub-economies are successfully challenged in the market and by public protest. First, many industries would be displaced or diminished as superior technologies are invented and sold on their merits. Cleaner and cheaper sources of energy for cars and power plants, for example, will increasingly pose the threat of displacement to large industries. So will safer and more effective non-chemical methods of pest control eventually diminish the chemical pesticides industry.

Second, new services are already emerging to show businesses how to reduce telephone, utility, and insurance bills, for example. These services give advice that the big companies should be providing themselves. They also show how to avoid dealing with middlemen who now stand between the producer and seller of a product or service, thus reducing costs now passed on to the consumer. Recently a small company was started to give advice to users of Xerox machines on how to save money by buying ink, paper, and other items independently, rather than through the Xerox company; and on how to obtain the most efficient service with the best combination of reproduction machines, something the Xerox company itself fails to point out.

These, it should be said, are just the kinds of changes that are called for by the theory of capitalism; they are what Joseph Schumpeter, perhaps the leading theoretician of the capitalist economy, had in mind when he wrote of the "creative destruction" of inferior or obsolete industries under capitalism. But in fact, such developments are being discouraged and suppressed by politically entrenched corporate institutions.

6. The *expendable sub-economy* is composed mostly of poor people who are being excluded from the services of the economy at large. It is not simply that the poor pay more: they are not being allowed to buy. In Washington, Baltimore, New York, in fact in every large city, insurance and banking firms commonly "red line"—or refuse to do business with—people in the poor districts. What has happened is that *Fortune*'s Five Hundred largest corporations have decided that they have less and less need for the business of the poor. But by cutting off the funds needed for housing, for financing small business, and for municipal bonds in the low income areas of the cities, the banks and other lenders are causing the deterioration of the urban economy and injuring the well-being of millions of people.

The government, moreover, has become a willing partner in such discrimination. It provides fast tax write-offs for airplanes, computers, bulldozers, and trucks, causing loan money to flow in these directions and not toward loans to the poor and those who have more urgent needs. It provides tax inducements for slum landlords who are allowed to depreciate slum property at an accelerated rate and to pay capital gains taxes on profits from sales—a process which is quickly repeated by the next slum landlord.

The federal government artificially restricts the money supply in order to control inflation. It should ensure that all segments of the borrowing public be given equitable treatment so far as restrictions on borrowing are concerned. Several methods are available to accomplish this. One is to provide for different Federal Reserve Board requirements for different kinds of loans. Such reserve requirements specify the percentage of their demand deposits which banks must set aside at the District Federal Reserve banks. For example the FRB could require a reserve requirement of 5 percent against residential loans and one of 20 percent against nonproductive corporate loans, such as loans to conglomerates to acquire yet another company. Reserve requirements can be used in this way to encourage loans to sectors of the economy badly in need of funds.

Another method would be to link certain kinds of deposits to certain kinds of loans. For example, savings and loan association deposits are now required by law to be used heavily for housing loans.

Banks have similar deposits—so-called "time deposits" by individuals. In return for the benefits they receive from the federal ceilings on interest rates, as well as from other government programs, the banks could be required to make time deposits available when there is a shortage of funds for home mortgages and home construction.

Like so many of the other economic forces I have dealt with here, the banking system needs systematic surveillance and is not getting it. Banks in New York City, for example, often encourage industrial mergers which result in deposits being transferred to New York from regional or local banks all over the country. These regions find their local banks drained of funds, unable to extend credit, and the local economies suffer as a result.

Not long ago the large New York conglomerate called Teledyne Inc., a customer of the First National City Bank, bought up the Monarch Rubber Co. in Hartville, Ohio. The banks in Canton, Ohio, lost Monarch's deposits and its $2.5 million pension fund to National City. Money that should have been available for local borrowing was siphoned off to New York. The usual solution in such cases is for the local businessmen to appeal to Washington to come to the rescue—at the taxpayer's expense.

Apologists for the present corporate system will argue that the sub-economies I have described so generally here are justified because they support industries, create jobs, generate income. But it should be clear that their operations and the kinds of needs they satisfy are, to a great extent, neither desirable nor socially responsible; in many cases they are not legal. A safer traffic system would no doubt weaken the accident-injury industry, and that is as it should be. For most of this century there has been declared a national consensus in favor of competition, as well as numerous laws designed to encourage it, but both have been for the most part betrayed. When they have not, the benefits for the citizen have been dramatic.* Indeed each of the sub-economies I have described subverts values that are deeply rooted in American life.

What has been tragic is the general failure to understand how this has occurred. Fundamentally new ways must be found to make both government and corporations accountable. We should pursue the suggestion already made by some social critics for a "social accounts system" which would enable government and citizens to evalu-

---

*Last year, a new supermarket chain broke into the complacent food market of Washington, D.C., long dominated by three major chains. This episode and a detailed FTC report on monopolization of food prices in the Washington, D.C., area, according to an FTC report, saved Washington consumers $40 million in reduced prices in one year.

ate whether programs of education, medicine, and transportation, for example, were improving or deteriorating in quality. (The current inclusion of such activities in the gross national product has nothing whatever to say about their quality.)

Similarly computers should be made directly available to the citizen, and should be accessible both at shopping centers and by telephone. Such a cheap and simple source of information, which would give advice on the quality of products and of government and private services, could do much to squeeze the waste and deception out of the economy and give value to the dollar.

Senator Philip Hart has estimated that of the $780 billion spent by consumers in 1969, about $200 billion purchased *nothing* of value. By nothing of value he meant just that: over $45 billion was drained away by monopolistic pricing, for example, and over $6 billion by oil import quotas which drive up the prices of fuel oil and gasoline. His estimate, and it is only a preliminary one, shows how crucial is the need to evaluate how corporate and government wealth is being used—or misused—for individual and social purposes.

Such evaluations simply have not been made in our corporate political economy—not by our blinkered economists, certainly, and not by the government or the corporations themselves. Indeed the corporations have effectively blocked both the government and independent researchers from collecting and analyzing such information. Even the data on pollution must be fought for if it is to be extracted from corporations by government agencies and individuals bringing lawsuits. The task of the consumer movement now is to gather and analyze and disseminate this type of information by demanding it from the three branches of government and by mounting private actions by consumer groups to publicize it. Such information is the currency of economic democracy, the first tool for changing the perception of citizens and society itself.

PROLOGUE

Morton Mintz and Jerry S. Cohen

Calvin Coolidge once told us that "the business of America is business." The fashion has been to judge this notion quaint. But the late President is owed something better than condescension. He should be thanked for laying down an Orwellian stepping-stone to a perception of our true condition, Big Business *is* government.

To govern, the *Oxford Universal Dictionary* says, is "to rule with authority . . . to direct and control the action and affairs of (a people, etc.) . . . to hold sway, prevail . . . manage, order . . ." The constitutional government (a summary phrase intended to embrace the national and state and local governments) rules, directs, controls, sways, prevails, manages, orders. So does the giant corporation. This is an entity utterly unlike the ordinary business.

The constitutional government levies taxes. So, under a different name, does the giant corporation. "Men in America were so conditioned that they felt differently about taxes and about prices," the late Thurman W. Arnold said in *The Folklore of Capitalism.* "The former was an involuntary taking; the latter a voluntary giving. . . No one observed the obvious fact that in terms of total income of an individual it made no difference whether his money went for prices or taxes.''

In the period 1960–1966 consumer prices increased 14.1 per cent. This elicited protests. But the protests were directed largely at obtaining relief from the burden of taxes. Few perceived a relevant connection with inflated corporate profits which, after taxes, had increased 88 per cent, or six times as much as prices. What was little grasped, to put it another way, was that the price increases were substantially attributable to a *Profit* inflation. Unit labor costs in manufacturing could not be blamed. These had gone up only 2.1 per cent.

President Nixon, at his first press conference on January 27, 1969, rejected ''the suggestion that inflation can be effectively controlled by exhorting labor and management and industry to follow certain guidelines.'' Rather than intervene in price and wage decisions he would, he said, fight inflation with fiscal and monetary policy. The response of giant corporations to the Nixon signal illuminated the gap between them and ordinary businesses. In the President's remarks they divined a change in the rules of the game. No longer would they face, as they had in the Johnson Administration, the prospect of being summoned to the White House to be exhorted and pressured to restrain price increases. Promptly several giant corporations effected a series of price increases. The result was that eight months later copper, for example, was up 24 per cent. Zinc was up 11 per cent. Steel mill products, on the Wholesale Price Index, climbed 4.5 points. Little had changed in the three decades since Thurman Arnold wrote *The Folklore of Capitalism.* Public frustration did not take the form of demands for action to lower synthetically inflated prices, because these were perceived as ''voluntary giving'' rather than private taxes. Instead, public pressure welled up against public taxes, these being ''involuntary taking.''

In 1967 the nation's bill for repairing automobiles was running at an annual rate of between $5 billion and $6 billion. Edward Daniels, a specialist in auto insurance claims, estimated that $1 billion of the total was accounted for by the abandonment of bumpers that were functional for bumpers that were ornamental. These, General Motors acknowledged, met its standards if they protected surrounding sheet metal from the impact of a collision at a speed, if it can be called that, of 2.8 miles per hour. The $1 billion should be seen essentially as a tax levied in the form of elevated insurance rates. With hardly anyone noticing, the industry took another billion dollars in 1968 when it raised prices for ''captive'' parts—those obtainable only from the maker of the car—and other replacement parts.

When it sends men to war or to a penal death chamber the constitutional government takes life. The giant corporation also takes life. This is as dimly perceived as the similarity between a tax and an artificially high price. Because of this the corporation escapes blame and even criticism. Thought is given instead to the mysterious ways in which God moves His wonders to perform. The auto industry—meaning mainly General Motors—has provided memorable examples. Consider energy-absorbing steering assemblies. These prevent crushing of the driver in event of accident. Advanced designs were patented in the 1920s. Yet a curious apathy persisted until recent years, although a very large price in blood was being paid.

Finally the industry was embarrassed and prodded by hearings held in July 1965 by Senator Abraham A. Ribicoff (D–Conn.); by the publication, a few months later, of Ralph Nader's *Unsafe at Any Speed*; by the unexpected disclosure of the harassment of Nader by private detectives retained by GM, and by the awkward publicity that attended these matters. Stirred at last, the industry decided it could offer the energy-absorbing assemblies, first on certain 1967 models and then on all new cars manufactured after December 31, 1967. The National Highway Safety Bureau made a preliminary calculation of what this promised. If all rather than a negligible proportion of the motor vehicles in use were equipped at that moment with the safety devices, Deputy Director Robert Brenner said, "instead of 53,000 annual traffic deaths, there could be less than 40,000, a saving of 13,000 lives a year." The prevention of injury would be on a vastly greater scale, the steering assembly accounting for more than 40 per cent of all injuries to drivers. Lowell K. Bridwell, while Federal Highway Administrator, said that over past decades "hundreds of thousands" of drivers had been killed by unyielding steering assemblies. "Most of these deaths need not have occurred," he told the Senate Commerce Committee. His indictment has not been seriously challenged.

Nader said it would be "insulting" to auto industry engineers to suggest that they could not have perfected the steering device for mass produced automobiles over a decade ago. What he called the "suppressed creativity" of industry engineers had found other outlets. On the road are many millions of cars with cleverly designed hood ornaments, phallic bumper guards and other pieces of protuberant metal. While director of the National Highway Safety Bureau, Dr. William Haddon provided manufacturers with evidence, including color photographs, of needlessly grave and hideous wounds. Yet vast numbers of Pontiacs, to take an obvious example, continued to be armed with protruding center grilles shaped like meat cleavers. Seeing such a car, a pedestrian should be advised to be extra nimble in getting off the road, or the warpath. While doing so he might contemplate whether his fate was in the hands of the mighty rather than the Almighty.

Turn to an item as humdrum as windshield wipers. Naked they had always come. No one was offended. Especially in the era of the miniskirt there were more erotic distractions. However, General Motors decided that sales of its more ostentatious cars would be helped by concealing the wipers. In part, GM accomplished this by putting an upward curve in the rear of the hood and the adjoining fender corners. Unfortunately, this means that a front-end accident thrusts one or more of these pieces toward glass rather than steel. The result is that with a moderate impact the windshield breaks, adding $100 to the cost of repair. Inexorably, the cost of insurance rises, even for owners of cars with naked wipers. Thus GM has exercised a private power to tax. Suppose the accident is severe. The hood or fender then is rammed through the windshield into the passenger compartment. GM may also have exercised a private power to imperil life.

Other industries also merit attention. Let us turn first to the pharmaceutical industry. During the 1950s epidemics of serious and fatal staphylococcus infections were widespread. The most prominent cause was an exuberant overprescribing of antimicrobial agents, the sulfonamides and the early penicillins, that allowed proliferation of strains of bacteria resistant to treatment. Although the epidemics subsided with development of a new class of penicillins, the semisynthetics, a threat of new proliferations of resistant strains became apparent in the late 1960s. Dr. Calvin M. Kunin, a specialist in the treatment of infectious diseases and chairman of a National Academy of Sciences–National Research Council review panel on fixed combinations of antibiotics, has warned of possible peril to "all society."

The pharmaceutical industry was mainly responsible for creating the danger and, for fifteen years, perpetuating and expanding it. (To be sure, the Food and Drug Administration, which in 1970 finally secured a withdrawal of such irrational mixtures from the market, had disgraced itself by ever allowing the products to go on sale. This was an act so tainted that a federal grand jury undertook an investigation of the official involved. But the corrupting force was the industry; and the fount of the bitter-end resistance to withdrawal again was the industry.)

One of the therapeutically irrational but lushly profitable mixtures combined, in fixed ratios, two antibiotics, penicillin and streptomycin. The "widespread" and "indiscriminate" use of such products, which was a direct result of industry promotion, "almost led to disaster," Dr. Kunin said. But not until June 1970, when further resistance would have been futile or counterproductive, was an administrative and court battle abandoned by Wyeth Laboratories, one of two prescription-drug divisions of American Home Products, which in the preceding year was the nation's ninety-fourth largest industrial corporation. Similarly, the Bristol-Myers Company—until the FDA, in a rare act of courage, faced it down—used a massive promotional campaign to encourage physicians to switch their loyalties from other effective agents to Dynapen, a semisynthetic penicillin, even though overuse of such an admittedly excellent medicine needlessly increased the risk of staph epidemics. The Upjohn Company enlarged the peril with Panalba, yet another therapeutically irrational but exceedingly profitable mixture of antibiotics (tetracycline and novobiocin). As if this was not enough, the commissioner of the FDA testified that Panalba annually caused hundreds of thousands of needless injuries, a few of them lethal. Similarly, the needless use of streptomycin, usually in combination with penicillin or with a sulfonamide, creates a needless risk of irreversible deafness in some patients, particularly children. In passing, it may be noted that this entire situation probably could not have developed had not the pharmaceutical industry been able to govern a significant element of the medical profession. Such control was achieved, and is maintained, through devices that create dependency and stifle criticism, including gifts to medical schools and the placement of vast quantities of lucrative advertising in the *Journal* of the American Medical Association and other medical publications.

A giant corporation can affect the quality of life and the environment just as surely and profoundly as an elected government. In 1964 in Los Angeles County 3.5 million motor vehicles were daily burning more than 7 million gallons of gasoline and depositing about 800,000 pounds of contaminants into the atmosphere. Even before this, physicians, in a single year, had advised ten thousand persons in vulnerable health to move away. In June 1964 S. Smith Griswold, the county's air pollution control officer, put major blame on the auto industry. "Everything that the industry is able to do today to control auto exhaust was possible technically ten years ago," he told a meeting of the Air Pollution Control Association in Houston. "No new principles had to be developed; no technological advance was needed; no scientific breakthrough was required."

The speech set off an intricate series of events beginning with a visit by Ralph Nader to the Justice Department. He argued persuasively that, though it may have been done inadvertently, Griswold, an engineer, had provided the groundwork for a case of product-fixing as clearly in violation of the antitrust laws as price-fixing. In January 1965 the Department served the industry with initial demands for records. Samuel Flatow, an Antitrust Division lawyer who since has died, was assigned to lead an investigation. His findings were so serious that a grand jury was convened in Los Angeles. The grand jury heard evidence from July 1966 to December 1967. Finally Flatow requested permission to ask the grand jury to return an indictment. Washington refused the request. But on January 10, 1969—in the late twilight of the Johnson Administration—the Department filed a civil complaint charging the four leading manufacturers and the Automobile Manufacturers Association with having conspired to impede development and installation of anti-pollution devices and technology. The enormity of the charge should require no elaboration. It speaks, unspeakably, for itself. The suit never was tested in an open trial. It was settled in the fall of 1969 with a consent decree. As is customary with this remarkable legal invention, the defendants were enabled to avoid saying whether they had committed the offenses charged by the government while promising not to commit the same offenses thereafter.

It is natural that the power to tax, take life, and drastically affect the environment should be present in a giant corporation. It is natural, that is, in an entity with the proportions of a sovereign state. General Motors is the world's largest industrial corporation. Its annual revenue is greater than that of any foreign government except the United Kingdom and the Union of Soviet Socialist Republics, and greater, as well, than the gross national product of Brazil or Sweden. In 1965 GM's sales of $20.7 billion "exceeded the *combined* general revenues of the state and local governments of New York, New Jersey, Pennsylvania, Ohio, Delaware, and the six New England states." This figures out to $2.3 million per hour, 24 hours a day, 365 days a year (by 1969 it was 2.8 million). On the same hourly basis, its profit after taxes was $242,649.

Thurman Arnold, who in the New Deal was Assistant Attorney General in charge of the Antitrust Division of the Department of Justice, once characterized the Ford Motor Company and Chrysler Corporation as "satellites of General Motors. General Motors will let them live as long as they do not grow too much at its expense."

Major international implications flow predictably from corporations that are big enough to be fairly compared with nations. Here is a ten-billion-dollar example. In the late 1950s the demand for steel declined. By 1958, a recession year, mills in the United States were operating at less than 50 per cent of capacity. Yet in August of that year the industry *raised* the price by $4.50 a ton. Only a concentrated industry (or a monopoly) could do that. In the six member countries of the European Coal and Steel Community, steel producers behaved quite differently. They also had experienced a decline in demand. But they reacted with *lower* prices. So it came about that the United States, which had been exporting more steel than it was importing, reversed its role and entered the 1960s as a net importer. For many years American mills operated at less than two-thirds of capacity. Yet prices remained rigid or were slightly increased. In Europe, where prices fluctuated with demand, steelmakers operated continuously at or near capacity. To be specific: In the year 1960–1963 the export price of American steel was held at $126 to $127 a ton. In the same years in Europe the export price fell from $147 in 1960 to $93 in 1963. Claims of higher costs in the United States do not stand up. For one thing, coking coal was substantially cheaper in this country and iron ore was no more expensive. The foregoing is a summary of the background that Professor Egon Sohmen gave the Senate Subcommittee on Antiturst and Monopoly for this astonishing finding:

> Had the [American] industry worked at capacity during the early sixties, and had it exported the additional steel at world market prices, the additional export revenue (taking into account the fact that steel prices on the world market would have been somewhat lower as a consequence) would have eliminated the U.S. balance-of-payments deficits during these years. *One need hardly go into the details of what the United States would have been spared in this event. [Emphasis supplied.]*

A few of the details should be given. In the years 1960–1963 the aggregate deficit in the balance of payments was $10.6 billion. There would have been no deficit at all had the steel industry, in each of the four years, sold an additional 30 million tons of steel at world market prices of at least $90 per ton. Indeed, a $200 million surplus would have accrued. Professor Sohmen testified that the industry could have succeeded in this competition "without difficulty." Even the $10.6 billion understated the stakes. Sohmen explained why:

> If steel prices in the United States had uniformly been at the lower world market levels, many important American industries using steel (the automobile or the machinery industries, to name a few) could have reduced their prices. This would have entailed a rise in exports of those industries and a fall of competing imports, further improving the U.S. trade balance.

To function effectively and reliably as private governments, giant corporations must govern constitutional governments. During the era of the Progressive movement, which rose in the 1890s and peaked in 1912, "the Republican party of Wisconsin was neither more nor less than a railroad machine," Grant McConnell has written. "In California railroad domination was even more complete. The Southern Pacific virtually owned both parties." Today matters often are handled with more discretion. Aspirations are more modest. Rather than ownership, a potential for control is deemed sufficient. It is, for example, extravagant to want to control every member of a congressional committee on every issue; it is enough to be able to control a crucial vote on important issues. A campaign contribution, offered in an hour of need, can become one of the shrewdest of investments. A timely decision to locate an industrial plant in a particular state or congressional district can earn undying, and tangible, gratitude. No one has dealt with these matters more bluntly than Woodrow Wilson. "The masters of the government of the United States are the combined capitalists and manufacturers of the United States," he said during his first campaign for the Presidency. "It is written over every intimate page of the record of Congress, it is written all through the history of conferences at the White House, that the suggestions of economic policy have come from one source, not from many sources. . . . The government of the United States at present is a foster child of the special interests."

A similar complaint would have point today. In 1968 the Poor People's Campaign came to Washington. The reception was cold. Members of Congress accused leaders of the campaign of wanting handouts or other forms of special treatment. Senator Philip A. Hart (D–Mich.), chairman of the Senate Subcommittee on Antitrust and Monopoly, was struck by the contrast with the reception accorded a segment of industry that, say, has lost an antitrust case in the courts: "There is no hesitancy to ask antitrust amendments to take care of its special problems," he said. "Its arguments win general acceptance. It does not have the bad flavor of the poor, non-corporate petitioners."

In 1969, in the Supreme Court, a segment of the newspaper industry lost just such a case. Profit-pooling and price-fixing under a joint operating agreement by separately owned newspapers in Tucson, Arizona, were declared illegal. Similar agreements in twenty-one other cities thus were threatened. A bill to overturn the ruling was introduced in Congress, and wide congressional support was attracted. Liberals found it just as difficult as conservatives to antagonize such supplicants as the Hearst and Newhouse and Scripps-Howard chains. But the Department of Justice was opposed to the bill. Its testimony on Capitol Hill—cleared by the Budget Bureau, meaning the White House—was forceful. The bill would entrench "absolute monopoly," "flout the basic principles of the free enterprise system" and impair the vital newspaper function of "acting as a watchdog on government," the Justice Department said. One day in the autumn of 1969, Richard Berlin, president of the Hearst Corporation, visited President Nixon at the White House. A few days later the Department of Commerce, out of the blue, endorsed the bill, the Newspaper Preservation Act. Although no one could recall a precedent for the Commerce Department's speaking for the White House on an antitrust matter, it did emphatically speak for Mr. Nixon on this occasion.

Although there is some awareness that the oil and gas industries govern through the executive branch and the Congress, the awakening is a relatively recent development. The principal precipitating cause was the great fuss in 1968 and 1969 about the oil depletion allowance and such extraordinary arrangements as those that allowed Atlantic Richfield to earn a total of $797 million in net income in the years 1962 through 1968, pay no federal tax whatever in the first of those six years, and pay at the rate of 1.2 per cent in the seventh year. The following cases will fill out the literature on government by oil and gas.

The upkeep of President Eisenhower's farm at Gettysburg was paid for by three oilmen—the late Alton W. Jones, chairman of the executive committee of Cities Service; B. B. (Billy) Byars of Tyler, Texas, and George E. Allen, a heavy investor in oil. This has been documented by the late Drew Pearson and Jack Anderson. "They signed a strictly private lease agreement, under which they were supposed to pay the farm costs and collect the profits," the newsmen said in *The Case Against Congress.* They continued:

> *Internal Revenue, after checking into the deal, could find no evidence that the oilmen had attempted to operate the farm as a profitable venture. Internal Revenue concluded that the money the oilmen poured into the farm could not be deducted as a business expense but had to be reported as an outright gift. Thus, by official ruling of the Internal Revenue Service, three oilmen gave Ike more than $500,000 at the same time he was making decisions favorable to the oil industry.*

One must be exceedingly reluctant to impute a trace of impure motive to the late President. Oilmen were his friends. But one must credit the accuracy of Pearson and Anderson in saying that during his years in the White House, "Dwight Eisenhower did more for the nation's private oil and gas interests than any other President." In 1959, by executive order, Mr. Eisenhower imposed a system of oil import quotas. Reasons of national defense were cited. These proved to be insubstantial at best and preposterous at worst. The quotas severely restricted imports of foreign oil. The principal beneficiaries were the major oil companies. Over the years they managed to defuse every effort to overturn the system. They had what Senator John O. Pastore (D–R.I.) called "raw political power." By 1969 the quotas were costing the public $7.2 billion a year. This estimate, made by Dr. John M. Blair, then chief economist of the Senate Subcommittee on Antitrust and Monopoly, was carefully constructed from data on the comparative prices of American and Middle Eastern crude, laid down on the East Coast of the United States. Before almost deserted press tables at a subcommittee hearing, he showed that the quotas added about five cents to the price of each gallon of gasoline ($35 a year for the average motorist), and almost four cents per gallon to the price of fuel oil ($58.50 a year for an average homeowner with oil heat). These homely statistics drew trivial attention in major news media, which simultaneously were devoting massive attention, day after day, to the surtax. Thurman Arnold would have appreciated the irony. The inflated gas and oil prices were a "voluntary giving." The surtax (which, relatively, involved not very much more—about $9 billion) was an "involuntary taking."

On March 4, 1965, a pipeline carrying natural gas under high pressure exploded near Natchitoches, Louisiana. Seventeen persons were killed. Thirteen acres were devastated. Senator Warren G. Magnuson (D–Wash.), chairman of the Senate Commerce Committee, responded by proposing the first legislation to set federal safety standards for gas pipelines. In 1967, by a vote of 78 to 0, the Senate passed the bill. The unanimity of the vote by no means indicated that the bill was acceptable to the industry. To the contrary, the industry was highly displeased. But it chose to fight in the House. There its strategy was vindicated when the desired evisceration was accomplished in the Committee on Interstate and Foreign Commerce. Members of the defeated minority of the committee took the unusual step of writing a letter to the *New York Times* which was published on May 3, 1968. "In our opinion the bill was essentially gutted at the behest of the gas pipeline lobbies most of whose proposals were adopted verbatim," the congressmen said. They made efforts to strengthen the bill on the House floor but failed. The industry was openly pleased. "Certainly it isn't altogether what we'd like if we'd sat down and written the bill ourselves," a spokesmen told *Congressional Quarterly.* Fortunately, the Senate succeeded in significantly strengthening the bill before it became law. Yet the industry still may be reasonably pleased, because Congress has not provided adequate funds for enforcement.

John W. Gardner, the former Secretary of Health, Education, and Welfare, has urged that "each government agency honestly appraise the extent to which it has built an empire rather than served the public. And let it ask how much risk it has taken in fighting for good causes." His tone was not optimistic. "The natural state of the bureaucracy is to be unbloody but bowed," he said. "It would look better with some honorable scars." Gardner should be heeded. The importance of regulatory agencies, and of regulatory operations within the Executive, is too often downgraded or forgotten. They deal with the quality and purity of the air, water, food, and drugs; with the safety of aircraft, trains, buses, cars, trucks, tires, pipelines, chemical warfare agents, atomic energy facilities, medicines, pesticides, and food additives; with radiation from color television sets, microwave ovens, and X-ray machines; with the uses of the public's airwaves, with deceit in the marketplace, with the injection of water into hams, with the potential for power blackouts, and with the prices of power and natural gas.

It should be remembered that unlike the Supreme Court, which publishes majority and minority opinions for all to see, regulatory agencies and Executive regulatory operations sometimes operate in secrecy. A discreet phone call betweeen an official and a corporation can, in an operation such as the Food and Drug Administration, abort a necessary regulatory action. As it is, the subject matter can be so arcane as to defy comprehension by laymen. If the lax procedures standard in the FDA during the reign of the late Commissioner George P. Larrick had prevailed, Dr. Frances O. Kelsey would have yielded to the pressures exerted by Richardson-Merrell, Inc., and let thalidomide go on sale. By the time the capacity of the sedative to deform had been recognized, an estimated ten thousand limbless babies would already have been born to parents living in the United States. "Government itself develops vested interests which become more concerned with self-perpetuation than with social values," Senator Edmund S. Muskie (D–Me.) has observed. "Sometimes economic interests and government agency interests become so intertwined that the public cannot distinguish between the two." Three cases of intertwining:

Since 1938 a manufacturer wishing to market a medicine has been required first to demonstrate to the satisfaction of the government that the product is safe for its intended uses. For almost a quarter-century thereafter, however, there was no requirement of a demonstration of efficacy—meaning substantial evidence that a drug would live up to the claims allowed in the labeling. Predictably, many thousands of ineffective preparations went on sale. "There is no way of measuring the needless suffering, the money innocently squandered, and the protraction of illnesses resulting from the use of such ineffective drugs," President John F. Kennedy said.

In 1962, reacting to the thalidomide warning, Congress enacted the Kefauver-Harris Amendments. Among other reforms, the need for which was developed in two and a half years of hearings by the late Senator Estes Kefauver, these required manufacturers, after a two-year grace period, to submit substantial evidence for the claims of efficacy made for drug products marketed in the 1938–1962 period. These products account for more than 80 per cent of the preparations dispensed today by prescription and over the counter. A crucial role would be played by the director of the FDA's Bureau of Medicine. Yet the post had been vacant since August 1962, eleven months after notice of resignation had been served by the last physician to fill it. Primary responsibility for filling the vacancy rested on Boisfeuillet Jones, then special assistant for medical affairs in the Department of Health, Education, and Welfare. The Commissioner of the FDA at the time, George Larrick, had nominated Dr. Charles D. May, a distinguished pediatrician. However, the doctor had offended the pharmaceutical industry with critical testimony before Senator Kefauver and with an article pointing out that promotion of prescription drugs, including activities indistinguishable from payola, was costing three and a half times as much as all of the educational programs in medical schools. Jones "won the confidence of the pharmaceutical industry by blocking the appointment of Dr. Charles May," *Drug Research Reports* said in June 1964. Even before this, Jones had acknowledged to a reporter what his priorities were. He was looking, he said, for a director of the Bureau who would be "acceptable to the industry, the consumers and the academic world, but [HEW was] not trying to satisfy the industry *per se*."

Jones's patience was rewarded and his priorities met when, in April 1964, he chose Dr. Joseph F. Sadusk, Jr. Once in office as the FDA's top physician, Dr. Sadusk did everything within his power to frustrate the intent of the efficacy legislation. His services were properly esteemed by his constituency and, after leaving the agency, he became vice president of the pharmaceutical firm of Parke, Davis & Company. At the FDA he had made an almost immeasurable contribution to the unconscionable delay in taking nostrums off the market. Of almost four thousand preparations evaluated for efficacy by the National Academy of Sciences–National Research Council at the FDA's request in the years from 1938 through 1962, a "considerable number" failed to meet one or more—or even all—of the therapeutic claims made for them. As of early 1970 virtually all commercially significant medicines in this group were still on sale, and as of early 1971 most were.

Over a period of three decades producers of hot dogs and bologna increased the average fat content from 18.6 per cent to 32.2 per cent. This gave reason for concern. Large numbers of people consume these foods in vast quantities. They are mainstays for, among others, the poor and school lunch programs and institutions. A decline in nutritional value consequently was a threat to health. In addition, medical authorities warned that a greater intake of animal fats would enhance the bodily environment for heart disease. In December 1968 the Department of Agriculture proposed to limit the fat content of frankfurters and bologna to 30 per cent. The meat industry lobbied against the proposal. The Department backed down and proposed a 33 per cent limit, which was what the industry wanted. Only extraordinary counter pressure—from publicity and consumer forces—led the Department to revert to 30 per cent.

President Nixon was on the side of the public in the hot dog episode. But in key broadcasting issues he has been on the side of the fat and fatuous. Late in 1969 he made two appointments to the Federal Communications Commission. His choice for chairman was Dean Burch, a former aide to Barry Goldwater and chairman of the Republican National Committee during the senator's pursuit of the Presidency in 1964. Mr. Nixon's choice for commissioner was Robert Wells, a broadcasting executive. In making these appointments Mr. Nixon ignored the National Citizens Committee for Broadcasting and other public interest forces—but cleared Burch and Wells with the broadcasting industry. He was by no means the first President to have taken such a precaution with one or another true constituency, but this time the consequences promised to be particularly dispiriting. "Of all those Americans who are trying to get more out of life than they have put into it and who are laying waste their country in the attempt, none has appeared more successful as a group than the broadcasters," the jurors for the *Survey of Broadcast Journalism 1968–1969* said. "In what other business can a moderately astute operator hope to realize 100 per cent a year on tangible assets, or lay out $150 for a franchise that in a few years' time he can peddle for $50 million—should he be so foolish as to want to sell. The most fantastic rewards associated with broadcasting in many instances grow from enterprises that do as little for their fellow countrymen as they legally can."

The television industry has been providing more hours of "education" to an average child before he enters kindergarten than he will spend in college classrooms earning a bachelor's degree. In a single week of evening programs television may continue to offer, as it did by count of the staff of the *Christian Science Monitor* in October 1968, "254 incidents of violence, including threats, and 71 murders, killings and suicides," Assuredly the unrelenting exposure to violence will go on begetting violence, just as exposure to television advertising will go on begetting demands by children on their parents for advertised products. Children will go on being taught, as Commissioner Nicholas Johnson of the FCC put it, "that the single measure of happiness and personal satisfaction is consumption," that "success" derives from the purchase of a mouthwash or deodorant, and all the rest. "What are these network executives doing?" he asked in a statement to the National Commission on the Causes and Prevention of Violence. "What right have they to tear down every night what the American people are spending $52 billion a year to build up every day through their school system . . . ?" The "right" is much the same as the "right" of other industry executives to govern.

A few giant corporations dominate most basic industries, which, as a result, are called concentrated industries. At the same time, a relative handful of the same corporations dominate most of mining and manufacturing. This is called overall concentration. The near omnipresence of concentration may be obvious to a casual observer of the economy. But that presence requires emphasis and even reemphasis because of the frequent pretense of influential and sophisticated observers that it isn't there. It is a pretense that inhibits understanding. "Instead of reckoning with large and concrete corporations, economists and government officials prefer to shape policy around large and impersonal abstractions," Bernard D. Nossiter says in *The Mythmakers*. "They think in terms of total demand, total employment; they manipulate broad-gauged tools like taxes, spending and the supply of money and credit." But why has the crucial fact of concentration been snubbed? "This is, after all, a sensitive subject because it involves power," Nossiter says. "For a policy maker to cope with concentration can mean conflict with the strongest institutions in America."

To concentrate economic power in *either* private or public hands is to concentrate political power in the same hands. Concentrated political power, no matter in whose hands, weakens and may destroy democratic institutions. Claims of originality would be unbecoming. The Founding Fathers were fully aware of the dangers of concentrated power in their day—roughly a century before the United States became an industrial nation—and took admirable precautions against it. "The accumulation of all powers, legislative, executive, and judiciary, in the same hands, may justly be pronounced the very definition of tyranny," James Madison said. An accumulation of economic power so great that it becomes political power likewise can be tyranny. We have been adequately warned about the state that functions as a super-corporation. We have been inadequately warned about the super-corporation that functions as a state. In setting antitrust policy, Congress long has recognized "that concentration of industrial power may lead to the police state," William H. Orrick, Jr., said while head of the Antitrust Division of the Justice Department. "Can anyone doubt that the prewar experience of Germany, Japan, and Italy have proven the wisdom of the nation's concern over concentration of economic power?"

But concentration grows. One of those who have expressed concern is Attorney General John N. Mitchell. In a speech on June 6, 1969, he reviewed the record: In the previous two years the number of corporate mergers "more than doubled" and, more importantly, "involved an increasing number of large firms"; the assets of acquired firms increased from $4 billion in 1966 to more than $12 billion in 1968; among firms with assets exceeding $250 million, only five were acquired from 1948 to 1966—compared with six in 1967 and twelve in 1968; increasingly, the largest firms were playing a prominent role in acquisitions, as shown by the statistics for 1968. In that year companies among the two hundred largest made 74 of the total of 192 acquisitions of enterprises with assets of at least $10 million. Mitchell went on to say:

> In 1948, the nation's 200 largest industrial corporations controlled 48 percent of the manufacturing assets, Today, these firms control 58 percent, while the top 500 firms control 75 percent of these assets.

> The danger that this super-concentration poses to our economic, political and social structure cannot be over-estimated. Concentration of this magnitude is likely to eliminate existing and future competition. It increases the possibility for reciprocity and other forms of unfair buyer-seller leverage. It creates nation-wide marketing, managerial and financing structures whose enormous physical and psychological resources pose substantial barriers to smaller firms wishing to participate in a competitive market.

> And, finally, super-concentration creates a "community of interest" which discourages competition among large firms and establishes a tone in the marketplace for more and more mergers.

> This leaves us with the unacceptable probability that the nation's manufacturing and financial assets will continue to be concen-

trated in the hands of fewer and fewer people—the very evil that the Sherman Act, the Clayton Act, the Robinson-Patman Act, and the Celler-Kefauver Amendment were designed to combat. [Emphasis supplied.]

The fear of concentration expressed by the Republican Attorney General differs in no significant respect from the fear expressed by men whom, on other issues, he would not count among his admirers. President Franklin D. Roosevelt said, "I am against private socialism of concentrated economic power as thoroughly as I am against government socialism. The one is equally as dangerous as the other; and destruction of private socialism is utterly essential to avoid governmental socialism." But how distant was this from President Herbert Hoover: "Likewise the basic foundations of autocracy, whether it be class government or capitalism in the sense that few men through unrestrained control of property determine the welfare of great numbers, is [*sic*] as far apart from the rightful expression of American individualism as the two poles."

President Johnson's Cabinet Committee on Price Stability: "Further merger-achieved centralization of economic power and decision-making may seriously impair the proper functioning of our competitive, free enterprise economy, as well as threaten the social and political values associated with a decentralized economic system." Manuel F. Cohen, while chairman of the Securities and Exchange Commission: "A decision to hold back vital goods and services or to set prices at exorbitant levels then becomes not a simple business decision, but an irresponsible abuse of political power."

The late Senator Estes Kefauver: "Through monopolistic mergers the people are losing power to direct their own economic welfare. When they lose the power to direct their economic welfare they also lose the means to direct their political future." Senator Philip A. Hart, who in 1963 succeeded Kefauver as chairman of the Senate Subcommittee on Antitrust and Monopoly: "In this society of ours, we depend on diffusion of power as the best means of achieving political democracy. . . . If we fail the danger is clear to anyone who has studied history—particularly that of the Axis powers prior to World War II." Senator Gaylord Nelson (D–Wis.), head of a Senate small business subcommittee: "Americans, ever suspicious of concentrated political power, have permitted concentrations of economic power to develop, substantially unchallenged, that would make a Roman emperor gasp."

The late T. K. Quinn, who was a vice president of General Electric: "Big business breeds bureaucracy and bureaucrats exactly as big government does." C. S. Lewis: "The greatest evil is not now done in those sordid 'dens of crime' that Dickens loved to paint. It is not done even in concentration camps and labour camps. In those we see its final result. But it is conceived and ordered (moved, seconded, carried and minuted) in clean, carpeted, warmed and well-lighted offices, by quiet men with white collars and cut fingernails and smooth-shaven cheeks who do not need to raise their voices. Hence, naturally enough my symbol for Hell is something like the bureaucracy of a police state or the offices of a thoroughly nasty business concern."

The bond between men as diverse as those quoted in these pages is of course a common concern about power which is neither checked nor balanced. We are but pawns of such power. The rulers of the great corporations do not have to stand for election. The individual stockholders, the men and women popularized in institutional advertising, do not have control. "In General Electric the election of directors was only formalized at stockholders' meetings," T. K. Quinn said. "The directors were in every case selected by the officers. We had then, in effect, a huge economic state governed by nonelected, self-perpetuating officers and directors—the direct opposite of the democratic method."

In major respects little seemed to have changed by May 22, 1970, when General Motors held its annual meeting of shareholders in Detroit. But spokesmen for the "Campaign to Make General Motors Responsible" were determined to press GM chairman James M. Roche about how the corporation selected directors. Barbara J. Williams, a black law student, demanded to know why no black person ever had been named to the board.

"No black has been nominated and no black has been elected," Roche said. "Our directors are elected by our stockholders."

Miss Williams asked, "How are they nominated?"

"They are nominated at the annual shareholders meeting just as they were today" (in January 1971 GM did elect a black director, the Rev. Dr. Leon M. Sullivan of Philadelphia).

Miss Williams, who was, of course, trying to bring out how closely held the whole process is, then inquired, "Why are there no women on your Board of Directors?"

Roche replied, again vaguely and circuitously, "Our directors are selected on the basis of their ability to make a contribution to the success of General Motors."

Later, Harry Huge, a Washington lawyer, cut through Roche's semantic maze. "Mr. Roche," he said, "*you* nominate the Board of

Directors, because eleven [of twenty-four] members of the Board are your officers and former officers of the Board of General Motors." When Roche demurred, saying he merely "can make my recommendations," Huge challenged him to show that "you don't get your way." He asked, "Have you ever had a recommendation that wasn't acted upon favorably?" Roche said he had—but did not assert that the Board ever had rejected a recommendation of his for the Board.

Geoffrey Cowan, a "Campaign GM" coordinator, elicited an amplification. "Different members of the Board," Roche said, "get together and agree on the proposed candidates submitted to the entire Board for their approval." In politics such a practice commonly is derided as "cronyism."

Yet, even though the GM meeting of 1970 supports Quinn's diagnosis of 1953, that diagnosis must be sharply qualified. In many giant enterprises stockholders have acquired control or a potential for control. Such stockholders, however, are the great institutional investors, principally banks, insurance companies, mutual funds and pension funds, not individuals. Such stockholders have caused power to pass from a few hands into fewer hands. The situation was illustrated in a staff report for the Subcommittee on Domestic Finance of the House Committee on Banking and Currency. The staff found that in 1967 institutional investors held $1 trillion in assets. Of this sum $607 billion, or 60 per cent, was held by the trust departments of the forty-nine commercial banks which the staff surveyed. Six banks in New York City alone held $64.4 billion. One of these banks, the Morgan Guaranty Trust Company, by itself accounted for $16.8 billion. Each of the six New York banks held stock in the others. And each of the six banks, along with major banks in other principal cities, held stock in and shared directors with companies selling competing products or services. Together, the Subcommittee staff found, the forty-nine banks in the survey held at least 5 per cent of the common stock of each of 147 of the 500 largest industrial corporations. The same banks had a total of 768 interlocking directorships with 286 of the 500 largest corporations, or "an average of almost three directors for each corporation board on which bank director representation is found." Thus concentration has tended to evolve into super-concentraion.

Such professed conservatives as Governor Ronald Reagan have faith in the benign nature of business. His adviser on consumer affairs in Sacramento, Mrs. Kay Valory, counsels the disgruntled to seek solace in pamphlets prepared by the National Association of Manufacturers. Not that such faith is unique to the Reaganesque portion of the political spectrum. Such putative liberals as Adolf A. Berle, Jr., also put faith in the benign nature of giant corporations. The expression of such reverence may have taken its finest form in a book which, despite the title, is not always to be found in the libraries of theological seminaries. The book is *United States Steel: A Corporation with a Soul*. The author, Arundel Cotter, official biographer of United States Steel, wrote the book a half-century ago. At the time men in the mills worked a twelve-hour shift six days a week and an unbelievable twenty-four-hour shift every second week. Cotter says that the attitude of Elbert H. Gary, chairman and chief executive officer, toward labor "was well known. He believed in 'leaning over backward' in the matter of giving justice to the worker." More, the corporation "was, in a modified sense, an experiment in popular ownership, the ownership of industry by the worker." Admittedly, firmness on occasion had to be shown: "While the colored man often makes a satisfactory worker if properly 'bossed,' he is unreliable and too often has as his motto, 'never do to-day what you can put off until tomorrow.' " Yet, because his "sense of justice" was "the supreme passion of his life," Gary "treats everyone 'white.' " That being so, "the Steel Corporation is a true democracy." In 1906, when the corporation incorporated the town (later city) of Gary, it brought more than democracy to Indiana. It "made Gary at least an attractive, if not a beautiful, residential town," one which a visitor "is never allowed to leave . . . without seeing the Y.M.C.A." A visitor might also see the "patch," a small section in the heart of Gary "full of saloons and dives." This was oppressive to the corporation. It had not acquired the site "because of some question as to the validity of title" and consequently "has no power of restriction over its development. Gary men have long hoped that some means of cleaning up the section would be found. Prohibition seems to be doing it." In World War I the average wage at United States Steel increased from $905.36 in 1914 to $1,684.58 in 1918. Net income increased from $71,663,615 in 1914 to $199,350,680 in 1918. "Of course, United States Steel made large profits out of the war. . . . But always its officials put patriotism before profits."

Unlike Governor Reagan and Adolf A. Berle, Adam Smith two centuries earlier was an agnostic about the goodness of business. Indeed, Smith wrote of "the mean rapacity, the monopolizing spirit of merchants and manufacturers, who neither are nor ought to be the rulers of mankind." He put his trust in classic competition. This would make the spirit of merchants and manufacturers, rapacious or not, beside the point, because competition would prevent them from becoming rulers. Classic competition is easily described. Here is the model in a lucid definition by John Kenneth Galbraith: ". . .

the market where sellers are numerous, capital requirements are modest, technology generally available, entry in consequence not difficult, the products of different sellers largely substitutable and where in further consequence no seller has the power to influence appreciably the price at which he sells. That is to say he has no market power. All sell at an externally and impersonally determined price." This precludes concentration of economic power and therefore of political power in business and industry.

Because General Motors claims to fit the competitive model it is time to refresh one's perspective about GM. This can be done without redundancy. It sells more than half of the automobiles sold in the United States. In 1965 its 735,000 employees, at work in the United States and twenty-three foreign realms, earned $5,448,343,000, or more than double the personal income of all of the citizens of Ireland.

The occasion for GM making the claim that it fits the classic competitive model arose in 1968 when two subcommittees of the Senate Select Committee on Small Business began hearings on "The Question: Are Planning and Regulation Replacing Competition in the American Economy? (The Automobile Industry as a Case Study)." GM's answer was a ninety-eight-page statement, formidably entitled: "The Automobile Industry: A Case Study of Competition." This document was intended to show that "competitive rivalry in the industry, far from being replaced by planning and regulation, has intensified." The statement also undertook to show "the error in any claim that General Motors has market control."

The statement ignored the category of oligopoly, which economists have recognized for thirty-five years. Again, Galbraith's definition: "A small number of firms have the market rivalries semantically associated with competition. But the firms are interdependent in their pricing—the price set by one affects the prices that can be charged by all. And recognizing this interdependence, each firm thinks, inevitably, in terms both of its own good and that of the industry. It avoids setting prices that are mutually destructive; it aims for prices that maximize its returns and by the same token those of others. Since such calculation is imperfect and overt communication illegal, the resulting price may differ from the monopoly price. But it approximates it in some fashion. And . . rivalry continues in advertising, product improvement, gadgetry and the like where it is not destructive."

The subcommittees submitted the GM statement to some eminent economists, including Galbraith. His comments were acerbic. "The automobile industry with three large and strong firms and one weaker one is cited more often than any other as the classical manifestation of oligopoly,'' he said. GM should not attempt ''to be identified in competitive structure with the apple grower or peanut vendor.'' That such a statement ''could come from a wills and deeds lawyer in the most remote boondock would be surprising,'' he said. ''I confess to total puzzlement as to how this could happen.''

Professor Galbraith's total puzzlement may have to do with a dreamy notion he expressed in *The New Industrial State*. There he had astutely recognized that *something* has to protect the country against arbitrary corporate government, or to put it another way, private government without the consent of the governed. But his nomination was the intellectual in politics, the ''educational and scientific estate, with its allies in the larger intellectual community.'' The mocking phrase of Professor Walter Adams of Michigan State University was ''platonic philosopher-kings.''

But there may have been no need for puzzlement about why General Motors claimed to fit the model of classic competition. To start with, it would have been reasonable to assume that for GM, as for any giant corporation, ''competition'' is the only fig leaf around. GM was being pressed by the chairmen of the subcommittees at the time, Wayne Morse of Oregon and Gaylord Nelson of Wisconsin, both intelligent and tough-minded men. It would be too painful to admit the naked truth, which, as stated by Carl Kaysen, a former colleague of Galbraith's at Harvard, is that ''the power of corporate management is, in the political sense, irresponsible power, answerable ultimately only to itself.'' GM sensibly would avoid the silly claim that it is a democracy run by its 1.3 million stockholders. Could GM lightly concede that it is, in the phrase of Professor Adams, ''a self-serving, self-justifying, and self-perpetuating industrial oligarchy''—or *any* kind of oligarchy—but that the educational and scientific estate protects the country? No. In an imperfect world even GM on occasion must settle for the least of evils. Better to say it competes, even if that means being classified with the apple grower and the peanut vendor. Better to wear a fig leaf called ''competition,'' even if it is transparent.

The First Amendment protects what the philosopher Hannah Arendt called ''the sense by which we take our bearings in the real world.'' Survival, she said, requires ''men willing to do what Herodotus was the first to undertake consciously, namely, *legein ta eonta,* to say what is.'' Not even total immersion in the prose of Arundel Cotter, which deserves a prominent place in the treacly annals of corporate religiosity, can detract from the towering importance of the guarantee of a free press. John Kenneth Galbraith said of the American government that it "works far better—perhaps it only works—when the Federal Executive and influential business and the respectable press are in some degree at odds. Only then can we be sure that abuse or neglect, either public or private, will be given the notoriety that is needed. In the time of Coolidge and Hoover, the Federal Executive, business, and the press were united. These are times in our democracy when all looks peaceful and much goes wrong." And so we must look into how the First Amendment is used to check corporate power.

During the 1968 presidential campaign, newsmen questioned Richard Nixon, Hubert Humphrey and George Wallace on *Face the Nation* and *Meet the Press.* It is anything but routinely possible for the public to see newsmen confront those who exercise substantial private power. "The individuals who hold the reins of power in any enterprise cannot trust themselves to be adequately self-critical," John W. Gardner has said. It would be instructive to see, on television, critical questioning of the president of General Motors about the long gestation of the impact-absorbing steering assembly. The president of United States Steel might be asked about the contribution of his industry to the balance-of-payments crisis. The presidents of the Upjohn Company and American Home Products might want to try to persuade us that it was necessary to go to court to prevent interruption of the marketing of antibiotic combinations that expose large numbers of persons to needless injury and even death.

For that matter, leaders of the news media, in an open society, might agree that it would be only fair for them to be publicly questioned about their performance. The outlook for such even-handed checks on private power is never particularly luminous, but a balanced judgment must be that it is generally and reliably enhanced neither by concentrated ownership of news media, whether on a local, state or national basis, nor by enlarging opportunities for corporations with non-media involvements to control news media. The agencies of mass communication, the Commission on Freedom of the Press suggested two decades ago, "can facilitate thought and discussion. They can stifle it. They can advance the progress of civilization or they can thwart it. They can debase and vulgarize mankind. They can endanger the peace of the world; they can do so accidentally in a fit of absence of mind." All of which is an elaboration on the recognition that the selection of what to report and what not to report, of what to emphasize and what not to emphasize, of the point in time at which significant disclosures will be made—all such decisions are an exercise of the power *legein ta eonta*, to say what is.

Clearly this is a very special and most important kind of power. In 1968 and 1969 the National Commission on Product Safety held a series of hearings on needlessly hazardous products used in and around the household. One of these hearings concerned unsafe glass doors. These alone were estimated to injure children, sometimes fatally, at a rate of 100,000 per year. The remedy for new construction was simple: the Federal Housing Administration, under its rule-making power for guaranteeing mortgages, had but to require, at an extra cost of a few dollars, the use of extra-strength glass which, if it breaks at all, crumbles into pebbles, rather than splitting into shards. As a practical matter, this would control the practice throughout the home-building industry. Parents of victims came forward to testify, hoping thereby to spare other children. A Georgia couple told how their daughter, playing at a neighbor's house, had crashed through a sliding door of cheap glass. Her wounds were so severe that she very quickly bled to death. A Capitol Hill policeman told of terrible injury done to his little boy when, in an unfamiliar new apartment, he too went through such a door. It happened that a newspaper story on the hearing was seen by Representative Benjamin S. Rosenthal (D–N.Y.). He was struck by, among other things, testimony showing that the National Association of Home Builders, like the FHA, was not supporting safety glazing, and by evidence that on leaving the government some FHA officials have found a snug harbor in the NAHB. Rosenthal summoned the FHA officials involved to a meeting. This, along with the hearing and the news story, helped to overcome, rather swiftly, their reluctance to act.

It must be noted that many major news media did not cover the hearing although, having been held in the New Senate Office Building, it was not inaccessible. Noncoverage of such important matters is commonplace. News resources—reporters, space and time to accommodate their product—are highly limited. News opportunities are not. The point remains, however, that to be able "to say what is" is to exercise formidable power.

It is right to abhor control by the state of "the power to say what is." It is also necessary to recognize the significant potentials for abuse that lie in private control of the same power. One such potential exists in advertising. Although this is too well known to require elaboration here, an example will not overburden the point. The advertising message that Ultra-Brite "gives your mouth sex appeal" helped to win that "whitener" toothpaste nearly 10 per cent of a $350 million market. The disinterested message of the Council on Dental Therapeutics of the American Dental Association was treated as if it had bad breath. That message was that "whitener" toothpastes may be too abrasive and may increase susceptibility to decay in the one adult in four over thirty-five whose gums tend to recede and expose the vulnerable cementum.

Our principal concern is with ownership of news media by large corporations with conglomerate interests. The problem may be made clear at once with a couple of chilling statistics. Each year occupational accidents kill 14,000 persons and disable—for as long as a lifetime—2.2 million others. These figures are almost universally acknowledged to be conservative; furthermore, they exclude casualties from occupational disease, such as coal miner's "black lung." Other things being equal, is the prospect for thorough reporting of this situation likely to be as great by a news medium with corporate ties to manufacturing or mining as by a news medium without such ties? We need not deal only in hypotheticals. The case was powerfully laid out on the public record a few years ago when the International Telephone and Telegraph Corporation made (but ultimately abandoned) an effort to acquire the American Broadcasting Companies. Here is a concise contemporaneous description of the two corporations:

> ITT is a sprawling international conglomerate of 433 separate boards of directors that derives about 60 percent of its income from its significant holdings in at least forty foreign countries. It is the ninth largest industrial corporation in the world in size of work force. In addition to its sale of electronic equipment to foreign governments, and operation of foreign countries' telephone systems, roughly half of its domestic income comes from U. S. Government defense and space contracts. But it is also in the business of consumer finance, life insurance, investment funds, small loan companies, car rentals (ITT Avis, Inc.), and book publishing. . . .

> ABC was born in 1941. . . . Today ABC owns 399 theaters in 34 states, five VHF stations, six AM and six FM stations (all in the top ten broadcasting markets), and, of course, one of the three major television networks and one of the four major radio networks in the world. Its 137 primary television network affiliates can reach 93 percent of the 50,000,000 television homes in the United States (more in prime-time evenings through secondary affiliates), and its radio network affiliates can reach 97 percent of the 55,000,000 homes with radio receivers. ABC has interests in, and affiliations with, stations in 25 other nations, known as the "Worldvision Group." ABC Films distributes filmed shows throughout this country and abroad. It is heavily involved in the record business, and subsidiaries publish three farm papers.

In proceedings before the Federal Communications Commission, ITT and ABC argued that the network would be granted an autonomous status to assure that ABC news and public affairs would be uninfluenced by other ITT business interests. The minority of three commissioners who fought the proposed merger were highly skeptical, especially because of a "subtle, almost unconscious process":

> *ABC newsmen and their supervisors will know that ITT is the boss, and that ITT has sensitive business relations in various foreign countries and at the highest levels of our government, and that reporting on any number of industries and economic developments will touch the interests of ITT. The mere awareness of these interests will make it impossible for those news officials, no matter how conscientious, to report news and develop documentaries objectively, in the way that they would do if ABC remained unaffiliated with ITT. Some of the newsmen will advance within the news organization, or be fired, or become officers of ABC—perhaps even of ITT—or not, and no newsman will be able to erase from his mind that his chances of doing so may be affected by his treatment of issues on which ITT is sensitive.*

> *Thus, the threat is not so much that documentaries or news stories adversely affecting the interests of ITT will be filed and then killed, or slanted—although that is also a problem. It is that the questionable story idea, or news coverage, will never even be proposed—whether for reasons of fear, insecurity, cynicism, realism, or unconscious avoidance.*

It should be borne in mind that the minority commissioners—Nicholas Johnson, Kenneth A. Cox, and Robert T. Bartley—were emphasizing a *potential* for abuse. Almost every day, men and women of courage and integrity do make their mark on news media owned by large organizations as well as small ones. The Westinghouse Broadcasting Company is part of the conglomerate Westinghouse manufacturing organization, has observed high standards, and has a commendable record of dealing with sensitive issues including consumer matters. On the very morning these words were written the *Washington Post* published a column in which Nicholas von Hoffman sharply criticized WTOP, which is owned by the Washington Post Company, for refusing to sell time for a brief message by the Business Executives Move for Vietnam Peace. In addition, the *Post* has published numerous editorial-page pieces critical of its own performance. But, again, it is the *potential* that is of foremost concern. The environment always to be sought is one which assures that ordinary men, not merely heroes, will reliably do what is necessary. The broadcast media did not do what was necessary in terms of news coverage of developments, many of them dramatic, about the largest prospective merger in the history of broadcasting. They treated the news negligibly when they treated it at all. ABC News "often sounded as if its stories about the mergers [*sic*] were dictated by management," the *Columbia Journalism Review* said. "Journalists can be relieved that two such managements did not get together." Thus the broadcast media lent substance to the concerns of the three commissioners, as well as to the Justice Department, which intervened against the merger. ITT's business operations, the Department said, "are bound to generate enormous pressure to intervene in areas of news coverage which threaten fundamental economic interests of the company."

But if doubt remained about a possible threat to the integrity of news at ABC it was removed by ITT itself when, in an incredible display of potential for abuse, it made brazen efforts to intimidate reporters who were beyond its internal system of reward and punishment. After the *Wall Street Journal*'s Fred L. Zimmerman broke the story, the Justice Department's antitrust lawyers, brilliantly led by Lionel Kestenbaum, subpoenaed three reporters—Eileen Shanahan of the *New York Times*, Stephen M. Aug, then of the Associated Press, and Jed Stout, then of United Press International—to testify at a hearing which the Commission had reluctantly convened.

In the aggregate the most serious incidents involved Miss Shanahan. On one occasion, she said under oath, an ITT official relayed a company comment on a development and said "something to the effect, 'I expect to see that in the paper, high up in your story.'" At her office in Washington, Edward J. Gerrity, ITT's senior vice president for public relations, asked Miss Shanahan if he could look at a story she was writing, a request which as a reporter she of course considered "improper." In a tone she described as "accusatory and nasty" he "badgered me" to try to get the *Times* to use the text of a certain FCC order. Gerrity inquired whether Miss Shanahan had been following the prices of ITT and ABC stock. Did she not feel a "responsibility to the shareholders who might lose money as a result" of her stories? Her response was, "My responsibility was to find out the truth and print it." Was she aware that Commissioner Johnson and Senator Gaylord Nelson were working "on legislation that would forbid any newspaper from owning any broadcast property"? (Johnson and Nelson each said that they had never met and had collaborated on nothing.) Gerrity told Miss Shanahan that she ought to pass the (false) information along to her publisher, the implication being that the *Times*, as an owner of radio stations, would see a threat to its own economic interests. There were other incidents of nastiness and misrepresentation, some of them involving John V. (Jack) Horner, ITT's public relations chief in Washington.

ITT offered no rebuttal to the sworn testimony of Miss Shanahan, who, needless to say, is a highly respected reporter. Neither did ITT concede that it had engaged in improper conduct. Miss Shanahan testified on April 20, 1967. Eight weeks *afterward* Horner was questioning friends and former employers of Miss Shanahan about her personal and professional life. Subsequently the FCC affirmed its earlier approval of the acquisition, again by a vote of 4 to 3. The Justice Department then filed a lawsuit to block it. On January 1, 1968, while the case was pending, ITT abruptly backed out of the proposed merger to move on to less troublesome acquisitions. The lawsuit had been appropriately entitled *United States of America v. Federal Communications Commission.*

Deservedly, there would be a poor market for a book on the theme that death is an outrage and should be abolished. And if great centralization of economic power is, in a modern technological society, inevitable, possibly our effort would not have much point. The fundamental question—one which should concern conservatives and liberals alike—is whether economic concentration is truly necessary. If we must have it, the outlook for the individual is bleak. He will not have a significant opportunity to shape the intricate corporate and governmental organizations which control his destiny. The democratic institutions which were carefully designed to allow him fulfillment increasingly will be seen as the hollow farce that the New Left asserts them to be.

Not just the New Left. During the 1968 presidential campaign Richard Nixon, describing complaints of "the alienated," found "a common thread." Although he was of course running it through the eye of a needle pointed at Democrats in Washington, his rhetoric was more encompassing, even if inadvertently. "The power to control decisions immediately affecting one's life is vanishing. . . . That unique, precious, indescribable thing—the *individual* human mind, heart and spirit—is being injured, or neglected, or slighted. . . . What we need is not one leader, but many leaders; not one center of power, but many centers of power." Compare this with Jeremy Larner, who was a speechwriter for Senator Eugene J. McCarthy in his campaign for the Democratic presidential nomination: "The idea is to break power down to small units, so that people can create more satisfying ways of living. That is why the cliché of 'control over the decisions which affect our lives' reaches people, whether it is spoken by Mr. Nixon,

Mr. [Richard N.] Goodwin, or Mr. [Tom] Hayden. But the new class [which is "searching for politics which can change the quality of life"] is going to find that meaningful participation is impossible without a radical democratizing of our decision-making institutions. *For the ethic of corporate power is blatantly incompatible with the distribution of power among equal citizens."* [Emphasis supplied.]

John Kenneth Galbraith contends that concentration of economic power must be accepted; modern technology makes it inevitable. Galbraith argued his case in *The New Industrial State.* It was published with deserved acclaim for its perception, style and wit, in 1967. This date must be accorded some attention. "I had nearly finished a preliminary draft of this book when President Kennedy asked me to go to India in 1961," he said. "With some misgiving I put the manuscript away in the vault of the bank." He returned to Harvard in 1963. A year later, Senator Hart, the Michigan Democrat who heads the Senate Subcommittee on Antitrust and Monopoly, opened hearings on economic concentration. *The New Industrial State* cites the hearings at a couple of points but, we believe, takes them insufficiently into account. In addition, Senator Hart productively continued the hearings in 1967, the year in which the Galbraith book was published, and each year thereafter, including 1970. The news media generally accorded them slight attention; not unexpectedly, public awareness of them is limited. Yet the Hart hearings provide an abundance of empiric evidence to refute Galbraith's thesis. The facts argue that the new technologies should be leading us not toward more concentration, and to preservation of existing concentration, but to deconcentration. That is their natural thrust.

> *Actually, big businesses are generally no more and no less efficient than medium-sized businesses even when the gains wrung by monopoly power are included in efficiency. This is the one general finding in comparative cost studies and comparative profitability studies. . . .*
>
> *When we recall that most big businesses have numerous complete plants at various points throughout the country, this finding is not surprising. Why should United States Steel be more efficient than Inland Steel, when United States Steel is simply a dozen or more Inland Steels strewn about the country? Why should GM be appreciably more efficient than say a once again independent Buick Motors?*

The foregoing excerpt appeared in an article entitled "The Case Against Big Business." The author was George J. Stigler, of the University of Chicago Law School, who headed the Task Force on Productivity and Competition appointed by Richard Nixon while he was President-elect. Exactly the same point was made—an identical phrase was even used inadvertently—by Professor Walter Adams:

The unit of technological efficiency is the plant, not the firm. This means that there are undisputed advantages to large-scale integrated operations at a single steel plant, for example, but there is little technological justification for combining these functionally separate plants into a single administrative unit. United States Steel is nothing more than several Inland Steels strewn about the country, and no one has yet suggested that Inland is not big enough to be efficient. A firm producing such divergent lines as rubber boots, chain saws, motorboats, and chicken feed may be seeking conglomerate size and power; it is certainly not responding to technological necessity. In short, one can favor technological bigness and oppose administrative bigness without inconsistency.

If technological efficiency collapses as a justification for concentration, then what justifications remain? "The size of General Motors is in the service not of monopoly or the economies of scale, but of planning," Professor Galbraith says. "And for this planning . . . there is no clear upper limit to the desirable size. It could be that the bigger the better." It will suffice—but only for the moment—to ask, we hope not unkindly, whether those concerned, for example, with planning the preservation of the environment care to entrust that delicate mission to the company which, through its vehicles and plants, produces 35 per cent of the country's total tonnage of air pollution. Or, for that matter, to General Dynamics, General Electric, General Foods or General Anything.

The last remaining major justification for "Brobdingnagian size," as Professor Adams has called it, is that it provides the necessary environment for invention, innovation, and technological progress. The empiric evidence simply does not bear this out. An extraordinary proportion of the important, radical developments have come from loners, men who worked outside large organizations or without their support. "The disk memory unit, the heart of today's random access computer, is not the logical outcome of a decision made by IBM management," Arthur K. Watson, formerly of IBM and now ambassador to France, has candidly acknowledged. "It was developed in one of our laboratories as a bootleg project—over the stern warning from management that the project had to be dropped because of budget difficulties. A handful of men ignored the warning. They broke the rules. They risked their jobs to work on a project they believed in."

The late Milton Lehman, biographer of Robert H. Goddard, said that this "sickly, frail unrecognized" inventor had accomplished more than any other in this century and "more than any man, opened the door to the age of space." Testifying before the Senate Antitrust Subcommittee, Lehman said that "the organization" of course frustrated Goddard. Yet, he made his rocket inventions with a total of $250,000 for "the salary of his crew, the cost of his 'hardware,' the fees for his patents, and the maintenance of his household—for more than 40 years. (And if you divide $250,000 by 40, it doesn't leave very much a year for inventing the modern space age.)" Walter Adams and Joel B. Dirlam did an analysis of the steel industry, which is one of the most concentrated in the United States. The findings were dramatic. Professor Adams later gave this summary:

> It spends only 0.7 percent of its revenues on research and, in technological progressiveness, the giants which dominate this industry lag behind their smaller domestic rivals as well as their smaller foreign competitors. Thus, the basic oxygen furnace—considered the "only major breakthrough at the ingot level since before the turn of the century"—was invented in 1950 by a minuscule Austrian firm which was less than one-third the size of a single plant of the United States Steel Corp. The innovation was introduced in the United States in 1954 by McLouth Steel [of Detroit] which at the time had about 1 percent of domestic steel capacity—to be followed some 10 years later by the steel giants: United States Steel in December 1963, Bethlehem in 1964, and Republic in 1965. Despite the fact that this revolutionary invention involved an average operating cost saving of $5 per ton and an investment cost saving of $20 per ton of installed capacity, the steel giants during the 1950's, according to Business Week, "bought 40 million tons of the wrong capacity—the open-hearth furnace" which was obsolete almost the moment it was put in place.

The natural thrust of the new technologies toward deconcentration, toward smaller units, toward a socioeconomic environment compatible, to repeat Jeremy Larner, "with the distribution of power among equal citizens"—this natural thrust has been frustrated. Instead the unnatural has been occurring, most prominently in the 1960s in the conglomerate merger movement. More than anything else this is a testament to the efficacy of synthetic stimuli. In the government sector these have included tax advantages and a long-standing failure to enforce the antitrust laws with the vigor encouraged by the Supreme Court. In the private sector the synthetic stimuli toward concentration have included such power plays as that after World War II when steel was in short supply. General Electric and General Motors could get steel for appliances. Small and medium-sized producers could not, and in significant numbers they died.

The concentration of economic power is well advanced. There is still time—probably not much—to halt the process and maybe even reverse it. If we fail to act swiftly, those who hold concentrated economic power will bring it increasingly to bear on our democratic institutions. They may come to dominate them. Such a manifestation of self-protection and aggression is their natural thrust. We may learn the hard way, and too late, that a free society and massive concentration of economic power cannot for long coexist. This power can be diffused. Its growth can be stunted. These are feasible goals. We will make suggestions looking toward their achievement. If these suggestions should strike the reader as less than ideal we can only offer him the consolation of Alexander Hamilton. "I never expect to see a perfect work from imperfect man," he said.

2

CORPORATE DISREGARD FOR LIFE

If corporations have been irresponsible in creating economic waste, they have been criminal in their abdication of human concern in the area of unsafe products. Unchecked by regulatory agencies, legal remedies, and so-called marketplace pressures, corporations both large and small, sometimes unwittingly and sometimes consciously, have marketed ill-designed products and left us a legacy of death and injury. Corporate-induced violence far outstrips the other kinds of violence that cause widespread concern: street crimes, for example, take 7,500 lives every year; automobiles take 55,000 lives, a majority of which could have been saved by safer cars.

Such irresponsibility on the part of manufacturers was facilitated by the innocent confidence consumers had in corporate integrity and technological achievements. Consumers believed—and generally still do—that industry makes products as safe as possible, and that if products weren't safe the government would prohibit their sale. Both of these suppositions are false. Although federal legislation in specific areas since the mid-1960s has made certain products such as automobiles safer in design, there is no comprehensive law requiring safety standards for all products. Even laws that have been passed are weakly enforced. For example, the deadline for federally-required installation of the air bag, or an equivalent system, which would save thousands of lives in auto crashes has been thrice delayed until the 1976 model cars. And so many products which are patently hazardous or ill-designed for reasonably safe performance continue to be sold. It is apparent that a federal law must be passed to include all products: one that will set the highest standards practical technology permits and that will subject willful violators to criminal penalties. We cannot depend on industry to market safe products of its own accord as a long history of carnage attests.

Even when a danger is nationally exposed, corporate giants insist on pursuing profits—as in the face of a national cancer epidemic caused by cigarettes which the first article in this section, "Selling Death," by Thomas Whiteside illustrates. With scientific evidence against it, the tobacco industry has, since 1964 when the hazard was first exposed nationally, continued its insidious advertising of cigarettes to ensnare new smokers and to persuade people that, despite the Surgeon General's annual reports, smoking cigarettes is in fact healthy. Confronted with the evidence that tar is a cancer-causing ingredient, the industry reacted by producing longer cigarettes (the 100 millimeters) with greater tar content. As Whiteside reports in his article, "Selling Death," and in his book of the same name, since cigarette commercials on television and radio have been finally abolished by Congress, the industry has cynically transferred its advertising money to other media.

Nowhere has corporate disregard for life been more visible than in the automotive industry, as documented by three articles in this section. In early 1972 Volkswagen announced that more VWs have been produced than any other model car, surpassing the more than fifteen million Model Ts produced by Henry Ford. This can hardly be cause for rejoicing by any but the makers of Volkswagen, since studies show that the VW is probably the most dangerously designed car in common use in this country. Neither can American car manufacturers take comfort in their record. It has been seven years since my book, *Unsafe At Any Speed,* was published exposing dangerous auto design: in particular, General Motors' Corvair. Recent evidence confirms that GM officials knew at the time the Corvair was marketed (in the very early sixties) that it had dangerous defects, including a faulty heater that gave off deadly carbon monoxide and an instability that caused it to overturn easily. For years GM tried to hide the evidence (some of which is revealed in another article, "Confessions of a GM Engineer," later in this book). Still, as Colman McCarthy, editorial writer for the *Washington Post,* revealed in a series of articles, General Motors continues to produce dangerously defective vehicles—now it's school buses—and hopes it will not be discovered. (One of the McCarthy articles, "Bitter Tales from the GM Lemon Groves," is reprinted in this section.) In another excerpted chapter from *America, Inc.* "Crime in the Suites," Morton Mintz and Jerry Cohen put into historical and social perspective the long tradition of corporate crime in America, documented by some fascinating letters which the President of du Pont de Nemours Company and the President of General Motors exchanged in 1929. Mintz and Cohen also point up the difficulties of obtaining strict enforcement of the auto safety law.

Similarly, my article "The Burned Children" documents the laxity with which both government officials and fabric manufacturers regard the hazard of flammable clothing and other fabrics which easily catch fire, causing hideous scars and sometimes death. Since the early fifties manufacturers have known how to process fire retardant cotton that could prevent thousands of burn injuries and deaths.

Corporate powers managed to keep the dangers of products hidden so long by denying or minimizing existence of the hazards, and instead blaming death and injury on the *misuse* of products. Part of the cover-up was legitimized when industry set its own safety standards—at the lowest common denominator—giving the impression that industry was vitally interested in safety and that products were at a safety level consistent with technological knowledge. There were few statistics to refute these claims for safe products. This was changed by the Congressionally authorized National Commission on Product Safety which issued a significant report in 1970. For the first time figures were amassed and the testimony of experts and consumers was taken at hearings throughout the country. The figures and testimonies documented the enormous problem of product-involved deaths and injuries. Concluding this section is an introduction I wrote for the Commission hearings which were published in thirty-three volumes. The introduction not only recounts the negligence and callousness of many industries that the Commission uncovered, it also explains what various groups such as attorneys, product engineers, and consumers

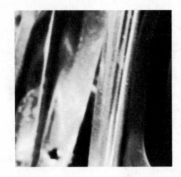

SELLING DEATH

Thomas Whiteside

In the period preceding the removal, by act of Congress, of all cigarette advertising from radio and television at the beginning of this
year, spokesmen for various tobacco companies were insistent, in
interviews with reporters, that the industry planned no undue increase
in the amount of cigarette advertising in the press when the ban on
cigarette commercials went into effect. Some weeks have now passed
since cigarette commercials were taken off the air. During that time
I have been interested in whether the press, and in particular magazines, would abstain from taking advantage of this situation by soliciting or accepting, for profit, any additional print advertising for a product that has been shown in medical studies (which have been reported
in the press itself) to be the leading cause of lung cancer among
men and a significant contributing factor to premature death from
coronary heart disease, emphysema and a number of other diseases.
I have also been interested in exploring the extent to which the tobacco manufacturers have felt themselves restrained, in planning their
cigarette-advertising campaigns in the print media for the period after
the ban on radio and TV cigarette commercials, by the realization
that any excessive increase in the number of print ads they took out
might provoke the Federal Trade Commission to take some kind of
regulatory action, for example requiring health warnings to be displayed in all print advertising.

By any such standards of restraint, the behavior of the tobacco
companies and the magazines alike since the ban on cigarette commercials went into effect has been alarming. A prime example exists
in the advertising pages of *Life*. In the fall of 1969, in response to

From *The New Republic,* 27 March 1971. Reprinted by permission of *The New Republic,* © 1971, Harrison-Blaine
of New Jersey, Inc.

a letter from Sen. Frank E. Moss of Utah, attempting to determine the attitude of various publishers to accepting an increased volume of cigarette advertising after a cutoff of cigarette commercials from the air, Andrew Heiskell the chairman of Time, Inc., publicly assured the senator that his company would continue to take cigarette ads but that it had no intention of accepting any "overwhelming" amount of cigarette advertising as a result of the TV cutoff. What has happened since this assurance can be gathered by the fact that whereas the first three issues of *Life* in 1970 carried twelve-and-a-half pages of cigarette advertising, the first three issues of the same magazine in 1971, immediately after the ban on cigarette ads on TV went into effect, carried twenty-two pages of cigarette advertising—all of them in color. And a comparison of the number of ads carried in the February 5 issue of *Life* this year with that in the first issue in February of last year shows that the number of cigarette ad pages has jumped from two to eight.

On February 8 of this year, *Life* carried a full-page ad in *The New York Times* in praise of what it called "Life's Editorial Power." The ad asked, rhetorically, "Who else had the photo of the National Guard about to fire at the Kent State kids? The reminiscences of Nikita Khrushchev? The 242 pictures of one week's American war dead in Vietnam?" It went on, "That kind of editorial excellence gives *Life* more impact than any other magazine. And gives your ad more impact than it can get anywhere else."

How can any responsible publishing corporation use a claim of editorial excellence to hold forth the unblushing assurance, applying in this case to cigarette manufacturers, that ads for a product, the use of which is officially recognized as a major cause of disease and death each year, would have "more impact" than anywhere else? If *Life*, which carried those "242 pictures of one week's American war dead in Vietnam," were to carry pictures of the number of American cigarette smokers who succumbed to lung cancer alone in the course of an average week, it would need not 242 pictures, but at least four times that number. How can any publisher—anyone—*make money* out of selling advertisements for a product that is known to cause death on a disastrous national scale year after year? The record of *Time* is no more encouraging than *Life* in this respect. The first three issues of *Time* for 1970 carried eight pages of cigarette advertising. The first three issues of the same magazine for 1971 carried a little less than 21 pages of cigarette advertising. And *Newsweek* is not much better than *Time*. In the first three months of 1970, *Newsweek* carried 23 pages of cigarette advertising, and for the first quarter of 1971, *Newsweek* has scheduled 50 pages of cigarette advertising—an increase of 108 percent. And nobody can accuse the editors of *Newsweek,* any more than one could accuse the editors of *Time* and *Life,* of not knowing the facts about the causal relationship between cigarette smoking and lung cancer and other fatal diseases. Nor can the editors of *Look* claim innocence about the facts concerning cigarette smoking and disease. The fact that *Life* and *Look* are in financial trouble can hardly be viewed as an acceptable excuse for their trying to prop up their corporate health at the expense of the health of their readers.

With certain honorable exceptions, such as *Mademoiselle* and *Glamour,* two Condé Nast publications that, because they are meant to appeal to young women, have decided against taking cigarette advertising, the women's magazines as a whole are soliciting and accepting a new flood of cigarette advertising. What makes the use of this medium of advertising so particularly detestable is the knowledge that although women are less prone to lung cancer than men, the lung-cancer rate among women smokers in the last fifteen years has shown an alarming rise. Further, women, when they try to stop smoking, appear to have greater difficulty than men in breaking themselves of the habit. To counteract the trend among the smoking population generally toward cutting down on cigarette consumption, tobacco manufacturers are making great efforts to develop the market among women—in particular by putting out new brands of cigarettes "imaged" in such a way as to seem particularly attractive in the female market. Huge sums have been poured into the promotion of new "women's" cigarettes such as Virginia Slims, put out by Philip Morris, and Eve, which Liggett & Myers has introduced this year on a national scale with huge double-page color spreads in the major magazines of general circulation and in the women's magazines. The introductory ads for women are headed, "Farewell to the ugly cigarette. Smoke pretty. Eve." The accompanying copy goes on, "Hello to Eve. The first truly feminine cigarette—it's almost as pretty as you are. With pretty filter tip. Pretty pack. Rich, yet gentle flavor . . . Women have been feminine since Eve. Now cigarettes are feminine. Since Eve." The ad is illustrated with a color picture of a woman's hand, amid wild flowers, holding a pack of Eve, and the pack design shows the head of an innocent-looking woman gazing out from a profusion of flowers and greenery depicted in mock-tapestry style. The deliberately contrived themes in this particular advertisement of innocence and of temptation, and an equally deliberate concealment, by the hand that is shown holding the package, of the message printed on the side, "Warning: The Surgeon General Has Determined That Cigarette Smoking Is Dangerous to Your Health," surely make this one of the most deceitful cigarette advertising campaigns yet devised.

What is perfectly clear from all this is that the legal measures that have been taken so far to bring some measure of governmental control over cigarette advertising are altogether insufficient to restrain the tobacco industry from huge advertising campaigns in the further-ance of what can only be regarded—considering what is known about the relationship between cigarette smoking and various diseases—as manslaughter on a massive scale. And the press as a whole has been undeterred from acting as co-conspirator in this manslaughter for the sake of whatever additional profits publishers have been able to seize as a result of the ban on cigarette commercials on the air. Obviously, some drastic action has to be taken to correct this situation. Under the Public Health Cigarette Smoking Act of 1970 the Federal Trade Commission is preempted until July 1, 1971 from prohibiting cigarette advertising or even from requiring that health warnings be plainly visible in all cigarette advertising; thereafter, if the FTC wishes to act in these respects, it must give Congress six months' notice of its intention to do so. This preemption was inserted in the Act through the pressure of tobacco industry lobbyists, who calculated that any such moves by the FTC might be forestalled in Congress with the help of the tobacco industry and its commercial and political allies. Even if such moves against cigarette advertising by the FTC were permitted by Congress, the resulting delay of approximately one year in controlling or prohibiting cigarette advertising would certainly have a contributory effect on the scores of thousands of human fatalities that occur in this country each year as a result of cigarette smoking. Under the circumstances, it does not seem to me that the FTC is in a position to bring an effective end to the systematic promotion for profit of this clearly lethal product. Consequently, I suggest that the problem of cigarette advertising be placed under the jurisdiction not only of the FTC but also of the Food and Drug Administration, and that all cigarette advertising in this country be banned under the provisions of the Federal Hazardous Substances Act, which author-izes the FDA to ban or control the sale or promotion of substances that because of their toxicity are hazardous to public health. The toxic substances covered by the terms of the Hazardous Substances Act include those that are capable of causing harm to humans "through inhalation." This definition fits cigarettes and cigarette smoking quite precisely, and I believe that if the Food and Drug Administration does move promptly to place cigarettes and cigarette smoking under the provisions of the Hazardous Substances Act for the purpose of bring-ing the promotion of cigarettes under adequate federal regulation, the Federal Trade Commission would then also be able either to ban all cigarette advertising or to require that strong health warnings be prominently displayed in the cigarette advertising that is allowed.

THE BURNED CHILDREN

Ralph Nader

A five-year-old boy was playing in the kitchen while his mother was outside putting wash on the clothesline. The next time his mother saw him, the child was running into the yard and his body was totally black. At first she thought he had been playing with ink or paint. But as she got closer, she realized that his pajamas had burned. All that was left of them were the cuffs burning around his ankles. Later she found bits of charred cloth scattered through the house where the child had run wildly after the pajamas caught fire, apparently on the stove. Four weeks later, the boy died.

This tragic incident occurred just before Christmas last year. It is not an isolated case. Approximately 3000 people die every year after their clothing catches fire. Over 150,000 are injured in the same way. When all fabric fires are included more than 250,000 people suffer injuries and 4000 die each year. An unusually high proportion are children and elderly people. More children under the age of five die from fires and explosions than from any other kind of injury.

Despite the fact that physicians and public health officials have been pointing out these facts for years, and citing instances as shocking as the case of the five-year-old boy, consumers still have little protection against the hazards of flammable fabrics.

From *The New Republic*, 3 July 1971. Reprinted by permission of *The New Republic*, © 1971, Harrison-Blaine of New Jersey, Inc.

The Flammable Fabrics Act passed in 1953 has long been recognized by safety experts as a sham. William White, former chairman of the National Commission on Product Safety, has noted that the Act "is famous for allowing 99 percent of all fabrics marketed in this country to pass the test. It is well known to the plastic surgeons who repair the burned children who were wearing the clothing made from fabrics that always pass this test."

In 1967 attempts were made to correct this situation. The Flammable Fabrics Act was amended to include home furnishings and wearing apparel such as shoes and hats which were not previously covered, and to provide for new flammability standards to be set by the Department of Commerce. Today, three-and-a-half years later, only one new standard has been set and not a single new standard for clothing. The Secretary of Commerce did not even call a meeting of his advisory committee on flammability standards until May of 1969, nearly one-and-a-half years after the amendments were passed.

All the department has done with regard to clothing is to propose a standard for children's nightwear which is so restricted that by industry's own count it will eliminate only 1 percent of the total clothing-related burns. The standard applies only to sleepwear up to the size of 6X. (Yet even many five-year-olds wear larger sizes.) It is less inclusive than England's regulation, in effect since 1967, that *all* children's sleepwear be flame-retardant and that all adult sleepwear be labeled if it does not pass the tests.

The formal administrative procedures to set a new standard for children's sleepwear began in January, 1970. Department of Commerce officials, after many unwarranted delays, now say that a mandatory standard will be set within a few weeks. However there may be yet another delay; the effective date of the standard may be extended from 1972 to 1973 to allow more time for industry to comply.

The only standard the Department has actually set under the 1967 amendments is a test for rugs and carpets that went into effect April 16, 1971. This test was heartily endorsed by the carpet and rug industry because it is so weak most of their products can already pass it. Even the National Bureau of Standards, not known for its vigorous safety efforts, considers the "pill" test for carpets to be inadequate. This test utilizes an aspirin-sized methanamine tablet as a timed ignition source. The National Bureau of Standards calls it a "first generation test," since it "fails" only those carpets that can be easily ignited by a flame as small as that of a cigarette. It does not measure the reaction of a carpet to a larger fire. The carpet that contributed to the deaths of 32 nursing home patients in Marietta, Ohio, in 1969 would have passed the "pill" test.

Rugs that might have trouble passing the test—small machine-tufted carpets—are virtually exempt. The Commerce Department has ruled that such rugs can still be sold whether or not they pass the pill test. The only "safeguard" for the consumer is a requirement beginning December 8, 1971, that small rugs which fail the test be so labeled. These small rugs, less than 4 x 6 feet, account for 18 percent of the market, with approximately 55 million sold every year. Shag rugs, some of which present the greatest flammability hazard of all rugs, are often made in this size range. According to industry's own statement, 80 to 90 percent of these small rugs are made of cotton or rayon and would fail the pill test.

The final loophole in the standard is that carpets produced before April 16 may be sold without being tested or labeled, so consumers can't tell whether a rug has even undergone the pill test. The Department of Commerce hasn't alerted the public to this fact.

The industry has successfully resisted meaningful flammability standards primarily by persuading the Department of Commerce that consumers should bear the burden of protection. The remarks of George S. Buck, Jr., research director for the National Cotton Council, are typical. Mr. Buck alleged at hearings before the Department of Commerce in January, 1971, that "consumers don't give a damn about inflammable fabrics. . . . They are much more interested in comfort, wear-life, and style than . . . fire-resistance."

Even more blatant was the statement of an industry representative who wrote to the Department of Commerce protesting proposed flammability standards for children's nightwear: "It is impossible for industry or government to completely insulate a child from the hazards caused by careless and negligent parents or guardians that allow a child to become dangerously close to a source of flame. This small minority of parents and guardians who fail in their duty should not force the majority of careful and sensible parents to bear the cost of the hardship."

Passing the burden to the consumer is one of the oldest tricks of the marketplace. In reality, the consumer has almost never been offered a meaningful choice in flammable fabrics. It is virtually impossible to outfit a family and furnish a home in flame-retardant material, even though many fabrics can be made flame-retardant. Nor does the consumer have the information to enable him to make a choice between safe and unsafe fabrics. Few consumers think about flammability when they read advertisements that talk of nothing but style and comfort. How many manufacturers have attempted to sell safety in the way they sell fashion and convenience? The answer is virtually none. Even the Department of Commerce, charged with regulating flammability hazards, devotes an entire page in its textile "consumer guide" to "the exciting world of fibers and fabrics" and another page to wash-and-wear miracles. No page is devoted to warning the consumer about the hazards of flammability.

Most people learn about the hazards of flammable fabrics when tragedy strikes their own family. It is almost inevitably a costly lesson. One family in the state of Washington lost two children—a 13-year-old girl and her younger brother—in separate incidents that involved clothing that caught fire.

There are few injuries more traumatic than severe burns—and few burns more serious than those involving clothing ignition. The pain, the scars, the difficult and expensive medical treatment are excruciating burdens for burn victims and their families. And the opportunities for fires are all too prevalent in the home, where 80 percent of all burns occur. Another family lost their only child after his pajamas ignited from touching or coming near the burner on an electric stove. The two-year-old child lived for 69 days with third-degree burns over a large part of his body. In most of these cases, it would have been difficult for the parents to protect their children without totally unrealistic precautions.

Such accidents are not restricted to the young. An 86-year-old retired physician sustained burns over nearly half of her body when the sleeve of her nightgown caught on fire after coming in contact with the burner on an electric hot plate. She died after 22 days in the hospital.

Even when burns are not fatal, in addition to their anguish, families often have astronomical medical bills. One girl was burned when her jacket caught fire; she sustained second and third degree burns over 45 percent of her body. An HEW report stated that reconstructive surgery for her face, hands, and arms could cost $50,000 or more.

Time after time, physicians have brought in evidence of severe burns that could have been less serious or even avoided if the clothing had been flame-retardant. Two electricians were burned when a flash emitted from the high-voltage fuse panel they were servicing. One suffered a severe 40 percent body burn because his flannel shirt caught fire. He was in the hospital for three months and required several skin graft operations. The second man was wearing a heavy cotton work shirt and suffered only second degree burns to his hands and face. He was in the hospital for 25 days and required no grafts. Dr. Abraham Bergman, a Seattle physician, asked at Senate hearings in June 1970: "How many bodies have to be stacked up before effective action is taken to prevent clothing burn injuries?"

Efforts to improve consumer protection have been hindered by the fact that the magnitude of the fabric-burn problem has been concealed through lack of precise data. Statistics are still collected so haphazardly that current figures on burn injuries may underestimate the real picture. The National Commission on Product Safety took an important step toward correcting the dearth of injury information by instituting a system of hospital reporting, now operated by the Food and Drug Administration. But there are ominous signs that FDA is actually regressing in the investigation of reported burn cases. It has allowed its specialized teams that make in-depth investigations of injuries to deteriorate to the point where both the Boston and Denver Injury Study Units are operating at half their former level. Many injury investigations are now being carried out by FDA field inspectors who have no expertise at all in the area of consumer product safety.

The Department of Health, Education, and Welfare has been woefully inefficient in submitting its reports to Congress on injuries and deaths associated with the use of fabrics. These reports should be made annually under the 1967 amendments to the Flammable Fabrics Act. The first report was due in 1968 and was not delivered until after the second report was due in December 1969.

A chief block to greater safety remains weak government standards, often with loopholes so that manufacturers can avoid meeting even those regulations. The setting of weak standards initially makes it even harder to improve them, a fact recognized by the industry since 1953. The Department of Commerce, one of the least responsive of all government agencies to needs of consumers, has gone along like putty in the hands of manufacturers. Senator Warren G. Magnuson, author of the original Flammable Fabrics Act and Chairman of the Senate Commerce Committee, commented recently on the performance of the Department of Commerce in implementing the Act. He said: "No single bill with which I have been associated has been so bitter a disappointment. . . . A National Commission on Product Safety report last year reached two basic conclusions: the powers contained in the Act are adequate; the Department of Commerce is grossly inadequate."

Regulation has been reduced to an impotent approval of products that are cheapest for industry to make and will yield the highest profits. Low or nonexistent standards have made possible a controlled market where the innovative manufacturer who develops a safer fabric can be undercut by competitors who lower their prices temporarily and drive him off the market. Furthermore, manufacturers have frightened consumers by telling them that prices will go up for flame-retardant clothes (without mentioning that millions of dollars would be saved if burn injuries decreased). The available evidence suggests that the projected price increases are, in large part, either bluff or so much in excess of costs that manufacturers would be able to sustain them only by colluding. One garment manufacturer we contacted, for example, anticipates a $1.70 price differential between flame-retardant and regular pajamas. But cost data which he later provided shows that the additional cost of producing flame-retardant pajamas amounts to little more than the extra 55 cents per pair required to buy chemically treated fabric. Instead of intervening on the side of the innovative manufacturer and the consumer, Commerce has been a loyal defender of these textile interests who say they "cannot afford" to provide safety.

Two things are urgently needed if there is to be any change. First, the Department of Health, Education, and Welfare is going to have to provide more vigorous data collection on burn injuries and renew its almost dormant research function. Consumers will have to demand that information collected by HEW be made public and that specific brands be named as market guides, according to their flammability hazards or their safety improvements.

Second, concerted consumer pressure will be required if the Department of Commerce is to be moved to enforce the law. Congressional hearings to inquire into the protracted delays in setting standards is one step. Another step is citizen petitions to the Department to activate administrative procedures to set meaningful standards. The insurance industry could be of key assistance here. It may well be that a legal challenge to the Department's failure to move expeditiously in this area will be required or that the regulatory function should be placed elsewhere. It is Senator Magnuson's firm judgment that "the flammable fabrics program should be taken from the Department of Commerce and merged with the overall product safety program in an agency which is willing and capable to do what must be done."

Many deaths could be prevented and injuries greatly reduced in severity. We know how to make fabric less flammable. We know too that it is more efficient to make clothing safer than to keep children from climbing on stoves or persuade mothers not to buy frills for little girls. In few areas have industry and government been less responsive to consumers.

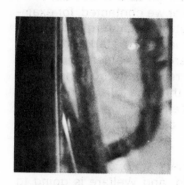

THE BEETLES

George Lardner

Ralph Nader and General Motors have found something on which they can agree: too many Americans are buying Volkswagens, some 3.2 million of them wriggling through heavy traffic and sandwiching themselves into small parking spaces. The chagrin in Detroit is economic, for only Ford, Chevrolet, Plymouth, Pontiac, and Buick are still outselling VW. Nader's concern is more basic: the Beetle is "more likely to cause serious or fatal injury in any collision than virtually any other car in common use in this country."

Accustomed to Nader's barbs, Volkswagen of American insists that its imports offer "safe, dependable and economical transportation" and sniffs that Nader, "has been making similar allegations about our products since 1966." The documentation this time may not be so easy to ignore. Compiled by Nader and 10 of his colleagues at the Center for Auto Safety, it has been put together in a 200-page report that flatly accuses Volkswagen of trying to "cover up or repress the engineering truth about its vehicles."

Take, for example, a 1968 study of the Beetle commissioned by the Volkswagen organization and undertaken by Cornell Aeronautical Laboratory's Automobile Crash Injury Research Project. Confined primarily to pre-1966 sedans, it found the cars especially prone to damage from rolling over after a collision or even in the absence of a

From *The New Republic*, 9 October 1971. Reprinted by permission of *The New Republic*, © 1971, Harrison-Blaine of New Jersey, Inc.

crash. According to the Nader report, it also found Beetle occupants tossed out of their cars in an accident more often than riders of any other foreign or light American car except the Renault Dauphine. The chances of fatal or dangerous injury among ejectees, the ACIR study added, "generally was three to six times greater than among nonejectees."

"As you can readily determine by reading our final report," the Cornell laboratory's research chief, Robert A. Wolf, wrote to Senate Commerce Committee Chairman Warren G. Magnuson (D–Wash.) on Jan. 10, 1969, "it is hardly laudatory of Volkswagen." Volkswagen of America, long established as the sole importer of VWs, determined otherwise, telling its dealers: "We believe that this study . . . demonstrates that our car is the safest small car in the world." And the *VW Dealer and Industry News* happily proclaimed in an article last Feb. 22: "So VW is a safe car."

VW customers may be less familiar with a deposition taken 12 days earlier from Ulreich Seiffert, Volkswagen's chief test engineer, for a federal court case in New Mexico. The suit, filed against Volkswagenwerk AG, was prompted by a September 1967 crash in Albuquerque in which a 1966 VW allegedly rolled over, lost its gas cap and caught fire. Two people in the VW were killed.

Seiffert disclosed that Volkswagen AG had conducted barrier crash tests of 1965 and 1966 Beetles with somewhat disquieting results. The gas filler caps had come off in every one of five tests conducted at slightly more than 30 miles an hour. The experiments were started a year before the Albuquerque crash and completed a month after it. According to the Nader report, the National Highway Safety Bureau had asked Volkswagen of America in the summer of 1969, nearly two years later, for information on all the laboratory tests involving the gas caps on its 1961-1967 models, but the findings that Seiffert mentioned at his deposition were not supplied. Stronger caps were designed and installed on 1968 and later-model Beetles, but Volkswagen of America, according to the Nader report, refused to alert owners of older VW's to the hazards of keeping their original caps. By contrast, the VW distributor in Sweden, evidently under pressure from the official Swedish Council on Road Safety, offered the improved caps free to all 250,000 owners of 1961-1967 Beetles in that country. Here in the US a new one will cost $2.10 at your friendly Volkswagen dealer.

The allegedly defective gas caps, Nader says, are illustrative of most of the Beetle's shortcomings: small, even trivial, but "highly tragic" in their consequences. A filler cap can pop off in a collision, especially when the car has its gas tank up front like the VW. A study of fire crashes in Sweden in which 72 victims were burned and 38 died, concluded: "Excluding the fires from reserve tanks, it is found that front tank cars are responsible for 80 percent of the burns and 88 percent of the fatal burns in these cases."

The Beetle's "distinctive hazards," as the report calls them, keep cropping up. An estimated two million VW's remain without safety rims on their wheels although the original patent for them entered the public domain back in 1957. The VW's "fair-weather" door latch is another example. American auto manufacturers began using interlocking door latches in 1955 to cut down the chances of car doors popping open in a crash. Again, the report notes, "Volkswagen waited 10 years before they adopted this inexpensive safety item on their cars. In the meantime . . . many people were being killed and injured by ejections from Beetles. . . ." Even the new latches, Nader maintains, may fall short of the government's tepid safety standards.

Perhaps an even more pervasive problem involves the VW seat tracks and seat backs that give way too easily in rear-end collisions, hurling occupants against the back of the car or even out the rear window. "All Beetles from 1959 through 1970 are affected by these seat defects, and the pre-1959 models and VW Squareback and Fast-back models are affected as well," declare Nader & Co. Lawsuits seem to be mushrooming. A Honolulu jury recently settled one complaint by finding Volkswagen almost as much at fault as the driver of the other car. The suit stemmed from the collision of a 1956 Chevrolet with the rear end of a 1965 VW Squareback that happened to be standing still. The VW's seat came loose from its tracks, spilling the plaintiff into the back of the car where she suffered head injuries. The jury ordered the driver of the Chevy to pay 60 percent of the damages and Volkswagen, 40 percent. According to Volkswagen of America vice president Arthur R. Railton, the seat tracks of 1971 VW's have been "redesigned to provide greater strength and ease of adjustment," a step which may or may not prove adequate.

Meanwhile, VW can still claim that the seats in its earlier models meet federal standards. The regulations, the Nader report protests, do nothing more than prevent seat failures "at speeds not much higher than parking lot maneuvers."

Other hazards of the Beetle, Nader says, are too ingrained for correction in the current design, such as its instability in crosswinds and its propensity for rolling over. The sluggish lightweight VW Microbus, he adds, is even worse, "so unsafe that it should be removed from the roads." Much could be done to make the millions of Beetles now on the roads less dangerous, Nader says; the modifications would cost Volkswagen of America $184 million, or an average of slightly less than $60 a car. The company seems unlikely to respond. "Our products," said a Volkswagen spokesman, "meet or exceed all safety standards."

It is a claim that has come to serve the auto industry as an endorsement, like government-graded beef. It appears to mean about as much. More than 30 auto safety standards have been issued since the first of them went into effect Jan. 1, 1968. According to the Nader report, VWs have been given compliance tests for just 10 of these standards and of the 25 tests conducted, "there were 14 failures," half of them still awaiting investigation and the other half either resolved with "no action" or concluded with "a mild letter to Volkswagen."

VWs may get closer scrutiny in the months ahead. The National Highway Traffic Safety Administration has been conducting stability tests on the Beetle, as part of a long-overdue check on the similarly designed 1960-63 Corvairs which Nader condemned in *Unsafe at Any Speed:* The agency is taking the new Nader report "very seriously."

There was apparently no chortling among the domestic automakers over Nader's indictment of the competition, however. When one manufacturer is attacked on safety grounds, says one longtime industry-watcher, "they all kind of wince." Both GM and Ford are said to have conducted their own crash tests on VWs which Nader challenged them to disclose, but both GM and Ford also have plants in West Germany and it is doubtful that they would wish to antagonize VW. The industry attitude, Nader suggests, is "a case of 'you scratch my defect and I'll scratch yours.' "

Even so, there have been rumblings at Volkswagen AG, which exports 30 to 35 percent of its production to the United States. The day after the Nader report was released, VW Chairman Kurt Lotz resigned from his $180,000-a-year post, concluding weeks of rumors that he was about to be fired. Although US sales of VW's various models reached an alltime high last year of 569,182 cars and Microbuses, the company's net profits fell sharply. Another drop was forecast this year even before President Nixon announced his new surcharge on imports, a step more to Detroit's liking than niggling over auto safety.

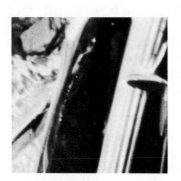

BITTER TALES FROM THE GM LEMON GROVES

Colman McCarthy

Last week, General Motors issued a recall of 4,269 school buses for possible brake defects. The recall followed a six-week nationwide survey by GM which was originally prompted by two articles on this page in December detailing the endless safety and mechanical breakdowns of three new GM school buses. These were owned by John Donovan, a local school teacher with an immense frustration capacity.

By taking a survey, GM wanted to know whether Donovan's problems were a local fluke or a national epidemic. If the latter, a recall would be made. Martin Caserio, a GM vice president and a Detroit veteran who had been through the recall ritual many times, said that GM was deeply concerned about safety. However, he told a Washington press conference in December he did not think John Donovan's repeated brake failures, rattling transmissions, hanging exhaust pipes, faulty tires, etc., were "safety-related" problems.

After some confusion and delay, GM supplied the press with a partial list of GM bus owners. Entitled "School Bus Owners operating five or more 1969 GMC conventional model school buses," it contained 44 names. These owners were from only 16 states and pos-

From *The Washington Post,* 23 February 1970. © *The Washington Post.* Reprinted by permission.

sessed a total of only 504 buses. This meant that some 3,500 other 1969 model buses could not readily be checked.

On receiving the list from General Motors, The Washington Post began contacting by phone the 44 owners. Apart from the one owner who couldn't be reached because he had been dead four years and the four others who were listed by GM as owning a total of 35 vehicles but in reality owned none, the majority of respondents were unhappy or frustrated over the performance of their new buses. Repeatedly, they told of the time and money wasted hauling the buses to garages for repairs; often they were repairs of repairs. It soon became clear that the safety and mechanical problems of the '69 GM school bus were not isolated in Washington. They were nationwide, all the way from the enraged owners of the Beirns Bus Service, Kenilworth, N.J., whose six new buses failed the New Jersey State inspection because of faulty brake equalization to the stoic in Roslyn, N.Y., who said, "I was a GM man at heart, but no more. I don't know what they've done to these buses, but I've bought my last one."

It was quickly discovered that GM's list was incomplete. Regularly, an owner on the list would supply the names of the other multiple-owners in his area who were not on the list. Often, it was obvious why they were omitted. Raymond Wilson—a pseudonym—is a GM dealer who owns 15 of the 1969 buses. He saw the stories about Donovan in his local paper in December and was "delighted that the truth was finally being told about GM." He has had massive safety and mechanical problems also. "The power steering cannot be fixed, no matter what;" one new bus being driven back from the factory nearly killed his driver because the gas tank had a hole in it that dropped the fuel onto a heated exhaust line; "the brakes aren't worth a damn and won't stay adjusted. Overall, things have gotten to the point that I hate to face customers."

Other people that Wilson hates to face are reporters. The same morning he read the story about Donovan, he was called by the local GM representative and told "to keep my mouth shut if any newsman called. The rep. told me this kind of publicity could hurt us all." Wilson agreed to talk to the Post only if strict anonymity was given his name and location of business. Even though he is a GM dealer, he is convinced that if the company finds out he has spoken to anyone they will "get even."

Another GM dealer—also not on the list—was so fed up with his seven 69s that this year he bought Fords. Asked if he thought it odd that a GM dealer would buy a competitor's product, he answered:

"What should I do—keep on buying buses that I know are nothing but trouble?"

Not all the GM owners on the list were unhappy. A spokesman for the Long Island Bus Co., East Farmingdale, N.Y., said that his mechanics "have been big on preventive maintenance, so we have little trouble." Another owner, the Pace School Bus Service, Independence, Mo., said that aside from frequent clutch adjustments everything was fine. Asked about his exhaust pipe hangers, he replied: "Oh, them. They were so weak when the buses were sold to us that we just tied them up with baling wire. And that was that." The mechanic for the five buses owned by the Lake Orion, Mich., schools said he had no serious complaints. "The brakes are hard to push and get sluggish. But they're safe enough; the driver just has to get used to them."

With a few chilling exceptions, all the dissatisfied owners said they received prompt and polite service from the local GM dealers. Warranty repairs were paid for with little fuss. But what GM does not pay for is the large amounts of time needed to haul the buses to the garage or pick them up after highway breakdowns; nor is there compensation for the always-present frustration. Ben Stanski, with 10 of the 1969 models, of the Berkshire Gray Line, Pittsfield, Mass., has been constantly bedeviled by burned-out clutches. Some have gone at 3,000 miles, when they should have lasted 25,000 or more. But the main irk is getting the buses started in the morning during the winter. "Here they are," said Stanski, "brand new buses. And a crew has been having to come in at 4 a.m. to work on them so they start up. If we let the buses sit until the regular drivers come in, the kids would never get picked up."

One person who conceivably should have no trouble making his voice heard by GM is a mechanic for the Pontiac, Mich., School District, in the very town where GM makes its buses. The mechanic said that along with radiator, electrical and tail pipe problems, he is plagued with brake troubles. The buses on which many children of GM employees ride every day have had no accidents yet due to brake failure, but this may be due to the mechanic's diligence. "If I keep adjusting them every month, they're O.K. When the brakes are the least bit out of adjustment, which happens frequently, they are hard. When you put your foot on them, you think you have plenty of pedal left. But the only problem is you can't stop. So I adjust them every month."

The most recurring complaint of the 39 owners was the tail pipe hanger. This device is on the rear underside of the bus and keeps the exhaust pipe secure. When it is not strong enough, the pipe will jangle until it snaps. The poisonous exhaust fumes are then leaked forward under the passenger compartment. Most states consider a weak pipe hanger a safety hazard and inspectors will flunk any bus that has one. Two months ago, a Washington GM representative admitted to a reporter that the hangers on the '69 buses were too weak to hold the pipe safely. "The factory made them just too flimsy," he said. When Martin Caserio was asked at the December press conference about this problem, he said a weak pipe hanger was certainly a bother, "but it was not safety related." When a pipe broke, said Caserio, the bus driver would surely be alert enough to hear the thing clattering along the ground and have repairs made before any harm might be done to occupants.

From the response of the 39 owners on the GM list, and the many others mysteriously excluded from the list, a fair conclusion is that something is inherently wrong with the 1969 GM school bus. Too many owners in too many places reported too many breakdowns for the problem to be passed off as "one of those things, sorry about that."

Last week, after General Motors had reached the same conclusion and ordered a recall of 4,269 new buses for "possible brake defects," a GM public relations man said that his company had made a survey of 850 buses in December and January and discovered that one bus—only one—had defective brakes. Evidently, though strangely, GM used a different list of owners from the one supplied the press, or else they would have found many more than "one" owner with brake problems—starting with their neighbor in Pontiac, Mich., and including the Beirns Bus Service, the Community Charter Bus Co., Stanton, Calif., the Schaunburg Trans. Co., Roselle, Ill., the Guasti School, Guasti, Calif., Morris Hills School District, Rockaway, N.J., the anonymous GM dealer, a private owner in Olean, N.Y., and others. Although none of these had the numbing scare of Mrs. Warren McConnell of Springfield, Va.—last fall, one of her '69 GM buses had total brake failure and ran into a pasture to stop—they all said their brakes had given, or are giving, them serious trouble.

Since the GM recall involves only brakes, questions are raised about other complaints of owners. First, the tail pipe hangers. In a letter to Virginia H. Knauer, special assistant to President Nixon for consumer affairs, on Feb. 11, Martin Caserio admitted that some 300 out of 850 1969 buses had their hangers replaced. Yet, in the recall, this defective part was not mentioned.

A second major complaint not mentioned in the recall involves clutches. Caserio's Feb. 11 letter acknowledges that in some cases "clutch durability (is) unsatisfactory." But rather than admitting the clutches are mechanically flawed, and then recalling them, the GM vice president repeats the standard implication that clutch trouble is usually caused either by foot-happy drivers or by lack of maintenance. But when the anonymous GM dealer has five of seven clutches burn out, even though he adjusts them "every day"; or when a Fullington, Tenn., owner has had to replace four out of six clutches—including one that didn't last 1,000 miles; or when an El Centro, Calif., owner has to adjust his clutches every 600 to 1,000 miles; when complaints like these are regularly heard, something more than foot-happy drivers are to blame.

Last December, GM president Edward Cole said that if his company's survey showed that a recall was necessary, well, a recall it would be. As Martin Caserio said during his press conference, "We'll step up to our responsibility." This is indeed praiseworthy, but the concept of a recall—an outrageous idea in itself, but which a cowed public now accepts calmly—raised fundamental questions. Where was GM's responsibility when their product was being made? Why wasn't it stepped up to then? This is the third consecutive year a recall has been made on GM's school buses, so the notion that something might be wrong in design or in the assembly line must have occurred to someone at GM.

Even when a recall is made, the question comes up about retribution for other things besides free labor and parts: such as time spent hauling broken buses in from the roadside waiting at the garage, the mental worry of driving children on vehicles that may be unreliable, the time lost to one's family because the bus needs to be tinkered with or carted to the garage.

CRIME IN THE SUITES

Morton Mintz and Jerry S. Cohen

"Went to Nauset Light on the back side of Cape Cod," Ralph Waldo Emerson said in his *Journal.* "Collins, the keeper, told us he found obstinate resistance to the project of building a lighthouse on this coast, as it would injure the wrecking business." A century later, the world's largest industrial corporation was advertising the slogan "General Motors Is People." Both messages—that business deliberately sacrifices life for profit, and that GM is Just Folks much like, perchance, the apple grower and the peanut vendor—essentially are caricatures of reality. There is a more serious objection. It is that such oversimplifications lead us away from, rather than toward, a few truths which are indispensable to understanding corporate behavior.

Large corporations commonly engage in criminal behavior, although sustained underreporting of this fact in communications media severely limits public appreciation of it. Crime is behavior which the state regards as socially harmful and for which the law provides penalties. That is the legal definition. If an act is punishable it is criminal even if punishment is not invoked, and it is criminal regardless of the particular administrative procedures that are prescribed to deal with it. Corporate crime is socially harmful behavior by corporations for which the law provides penalties. This was the definition used by the late Edwin H. Sutherland, who made the first systematic study of corporate crime and, in 1949, published his classic *White Collar Crime.* This phrase means crime committed by "persons of respectability and high social status" in the course of their occupations. He based the book on his study of the life careers of seventy of the largest manufacturing, mining, and mercantile corporations. His sources were official records of violations of laws governing restraint of trade; misrepresentation in advertising; infringement of patents, trademarks, and copyrights; fair labor practices; rebates; financial fraud; conduct in wartime; and some miscellaneous categories. The average age of the seventy companies, none of which was an oil company, and none of which, regrettably, was named, was forty-five years. The terminal date of the analysis was, generally, 1944.

"Of the seventy large corporations, 30 were either illegal in their origin or began illegal activities immediately after their origin," Sutherland said. Forty-one of the companies were convicted in criminal courts a total of 158 times, or an average of 4 times each. "In many states," he noted, "persons with four convictions are defined as 'habitual criminals.' " In addition to the convictions, a total of 822 adverse decisions were rendered against the seventy corporations, including 296 in civil courts and 129 in equity courts. The balance, 397, were orders, confiscations or settlements by one or another official commission. In all, an average of 14 adverse decisions had been rendered against each of the seventy companies, and in one case there were 50.

These figures grossly understate the reality. Not all violations are recorded. Some of the laws that were violated were not enacted until the New Deal came to power in the 1930s. In addition, Sutherland pointed out, "vigorous prosecution of corporations has been concentrated in the period since 1932." Of the grand total of 980 adverse decisions against the seventy corporations only 292, or less than one-third, were rendered in the first three decades of the twentieth century.

This chapter will present numerous specific examples of criminal and antisocial, or harmful, behavior. This will serve several precise purposes. Each example involves an impact on people that, in itself, argues for its inclusion, and, in addition, illuminates one or more aspects of a large and complex whole. The assembly of specific examples in one place will assist appreciation of the enormity and pervasiveness of corporate conduct which violates the legal and ethical codes that supposedly guide society. The presentation may also contribute to a more balanced perpective on law and order than currently prevails. Most importantly, this chapter is intended to enlarge public understanding about conscience in an entity that lacks a soul. The public depends significantly on the corporate conscience to protect their lives, health, and pocketbooks. This tends to be counterproductive. It delays the advent of the kind of mature economic and political processes which would require more corporations, more of the time, to behave *as if* they had consciences.

Rarely, an individual of conscience has found it possible to transfer his personal standards to the business under his control. That was the case with William H. Danforth, who died in 1955, and his company, Ralston Purina. Ferdinand Lundberg, who does not casually bestow compliments, said:

> *As far as the record shows, Danforth (unlike many of his prominent business contemporaries) never engaged in any shady practice, was never involved in any swindles, was never the defendant on criminal charges and was never accused of exploiting his workers. Nor was he, it seems, ever seriously criticized, knocked, called to account or rebuffed in good times or bad. For a portrait of the American capitalist as an extremely good, wholesome, honestly Christian earnest outgoing dogooder one must turn to William H. Danforth.*

Those who see Ralston Purina or another corporation as "good" tend to see yet other corporations as "bad." This accords with the phenomenon of "The Personification of Corporation," to use the title of a brilliant chapter in Thurman Arnold's *The Folklore of Capitalism.* "The ideal that a great corporation is endowed with the rights and prerogatives of a free individual is as essential to the acceptance of corporate rule in temporal affairs as was the ideal of the divine right of kings in an earlier day," he said. Arnold, writing in New Deal days, continued:

> *Men have come to believe that their own future liberties and dignity are tied up in the freedom of great industrial organizations from restraint. . . .*
>
> *The origin of this way of thinking . . . is the result of a pioneer civilization in which the prevailing ideal was that of the freedom and dignity of the individual engaged in the accumulation of wealth. The independence of the free man from central authority was the slogan for which men fought and died. This free man was a trader, who got ahead by accumulating money. . . . Men cheerfully accept the fact that some individuals are good and others bad. Therefore, since great industrial organizations were regarded as individuals, it was not expected that all of them would be good. Corporations could therefore violate any of the established taboos without creating any alarm about the "sys-*

tem" itself. Since individuals are supposed to do better if left alone, this symbolism freed industrial enterprise from regulation in the interest of furthering any current morality. The laissez faire religion, based on a conception of society composed of competing individuals, was transferred automatically to industrial organizations with nation-wide power and dictatorial forms of government.

To personify large corporations is to obscure the important fact that they must march to different tunes than William Danforth's. He was moral and they are amoral. In his special circumstances his conscience was his guide, and his conscience was Ralston Purina's guide. In the circumstances of giant corporations profit must be maximized. This may or may not accord with the individual consciences of the owners and managers. The crucial difference is that while Danforth owned Ralston Purina, had the freedom to manage it as he wished, *and* was enormously successful, a similar set of conditions does not prevail for most corporations. Ownership is separate from management. Directors and executives do not have a freedom such as Danforth's. A corporate director, Benjamin N. Cardozo, the late Associate Justice of the Supreme Court, once said, owes a "duty of constant and unqualified fidelity" to the corporation and its stockholders who, of course, are seeking the best possible return on their investment dollars—an earthly rather than a heavenly reward. After researching the literature on the subject, the Library of Congress found that a director "must exercise his unbiased judgment, influenced only by considerations of what is best for the corporation. . . . Many courts have spoken of the rule as being that a director owes a loyalty that is undivided and an allegiance that is influenced in action by no consideration other than the corporation's welfare."

The corporation's welfare traditionally has been defined in terms of its financial statement. And, Bernard D. Nossiter has said, "there is nothing in the logic or practice of concentrated corporate industries that guides or compels socially responsible decision-making." To be even blunter about it, the rule of thumb is that if conscience is operative in a corporation it is because conscientious conduct pays, and if conscience is absent it is because *that* pays.

The point was memorably made by two titans of business in an exchange of letters that has drawn remarkably little public attention. The correspondence began four decades ago. The principals were Lammot du Pont, president of E. I. du Pont de Nemours & Company, and Alfred P. Sloan, Jr., president of General Motors Corporation. On August 5, 1929, the two executives had a conversation about the possible use in Chevrolets of safety glass, one of the single most important protections ever devised against avoidable automotive death, disfigurement, and injury. The next day, Lammot du Pont initiated the exchange of letters. Noting that the production capacity of his company was, at that time, limited, du Pont urged Sloan to try at once "to come to a decision" as to whether it wanted safety glass, or Pyralin for making safety glass, for Chevrolets.

August 7: Sloan acknowledged that "non-shatterable glass is bound to come." But, he told du Pont, for GM "to take an advanced position" at a time when production volume is increasing "at a decelerated rate" cannot "do other than to materially offset our profits."

> *We have always felt, rightly or wrongly, that it was not in the interest of the industry and to ourselves to advertise improvements in safety control through the exploitation of accidents. We all know that there are a very large number of automobile accidents. Every once in a while it looms up in such a way that it appears as if it would have more or less serious consequences. The only way I know we can bring the public to a realization that they are willing to pay a substantial amount more for a car that has non-shatterable glass as compared with one that has not, is to exploit in some form or other this general idea.*

Sloan went on to point out that in the past year GM's Cadillac division had equipped La Salles as well as Cadillacs with safety glass, that Packard, a competitor, had not, and the Packard's sales had not been materially affected. "In other words, I do not think that from the stockholders' standpoint the move on Cadillac's part has been justified. I believe that when any of us are dealing with safety matters we should perhaps not be commercial yet it is hard to avoid that phase of the question."

August 9: The point of advertising about safety glass, du Pont replied, would be "not to call attention to serious accidents, but to press the minor accidents which would not count for anything more than running over a stone in the road, were it not for the fact that the glass breaks, someone gets slightly cut, or cut in such a place as to constitute a permanent disfigurement. Can't the advertising stress *that feature* rather than what [the fear] most people have of the dangers of automobiles namely serious accidents and someone getting killed."

August 13: "Accidents or no accidents, my concern in this problem is a matter of profit and loss," Sloan told du Pont. He especially feared, he said,

> *that the advent of safety glass will result in both ourselves and our competitors absorbing a very considerable part of the extra*

> cost out of our profits. You, of course, are familiar with the comparatively large return the industry enjoys and General Motors in particular. I think you will agree with me that it is a very easy thing to reduce that return. I am fighting it not only every day but practically every hour of every day.

After explaining that production costs had gone up without a proportionate increase in production volume sufficient to absorb the cost increases, at least to the same degree as in previous years, Sloan said:

> I may be all wrong, but I feel that General Motors should not adopt safety glass for its cars and raise its prices even a part of what the extra cost would be. I can only see competition being forced into the same position. Our gain would be a purely temporary one and the net result would be that both competition and ourselves would have reduced the return on our capital and the public would have obtained still more value per dollar expended. I feel that it is much better to let the thing take its logical course and do what seems necessary when the necessity arises. . . . Naturally, from your standpoint . . . it is to your interest to have safety glass go in a large way irrespective of how it may affect the profit position of the automobile manufacturers but, of course, that is not my position and it is not your position in a broader sense.

August 20: Du Pont was "inclined to agree" with Sloan "that the adoption of safety glass, as well as the adoption of other improvements, is almost sure to result in the long run in lower profits to General Motors. I have entire confidence, however, that whether General Motors adopts it now or not, safety glass will be forced upon them."

The two men then apparently stopped corresponding about the matter for almost three years. On April 11, 1932, du Pont revived the question. In a letter to Sloan, he said that GM should encourage the use of safety glass, "rather than discourage or be apathetic. I understand that the new Ford models all have safety glass in the windshield and all the sports models have it all over. I think we should keep our 'eyes open' and 'ears to the ground,' so that we won't lose out in the procession if safety glass becomes popular."

Replying four days later, Sloan said that Ford for years had used safety glass in windshields, but "that is no reason why we should do so. I am trying to protect the interest of the stockholders of General Motors and the Corporation's operating position—it is not my responsibility to sell safety glass." Instead of burdening the stockholders, Sloan said,

> *I would very much rather spend the same amount of money in improving our car in other ways because I think, from the standpoint of selfish business, it would be a very much better investment. You can say, perhaps, that I am selfish, but business is selfish. We are not a charitable institution—we are trying to make a profit for our stockholders.*

Although Sloan's resistance to the adoption of safety glass presumably was responsible for a large number of preventable deaths and serious injuries, he violated no law and, indeed, was obeying the dictates of a conscience which did not let him forget his obligation to GM's stockholders. Yet, obviously, his conduct had harmful and antisocial results. Nothing has happened in the four decades since the safety-glass episode to diminish the point that there is no sensible relation between the harmfulness of certain corporate behavior and its legality.

Some years ago Congress passed a law making it a criminal offense to adulterate motor vehicle brake fluid, a practice with grave potential to cause brake failure without warning. This legislation was absorbed by the National Traffic and Motor Vehicle Safety Act of 1966. Before this measure was enacted, Senator Warren G. Magnuson (D–Wash.), chairman of the Senate Committee on Commerce, and Senator Vance Hartke (D–Ind.), a member of the committee, led a fight to provide criminal penalties not only for adulteration of brake fluid, but for all *willful and knowing* violations. They were defeated by the auto industry, whose principal Senate advocate on this issue was John O. Pastore (D–R.I.). Civil penalties, in the form of fines, were provided instead. The primary concern here is not with whether it was objectively and practically right to provide criminal or civil sanctions, or both, but that an act as terrible as willful and knowing adulteration of brake fluid could be, helter-skelter, a criminal violation one day and a civil violation another day—while being potentially calamitous any day.

Until the Safety Act of 1966 was adopted a manufacturer violated no law in, again knowingly and willfully, selling an automobile with safety-related defects (and, certainly, it was not an offense to sell cars, the Corvair being a classic example, which embodied what Ralph Nader has called "designed-in dangers"). Further, no law was violated by a standard industry practice, a non-action of not notifying customers when a defect was discovered. In 1959, for example, the Michigan

Supreme Court ruled against General Motors in a case that was initiated by a dealer mechanic whose leg was crushed by a 1953 Buick Roadmaster which, because of a defect, had lost its braking capacity. "Defendant Buick division warned its dealers," the court said. "It did not warn those into whose hands they had placed this dangerous instrument and whose lives (along with the lives of others) depended upon defective brakes which might fail without notice." If the number of repair kits distributed afterward by Buick to its dealers is a reliable guide, 54,000 of these dangerous instruments were on the highways.

In a case involving the Chrysler Corporation, a manufacturer's bulletin urged dealers to recall for inspection 30,000 already delivered 1965 Chryslers, full-size Dodges, and Plymouth Furys with particular serial numbers. The purpose of the inspection was to determine if it was necessary to reweld a mounting bracket for the steering gear. The company neither notified the owners directly nor ascertained how many of the possibly hazardous cars actually were brought in to dealers' shops.

Once the Safety Act was in force automobile makers were compelled, for the first time, to notify buyers of safety-related defects. These turned out to exist on a huge scale. In less than three years, "very limited investigations" by the National Highway Safety Bureau showed, manufacturers notified purchasers of 12 million vehicles of safety-related defects, including 2 million which had been brought to the industry's attention by the Bureau, a pathetically understaffed, underfinanced unit of the Department of Transportation.

Working under a contract from the Department, a research firm reviewed 287 separate campaigns by manufacturers to notify buyers of defects. Of the 5.5 million vehicles involved in the period in question, the two years ended September 30, 1968, the number recalled for inspection and possible correction of defects was as follows:

Defects that would or could cause loss of control *without warning:* 1,177,408.

Defects that would or could cause loss of control, but *with* warning: 4,000,620.

Defects that could cause control to deteriorate: 349,021.

The component most commonly involved was the steering system, although more than one defect sometimes figured in a single notification campaign. In all, 2,859,221 vehicles were recalled for possible defects in steering systems. Other categories included service brakes, 799,831 vehicles recalled; parking brakes, 33,539; and suspension systems, 277,085.

One case stands out. It involved 1960 through 1965 model Chevrolet and GMC three-quarter-ton pickup trucks—200,000 of them. Apparently as a cost-cutting measure, General Motors equipped these trucks not with standard one-piece wheels, but with three-piece disc units, in the 15 × 5.50 size, made by the Kelsey-Hayes Corporation. In September 1968 Ralph Nader submitted evidence to the Safety Bureau that a number of the wheels had collapsed without warning. Bureau engineers made an investigation that confirmed the evidence. They said the wheels had an inherent metallurgical defect that made them "prone to failure . . . at unpredictable times" even when used on "straight" pickups, i.e., those which were not equipped with "camper," van, or other heavy bodies. Consequently, the engineers warned, a hazard existed not only for occupants of the vehicles equipped with the wheels, but also for other motorists, pedestrians, and bystanders. GM, denying the existence of an inherent fault, insisted that only the use of heavy bodies and improperly inflated tires could create a safety-related defect.

Because the Bureau had not yet been separated from the Federal Highway Administration, the issue came to the administrator of that agency, Francis C. Turner, for decision. He ruled for GM. In doing so, in October 1969, he announced in a press release that the corporation had agreed to replace without charge the wheels on 50,000 of the 200,000 trucks—those on which heavy bodies had been installed. According to unofficial Bureau estimates which GM later said were low, the cost to the company would be $5 million; but it would save triple that amount if it could avoid replacing the wheels on the 150,000 "straight" vehicles.

The Bureau engineers, in their investigation, had found fifty-six trucks—fifty-four of them equipped with special bodies—on which the three-part wheels had collapsed without warning. Serious injuries sometimes resulted. Urging Turner to require GM to notify all 200,000 owners of a safety defect, the engineers said, "There is every indication that 96 per cent of all known wheel failures have occurred *under loads which are below the design wheel strength level specified by the truck builder.*" [Emphasis supplied.] Yet Turner, in his press release, claimed there was "some doubt at this time as to whether it could be said that a safety-related defect existed." Nader, in a letter to Secretary of Transportation John A. Volpe, denounced this claim as "utterly false."

Rather than letting it go at that, Nader and some allies—the Center for Auto Safety, Physicians for Auto Safety, and Larry J. Silverman of Nader's Study for Responsive Law, all represented by the Center for Law and Social Policy and the law firm of Arnold and Porter—filed a suit in Federal Court in Washington. The action, which included Volpe and Turner as defendants, essentially sought an order to make the Department of Transportation and its subdivisions enforce the auto safety law as Congress intended it be enforced.

On June 30, 1970, Judge Joseph C. Waddy not only held that Turner had made "a mis-statement" of the findings of his own engineers in the Safety Bureau, but issued an order that was both unusual and important. The order looked behind a settlement made by a federal regulatory operation and a regulated company, and it authorized Silverman to participate in subsequent proceedings (which the Department had not allowed him to do up to that time). Most importantly, the judge ordered the Department to complete or reopen its investigation of the wheels, to take such remedial steps as the investigation should warrant, and to report back to the court *why* it was taking such actions as it would decide to take. With this, the Department began to abandon its former position and move toward requiring GM to notify the owners of 150,000 "straight" pickups of a safety-related defect (the auto safety law does not empower the government to require a manufacturer to *correct* a defect).

In a report filed with the court on September 15, Bureau engineers said that they now had learned of fifty-two wheel failures on twenty-four trucks that had not been overloaded, that as of August 29 there had been a grand total of ninety-eight failures on twenty-four "straight" pickups, that failures must be presumed to have eluded their surveillance, and that additional failures surely were occurring. In one case, they said, a wheel collapsed only one day after the owner took delivery. The truck turned over one and a half times, struck an oncoming vehicle, and was demolished. Five persons were injured. The engineers also said that contractors engaged to examine the fifty-two wheels found that ten of them failed under loads of less than 1,520 pounds each—although the claimed design strength was 2,060 pounds.

At an informal Safety Bureau hearing on September 30, GM refused to present engineering testimony but claimed the Bureau had "no evidence" of an inherent defect in the wheels. It asked that the investigation be dropped. But two Syracuse University professors who made a study of the three-piece design, engineer Martin E. Barzelay and metallurgist Volker Weiss, said that the "factor of safety" was "far below commonly accepted practice."

Finally, on November 4, Douglas W. Toms, director of the Safety Bureau, said that the wheels made the 150,000 "straight" pickups subject to "sudden and catastrophic failure resulting in an unreasonable risk of accident, death and injuries to persons using the highways." He asked GM to notify the owners that the wheels were defective. The company responded, the same day, by filing a suit to block the action in Federal Court in Wilmington, Delaware—an effort to bypass Judge Waddy, who had retained jurisdiction in the case that had been brought in Washington. Two days later, the Justice Department, in behalf of the Safety Bureau, asked the Federal Court in Washington to impose civil penalties on GM of $400,000, the maximum allowed. It was the first action of its kind. While it was pending, Judge Caleb M. Wright in Wilmington threw out GM's suit. General Motors, which has spent millions of dollars to promote the claim that GM is the "Mark of Excellence," spent tens of thousands more to resist the Safety Bureau in Federal Court in Washington, while allowing the uninterrupted use on the highways of trucks with wheels subject to "catastrophic failure."

Over the decades in which manufacturers discovered defects—no one knows how many—in cars, school buses, and trucks, but failed to notify the owners because they were not forced to do so, they financed "traffic safety" campaigns. These cost relatively little. They may even have had a certain limited value. But they were also a decoy. They deflected attention from the role of quality control and of automotive design, even from dangers as obvious as the millions of knobs which needlessly protruded toward knees and skulls. There was too much emphasis on "the nut behind the wheel." There was no emphasis at all on the nut behind the system.

The news media are owed some of the blame. In 1956 Representative Kenneth A. Roberts, a conscientious Alabama Democrat who headed the health subcommittee of the House Committee on Interstate and Foreign Commerce, opened hearings on the relation of automotive designs to safety. He continued the hearings into 1963 (and the next year was defeated for reelection by a Goldwater Republican). In conducting the hearings Roberts "was surrounded by apathy and opposition in Congress and with hostility from the automobile industry and its traffic safety establishment," Ralph Nader said. The apathy, opposition, and hostility would not have been so effective had the news media told the public about the hearings, but they gave them negligible attention. The price paid, as reflected in the toll of highway death and injury, can only be conjectured.

In 1970, after an investigation of new-car warranties, the Federal Trade Commission said in a report to Congress that the industry had failed "to meet its obligation to provide the public with defect-free cars." All five members of the Commission, including Caspar Weinberger, the first chairman appointed by President Nixon, approved the report. The report said that "quality control of automobiles is unsatisfactory, the warranty coverage putatively provided by manufacturers is inadequate, and the industry response to the problem insufficient to protect the public."

If a thief breaks into your house and steals money the loss is obvious. But how does a manufacturer who has designed an appliance, an automobile muffler, or a light bulb to give out with all deliberate speed demonstrate moral superiority over a burglar? Questions of this kind could cause difficulties for those who overprice, impose usurious finance charges for installment buying, or inflict widespread harm, say, by polluting the biosphere, putting untested or inadequately tested additives into foods, or by loading excessive fat into 15 billion hot dogs a year, as was done until recently. But such questions pose no great difficulties for a youth who is a member of a gang and who, Robert C. Maynard said in the *Progressive*, "tends to see the world as a series of gangs, a few of them on his side but most of them arrayed against him . . . including the corporations that will not hire him into their hustle." Maynard, a reporter for the *Washington Post*, told of an afternoon in Chicago when he talked on a street corner with a dispirited member of the Black P Stone Rangers, one of the biggest gangs in the country:

> This young man wanted out of the whole business of the streets but he had no place he knew of to go.
>
> "All of the good shit," he told me, "is either staked out or played out." To him, the law was an instrument of the rich to protect what they had for their own against the incursions of the likes of him. "They don't pay no attention to no goddamn law unless they want to. . . .
>
> "The law," the Ranger sneered. "When last you hear of a millionaire going to the electric chair? When last you hear of the president of one of those big old corporations"—he sneered again at the sound of that word—"going to jail for fixing prices or selling people rotten meat that could kill them or even for income-tax evasion? When you hear anything like that?"

It is, unfortunately, an everyday occurrence for judges to impose brutal, even sadistic sentences—twenty years for possession of marijuana, fifteen years for stealing a Social Security check, and the like. Even an arrest for a trivial offense can imperil a man's livelihood. If convicted, a man realistically may expect to be derisively referred to thereafter as an "ex-con."

Such harshness does not attend corporations, even those that may massively steal and inflict violence. For what they like to depict as the war against crime, such men as Attorney General John N. Mitchell and Senator John L. McClellan say that wiretapping and preventive detention are essential. They are not talking about corporate crime. They do not intend to allow policemen to snoop on the phone conversations of business executives. They have no thought of detaining officers and directors of recidivist corporations in jail in order to prevent these organizations from committing new crimes. If a violation is charged a corporation can be fined, but, on the basis of ability to pay, the amounts usually are trivial. It will have the best of lawyers. Its career is not likely to be ruined or even set back. It cannot be put on a rock pile, be wrenched away from its family, be deprived of a normal sex life or be put among, as the standard phrase has it, "hardened criminals." And even if recidivist it is not called an "ex-con."

8

TRUTH VERSUS PROFITS IN ADVERTISING

In its 1968 January-February issue, the *Harvard Business Review* published an article so amazingly frank that it produced one of the greatest responses in that magazine's history. Titled "Is Business Bluffing Ethical?" by Albert Z. Carr, a former businessman, the article deserves to be read in its entirety, but the following excerpts will reveal its tone. Essentially, the author contends that deception is a necessary business ethic:

> *Most executives from time to time are almost compelled in the interests of their companies or themselves, to practice some form of deception when negotiating with customers, dealers, labor unions, government officials or even other departments in their companies. By conscious*

*misstatements, concealments of pertinent facts, or exaggera-
tions—in short by bluffing—they seek to persuade others to agree
with them. I think it is fair to say that if the individual executive
refuses to bluff from time to time, if he feels obligated to tell the
truth, the whole truth and nothing but the truth—he is ignoring
opportunities permitted under the rules and is at a heavy disadvan-
tage in his business dealings.*

*That most businessmen are not indifferent to ethics in their private
lives, everyone will agree. My point is that in their office lives they
cease to be private citizens; they become game players who must
be guided by a somewhat different set of ethical standards.*

*In the last third of the twentieth century even children are aware
that if a man has become prosperous in business, he has sometimes
departed from the strict truth in order to overcome obstacles or
has practiced the more subtle deceptions of the half-truth or the
misleading omission . . .*

Although Mr. Carr spoke of business in general, nowhere is the ethic
he advocates more visibly operant than in the corporate advertising
that daily inundates us with messages of "subtle deceptions . . . half-
truths . . . misleading omissions."

Deception through advertising reaches all segments of society. For
example, physicians as well as ordinary consumers can be deceived
by misleading drug advertising with disastrous consequences for their
patients. One particularly outrageous example of the misleading advertising of potent drugs is revealed in "The Peculiar Success of
Chloromycetin" from *Consumer Reports.* This drug is dangerous and
should be prescribed only for rare diseases like typhoid fever; yet,
because of persistent promotion over the years by Parke, Davis &
Co., Chloromycetin is still prescribed for millions of Americans with
minor ailments including the common cold.

Just as many consumers believe products are made to be as safe
as possible, they believe advertising claims have some factual basis:
when Sterling Drug asserts "Bayer aspirin is the best pain reliever
on earth," there must be some evidence to support Bayer's superiority
over other products. In truth, most advertising statements have very
little substance in fact and mislead buyers into choosing inferior or
totally ineffectual products. To determine how extensively companies
could and would supply the results of clinical tests to support claims,

Aileen Cowan, a pre-law student, and I sent letters to fifty-eight companies asking for substantiation of their claims. Their responses are outlined in "Claims Without Substance," an edited version of the petition we presented to the Federal Trade Commission. The petition asked the agency to establish a trade regulation rule requiring national advertisers to make their back-up scientific information available to the FTC and through the FTC to the public at the time advertising claims are made. The FTC did not make a trade regulation rule but in an unprecedented action, it did direct a number of major manufacturers to supply back-up information in support of advertising claims. By early 1972, the FTC had requested back-up data for about sixty advertisements, including those for automobiles, men's electric shavers, and air conditioners.

A particularly insidious form of advertising is that directed at children. In 1970, Washington consultant Robert Choate launched an attack on the cereal industry by testifying before a Congressional committee that forty of the sixty cereals being sold were so nutritionally deficient as to be "mostly calories and little else." His testimony was a bombshell, widely publicized and counterattacked by the industry. Less publicized was another part of Choate's testimony, an analysis of the advertising of cereals to children. He found that by such advertising less nutritious products were deliberately sold to children and that children were, in effect, programmed to demand sugar and sweetness in every food, thus being countereducated from nutrition knowledge. Mr. Choate discovered that the very worst cereals from a nutritional standpoint were advertised to children rather than to adults. His thought-provoking testimony, "Seduction of the Innocent," is reprinted here in its entirety.

Widespread deceptive advertising results in enormous waste to consumers and is often the result of monopolies which encourage the proliferation of products with little differentiation. Four companies, for example, dominate over 90 percent of the cereal industry. (More about the relationship between advertising and the giant corporations is found in the selection "Monopoly" later in this book.) Thus has much advertising abandoned its purpose of providing product or service information; it gives consumers little more than fictitious information with which they make wrong choices. Such falsehood is not, as businessman Carr suggested, good business. It makes a mockery of the enterprise system and prevents the practice of honest business. It is wasteful, morally and physically dangerous, and amounts to nothing more than calculated and organized thievery planned and imple-

CLAIMS WITHOUT SUBSTANCE

Ralph Nader and Aileen Cowan

Beginning in December 1969, two researchers with the Center for the Study of Responsive Law (one of them, Aileen Cowan) tape recorded and wrote descriptions of hundreds of commercials telecast by the four commercial stations in the District of Columbia, taped approximately 50 radio commercials, and clipped newspaper and popular magazine advertisements which seemed to make inflated statements or claimed to be based on clinical evidence. The researchers also obtained copies of advertisements for tires, automobiles, cereals, mouthwashes, toothpaste, and other products from the Federal Trade Commission.

Ralph Nader and Aileen Cowan then sent letters to 58 companies asking for supportive evidence for about 68 promotional claims. The letters, addressed to the presidents of the companies, requested information that would help ascertain: the extent to which data substantiating advertising claims are available to the public, the willingness of corporations to clarify vague promotional statements, the availability to the public of information about competitive brands to which manufacturers allude in their advertisements, the explanation why documentation was not provided (if it was not), the suggested recourse available to consumers interested in substantiating advertising claims, and the availability of sales figures and advertising expenditures.

To determine the availability and quality of clinical evidence substantiating promotional claims, petitioners Cowan and Nader asked companies to provide details and conclusions of their test data. These

Claims Without Substance by Ralph Nader and Aileen Cowan is a petition that was delivered to the Federal Trade Commission.

companies included Beecham Inc., which asserts that studies of a "major dental clinic" show that its dentifrice, Macleans, gets teeth "whitest"; Bristol-Meyers, which assures viewers that "a study of hospital patients showed: two Excedrin more effective in the relief of pain than twice as many aspirin"; Lewis-Howe, which states that "tests at a famous college" have shown that Tums "neutralizes excess acid in a matter of seconds"; and the Block Drug Company, which claims that "Nytol dissolves twice as fast as the other leading sleep tablets."

Other advertisements make claims for products without explaining how the claimed qualities of the product produce the benefits suggested. For example, the Warner-Lambert Company stresses Listerine's ability to kill "germs by the millions," and Richardson-Merrell Inc. asserts that Lavoris "scrubs your breath clean." Both advertisements attempt to convince consumers of the potency of the two products but do not explain whether or how the killing of bacteria and the "scrubbing" of one's breath substantially eliminate mouth odor.

Cowan and Nader also sought information about advertisements which included vague and unclear statements. Several unclear statements involved the use of dangling comparatives—implied comparisons for which the basis of the comparison is not revealed. For example, the Firestone Tire and Rubber Company states that its new "78" goes "thousands and thousands more miles than you'd ever expect." The Dow Chemical Company assures the housewife that its oven cleaner has "33 percent more power." General Motors claims that the Toronado's engine gives "worry-free performance thousands of miles longer." Armour and Company tells viewers that Armour bacon "gives you a little more because it shrinks a little less."

These companies and others were asked to reveal evidence supporting the implications of their statements—such as the number of miles the Firestone Company was suggesting, how Dow had determined that its oven cleaner had 33 percent more power, the number of miles General Motors claims that the Toronado's engine will last. Further, the manufacturers were asked the basis of their comparisons—for example, General Motors was asked to indicate what other automobile gave less worry-free performance than Toronado, and Armour was asked to supply the tests comparing its bacon with other brands.

Nine companies, whose advertisements implied extensive comparative product testing, were asked to provide studies which compared their product to the products alluded to in their claims, and to identify by brand name the products to which their product was compared. The Clorox Company, for example, asserts that "Clorox gets out stains that enzyme detergents leave in . . . and gets out stains and dirt the presoaks leave in." The General Foods Corporation assures viewers that its detergent Enzyme la France "whitens and brightens better than bleach . . . and removes stains faster than presoaks." Procter and Gamble states that "Biz soaks out a lot of stains you can't wash or bleach out." Ford, which claimed that Torino was "the lowest priced hardtop in its class," was asked to name both the automobiles considered to be in Torino's class and the average amount a consumer spends to buy a brand new Torino with accessories. The Standard Oil Company was asked to elaborate on its statement that Esso Extra has "more smoothness ingredients than most other gasolines" by naming the gasolines which comprised "most other gasolines" and to provide data derived from comparative testing substantiating its claim.

Letters were also sent to competing manufacturers whose advertising promotes "product differentiation": attempting to distinguish physically identical items by persuading buyers that one product is superior to other brands. The over-the-counter analgesic industry currently under investigation by the Commission spends millions of dollars differentiating between nearly identical products. However, in an article entitled "A Comparative Study of 5 Proprietary Analgesic Compounds" published in the *Journal of the American Medical Association*, December 29, 1962, Dr. Thomas DeKornfeld and his associates found no differences. After comparing the pain-relieving ability of Anacin, Bayer, Bufferin, Excedrin, St. Joseph's Aspirin and a placebo, they concluded that within the limits of generalization permitted by the population studied there are no important differences among the five compounds studied in rapidity of onset, degree or duration of analgesia. Confirming these findings in a telephone conversation with petitioner Cowan on December 7, 1970, Dr. DeKornfeld stressed that "there was no statistically significant difference between the brands tested"—that any small differences which appear are likely to be due to chance and not due to any difference between the efficacy of the compounds.

In another interview, Dr. DeKornfeld criticized Bristol-Meyers' use of the chemical study:

> *I would say that the claims made for Excedrin show only one side of the story. It shows the conclusions of one study and completely omits any mention of the fact that other studies have not been able to show this difference and it is quite possible that the repetition of the study on which these present claims are based would also be unable to show this difference or cer-*

tainly a difference of this magnitude. And all conclusions drawn from single studies have to be taken with a great deal of caution and we can accept the results as valid only if they are supported by additional investigation.

Nevertheless, Bristol-Meyers spent approximately $9 million in 1969 promoting Excedrin, and is now asserting that "two Excedrin [are] more effective in the relief of pain than twice as many aspirin tablets." The Whitehall Laboratories Division of American Home Products, which spent $25 million in 1969 for Anacin advertisements, implies that its tablet is the most effective of the analgesics because "two Anacin contain more of the specific pain relievers doctors recommend most than four of the other leading extra strength tablets." Sterling Drug spent more than $22 million in 1969 trying to convince the public of Bayer's superiority: "Bayer Aspirin is the best pain reliever on earth."

Cowan and Nader asked a number of companies which manufacture products whose safety has been questioned by reliable scientific data to supply evidence that their product is safe for its intended use. Thus Procter and Gamble, Colgate-Palmolive and the General Foods Company were all asked to provide their testing data showing that detergents with enzymes are safe. Researchers have reported in leading British and American medical journals that enzyme detergents cause allergic reactions such as severe dermatitis and asthma.

Beecham Inc., makers of Macleans toothpaste, and the Colgate-Palmolive Company, makers of Ultra Brite, were asked to provide tests showing that their dentifrices with abrasives do not harmfully wear away the teeth of some users. *The Wall Street Journal* reported in its September 30, 1968 issue that two members of Indiana's Department of Preventive Dentistry found that new dentifrices with whiteners contain such strong abrasives that they may harmfully wear away the teeth of some people. The Council on Dental Therapeutics has found:

Cementum and dentin are much softer tissues and even more susceptible to loss due to abrasion. Ordinarily these tissues are protected by the enamel . . . but individuals with exposed cementum, dentin and the soft restorative materials may lose significant amounts of tooth substance . . . when the more abrasive dentifrices are used routinely.
[*"Abrasive Toothpastes,"* Washington Post, December 1, 1970, p. B1]

A few letters were sent to companies asking them to clarify advertising testimonials by providing evidence that one man's experience is a common phenomenon among users. The Goodyear Tire and Rubber Company was asked to provide such evidence to substantiate the claim by Mr. Allen that "I've had Polyglas tires for approximately two years, and I've had about 35,000 miles on them." Procter and Gamble was asked to substantiate a woman's claim that her daughter "fries practically grease free with Crisco Oil." The woman showed french fries that were fried in one cup of Crisco Oil and claimed that all of the grease "comes back except one tablespoon."

The responses received by Cowan and Nader can be organized into ten categories:

1. Sixteen companies sent no response whatsoever.

2. Six companies refused to substantiate their claims to consumers contending it was sufficient to do so to the appropriate government agency.

3. Four answers included cursory descriptions of company tests rather than detailed scientific data.

4. Fifteen companies purported to clarify vague and misleading statements in their advertisements.

5. Eight letters contained personal assurances by company presidents or other representatives that promotional claims were truthful but did not provide the scientific data requested.

6. One company response retracted an advertising claim.

7. Two companies offered to send representatives to discuss their advertising campaigns (one later retracted the offer by telephone).

8. One letter indicated future correspondence would be forthcoming (no subsequent correspondence was ever received).

9. One company completely refused to cooperate.

10. Three responses included clinical studies, the value of which was dubious.

For example, James H. Howe, president of the Lewis-Lowe Company, wrote one of the eight letters giving assurances that advertising was truthful. He replied to a request for a copy of the test "at a famous college" which showed Tums to neutralize excess acid in a "matter of seconds" with the following remarks:

> We want to assure you that we have avoided "the use of exaggerated or unprovable claims" in our advertising and have based all the claims we have made on good evidence and advice. In fact, we pride ourselves on the high standards we adhere to in all aspects of our business.

Mr. Howe not only omitted the requested scientific data, he also failed to indicate his reason for not providing it.

Similarly, David J. Fitzgibbons, president of the Sterling Drug Company, sent no details or conclusions of comparative analgesic studies to substantiate claims that Bayer Aspirin "is the best pain reliever on earth." Instead he replied:

Please be assured that we share your concern with the importance of providing the public as well as the medical profession with accurate and truthful information in advertising. The policy of our company is, and always has been, the accomplishment of this goal.

When he was asked again in a second letter for scientific data, his response was similarly evasive.

Alfred L. Plant, president of the Block Drug Company, was asked to document advertisements for Nytol tablets and Tegrin Medicated Shampoo. He explained his unwillingness to provide the information by noting that advertising undergoes rigorous scrutiny by the company's legal and technical departments, advertising agencies, television networks, radio, other media, and various governmental agencies, and "none of these overseers would permit . . . advertising claims which are exaggerated or unprovable."

The J. B. Williams Company, manufacturer of Geritol, was asked twice to provide clinical evidence verifying claims made for Proslim, a diet wafer. A magazine advertisement asserted that "average weight loss [with Proslim] was nearly five pounds the very first week [and] doctors report pounds and inches lost in 7 days." The company was requested to provide such information as the names of the doctors reporting the success of Proslim, tests comparing the weight loss of people taking Proslim (plus the prescribed diet) with the weight loss of subjects taking the prescribed diet alone, and a full explanation of the test on which the "five pound average loss" was based. To discourage further questioning, Mr. Roger A. Schultz, Vice President Law, replied in his second letter:

Your original letter contains requests for such detailed scientific and medical information as to indicate a substantial lack of confidence in our product and our company. We would like to suggest that you consult your physician and develop alternate methods of reducing your weight.

Three companies provided cursory descriptions of their test procedures. The Ralston-Purina Company was asked to describe in detail the test upon which they based their claim that Meat Plus is "so good dogs chose it six to one in a recent test over the leading competitive variety." Mr. J. E. Corbin, director of the Purina Pet Care Center, sent the following reply:

> That test was conducted, under my direction, in July, 1968, at the Purina Pet Care Center, Gray Summit, Missouri. In this test, involving a statistically projectable sample of dogs of various sizes, ages, and popular breeds, Purina Meat Plus Beef and Meat By-Products, the variety featured in our advertising was tested against Alpo Beef and Meat By-Products, the leading competitive variety, in accordance with standard testing procedures. The dogs demonstrated a six to one preference for Meat Plus.

Since Mr. Corbin's explanation lacked significant information, such as the number of dogs tested and the circumstances under which the experiment was conducted, he was requested to provide more comprehensive information about the test. In his response, Mr. Corbin indicated that the research and techniques utilized in the test had to remain confidential.

The Ralston-Purina correspondence was sent to Robert E. Hunsicker, the President of the Allen Products company which produces Alpo Beef. He was asked if he believed the testing procedure of his competitor to be a reliable method to determine the preference of dogs for food. Mr. James G. Schmoyer, vice president for Research Quality Control, replied, "It is Allen Products Company's policy not to engage in disputes with our competitors."

Other manufacturers, like R. B. Shetterly, president of the Clorox Company, were asked to comment on the claims of competitors which seemed to conflict with their advertisements. Responding as did the others, Mr. Shetterly indicated that the policy of his company was "not to comment on copy claims of other manufacturers."

Of the nine companies asked to identify the specific products compared to their product in advertisements, only Ralston-Purina would even mention the other brand name.

Howard J. Morgens, president of Procter and Gamble, stated that the kind of information requested—such as scientific substantiation of advertising claims and test data concerning product safety—was only supplied to authorized government agencies:

> Since the [Federal Trade] Commission has been assigned by statute the responsibility for reviewing our advertising claims, we feel that our obligation in this respect must be to continue to respond fully and cooperatively to the designated agency of government, and that any duplication of this effort with private groups could hardly be expected to provide additional protection of the public interest.

Similarly, A. E. Larkin, Jr., president of General Foods Corporation, said that he "would have no reluctance to supply testing information to any duly authorized regulatory body with its attendant administrative safeguards." He would not, however, supply the details and conclusions of tests to the public.

The American consumer is faced with a virtually hopeless situation. He buys hundreds of different items in hundreds of different lines of products. In making each purchase he must decide which products to buy and then what brand to buy. He must distinguish between brands which on their face seem completely or substantially identical—like gasoline, paint, or milk—or whose differences are too complex for laymen to readily understand—like the internal workings of an automobile engine. He must weigh price, effectiveness, taste, warranty, ease of repair, consistency with or contribution to health, and many other factors. Advertising is supposed to supply the consumer with the vital information he needs to choose between competing products and brands.

Advertising should also provide a means by which business men are encouraged to compete. The company which provides the best product at the lowest price can truthfully describe its products to consumers and thereby increase its volume and profits. Advertising, it is therefore said, is vital to a free enterprise system based upon vigorous, effective competition.

In fact, however, as Americans know from their experience as consumers, and as the study of petitioners Cowan and Nader confirmed, advertising does not foster effective competition. Advertisers do not supply the consumer with information which would allow him to make an intelligent choice between products and low prices. Advertisers make vague claims which give consumers no real understanding of the products' performance, invoke clinical tests with little scientific basis to substantiate claims, and otherwise deliberately mislead and confuse the consumer.

At the very least, manufacturers do not provide facts needed for the consumer to make informed market choices. Instead, many buyers are ingeniously induced by misleading claims to buy an inferior product or a similar product at a higher price. Competition in the marketplace is rapidly being reduced to competition in advertising as businessmen spend more and more money on inflated or deceptive advertising claims rather than improving products or lowering prices. The result is both the exploitation of the consumer and the undermining of serious, meaningful competition.

THE PECULIAR
SUCCESS OF
CHLOROMYCETIN

CONSUMER REPORTS

Two years ago, a California physician journeyed to Washington to tell the Senate Committee on Small Business about the death of his 10-year-old son in 1952. The boy died after his father had given him the drug *Chloromycetin* for a mild urinary infection. As the father explained it, practicing physicians receive from 75 to 80 per cent of their information regarding drugs from drug company salesmen, called detail men, and from advertisements in medical journals. A few days before his son's ailment, the father was visited by a Parke, Davis & Co. detail man, who gave him a supply of *Chloromycetin* and assured him that it was a perfectly safe antibiotic. Yet only three days before that, the father said, the same detail man had been informed by a local pharmacist that *Chloromycetin* had been responsible for the death of a woman in nearby Pasadena.

"He deliberately lied to me that the drug was harmless," the father told the subcommittee.

The weight of medical evidence shows a correlation between the use of *Chloromycetin* and the incidence of aplastic anemia, a frequently fatal condition in which the bone marrow ceases to produce white cells, red cells and platelets (necessary for proper clotting).

There is no known method of determining beforehand a patient's susceptibility to *Chloromycetin* injury. Blood studies done during administration of the drug may suggest bone marrow depression, but even when it is recognized, the condition is often progressive. According to Dr. John M. Adams, of the department of pediatrics at UCLA, "Contrary to the belief of many doctors, *Chloromycetin* has an effect which is harmful in varying degrees to the bone marrow of all persons who take it."

The chances of dying of aplastic anemia as a direct result of taking *Chloromycetin* are fairly remote. A California study estimated the risk at between 1 in 24,200 and 1 in 40,500. Still, those seemingly slender odds should be regarded in the light of two other facts. First, the chances of dying of aplastic anemia, without any contribution from *Chloromycetin*, are less than 1 in 500,000. Second, according to the National Research Council, which investigated *Chloromycetin* for the U.S. Food and Drug Administration, *Chloromycetin* can no longer be considered the drug of choice for any illness except possibly typhoid fever (170 cases reported in the U.S. in 1969). Apart from that rare and not wholly substantiated exception, only in a few life-threatening conditions where other drugs have failed is there any justification for prescribing *Chloromycetin*. Yet it has been prescribed for and is being prescribed for millions.

MEDICAMENTA VERA

Medicamenta Vera (True Medicines) has been the Parke, Davis motto since the company's founding in 1866. In the 1940's, Parke, Davis scientists discovered that certain Venezuelan soil samples contained molds that yielded an antibiotic, chloramphenicol. It was found to be effective in treating various diseases, including typhoid fever and certain rickettsial diseases such as scrub typhus. Shortly thereafter, a Parke, Davis research team learned how to produce chloramphenicol synthetically for less than 10¢ a capsule. That was the first commercial synthesis of an antibiotic drug from soil molds. Parke, Davis rushed construction facilities for manufacturing chloramphenicol. It bestowed the trade name *Chloromycetin* on the drug and was granted a 17-year patent. Soon it had *Chloromycetin* in production at plants in Detroit and Holland, Mich., and in Hounslow, England.

When *Chloromycetin* was introduced on the American market in 1949, it won widespread acceptance for its effectiveness as a broad-spectrum antibiotic. It was also hailed for its apparent lack of adverse side effects. The first year, *Chloromycetin* sales exceeded $9-million.

The next year, sales increased to over $28-million. By 1951, *Chloromycetin* sales reached $52-million, which helped make Parke, Davis the world's largest pharmaceutical manufacturer.

Beginning in the early 1950's, however, medical authorities became alarmed over reports about the drug. An editorial in the *Journal of the American Medical Association (JAMA)* in June 1952 noted that aplastic anemia "has occurred in patients who have previously received one or more courses of chloramphenicol [*Chloromycetin*] without untoward effect. When the drug was subsequently administered, even in small doses, a severe blood abnormality has appeared. Even deaths have been reported." The editorial warned physicians to be on the alert for reactions following therapy with chloramphenicol. The editor of *JAMA* at that time was Dr. Austin Smith. Today Dr. Smith is president and chairman of the board of Parke, Davis.

In June 1952, after reviewing a number of case histories associating *Chloromycetin* with serious blood disorders, the Food and Drug Administration refused to approve any additional shipments of the drug, pending an investigation by a committee appointed by the National Research Council. The FDA reported in August of that year that the committee had "considered the records of 410 cases of serious blood disorders, of which 177 were definitely known to have been associated with *Chloromycetin.*" Half of those blood disorders were reported to have been fatal.

Nevertheless, the FDA decided to permit the continued sale of *Chloromycetin* on grounds that the drug "should continue to be available for careful use by the medical profession in those serious and sometimes fatal diseases in which its use is necessary." In order to prevent the indiscriminate use of *Chloromycetin*, estimated then to have been given to some eight million Americans, the FDA announced that the labeling would be changed to indicate that serious blood disorders had been associated with administration of the drug, and that *"Chloromycetin should not be used indiscriminately or for minor infections."*

SETBACK AND COMEBACK

Chloromycetin sales dipped sharply following the FDA investigation. In 1952, *Chloromycetin* sales dropped $5-million. In 1953 and 1954, sales were below the $25-million mark; the Holland, Mich., plant was closed, and Parke, Davis dropped from first to fifth place in total industry sales.

As time passed, the medical world should have been increasingly alerted to the dangers of *Chloromycetin*. For example, a study reported in *JAMA* in 1959 revealed a five-fold increase in the death rate of premature babies following prophylactic antiobiotic therapy in an Alabama hospital. In a four-month period, 160 newborns received such treatment. Twenty-eight died, and all 28 had received *Chloromycetin*. When its use was discontinued, the study revealed, "the neonatal death rate dropped back to and remained at about the level present before the use of chloramphenicol."

But even as the warning signals were being raised by the FDA and independent medical investigators, Parke, Davis was countering with a particular kind of marketing strategy. The company's president at that time, and its former sales manager, was Henry Loynd. In a series of letters to Parke, Davis's 980 detail men, Loynd pointed out that "with so much interest and attention being focused on *Chloromycetin* . . . the subject is doubtless being brought up by almost everyone on whom you call." Loynd went on to tell the detail men in a following letter that *Chloromycetin* had been officially cleared by the FDA "with no restrictions on the number or the range of diseases for which *Chloromycetin* may be administered." That, of course, was directly counter to the FDA's intent in warning against the drug so strongly.

Loynd's letters were followed by instructions from the company's sales director. He suggested that the detail men inform doctors that the FDA investigation had "resulted in the unqualified sanction of continued use of *Chloromycetin* for all conditions in which it had previously been used." However, he cautioned the detail men not to discuss the drug "unless the physician brings up the subject or unless you know that he has ceased prescribing *Chloromycetin*. Your efforts should all be directed in a positive direction designed to provide facts which will induce physicians to use *Chloromycetin* in a wide range of infections in which it is effective."

The marketing strategy was apparently more influential than the intelligence printed in medical journals. *Chloromycetin* sales began to rise. More than four million Americans were treated with the drug in 1959. In 1960, its sales were some $86-million. That was at a time when *Chloromycetin* was considered the drug of choice only for such rare diseases as typhoid fever and Rocky Mountain spotted fever.

ROUND TWO

The 1960 hearings on the drug industry conducted by Senator Estes Kefauver dealt *Chloromycetin* another setback. There it was revealed that, although Parke, Davis had included the FDA warning for *Chloromycetin* in advertisements carried in medical journals, the company had watered down the warning in direct-mail ads to physicians. Testimony from the hearings also indicated that some detail men were employing a somewhat warped sales track, alleging that *Chloromycetin* was no more dangerous than any other antibiotic and insisting that their information was "based on figures supplied them by their home office." In a letter to Parke, Davis, the FDA noted that it had received complaints from physicians "about your detail men playing down or minimizing the side effects of this drug."

In 1961, *Chloromycetin* sales declined by more than 20 per cent. In an interview published in a Detroit newspaper, the president of Parke, Davis blamed the Kefauver hearings, which, he said, "caused some very unfavorable publicity, I might say unjustified and some of it ridiculous, which cost us a volume loss on *Chloromycetin* of about $15-million." He expressed the hope that the matter would die down.

He also acknowledged that year that Parke, Davis had been or was involved in 25 law suits, some of which had been settled out of court. The first case to come before a jury was pressed on behalf of a woman whose doctor had prescribed *Chloromycetin* for a sore gum after a tooth extraction and again for a bronchial condition. She contracted aplastic anemia and died. In rendering a judgment against Parke, Davis, the court noted that "there was evidence that the 1952 warning label, the one on the drug at the time prescribed by [the doctor in the case], was ambiguous, inadequate and incomplete and that Parke, Davis was aware thereof." The doctor testified that he had been misled by Parke, Davis detail men and promotional materials.

Some of the suits got quite expensive, not only for the drug company, but for prescribing physicians. In 1962, a verdict of $215,000 was awarded against Parke, Davis and two doctors following the death of a 7-year-old girl who was given *Chloromycetin* for a series of minor infections over a three-year period. Here it was argued that Parke, Davis had misled physicians into using the drug indiscriminately, in disregard of the potential toxic effects of the antibiotic, for conditions where drugs of lesser toxicity should have been used.

In 1964, to cite one more instance of substantial reparations, Parke, Davis reached an out-of-court settlement of $12,600 with a California newspaper publisher. His 19-year-old daughter died after being treated with *Chloromycetin*, first for a sore throat and later for a mild urinary infection. Three doctors involved paid a total of $22,400.

But neither unfavorable publicity nor the threat of litigation could dissuade Parke, Davis from encouraging doctors to prescribe *Chloromycetin*. And, for the second time in nine years, sales bounced back. In 1967, some 3,700,000 Americans received the drug.

As before, some clever promotional devices undoubtedly contributed to the comeback. In 1962, Parke, Davis deleted from "Physicians' Desk Reference," a commercial publication containing drug information provided by the various drug companies and distributed free to physicians, all reference to the hazards of *Chloromycetin*. Instead, the company inserted a statement advising doctors that they could get information on "dosage, administration, contraindications and precautions" from the package insert, the detail men, or the company. A doctor prescribing *Chloromycetin* capsules, however, normally would not see the package inserts, since the inserts were sent to the druggist. And Parke, Davis and its detail men had long since made it clear that they would like to see almost unlimited use of the drug.

In 1962, Congress passed the Kefauver-Harris act, which required all prescription drug advertisements to include a statement concerning possible side effects. That didn't faze Parke, Davis. The company obscured the warning for *Chloromycetin* in a mass of fine print and ran a series of so-called "reminder" ads, which, it insisted, did not come under the terms of the Kefauver-Harris act. An ad would be headlined "When it Counts" and would be followed by the word *Chloromycetin* and a phrase "Complete information for usage available for physicians upon request." That was all—no warning. Other headlines read "Among the Most Significant Drugs in Use Today" and "A Name You Can Count on When It Counts." Another technique was to include a picture of a bronchoscope in *Chloromycetin* ads, implying that the drug should be used for respiratory infections.

ROUND THREE

The 1968 Senate hearings, under the chairmanship of Senator Gaylord Nelson, took some of the wind out of that kind of advertising. Medical authorities who testified estimated that *Chloromycetin* therapy was uncalled for in 90 per cent of the cases in which it had been prescribed. One doctor put the figure at 99 per cent. The committee learned of cases where physicians prescribed *Chloromycetin* for acne, tonsillitis and minor gum infections. The senators heard of one instance in which a doctor told a woman, who later developed aplastic anemia, to take *Chloromycetin* whenever she had a cold. Hardly surprising, in view of a study reported in *JAMA* in 1967; out of 288 cases of aplastic anemia associated with *Chloromycetin*, 12 per cent of the patients had been treated with the drug for the common cold.

The most immediate effect of the Nelson hearings, and the publicity that attended them, was a sharp decline in *Chloromycetin* sales. Sales of capsules (by far the most popular form in which the drug is dispensed) dropped 70 per cent in the first nine months of 1968. But Parke, Davis, having been through all this twice before, seemed unconcerned. The company's president, Dr. Smith, advised a group of security analysts not to worry since there would probably be a recovery "after a reasonable period of time."

Dr. Smith apparently knew what he was talking about. The latest FDA figures show a five-fold increase in the certification of *Chloromycetin* capsules in June of this year compared with June of last year, enough to treat from 16,000 to 31,000 people a month. And now that Parke, Davis's patent has run out, two rival companies are making their own chloramphenicol products. McKesson Laboratories calls its drug *Amphicol*; Rachelle Laboratories markets its under the trade name of *Mychel.*

The medical literature so abounds with evidence of the dire consequences of taking *Chloromycetin* and similar chloramphenicol products that it's inexcusable for physicians to prescribe those drugs promiscuously. Yet it's clear that some physicians do prescribe them promiscuously and will continue to do so, despite the hottest glare of adverse publicity on the drugs and direct warnings published in medical journals. It's equally clear that the manufacturers are hardly interested in curbing the distribution and demand for a rarely indicated and potentially deadly—but eminently profitable—product.

WHAT TO DO ABOUT IT?

Dr. Raphael Shulman, a member of the FDA's hematology advisory committee, points out that "as long as the drug is available it will be not only used but abused." The 11-man committee reported in March 1969 that its members were generally agreed that the Commissioner of Food and Drugs "should give further consideration to the possible restriction of this drug to hospital use." That seems like a sensible step. Treatment with chloramphenicol is presently advisable for only a few very severe conditions and under certain particular circumstances; you would expect that the few people who could possibly profit by it would already have been hospitalized. Moreover, once the drug is exclusively under hospital control, a physician would be compelled to justify his choice of chloramphenicol to his colleagues; hospitals and the privileges they can confer to (or withdraw from) doctors could bring great pressure to bear.

There remains, however, a larger issue concerning a patient's right to know the risks associated with *any* drug that his physician prescribes for him. A doctor may not perform surgery without the informed consent of the patient or his next of kin. Drug therapy can be as dangerous as surgery; witness the sizable number of people hospitalized each year for adverse reactions to prescription drugs. The FDA now requires manufacturers of oral contraceptives to prepare pamphlets for patients explaining in lay language the major side effects and hazards of contraceptive pills. The Commissioner of Food and Drugs has said that this action "may or may not serve as a precedent" for other drugs.

CU believes that it should—that, where appropriate, patients should be informed, in plain, easy-to-read language, of the possible hazards of drugs. Had patients been informed about *Chloromycetin* years ago, many people might have declined *Chloromycetin* therapy for minor ailments and escaped the horrors of aplastic anemia.

SEDUCTION OF THE INNOCENT

ROBERT B. CHOATE

Mr. Chairman, my name is Robert Choate. For three years I have been very active on the issue of hunger and malnutrition in the United States. During that period I have scrutinized America's food policies and have tried to assess the best means of guaranteeing to every American an adequate and proper food supply. Working primarily on the issue of hunger, I have worked for Secretary Robert Finch in HEW, for the White House, and for the Senate Select Committee on Nutrition and Human Needs; when not so employed, I finance myself.

While I have been interested in the policies of American food companies for a long time, the six months' preparation for the White House Conference on Food, Nutrition and Health brought me into regular contact with some of the major decision-makers of the food industry. I met with many of the nation's top nutritionists; I conversed regularly with the more recognized food technologists and researchers. Studying nutrition education, I became appalled at the state of ignorance we all hold about food values.

During that period I urged reforms; I begged for new policies; I sought more imaginative and compassionate approaches to food

---

Seduction of the Innocent by Robert Choate is a testimony that was given before the Consumer Subcommittee of the Senate Commerce Committee.

problems, particularly those of the poor. Some of the results of this work can be found in the final report of the White House Conference on Food, Nutrition and Health. Numerous recommendations in that report urge reforms, changes, innovations. We are now almost 8 months past that Conference. The policies remain unchanged; the ignorance persists; the reforms are in neutral gear. In an effort to revitalize the needed changes, I have prepared this report on a segment of the American food industry. Unfortunately, it is representative of the great mass of food merchandising today.

Among the 6000 different items in your grocer's shelves are 60 different breakfast cereals. The consumer is entitled to know which are the best. She is also entitled to an explanation of the sales technique used to urge these products to her table. She should understand what is being done to her child. Since industry has not acted, despite repeated recommendations by industry leaders and nutrition professionals at the White House Conference on Food, Nutrition and Health, it is time to consider governmental action.[1]

Those leaders in the food industry who understand the need for reforms seem restrained by the fear of losing their competitive position. The food inudstry—America's biggest at $106 billion a year—is fragmented, unsecure and jealous of small portions of the market. The biggest five food companies (by sales)—Swift, Kraftco, Armour, General Foods and Borden's—together constitute less than 10% of the food industry. Leadership to initiate reforms is hard to inspire in such a competitive world. A major food company executive has told me that fear, not inspiration, may hold the key to food company reforms. If this is so, the American consumer may have to inspire that fear.

Under the usual economic restraints of corporate employment, we find a mass of well-intentioned but powerless food professionals. Those in the food professions hesitate to compare the nutritional worth of various foods; they are curiously reluctant to arm the buyer with protective knowledge against deceptive advertising, mislabeled boxes, and deceitful containers, or even to help him understand the new food technology. Most Americans are nutritional illiterates, and their lack of knowledge makes them an easy mark for segments of the food industry eager to conceal the comparative nutritive worth of their products. The cereal industry is a case in point.

---

[1] *White House Conference on Food, Nutrition and Health, Final Report, 1970. Government Printing Office, pp. 284–285.*

THE 60 CEREALS

A study of 60 ready-to-eat cereals reveals that they are primarily calorie sources, the nutrient content of 40 of the 60 being so low as to remind this observer of the term "empty calories," a term thus far applied to alcohol and sugar.[2] In short, they fatten but do little to prevent malnutrition. Calories per ounce—a typical serving—range from 75 to 113 with 109 being very common. Fat content, a prime source of calories even in grains, ranges from 0.5 to 2.7 grams per ounce. Calories are a measure of the energy volume of a food, but food must contain more than calories if one is to remain healthy. The human system needs nutrients in the form of proteins, minerals and vitamins.

Proteins, which are needed daily, vary in quality. Grain proteins can be as good as meat, milk and egg proteins, if they are complete. Protein Efficiency Ratios (PER's) indicate whether a protein is complete. Whole milk has a good PER of 2.5. It is a commentary on cereal company ethics that PER's are available only on seven of the 60 cereals. PER's are not made available by cereal manufacturers for any but their best products; the very low PER's of most cereals[3][4] are a carefully kept secret. There seems to be little desire on the part of government to educate the public on PER's. On June 20, 1962, the U.S. Food and Drug Administration published in the *Federal Register* a proposed formula for evaluating protein values. The Canadian Government adopted such a formula, and uses it today to inform consumers of protein quality. Despite revisions and much-delayed hearings, the United States did not adopt such a formula and the Food and Drug Administration seems to have lost interest in alerting the public to PER's of cereals and other grain products. Both the Food and Drug Administration (FDA) and the U.S. Department of Agriculture (USDA) have responsibilities; neither will act. One of the reasons given for FDA reluctance to establish minimum standards in all nutrient categories for cereals is that such standards "might connote recognition of these products as a source of good food values." It also may be opposed by the industry.

In each ounce of the 60 cereals, the protein content ranges from 1.5% to 9.5% of an adult's recommended dietary allowance (RDA).[5]

---

[2]*White House Conference on Food, Nutrition and Health, Final Report, 1970.* Government Printing Office, p. 57.
[3]*Sure, Barnett, "Nutritional Values of Proteins in Various Cereal Breakfast Foods," Food Research* 16 161–165 (1951).
[4]*Clarke, Juno-Ann Krohn and Kennedy, Barbara M., "Availability of Lysine in Wholewheat Bread and in Selected Breakfast Cereals," Journal of Food Science* 27 609–616 (1962).
[5]*Averaged to 60 grams per day, based on 1969 figures published by the National Research Council.*

Only 10 of the cereals have 5% or more of the RDA per one ounce serving. A child of 14 or a middle-aged adult may need approximately 60–65 grams per day. The three top protein cereals average 5.3 grams of protein per ounce, with PER's declared. The rest have less than 4 grams, with generally unstated PER's. Dry cereals, it appears, are a poor and expensive source of complete proteins.

All of the cereals contain iron ranging from 3% to 200% of an adult's minimum daily requirement (MDR). That more iron is needed in our systems is now recognized by the Food and Nutrition Board of the National Research Council. The MDR of iron is about to be raised. There is some difference of opinion on the forms and amounts of iron that can be ingested, particularly by those already anemic. These doubts led us to show iron content on the graphs that follow only up to 100% of present minimum daily requirements.

Calcium is found in most cereals, in amounts ranging from 0 to 14.1% of an adult's minimum daily requirement. Judged apart from the milk which may be used on the cereal, the 60 represent a poor and expensive source of calcium.

Vitamins can be added to cereals, but only 8 of the 60 cereals contain vitamins A, C or D. Those eight contain from 33% to 100% of the minimum daily requirement of one or more of those vitamins. Most of the cereals contain B vitamins, especially niacin and thiamine. About half also contain riboflavin. The thiamine is particularly needed in foods with high carbohydrate content; its absence, as is found in several cereals, is detrimental to the consumer, if not provided by other foods.

Nutrient percentages are frequently judged adequate if they relate favorably to the percent of total daily calories afforded by that particular food. Some nutritionists will therefore tell you that a food with 10% MDR in iron is O.K. if that food provides 10% of the day's needed calories. This is frequently falacious. Today many children, particularly poor children, get most of their calories from fats and sugars. These calorie sources have no nutrients—hence the term "empty calories." Other foods must make up for what they lack.

To compare the nutrient worth of various products is difficult. All told, there may be 30 or more different nutrients, all needed in various amounts and time periods. For simplicity's sake, we have analyzed and compared the cereals on the basis of the protein, iron, calcium, vitamins A, C and D, and the B vitamins thiamine, riboflavin and niacin in a typical one ounce serving. Recognizing the need for balanced nutrient intake, we have added together the individual nutrient percentages of a typical human's daily needs to ascertain a purely numerical rating for each cereal. For instance, if a one ounce serving of a given cereal provided 10% of a person's minimum daily requirement of each of the above nine nutrients, then that cereal would have a numerical rating of 90. (Ten points for each of the nine nutrients.) In this way we have been able to compare the nutritional merits of sixty dry cereals.[6]

We have tabulated below the 60 cereals by nutritional content, showing cumulative nutritional merits. We believe it is useful to provide such a graphic display of the comparative value of cereals, especially since the variations are so great. While such a graph oversimplifies the interaction of nutrients, it does portray what the cereal companies are boasting about on their own boxes. In short it uses their standards. Were one to be comparing cereals for use on a desert island over a six month period, a more sophisticated comparison analysis should be made. Within one food group, such a graph has some merit. It should not be used across food groupings. The total rating number is only a number and is not a percentage figure.

The graph has some natural divisions. Three of the cereals—Kellogg's Product 19, General Mills' Kaboom and Total—seem clearly the best from a nutrient standpoint.[7] An additional six, having high numerical ratings from a variety of nutrients, seem nutritionally meritorious. They are:

Nabisco, 100% Bran
Quaker Oats Life
General Foods Fortified Oat Flakes
Kellogg's Special K
General Foods Super Sugar Crisp
Kellogg's Sugar Smacks

Another eleven seem to have some redeeming features. The bottom 40 seem to warrant the term "empty calories." For a budget conscious family, they are a bad nutrient investment for the dollar. They have calories and little else.

The nutritional worth of a cereal is not related to its cost to the consumer. A recent study of cereal costs in Philadelphia showed the

---

[6]Two to four ounces of milk, either whole, skimmed, canned or reconstituted powdered, generally are consumed with these cereals. Vitamin D is added to the milk about half the time. The milk's contribution is itemized later. If cereals are advertised without milk, it seems correct to include a dry analysis.

[7]Now in the running for top honors is Quaker Oats' King Vitaman, which is new on the market and not included in the graph. It lists nutrient levels at 100% MDR of iron, niacin, thiamine, riboflavin and vitamins A, C, and D, but claims no protein.

price per ounce for dry cereals to range from 2.2¢ to 7.4¢. Kellogg's Bran Buds was the cheapest; Quaker Oats Puffed Wheat was the most expensive. The cost per ounce is shown in the righthand margin of the attached bargraph describing cumulative nutrient contents. The average price per ounce is 3.8¢ for the top twenty cereals, 4.5¢ for the middle twenty, and 4.4¢ for the bottom twenty.

Over 50 of the 60 cereals are sugar frosted, sugar coated, or otherwise sweetened at the factory. This has serious implications for children's teeth.[8] [9]

Packaging of cereals seems designed to confuse the customer on cost per ounce. The smallest packages—the one serving, eat-out-of-the-box group—are the most costly. The comparative prices quoted elsewhere are based on the largest box available in a major super-market. Box sizes, however, ran from 7 ounces to 18 ounces, with 12 and 15 ounce sizes being common. But does the industry have to have boxes in 7, 8, 9, 10, 12, 13, 15, 16 and 18 ounce packages? Even if the nutrients were comparable, what shopper could analyze the benefits per dollar expended?

To illustrate the wide range of benefits gained, I have listed some of the nutrients obtained from various cereals for a 10¢ investment.[10]

	Ounces (for 10¢)	Protein (no PER evaluation) grams	Calcium (Mg.)	Iron (Mg.)	Thiamine (Mg.)
Kellogg's Product 19	1.86	4.6	140	18.5	1.86
General Foods Fortified Oat Flakes . .	2.79	14.3	120	52.6	0.92
General Foods Raisin Bran	3.4	9.5	78	27.6	0.38
General Mills Wheaties	2.96	7.3	36	3.8	0.44
Nabisco Shredded Wheat	3.0	7.5	30	0.7	.0
Quaker Oats Puffed Wheat	1.35	5.4	11	1.6	0.22

[8]*Resolution on Sugar and Dental Cavities, House of Delegates of the American Dental Association, September 1953.*
[9]*White House Conference on Food, Nutrition and Health, Final Report, 1970 (Government Printing Office) Page 48, Recommendation No. 3, Panel 11–12.*
[10]*From Table 9, "An Evaluation of the Nutritional Quality of Ready-To-Eat Cereals," Morris C. Matt, D. Sc., The Academy of Food Marketing, Saint Joseph's College, Philadelphia.*

Several breakfast products do not fit the usual interpretation of "dry cereals." Two are worth mentioning: Kellogg's Concentrate and Kretschmer's Wheat Germ. They appear to be additives to upgrade cereals rather than cereals themselves. The former costs 8.1¢ per ounce, has 106 calories, and has an impressive number of nutrients per ounce: Protein, 18.9% recommended dietary allowance (RDA) (PER asserted to be 2.5—that of milk itself); calcium, 6.0% of minimum daily requirement (MDR); iron, 50% MDR; vitamin C, 50% MDR; and vitamins B_1, B_2 and niacin, 50% MDR. Wheat Germ costs 3.7¢ per ounce, has 106 calories, and also has good nutritional credentials: Protein, 31.5% RDA (PER asserted to be 2.5); calcium 0; iron 25% MDR; vitamin C, 9% MDR; vitamin B_1, 50% MDR; vitamin B_2, 19% MDR; and niacin, 14% MDR.

Genetically speaking, the bran cereals all rate in or near the top third. Corn cereals, reflecting corn's low nutritional worth, gravitate toward the bottom. All the shredded wheats seem anxious to stay at or near the bottom. Nabisco's Shredded Wheat doesn't list its nutrients and has, to this observer, highly questionable box labelling.[11]

A frequent defense of the dry cereal industry comes in the form of describing a cereal's nutrient worth in combination with the sugar and milk which may accompany it. If cereals are to be considered a meal unto themselves, the argument has some merit. Believing that such a meal should provide one third of the minimum daily requirements in major categories, we have analyzed in Graph Number 2 to what degree selected cereals fall short of providing one third of MDR's in the nine aforementioned categories. We have shown three meritorious, three average and three lower-grade cereals with 4 ounces of non-vitamin D milk added. It becomes quickly obvious that the average cereals—those outside of the top twenty—fail as a complete meal even with milk added. Even if the amount of cereal were doubled while the milk remained constant, the nutrient value of these meals would still be inadequate.

That some cereals are of greater nutritional worth than others should come as no surprise. But which cereals are advertised, and to whom? Since cereal eaters are often under 16, what is the nature of the sales effort made to the young American whose taste and food patterns are just being formed?

---

[11]*Nabisco Shredded Wheat label exhibited. Relative position of Shredded Wheat revised in later testimony.*

CEREAL ADVERTISING

Every Saturday morning the national networks carry extensive cartoons and adventure films. TV Guide says of this period:

In recent years, these Saturday morning programs have become colossal moneymakers for the networks—delivering, as they do, a demographically pure audience for the makers of toys and breakfast cereals. The total network profits are high—about $20 million a year—and to assure their continuance, TV programmers have been spending record amounts of cash to develop shows that will capture the allegiance of the Nation's small fry and therefore the money of advertisers who want to reach the small fry.

For practical purposes, Saturday-morning children's TV is a scale model of the prime-time ratings battle, with all the same factors in force. The object of the game (seen from a TV executive's chair) is to attract the largest share of the available audience, thereby maximizing one's profits and pleasing one's advertisers and stockholders.

Each and every Saturday morning, about 50 percent of all the Nation's 2-to-11-year-olds are in place before their TV sets. Even at that age, they comprise an important "market" in the great American mercantile structure. And where a market exists—in the inexorable logic of free enterprise—goods and services materialize to tantalize its special tastes.[12]

After recently reviewing the nature of the advertisements and products interspersed among 100 minutes of Saturday morning children's cartoons on both CBS and NBC, I believe that:

1. Our children are deliberately being sold the sponsor's less nutritious products;

2. Our children are being programmed to demand sugar and sweetness in every food;

3. Our children are being counter-educated away from nutrition knowledge.

On Saturday, June 6, 1970, during children's cartoon time, seventy-three spot advertisements of 100 minutes each on NBC and CBS television advocated purchasing cereals, candies, cookies, popcorn, soda pop and toys.

---

[12]Efron, Edith and Hickey, Neil. "TV and Your Child: In Search of an Answer," a series from 1969 issues of TV Guide Magazine, Triangle Publications, 1969.

In 100 minutes on CBS and NBC, the following breakfast foods were touted:

Kellogg's Corn Flakes
Kellogg's Sugar Smacks
Kellogg's Sugar Pops
Kellogg's Raisin Bran
Kellogg's Sugar Frosted Flakes
Kellogg's Cocoa Krispies
Kellogg's Rice Krispies
Kellogg's Puffa Puffa Rice
Kellogg's Froot Loops
Kellogg's Pop Tarts
Kellogg's Danish Go Rounds
General Foods Raisin Bran
Ralston Purina Sugar Frosted Chex
Quaker Oats Quake
Quaker Oats Quisp
Quaker Oats Cap'n Crunch
Quaker Oats Crunchberries
General Mills Cheerios
General Mills Cocoa Puffs
General Mills Trix

ABC, monitored two Saturdays later over a seventy-minute period, included only two cereal advertisements—Cheerios and Cocoa Puffs—among its Tastykake, Orange Crush, Slurpee, Milky Way and M & M candy messages. A much higher percentage of public service spots were included, such as anti-smoking, Smokey the Bear, YWCA, Cub Scouts and pesticide warnings.

On television, the visual part of the advertising message is important. Even if the advertisement verbally does not boast of muscle-building protein, the flexing of a bicep or the up-rooting of a tree while the cereal is being spooned from a bowl conveys to a child that the cereal can do wonders for his physique. And if the program hero is involved, the child viewer is convinced of the cereal's worth. The interchange of heroes from program plot to advertising scenarios is common.

The television message generally avoids verbalizing specific nutritional merits but stresses repeatedly: sugar, energy, sweetness, chocolate, vigor, frostedness, action, alertness and prizes. Half mentioned milk. Sample messages include:

"Golden flying saucers, sweet and crunchy and . . . loaded with quazy energy."

" . . . gives you lots of energy, good wind."

" . . . make breakfast taste like chocolate."

"Walking, stopping, digging, crawling, Jumping high and never falling, . . . corn flakes takes you all the way."

"Eat . . . and you'll be a tiger in no time."

" . . . colorful cereal circles, sparkling with sugar crystals."

Cereal advertisers, it should be noted, did not invent the advocacy of sugared products. Every mother who has threatened to withhold dessert from an errant child has, in effect, given the sweetest part of the meal a reward symbolism which makes it more attractive. Desserts, in general, have less of the nutrients needed in a marginal diet than do the other courses.

A child watching 73 spots in a total of 200 minutes of Saturday television would gather (1) that cereals with sugar are great energy sources, (2) that energy and action are equivalent to happiness, and (3) that ability and health are a product of eating ready-to-eat, preferably sweet, cereals. Is this true?

Cheerios, the nation's most advertised cereal, has a TV budget of $5,404,800 out of General Mills' total TV budget of $29,425,100.[13] In comparison with the other cereals, it ranks 25th out of the 60 in cumulative nutrient merits. It provides per ounce, 6.3% of the recommended dietary allowance (RDA) of protein. The protein efficiency ratio (PER) is 1.02. Also per ounce, it contains 6.9% of the minimum daily requirement (MDR) of calcium, 12.0% MDR of iron, 5% MDR of niacin, and 25% MDR of thiamine (B_1).

Rice Krispies, the nation's second most advertised cereal, has a TV budget of $3,609,200 out of Kellogg's total TV budget of $22,505,900. It contains no vitamin A, C or D and ranks 39th in cumulative nutrients among the 60 cereals analyzed. It provides 2.8% RDA or protein (no PER available), 0.9% MDR of calcium, 0.9% MDR of

---

[13]*All product and company advertising figures are taken from:* National Advertising Investment Report, 1969. *Leading National Advertisers, Inc.*

calcium, 5% MDR of iron, 20% MDR of niacin and 11% MDR of thia-mine.

Kellogg's Sugar Frosted Flakes, represented by Tony the Tiger, is the third most advertised brand, and Tony gets a TV budget of $2,738,000. Sugar Frosted Flakes has no vitamin A, C or D and falls to 58th among the 60 cereals in nutritional merit. It provides 2.2% RDA of protein (again no PER), 0.2% MDR of calcium, 3.0% MDR of iron, 6.0% MDR of niacin, and 12% MDR of thiamine. Tony, one critic reports, is today's anti-Popeye.

Then comes regular old line Kellogg's Corn Flakes. This product has a TV budget of $2,461,500. It too has dubious nutritional worth, being 38th out of the 60. Its protein boast per ounce is 3.5% RDA (no PER available). Its calcium content is 0.1% MDR, along with 7.0% for iron, 15% MDR of niacin, and 12% MDR of thiamine and 2.5% MDR of riboflavin. It contains no vitamins A, C or D.

Kellogg's Rasin Bran has a TV budget of $1,709,700. Well iden-tified on children's TV, it has a protein value of 3.8% RDA, calcium content of 2.0% MDR, 100% MDR of iron, 20% MDR of niacin, 12% MDR of thiamine and 2.5% MDR of riboflavin. It has no vitamins A, C or D. This cereal is 13th in the rating of the 60.

Kellogg's Sugar Smacks, which has a TV budget of $692,500, is rated ninth in comparison to the 60 cereals and is one of those counted nutritionally meritorious. It contains 2.3% RDA of protein (no PER), 0.5% MDR of calcium, 3.0% MDR of iron, and 33.3% each and Froot Loops, each stresses sweetness. The meritorious assessment of the first two places them down with Corn Flakes and Rice Krispees, while Froot Loops is 21st in nutritional merit.

Other Kellogg's products seen advertised on children's TV and having TV budgets over $500,000 are: Sugar Pops, Cocoa Krispies, and Froot Loops is 21st in nutritional merit.

Nine out of nine of Kellogg's cereals touted to children during the 200 minutes contain sugar or stress sweetness. Only two of them are in the top twenty, according to nutritional merit. One of them is in the top nine.

How about the other companies?

Big on Saturday morning kiddy cartoons are General Mills' Cheerios, Cocoa Puffs, and Trix. General Foods touts Raisin Bran.

Quaker Oats shouts Quake, Quisp and Cap'n Crunch. Each has a TV budget over $500,000 per year. None are in the top nine, nutritionally. All contain sugar. (General Mills' Wheaties, not seen on Saturday mornings, is a major advertiser, with $1,125,400. Nutritionally, it rates 29th out of the 60.)

Even a cursory review shows that the better cereals are advertised to older viewers. The rest are touted to the children, generally on a sugar-related message. Prizes further seduce those to whom sugar is no favor.

According to *Advertising Age* of August 25, 1969, these vast expenditures of advertising net the companies a gigantic percentage of the dry cereal market.

	Dry cereal TV budget	Dry cereal percent of market
Kellogg's	$18,778,500	43
General Mills	15,819,200	21
General Foods	7,680,400	18
Total	42,278,100[1]	82

[1]*For comparison of advertising expenditures: General Motors has a TV budget of $42,000,000 per year.*

Best sellers are:

	Percent of market
Kellogg's Corn Flakes	9
Kellogg's Rice Krispies	5
Kellogg's Sugar Frosted Flakes	5
General Mills Cheerios	7
General Mills Wheaties	4

These six cereals rate 38th, 39th, 58th, 25th and 29th in our nutritional rating order.

We do not state that the better cereals are not advertised. The following top nine cereals include many with healthy budgets. While the TV expenditure is the largest portion of their advertising cost, magazines and other periodicals also contain their ads. In this regard they are unlike the cereals sold primarily to children, which have budgets almost totally devoted to television expense.

TV budget

Kellogg's Product 19	$2,226,917
General Mills Kaboom	1,959,000
General Mills Total	2,567,200
Nabisco 100% Bran	?
Quaker Oats Life	846,700
General Foods Fortified Oat Flakes	?
Kellogg's Special K	2,484,900
General Foods Super Sugar Crisp	1,366,900
Kellogg's Sugar Smacks	692,500

A few additional points must be made on the advertising of cereals to children. A recent petition to the Federal Communication Commission by ACT (Action for Children's Television) of Boston included a study of television advertising practices on more than just the Saturday morning shows. Ralph M. Jennings reported that in city after city, weekday or weekend, cereals, candies and toys dominated the advertising message.[14] The only time when cereal advertising decreased was when the toy manufacturers bid the cost of the advertising time up to prohibitive levels just before Christmas.[15]

An insidious part of advertising to children—be it for cereals, candies or toys—is the practice of the hero character emerging from the plot or scenario of the cartoon or adventure and hawking his sponsor's products. The Banana Splits and Captain Kangaroo regularly do this. We have avoided mentioning the plot or scenario of the children's shows. Suffice it to say that the action is violent, repetitive and unreal. Entertainment, not education, is the message. The networks generally oversee the content of the programs; certainly they influence the content by virtue of matching advertiser to program. Ultimate responsibility for honesty and quality lies with the company; in children's shows the theme of the program is not so sacrosanct as to not be influenced by the advertising dollar.

---

[14]*Network TV: Brand, Product and Parent Company Schedule Detail and Expenditure Estimates for the Week Ending June 7, 1970.* (Broadcast Advertisers Reports, Inc., New York) Section 3, p. 27.
[15]Jennings, Ralph M., *"Programming and Advertising Practices in Television Directed to Children",* Prepared for Action for Children's Television (ACT), April 1970.

Lest one feel that messages directed to children carry little weight, I interviewed one Washington Safeway manager as to cereal merchandising. The gist of his remarks included:

There's no doubt it's the kids who select the cereals.

Sales volume shifts as television ads promote one product or the other.

The newer cereals seem to be making a dent in the old favorites.

Like the cereals, the pop-up products are influenced by fads.

Cereals occupy about one-thirtieth of our shelf space.

Our return, our earnings, from cereals averages out above most of the other departments.

Look at that checkout counter; that lady must be taking home six boxes of cereals.

These comments gain importance when one understands the extent to which children demand foods huckstered to them on television. They are further underscored when one realizes that many children today, particularly in depressed areas, do the shopping.[16] Medically important, the National Nutrition Survey under Dr. Arnold Schaefer found the incidence of malnutrition among the poor alarmingly high, particularly among children.

Once a cereal enters your home, the advertising changes emphasis. The back-of-the-box billboard, which is a medium unto itself, entices another purchase by hawking these rewards among the top nine cereals:

Esther Williams advice on nutrition
Decaffeinated Coffee and nutrition
Puppets
Pen Sets
Historic Documents
Racing Cars
Dolls
Jewelry
Knives

---

[16]During a panel meeting prior to the White House Conference a supermarket manager of an eastern city stated that a recent survey had shown 12% of his customers to be under 12 years of age.

Obviously nutrition education has entered the minds of few merchandisers. Among the least nutritionally meritorious cereals, the following back-of-the-box rewards appear:

Archie records
Knives
Jewelry
Puppets
Pennants
Dolls
Stamping and printing sets
Art miniatures

Perhaps these children-oriented rewards are offered because any nutritional message might be embarrassing. The seduction of the innocent encompasses more than sugar-coating.

(Not long ago, a major cereal manufacturer brought together his cereal sales managers with hucksters of toys, plastics, and other box inserts. The meeting topic was what next to add to the cereal box to persuade Junior to buy more flakes. A disgusted employee finally could take it no longer, and suggested to the toy manufacturers that they might do better by including a box of cereal in the next toy package, and thereby save them both a great deal of trouble.)

We claim that our children are deliberately being sold the sponsor's less nutritious products; that our children are being programmed to demand sugar and sweetness in every food; and that our children are being counter-educated away from nutrition knowledge by being sold products on a non-nutritive basis.

These practices dominate the cereal world. In part, they are found in the marketing of every major food group. The consumer is the victim. The industry shows little inclination to stress comparative food values. The industry shows little inclination to correct our nutritional illiteracy. Stark evidence of this is the emerging "new campaign" of the Food Group—a team of food merchandising interests which is studiously avoiding the mention of comparative food values. Excusing the vapidness of this effort, its leader, Clarence Adamy of the National Association of Food Chains, volunteered that "It's only an alert and aware campaign—to make the public think about food. Besides, what else could we do?" Food merchants and food producers seem to fear anything more specific than a campaign to eat "from four basic foods groups."[17]

---

[17]Dr. Jean Mayer, Special Consultant to the President on Nutrition, deplores the four food group approach as being unsound nutritionally and educationally.

WHO'S TO BLAME?

It would seem that the worst cereals are huckstered to the children on a totally anti-nutritional basis equating sweetness with health and ability, while the very few good cereals are sold to adults in a manner all but defying nutrient cost analysis. Is the research director or the sales manager at fault?

Conversations with food company officials indicate that while research departments know and can produce better quality products, in the main the sales departments dissuade the development of such products lest it "upset the established profit makers." The average American, it is believed, it impervious to a solid nutrition pitch.

It wasn't always this bad. Up through World War II we seemed more conscious of our food patterns. Still somewhat farm rooted, we had discovered pellagra in the Southeast, rushed to feed the world and suffered food rationing stamps. Henry Wallace was re-organizing the Department of Agriculture. We talked about food bargains and values.

Then several forces converged. Television discovered huckstering and we became persuaded to buy our foods more on the size, the shape, the smell of the box than on its nutritional content. Food was made "convenient," even if nutritionless. The Food and Drug Administration, handicapped by politics and a low budget, felt compelled to give drugs more attention than foods. It felt, and still feels, crippled by the dichotomy which gives the Federal Trade Commission authority over food advertising and the FDA authority over food labelling. "What," it asks, "is our role when a package label is shown on TV?" Food and Drug has no mandate to police nutrition; it does concern itself with honest labelling and product standardization. This pertains to ingredient identity, not nutrient values.

I feel the Food and Drug Administration must be authorized and financed to maintain a nutrient watch on American foods. And, its records should be made public.

Meanwhile the post-World War II production policies which fed the military machine rushed on undaunted and farm subsidies were raised to produce not protein-tons or iron-tons but plain tons. Volume and weight were rewarded, not quality. Lettuce heads became harder and coarser. Tomatoes became tougher. Beans and peas were sown better to fit the picking machine than our nutritional needs and taste desires.

Corn bushels per acre were all-important particularly when acreage was restricted. Corn volume rose, but not its nutrient content.

Only in 1969 did "Opaque 2" corn, a more nutritious corn, become whispered about among a handful of corn producers. Higher in lysine but lower in tonnage per acre, it will not achieve American farmer acceptance until subsidies change.

Food technologists have radically changed their profession in the last two decades. Food values now can be merged, as when two grains are blended in a cereal. Augmented foods, fortified foods frequently are better than their original, raw source materials. Grain proteins in particular can benefit by astute nutrient blending. Hence to teach food values from the basis of what raw ingredients went into a processed food may not only deceive the customer into thinking a processed food has the sum of the nutrients of its raw materials but may also hide the improvement in nutrient worth that an interested food producer may have carefully arranged to have added to his product. Fortified foods, augmented foods, and food using new nutrient technology are worth seeking out on the grocer's shelf. But first they have to be labelled; first they have to be advertised. And the consumer must be educated sufficiently to want to seek them out.

Incredible as it seems, there is in the United States no data bank where a citizen can seek a complete nutrient content analysis of any foods available to him at a local supermarket. Labels tell little; companies tell less. A citizen is defenseless in the face of a changing food technology.

Meanwhile the American consumer believes that his Food and Drug Administration is protecting him. FDA is not interested in nutrition; it conducts no regular review of nutritional content except to monitor the truth of food advertising. Its standardization practices have been more designed to assuage businessmen than to meet known nutritional needs among undernourished groups. For instance, bread manufacturers, not wanting nutritional competition but recognizing the need for re-establishment of nutrient values, asked FDA for "standards" and FDA obliged. Unfortunately, the FDA has not administered those standards in an enlightened manner to further the sales of extra-quality breads.

Food and Drug's role is not free of politics. Its budget is determined by Congress, and a shortage of dollars can restrict overambitious consumerism. The White House, by its power of appointment, also can influence the persistence of FDA in protecting the consumer in food matters. The citrus industry likes to represent itself as *the* source of Vitamin C. Fruit juice companies are not permitted to fortify citrus juices with Vitamin C. The same applies to tomato juice. All

SEDUCTION OF THE INNOCENT

juice may suffer Vitamin C loss in the processing; but FDA will not permit tomato juice to be fortified with C to a point where it might threaten citrus interests. Artificial juices, however, may be fortified.

Food and Drug since 1943 has relied on the ivory tower Food and Nutrition Board of the National Research Council to set its food policies. "Fortify only up to original, raw quality levels" was their myopic recommendation over the last quarter century. They also no doubt influenced the non-standardizing of cereals "lest it connote recognition of these products as a source of good food values." They may have influenced the keeping of nutrients out of popular soda pops.

Food and Drug does not let soda pop manufacturers advertise their products on a nutritional basis. They apparently feel soda pops are going to go away—a particularly shortsighted view when one comprehends their use by the poor in some areas of the country.

On fortification of foods which might lower the cost of a balanced diet to a money-short family, FDA has sought refuge in reiterating USDA's urging that we "buy from four basic food groups."

The record of USDA is not much better—take for example the department's advisory statements for foods to be used in conjunction with the recently expanded school breakfast program. While recommending that breads or cereals be included, the Department carefully avoids any language that might shed light on the nutritionally better cereals.

USDA and FDA apparently fear upsetting historic food sources. They have been worried more about the economics of the market place than about meeting the nutritional needs of the budget-dominated American family. Up until recently they would only permit the fortification of foods up to the nutrient value of the raw product. This meant that with such foods as corn, fortification was only permitted up to original low nutrient levels. This meant with grains having low PER's after processing, the customer was supposed to buy meats and milk products rather than get equally nutritious protein at half the cost from fortified grain products.

The disposition of the Department of Agriculture to have everyone taught about food values on the basis of "four basic food groups" may be rank evidence of the power of four major lobbying groups to dominate consumer knowledge. It also may be trapping the United States into some outdated food suppositions. Many of the foods on the market today have less nutrients than two decades ago because of volume-oriented genetic research; many of the processes which bring food to the market lower the nutrient values as foods are frozen, canned, baked, fried, or just packaged. These processes make our foods more convenient; we buy them for their size, their color or their smell—but seldom for their nutrient worth. In this regard the cereal industry is franker than most parts of the food industry. How many fruit juices, cake mixes or other prepared dishes advise the consumer of the nutrient contents?

SUMMARY

While some cereals have nutritional merit, those advocated to children seem to be of lower quality. They are advertised on a sugared basis, thereby creating a taste preference that may continue through life. The products advertised with them during the children's television show time also stress sweetness and sugar-energy. Despite warnings from dental authorities, today's TV watcher is programmed to want and trust in sugar for his health. Energy, sparkle, exhilaration and ability are equated with sweetness. This misinformation displaces any solid nutritional message which might give the youngster an understanding through life of the relationship between what he eats and how he feels.

In the home, the cereal box represents a domestic billboard. It could be a major educational force, but again it urges the purchase of certain foods based on rewards, toys and gimmicks and studiously avoids the ABC's of good nutritional knowledge.

Dry cereals are not a good buy for those on marginal budgets; their protein content and quality are generally low.

If a family likes dry cereals and can afford them, there are several with respectable nutritional content. But it is apparent in this first of several food industry analyses that we humans are viewed not as beings to be nourished, but as suckers to be sold.

I ask this Senate Subcommittee to investigate the policies of the cereal industry as it shapes the counter-nutritional message that is beamed to our children approximately 14 hours per week. I request that you analyze the content of the industry's advertising messages. I ask that you examine the reluctance of advertising agencies to stress nutrition; and I ask you to explore how both script and scenario writers and sponsors and networks alike can deliver this country from its nutritional illiteracy. Finally, I ask that you review the strange policies of the Food and Drug Administration, the Federal Trade Commission, and the Department of Agriculture, which perpetuate the misleading of the American consumer by those in the world of food production and marketing.

CONSUMER WASTE AND FRUSTRATION

The big issue of consumerism is comprised mostly of smaller issues. It is the small frustrations that push consumers to despair and anger: deceptive packaging, cancellation of insurance policies, ridiculous auto-repair costs, products that break down, credit snooping, lack of product information—all the things that daily touch our lives, consume time, and seem avoidable. There is no doubt that the consumer builds up hostility to corporations and merchants over such matters; that hostility is sometimes expressed in unforeseen ways. For example, the sharp rise in shoplifting by ordinary individuals is seen by some businessmen as a venting of anger over shoddy products and poor service. Time and again merchants hear the excuse from unrepentent shoplifters: "All of you deserve what you get."

Waste and frustration have become a national malady. According to Senator Philip Hart, in 1969 consumers spent about $200 billion for nothing of value, about one-fourth of that year's entire consumer spending. That meant that nearly 25 percent of the consumer dollar was totally wasted. When Senator Hart looked into the auto-repair business, he found even greater waste; he estimated that about one third or eight to ten billion dollars spent on auto repairs went for poor or unnecessary work.

In a series of hearings before the Antitrust and Monopoly Subcommittee and the Commerce Committee, Senator Hart and his colleagues heard William Haddon, Jr., President of the Insurance Institute for Highway Safety, document how the national auto-repair bill was due in great part, to poorly designed cars. In films of crashes at low speeds, it was shown that bumpers are merely cosmetic, not protective, that they surrender in crashes against barriers at only five miles per hour and less, causing extensive damage and high repair costs. On 1971 models tested, the repair bill for a five-mile-per-hour, front-end crash averaged $331; at ten miles per hour, when crashed front-into-side of a like model, the repair bill shot up to an average of $637. Haddon first exposed "Our Delicate Costly Cars," as he called them, in testimony in 1969; since then, with the support of the Institute, tests have continued on more recent models. The problem is particularly well presented in testimony Haddon gave in 1970, reprinted in this section. The tests that year received considerable publicity, and the following year some automakers advertised new, improved bumpers. The bumper on the 1971 Buick Skylark, for example, was touted as withstanding "four times as much force from any intruding or any impacting object than the 1970 models." Yet in a five-mile-per-hour, front-into-barrier crash—a man's *walking* speed—Haddon found that the Buick Skylark suffered repair costs of $427. "Some bumper!" he observed. Yet the industry has known for decades how to construct attractively designed bumpers that will withstand crashes of ten miles per hour with little damage. Such a situation is an excellent example of how the waste of consumer dollars is built into the structure—in this case the design-repair-insurance structure, for the losses are passed onto the car-owner in staggering insurance premiums.

Elsewhere in this section Jeffrey O'Connell, law professor at the University of Illinois, documents other reasons why drivers are confronted with soaring insurance rates. His solution is "no-fault" insurance. Betty Furness, former special assistant to the President for consumer affairs, expresses women's frustration in trying to determine what is in food by reading the labels. Jennifer Cross, author of the book *The Supermarket Trap,* explains in two articles how industry resists open-dating on perishable foods and erodes the consumer dollar on games of chance in grocery stores and gasoline stations.

Another kind of consumer frustration is the persistent corporate encroachment on personal privacy. Corporations refuse to share even the most vital information of public concern with citizens, but show no such compunction about prying into the lives of citizens by compiling extensive dossiers on their activities which they have gleaned from such unauthoritative sources as neighborhood gossip. The increased use of computers compounds the danger, and unless new controls are placed on corporate snooping (as I urge in the article "The Dossier Invades the Home"), there is bound to be a stifling effect on individual freedom.

The selections in this chapter are not meant to be all-inclusive; a cursory look at magazines and books could produce dozens more examples of consumer waste and frustration. They are meant merely to illustrate what the consumer is up against.

WHAT THE LABELS DON'T TELL YOU

Betty Furness

A woman who follows good recipes may cook a marvelous dinner from scratch. Or, God forbid, a poor one—but at least she knows what goes into it. If she buys "convenience" foods, she may get as good a dinner or even a better one. But finding out exactly what she's feeding her family can be more of a challenge than her stint at the stove.

There's a lot of talk today about food additives—sweeteners, flavor enhancers, preservatives, and so on. Leaving those aside for the moment, let's just try to see what basic foods and food elements are in the cans and bottles and boxes we buy regularly.

For dinner tonight, let's say it's corned-beef hash, salad with French dressing, and ice cream. A simple menu. Buying the food should take about two minutes. But instead of buying the first item on the shelf, let's try to make the best possible buy in canned corned-beef hash, bottled French dressing, and ice cream.

By "best buy" I really mean best value—from the viewpoint of nutrition, not just money. That will mean reading the labels to make an intelligent decision. But can we?

There's a federal law that requires food companies to list all the ingredients of what are called "combination" foods—stews, chili, meat

---

From *McCall's*, November 1970. Reprinted by permission of *McCall's* and the author.

pies. The ingredients must be listed in "descending order of importance," meaning we're getting the most of the item listed first.

Here are two cans of corned-beef hash, each weighing 15½ ounces. The one with the yellow label lists these ingredients: beef and cooked corned beef, water, dehydrated potatoes, salt, sugar, flavoring, sodium nitrate, sodium nitrite. Price: forty-nine cents.

The can with the white label reads: water, cooked corned beef, dehydrated potatoes, salt, flavoring, sodium nitrite. Price: fifty-five cents.

This looks like a pretty clear-cut case. Since the white-labeled can lists "water" first, you know that what you're buying the most of is water; and since it's corned beef you're after, the yellow-labeled can looks like the better buy, especially as it sells for six cents less.

But suppose both cans list water first or corned beef first. Then how do you know which to choose? You don't, because the food people are not required to tell you the percentage of each ingredient. There must be a minimum of 35 percent corned beef in corned-beef hash, but you have no way of knowing whether a can contains only the minimum (or even what the minimum is), or whether this particular company has been generous and given you more meat than is required. (One Department of Agriculture test found, for instance, that the amount of beef in a can of beef stew can vary from 41 grams to 87 grams in cans of exactly the same size.) You'll find that the food people tell you what the law says they must tell you, but they seldom give you additional information, even if it's to their advantage to do so.

Women tell me that they want to know the percentage of ingredients in combination foods.

Women are also becoming increasingly aware of the nutritional value in foods, especially the protein value. Protein is the one indispensable food element to ensure proper growth in children and to help all of us avoid malnutrition. It's also the most expensive element in our diet, so it would be nice to know how much protein is in such processed meats as frankfurters, such nonmeat items as cottage cheese, and—obviously—in the corned-beef hash we're having for dinner.

But we don't get that information today. The reason is that we're only people. Pick up a can of dog food, and you'll find not only the ingredients listed in descending order of importance, but a nutritional analysis of the contents, including the amount of protein, fat, calcium, moisture, and vitamins.

Who does Fido have to thank for that information? State legislatures that care about animals, that's who. And as farmers wouldn't think of buying feed for hogs or cattle without knowing the protein content, several states have laws that demand this analysis labeling. Since animal-food manufacturers want to sell in all states, it's easier to label all the food in the same way. So even in states that don't have such labeling laws, hogs and cattle are protected. So is your dog. But not your child.

Women want nutritional value on food labels.

Good luck in choosing the best value in corned-beef hash. Now let's buy salad dressing.

The basic ingredients of French dressing are oil, vinegar, salt, and pepper. So what do we find on the label? Vegetable gum, algin derivative, hydroxpropyl methylcellulose added; calcium disodium EDTA added as preservative.

You figure they've got to be kidding. Aside from additives that appear to come from ancient Greece, where are the oil and vinegar and salt and pepper?

Now we've inadvertently hit upon a truth. (Because we already know the basic ingredients of a number of foods, the federal government has established what it calls a "standard" for a lot of them. It has listed the possible basic ingredients for each standardized food in the Code of Federal Regulations, which you can read any time you're in Washington.) The food people do not have to list basic ingredients on labels; only optional ingredients have to be listed.

That goes for French dressing and about 400 other foods, such as canned fruits and juices, canned vegetables, margarine, mayonnaise, jellies, noodles, and cheeses, in all of which the major ingredients are supposed to be fairly self-evident.

However, there isn't a standard for Italian salad dressing—and I don't know why. The label on one brand of Italian dressing reads: vegetable oil, distilled vinegar, salt, sugar, dehydrated garlic, spices, lemon juice, calcium disodium EDTA added as preservative.

Italian? Aside from the garlic, that sounds like French dressing to me.

But whether it's French dressing that we know contains some kind of oil, or Italian dressing that contains "vegetable oil," we still don't know *which* vegetable oil.

With or without warnings from their doctors, many people are concerned about cholesterol in their diet and try to avoid eating saturated fats. Even in the vegetable oil family, the degree of saturation differs—with safflower oil being among the most unsaturated and coconut oil probably being the least.

I'm told that most salad dressings are probably made with peanut oil or soybean oil, but we have no way of knowing which vegetable oil is used. So if we care about the cholesterol problem, we may decide to choose the oil we think best for us and make our own salad dressing.

But chances are we don't have time or equipment to make our own ice cream, so let's buy some.

Ice-cream recipes list six or seven ingredients; and here again, having decided that we know pretty much what's in ice cream, the federal government has established a standard for it. The printed standard consists of about twelve pages of small type. You'd hate to use it as a recipe. It states how many solids must be in a gallon and says the weight must not be less than 4.5 pounds. And then it starts in on optional ingredients.

Under optional dairy ingredients, there are 28 items. My total count of optional ingredients such as sweeteners, caseinates, stabilizers, and emulsifiers may not be accurate, because I don't understand a lot of the terms, but I think it's 112.

Now, some of us would like to know which of the 112 possibilities we're about to eat. Some of us are simply curious; others may have allergies and need to know. A carton that states only the name of the maker and the word "vanilla" may be pristine in its beauty, but it doesn't tell us much.

Women would like to know what ingredients are in *this* ice cream.

The label on a carton of diet ice cream is a lot more chatty. It doesn't list all the ingredients, but it does tell you the type of dairy product it contains, because it's made for people who are on doctor's orders to avoid certain food elements—among them sugar and some types of fat. The label also lists the percentage of fats, protein, and carbohydrates, and the calorie count per hundred grams and per ounce, including the source of the calories.

Now *that's* labeling.

Though diet foods are all labeled with warnings that they are "intended for use by diabetics under medical advice" and explain that the artificial sweetener is "for use only by persons who must restrict their intake of ordinary sweets," a number of nondiabetics have seen and/or used these foods and are aware of the added information on the containers. And they like it.

The reason for all this lovely information is another law that states that if any claim is made about a food, such as calling it a "diet" food, or saying that it supplies daily minimum amounts of vitamins, minerals, or proteins, the maker must back up his claim by stating all the ingredients and the nutritional value of the food. That's why you find a lot of good information on cereal boxes.

So now we know how many calories there are in diet ice cream. But what help is that if we can't compare it with regular ice cream, and regular ice cream with ice milk, and ice milk with sherbet?

Women want to know how many calories there are per ounce, or serving, or container. And not just in ice cream.

At a recent hearing in Washington, an official from the Department of Agriculture was discussing food products for which there are published standards, such as chili, cooked sausage, meat stew. He admitted that the standard was not on the label of any can, and when asked how the housewife is supposed to know what the standard consists of, he said that "educational and informational releases are widely distributed. They go to newspapers and radio and TV stations, and high schools and colleges, and are the basis for news items about meat and poultry products that are in popular publications."

Swell. A lot of us aren't in school any more, and even if we read these news items, they aren't going to help us a month later at a food counter. It's enough to remember our shopping list without remembering the standards for meat stew.

Food manufacturers say we don't want all this information. They claim we buy by brand, habit, or as a result of their current advertising.

They also say they'd be hard put to squeeze all the facts I'm talking about on a small container. But I found one container telling me so much I phoned the company to ask why they're being so good to us.

Borden's Lite Line Yogurt says it contains half the calories of regular fruit yogurt. Between that claim and the fact the there's no federal standard for yogurt, they were stuck with telling us all they know about the ingredients, nutritional value, and calories. Which they did. But they went farther than they had to. In claiming only half the calories of regular yogurt, they then listed the calorie count of both kinds.

Remember, Borden's regular fruit yogurt doesn't list calories, because it doesn't have to, but you can get this information on a container of their Lite Line. (It's 255 in 8 ounces of regular, as opposed to 125 in Lite Line.)

So I asked them why this information is available not on the product's *own* container, but but on the container of *another* product. I was told it's because there's more space on the Lite Line box—but that they're considering putting calorie labeling on the regular yogurt, too.

Speaking on behalf of a lot of you who have told me you'd find this helpful, I urged them to go right ahead and do that.

So it turns out that making the best buy in canned corned-beef hash and bottled French dressing and store-bought ice cream isn't as simple as merely comparing prices. We can't see through the can or the carton or the intentions of each food manufacturer. And we can use our heads only to the extent of the information available to us.

There are two ways we can get the food-labeling information we want. First, we can try to persuade the food people that we really do want to know what's in everything, how much of it there is, how many calories there are, and what the nutritional value is.

If the food people don't hear us, or don't believe us, there are some Congressmen who do, and they've already drawn up some bills that would cause this information to become ours.

Until one or the other of these solutions is found, the woman trying to shop intelligently for her family is very like Oscar Wilde's definition of a cynic: She knows the cost of everything and the value of nothing.

LET THE BUYER (NOT ONLY) BEWARE (BUT BE GONE)

Jeffrey O'Connell

The prodigal waste of the auto insurance system creates especially acute problems for both individuals and society in that auto insurance is (1) so expensive, (2) so inflationary and (3) so necessary.

Automobile insurance costs have long been one of the fastest rising items in the nation's economy. A report in 1966 stated that the meteoric rise in medical care costs in the preceding ten years had been exceeded only by the rise in the cost of "automobile insurance, domestic help and local transit fares"—the latter two items, along with medical care, being legendary for their inflation in recent years. In 1970, the Cleveland Trust Company published a list of the 15 items in the consumer price index that have risen the fastest. The list included a "weight" factor to take account of the importance of the item in the consumer price index since, in the words of *The New York Times,* "obviously big items like food and housing have more weight than seldom used ones such as . . . an item like cracker meal." On the Cleveland Trust list, auto insurance ranked fourth behind meat, home repairs and mortage interest rates, but ahead of doctor's fees, local transportation, property taxes and hospital service. "Armed with this table," said *The New York Times,* "the consumer can take some specific actions to avoid goods or services where the price rise has been most significant." But alone on the list is an item *required,* in effect, by the government to be purchased and therefore truly unavoidable by almost all—namely auto insurance. Auto insurance is not, then—like steak—a dispensable luxury, or even—like medical care—an item one can often to some extent cut down on, but a compulsory item.

In the words of the recent report of the New York State Insurance Department, "[A]utomobile insurance is expensive. The average premiums for the liability insurance whose purchase is required by law is now $125 a year. For some one-car families the necessary insurance can cost as much as $429 a year." And note that such insurance covers only minimum compulsory coverage—$10,000 to cover the insured's liability to any one person injured in an accident, $20,000 to cover all liability of any number of insureds in the accident, and $5,000 to cover property damage negligently inflicted by the insured. But, given the nature of present day automobiles—machines that can accelerate from zero to 60 miles per hour in nine seconds and which can reach speeds of 100 miles per hour and above—and given the corollary amount of injuries and damage that even a minor accident can cause, coverage of $10,000 is very minimum average indeed. According to the New York State Insurance Department report, "Expensive as it is, the compulsory amount of automobile liability insurance is not enough either to assure victims of full compensation or to protect the vehicle owner against personal liability in case of serious loss. . . ." Truly adequate limits could cost an owner of a car with a good driving record as much as $1500 a year in New York City.

And costs continue to rise. The cost of automobile insurance has just about doubled in the last twenty years; and, according to the New York report, "the prospects are for it to continue to go up."* From 1950 to 1970, the typical average premium rate in New York State for compulsory automobile liability insurance has been:

Year	Amount	Per cent Increase from 1950
1950	$ 69.63	—
1955	86.98	24.9
1960	108.67	56.1
1965	112.87	62.1
1970	135.60	94.7

*Confirming this prediction is this item from the front page of The New York Times, *February 5, 1971:* "Automobile insurance rates will go up sharply throughout New York State by the end of this month or early in March." *For a pro and con discussion of a possible contrary indication for the immediate future, see* Wall Street Journal, *May 28, 1971, p. 1, col 6; June 11, 1971, p. 6 col. 6; July 6, 1971, p. 7, col. 1.*

Perhaps, then, it should not be surprising that the number one complaint concerning automobile insurance is its high cost. According to a recent survey done by the Survey Research Laboratory at the University of Illinois, when people were asked to list their complaints about automobile insurance, 41 per cent listed the high cost of auto insurance as their prime cause of dislike, with the second highest category (that insurance is often cancelled or made unavailable) reaching 10 percent. Some comments from the respondents to the Illinois poll are illustrative of public discontent:

> *"The premiums are too high. It is ridiculous what one has to pay for present-day [automobile] insurance."*

> *"[I]t keeps going up in price whether you have an accident or not."*

> *"You have to pay more for the insurance than the car is worth."*

Insurance men and lawyers often decry complaints about the high cost of auto insurance on the grounds that any rise in automobile insurance prices is explained by the fact that such costs only reflect the fast rising items which automobile insurance pays for—medical costs, lost wages, automobile repair costs, etc. They point out, for example, that during the same 20-year period that automobile liability insurance rates rose by 94.7 per cent, the U.S. Consumer Price Index for medical care rose by 114.4 per cent, and for automobile repairs by 83.1 per cent, while earnings for production workers and manufacturing establishments in New York State rose by 118.4 per cent. But the fact that automobile insurance is tied to some of the fastest rising items in the economy is all the more reason (1) to be concerned about its waste and (2) to search to find ways to cut its costs. This is still more essential when it is recalled that since automobile insurance is in effect required of every motorist in every state, rises in its cost adversely affect so many. And finally, it is even more essential given the fact that more and more Americans are being forced by our patterns of living to buy two or more cars, thereby greatly increasing the effect on them of inflation in auto insurance.

A further irony in all this is that despite soaring rates, auto insurance companies insist that they are losing huge sums. These plaints have often in the past taken on a somewhat disingenuous air when one realized that the companies were speaking only of their *underwriting* losses. They refused to take account—and, if they could help it, refused to let others, such as insurance commissioners, take account—of the millions they earn as investment income on the vast sums they hold as a result of carrying on automobile insurance. According to *Consumer Reports,* "[T]he insurance companies cry that they have lost billions of dollars over the years in their automobile liability underwriting—that is, they have paid out, in expenses and claims, more than they have taken in. They tend not to emphasize that the red ink is dyed black again by investment income."

But even including investment income in the rate making process—as some insurance commissioners, including New York's, have done—does not dramatically alter the overall auto insurance picture nor remove the undeniable price squeeze that auto insurers find themselves in. This was probably especially true recently, with reduction in portfolio values stemming from declines in the stock market.

Faced, then, with rising costs, insurers have naturally enough sought to get approval of rate increases from state insurance commissioners. But, because auto insurance costs so much and delivers so little, insurance commissioners, who are, after all, political appointees, have felt reluctant to allow price rises in a product so plagued with causes for dissatisfaction. Granting price rises—or at least price rises on the order requested by insurance companies—has been political dynamite. In the words of Professor Robert E. Keeton of the Harvard Law School, automobile insurance "is a basically unsatisfactory product. It is unattractive to consumers. . . . In turn, public dissatisfaction makes it difficult for insurance companies to obtain regulatory approval for premium rates that are adequate. . . ."

Faced with such a response, according to the recent New York State Insurance Department report,

> [A]utomobile insurers thrash around for ways to control their costs, to bring order to a seemingly irrational and unpredictable business environment. It is no wonder that when financial institutions the size of casualty insurance companies begin to thrash around, they can do real damage to their surroundings.

How do insurance companies thrash around? By refusing or shedding as insureds anyone they think will be a bad risk. In this respect, insurance companies have accelerated a trend which has long since rocked the automobile insurance industry. A little history at this point will help to fill out the picture.

Prior to World War II, nearly all drivers who sought insurance could readily purchase it. Most insurance was sold through old-line, sometimes rather sleepy, stock or mutual companies operating through independent insurance agents. These agents received a substantial commission (usually 20 per cent of the premium—generous recompense since the agents were selling a product, in effect, required to be purchased). Agents could place the business with any one of several companies they dealt with. There was little rate differentiation since insurance companies—considered by court decision and then by Congressional enactment exempt from the antitrust laws—all charged the same so-called "bureau" rates. (Bureau rates are set by a rating bureau which is, in turn, set up and supported by an aggregate of insurance companies.) According to a recent DOT study "Competition in the automobile insurance industry had been limited prior to World War II. Most insurers participated in cooperative rate-making arrangements; price competition was limited; and profits were favorable."

The period following World War II, however, saw a mushrooming growth both in the number of automobiles and in the number and cost of accidents. According to a DOT study,

In the intervening years [since World War II] the economic, social, and legal environment for the automobile insurance industry . . . changed radically. Automobile ownership is now widespread. Currently, 80 per cent of all households own one or more automobiles, with over one-quarter owning two or more. This represents a substantial increase over earlier years. In 1950 only 59 percent of all households owned one or more cars and only 7 per cent owned two or more. . . .

Concurrent with the growth in automobile ownership has been an enormous increase in the expenditures on automobile insurance. Premiums paid increased tenfold between 1938 and 1958 and doubled again through 1968. Current expenditures exceed $11 billion.

As insurance costs increased after World War II, an increasing number of insurance companies broke out of the old non-competitive mold and began to compete on the basis of lower prices. This was accomplished in two ways: First, a growing number of companies began to bypass the high expense of sales commission by selling directly to the consumer. So-called "direct writers"—the leading ones being State Farm and Allstate—captured more and more business from the so-called agency companies by using exclusive agents or salaried employees, as opposed to expensive independent agents working on commission. Other companies made marketing inroads by using mail order sales. As a result of such tactics, State Farm and Allstate, which in 1949 collected 5.1 percent of automobile insurance earned premiums, have raised that share to 20 per cent at the present time. Direct writers now write over 40 per cent of premiums written for automobile liability coverages.

If the new price-cutting marketing techniques had been limited to cutting down on expensive middle men, few—except the middle men—would have had cause for complaint. Unfortunately, the second price cutting technique pioneered by direct writers—and later copied by their increasingly desperate agency competitors—has spawned disastrous results for the public and, indeed, for the insurance industry itself.

Complementing their efforts to cut marketing costs, direct writers sought to reduce claims costs by writing insurance for only selected risks, i.e. insureds least likely to cause accidents. Thus the process of "creaming" the market began. It quickly spread to the old line agency companies who instructed their agents to restrict the type of business they wrote. But this selective process was often extremely crude in the way it operated, ruthlessly casting aside many perfectly adequate risks whose only offense was being young or old or black or divorced or living in the wrong neighborhood. According to the New York Insurance Department report,

> Insurance companies are large organizations, in which such mass operations as individual underwriting decisions [i.e., selecting those to be insured] have to be delegated to a large number of employees and agents. For that reason, insurance companies try to standardize the underwriting process and make it routine. They are forever casting about for simple, objective, readily identifiable, present characteristics of an insured that the subordinate underwriter or agent can conveniently use to distinguish a "good" from a "bad" future risk.

The result, in turn, was an often irrational and even outrageous denial of an essential commodity to millions of Americans. Reporter James Ridgeway has described how insurance companies

> are locked in ruinous competition to insure preferred risk drivers—people between 30 and 50 who don't drive their cars around much and haven't had any accidents. . . . Those not included in the prime risk category are paying more for insurance and in some cases find it hard to get policies from reputable companies. The squeeze is especially severe on people between 16 and 25 or over 65, or anyone owning a car living in a metropolitan center. Some companies will simply not write any business in poor Negro neighborhoods.

As former Pennsylvania Insurance Commissioner David Maxwell said recently, "Buying a car only takes money, but getting auto insurance is more like joining a country club"—with the addition that in

141

the case of auto insurance there are laws which, in effect, require you to find a club to join.

In the words of *The New York Times*, "Horror stories are widespread about how insurance companies treat their customers."

An Auburn, Washington, youth, age 19, with a perfect driving record had his coverage cancelled when he enlisted in the Air Force. He had the choice of giving up driving or taking a policy with a high-risk company, at twice the premium.

A Sibley, Iowa, farm couple in their 70s had their insurance company refuse to renew their policy. The husband had had one claim last year, the couple's first in 35 years of coverage with the company.

After a businessman had applied to an agent for auto insurance, the typical industry process followed whereby an investigator visited the businessman's home to speak with him. In writing up his report, the investigator mentioned that he had noticed several paintings of nudes on the wall. The businessman was turned down for the insurance as a moral hazard!

A man in Virginia was refused insurance after a neighbor had told an investigator that the applicant drank too much, a story that later turned out to be false.

Karl Herrmann, the insurance commissioner of the State of Washington, testified as follows before a U. S. Senate Committee investigating auto insurance when he was chairman of the Joint Interim Committee on Insurance of the Washington State Legislature:

Our committee is continually amazed at some of the deceptive techniques employed by a number of insurance companies to avoid fair treatment of the policyholder. One such case involves one of the biggest insurers of autos doing business in our state.

Our files have the complete record and photostat copy of the correspondence that took place in this particular case.

A graduate student in economics at the University of Washington, in Seattle, had his auto insurance suddenly cancelled. The letter, which lacked specific reasons for the cancellation, was signed by a Mr. "T. Case." The student tried to reach Mr. Case repeatedly by telephone, but could never locate the signer of the letter. He was always told by the insurance company's telephone operators that "Mr. Case is out to lunch," or "He's in conference" or "He's sick today."

One day the student was discussing his problem with an official of the university. A secretary whose husband worked as an adjuster for the company involved overheard the conversation and explained why it was that "Mr. Case" was always out. "That stands for 'Tough Case,' " she said. "There is no such person. It's the way the company has of avoiding further discussion with cancelled policyholders." Signing phony names on letters to customers is not the solution to the public's growing demand for better treatment at the hands of the auto insurance industry.

Nor are these isolated instances—shocking as they are. On the contrary, they are part of a planned, pervasive design by the insurance industry as a whole to restrict ruthlessly those who can obtain insurance.

Thus, Charles W. Gambrell, South Carolina's insurance commissioner, stated that in South Carolina there is a requirement that insurance companies disclose the "guides" that insurance agents follow in writing insurance policies. According to Gambrell, 83 per cent of the insurers writing 65 per cent of the insurance in this state will not write new business for aged drivers (between the ages of 62 and 70). Similarly, 16 per cent of the companies will not write divorced people. Gambrell hypothesizes that the categories of poor risks listed in the guides as "suspects" are applicable throughout much of the country and, in fact, are just a veiled way of discriminating against Negroes.

The following is from the transcript of testimony before a Senate Committee by Orman L. Vertrees, a reporter on the *Seattle Post-Intelligencer:*

MR. VERTREES: [*A series of articles on automobile insurance*] *triggered a staggering response from our readers. In a matter of just a few weeks, we received in excess of 500 letters and telephone calls on insurance matters, most involving complaints from the insurance consumer. . . .*

An analysis of insurance complaints received by the Post-Intelligencer *showed that automobile coverage was by far the most critical area. There were numerous instances of cancellation or failure to renew policies without any explanation from the company to agent or policyholder. There was evidence of mass cancellations. Seattle's central area, populated largely by minority groups, found its rates higher and coverage harder to obtain. Those in certain occupations, such as longshoremen, bartenders, servicemen, waitresses, entertainers, and of all people, air-*

craft workers—the Boeing Company employs thousands in the Seattle area, its headquarters—were frowned upon by some auto insurers. . . .

A little over a year ago, a Seattle insurance broker sent me a copy of a pamphlet, then in its 15th printing, entitled "Automobile Underwriting Pointers." The manual had been circulated by Safeco [Insurance Group] to several thousand of its agents. . . .

The manual warned agents to look with disfavor upon the "lower laboring classes, aircraft employees, longshoring classes, etc.," where auto insurance was concerned. It said that if someone liked to be called by a nickname, such as "Shorty" or "Scotty," he might not be conservative enough in outlook to qualify for auto insurance. It also warned that how a child's hair was cut should have a bearing on whether or not the family auto was to be insured.

THE CHAIRMAN [*Senator Warren G. Magnuson of Washington*]: *You know, back home I am known as "Maggie." I suppose that could have some bearing on my auto insurance.*

MR. VERTREES: *You might have trouble, Senator.*

Another factor exacerbating the restrictiveness of the auto insurance market is caused by insurance companies' worry about the kind of witness its insured will make in court. This is especially pertinent under auto insurance, given the much greater likelihood, relatively speaking, of litigation under this coverage. T. Lawrence Jones, President of the American Insurance Association, has admitted that examining each applicant for an insurance policy as a potential defendant in court ". . . unfortunately leads to the reluctance of some [insurance companies] . . . to make auto insurance available to young people, minority groups and people with occupations that are judged to be in less favorable light." This, coupled with the fact that insurance people tend to be prototypically middle class, conservatively oriented people, means that any deviance from the norm can be viewed with alarm.

A pervasive factor in restrictive auto insurance underwriting is race (or perhaps one should say racism). For example, Retail Credit Company, an Atlanta, Georgia based organization, in 1966 made 20,000,000 inspection reports on people who applied for insurance to determine whether the applicant should be given coverage. Retail Credit's Handy Guide lists the points that should be covered in the inspection report. Under a section headed "West Indian Island Races including Puerto Ricans, it asks:

Is applicant pure Caucasian or a mixture? Describe the individual if a mixture of races to show whether predominantly Caucasian or Negro. It is not practicable to attempt to estimate percentages.

And the guide has the following questions about applicants for insurance who are Mexican-Americans:

Is he a permanent resident or the floater type?

Does he occupy a hovel type of residence or a good substantial home?

Does applicant associate with Mexicans or with Anglo-Saxons?

References to race pervade the guide. On a church applying for fire insurance, for example, the inspector must note "whether Baptist, Episcopalian or Methodist, etc., and whether the congregation is composed of Negro or white people, or general racial makeup of congregation." On apartment houses, information according to the report, should include "racial descent" of tenants.

Upon being asked about the guide, W. Lee Burge, President of Retail Credit, replied that the company was revising "all the sections dealing with race in an effort to delete those references."

It is questionable, though, how much good that will do. According to an insurance commissioner of a midwestern state, one insurance company routinely assigns Negro applicants a code number beginning with the number seven, and he has discovered that a suspiciously large proportion of these "sevens" are turned down. "You can't prove discrimination," he says "because the word 'Negro' is never used on the application form."

BLIND DATES IN THE SUPERMARKET

Jennifer Cross

One of the most interesting items of mail to arrive on Capitol Hill recently was a jar of Heinz baby food, purchased last April by a woman in Louisiana. Was the sample an old one, she inquired, or had Heinz failed to comply with the Fair Packaging & Labeling Act by leaving the zip code off its address? It did not take much investigation to reveal the jar's guilty secret—it was more than eight years old and, of course, spoiled.

This case history, which now occupies pride of place in Rep. Leonard Farbstein's chamber of horrors, illustrates a problem every housewife faces when she goes shopping—how to be certain that the food is fresh? To be sure, little old ladies still pinch the produce, and millions of mothers continue to squeeze bread. Unfortunately, today such Yankee horse-trading techniques often do not work, since the revolution in packaging food technology either conceals the product from view or, by the ingenious use of chemicals, masks or retards spoilage. While most food is wholesome, almost everyone has at some time brought home a pound of rancid butter or a dubious brace of lamb chops, which may or may not have been returned to the store, and which the store may or may not have replaced.

The extent of this problem, and the amount of irritation it causes shoppers, did not make the headlines until after last November, when

From *The Nation*, 2 November 1970. Reprinted with permission.

Mr. Farbstein and fifty-eight other Congressmen introduced H.R. 14816, which would require manufacturers to mark canned and packaged food with the clear (regular calendar) date when it should be retired from the shelves.

In recent months thousands of consumers have complained to Mr. Farbstein about soup so old it almost had to be chiseled out of the can; milk that soured the day after it was opened; insects that lurked in packaged food; foul-smelling sausage or cottage cheese; addled eggs; stale candy, and a number of items which had been thawed and refrozen. Other people griped that although many packages already had a pull date on them, they were given in a jumble of code letters and numbers which neither they nor often the grocery clerks could decipher. Why should they have the bother and expense of making a return trip to the store, particularly as a few managers declined to make good on the merchandise?

The complaints of these shoppers were confirmed by two Congressional surveys in Washington, D.C., and by local newspapers in Minneapolis, Detroit, Rochester, N.Y., Richmond, Va., Phoenix, Philadelphia, Louisville, Chicago, Miami and the San Francisco Bay Area.

Very few of the stores inspected were without one or more items of perishable food which had outlived the code pull date. Suzanne Hovik of the *Minneapolis Star* summed it up: "Admittedly, unfresh food is the exception rather than the rule when the total number of items on the shelves is considered. Nevertheless, unfresh food is there for sale, often right next to fresh food. You could easily spend money on food that may not be as tasty as fresh food, may not be as nutritious, or worse yet, may not be safe." She added that the life of such food in shoppers' refrigerators was considerably reduced.

Mr. Farbstein also discovered that neither the food industry nor the government was being entirely honest in their advice to shoppers on the life of processed food. "How long will canned foods keep?" asked the National Canners Association in their handout booklet to the public. "Indefinitely, if nothing happens to the container to cause a leak," said the NCA, though both it and the Food & Drug Administration, which dutifully reprinted the message, conceded that "extremely long storage at high temperature may result in some loss of color, flavor, appearance, and nutritive value."

Alas, nothing lasts forever! A study made by the U.S. Army Laboratories at Natick, Mass., showed that in fact canned foods have a very variable shelf life, which can be halved or quartered by storage at high temperatures. Particularly vulnerable are high acidity foods, like tomatoes or sauerkraut, which may develop gas and bulging cans, and cold packed or dry foods, which eventually turn rancid or lose their water-soluble vitamins. The life span of frozen foods is similarly variable, said the Army, even at 0° F., the recommended storage temperature. Fragile items like frankfurters, patties and other processed meats, are good for no more than one to three months; frozen juice concentrate will last two to three years; most other foods expire somewhere in between.

On the face of it, nothing could be simpler than Mr. Farbstein's bill, which would both reassure customers that their food was fresh, and enable store personnel to remove stale merchandise without having to unscramble the codes, or wait for the delivery man to do it for them. Yet Mr. Farbstein has little hope that his bill, or Sen. Joseph Montoya's companion version in the Senate, will come to early vote. The issue of open dating has uncovered a mare's-nest of problems and disagreements throughout the food industry.

As of now, some eight supermarket chains have installed open dating on some perishable products. They are Safeway (which has had some open dating for years, but kept very quiet about it); Jewel, Hillmans (Chicago); Chatham Supermarkets (Warren, Mich.); Stop & Shop, and the Star Market Co. (Boston); Great Scott Supermarkets (Detroit), and Ralphs (Los Angeles). None of these will admit that *their* company has a problem with stale food; they are making the gesture in the interests of good public relations, and (privately) to improve profits and tighten up inventory control. So far, they seem to be doing well by doing good, at least if one judges by the Jewel Company's increased profits, and the success of Safeway's first publicity campaign about open dating of dairy products in Washington, D.C.

Other food industry reactions are typical of any big business under consumer attack, the rules of the game being to deny that the problem exists, to blame the customer for causing it, and finally to threaten that any solution will cost the public a packet. The line was laid down by that seasoned campaigner, Clarence Adamy, president of the National Association of Food Chains. The two District of Columbia surveys, he said, made no sense. Stores were in business to sell fresh food. A little while later he reassured a food industry convention: "We have nothing to hide. We have no reason to be defensive, because it is now and it has always been in our best interest to be fair and open and above board."

The *real* problem, said Mr. Adamy, and scores of retailers around the country, is the housewife. If we have open dating, she will paw over the shelves like some diligent raccoon, selecting the freshest food from the back. By ignoring perfectly good stuff at the front because its pull date is nearly up, she will *increase* the rate of spoilage, and end up paying more at the checkout counter.

While reactions from food manufacturers have been mixed, some, especially dairies and bakeries, are positively ferocious in their opposition to open dating. A spokesman for Christopher Milk screeched at a *San Francisco Bay Guardian* reporter that it would "raise the cost of milk 50 to 100 per cent for the poor people of the city." A Langendorf Bakeries distributor snapped: "Open dating is useless. You just get housewives confused. Fresh bread isn't good for you anyway—it's not healthy."

More seriously, Representative Farbstein reports a number of attempts by food companies to force the media to kill or modify news stories on the subject. *The Miami News* was blackballed by three major chains (Publix, Winn Dixie and Lucky), two of which withdrew their advertising. As a result of chain pressure, a critical article in the *Chicago Sun-Times* was rewritten, and a second in the *Chicago Daily News* was scrapped entirely.

This belligerent panic has blown up with very little supporting evidence from customer behavior. How can stores know in advance what shopper reaction will be to open dating? The fact is that few women read labels beyond a cursory look at the price and brand name. Fewer still would have the time to fetch items out from the back of a loaded display cabinet. A customer who *trusts* her supermarket is far more likely to glance at the pull date to make sure it is current. Only if she is suspicious will she grope for the freshest item.

Denmark, France and West Germany, which already have extensive open dating, find that it encourages customer confidence and improves sales. Early experience in this country suggests the same. Jewel has enjoyed larger profits and improved inventory control since its switch last July. Safeway reports improved sales and no rumpled merchandise; so does Pillsbury, which for some time has put open dates on its frozen dough products.

Then what is the food industry *really* afraid of? Are we eating even more stale food than the surveys suggest, or at least food that is past the prime of life? Are stores afraid that their farm-fresh image could not stand the shock of this revelation? The businessman is habitually reluctant to do anything when *forced* to it by the federal government, particularly if the change may not yield a profit. However, in this case, that is only part of the trouble.

One snag is a more or less chronic dispute between supermarkets and manufacturers as to which of them shall pay for spoiled and damaged merchandise. A recent industry survey shows that 70 per cent of all spoilage (including breakage) takes place before the goods reach the store. Obviously, much of the cost of this (though not the profit) can be recovered through insurance. But most stores would prefer a spoilage allowance or guaranteed refund from the manufacturer. At present these are granted for only a limited number of items, such as cookies, crackers, snacks, national brand (but not private label) bread, and for small, higher priced (but not bulk, low-priced) orders of milk. On high-spoilage items like meat, produce and frozen foods, stores must carry the whole risk. Stop & Shop, the Boston food chain which switched to open dating, ran a series of ads trying to persuade food manufacturers to foot the bill for out-of-code food. The response has been poor, leading a spokesman for the chain to complain that "manufacturers are not really interested in consumerism or sanitary food stores."

A second difficulty is the need to improve handling and sanitation standards throughout the industry, to reduce both food spoilage (unlovely but safe) and food contamination (which can cause sickness). At the manufacturing end, carelessness or lapses in control provoked Dr. James Goddard, a former FDA commissioner, to complain four years ago to the Grocery Manufacturers of America about flotsam and jetsam left by rats, birds and insects, and to inquire: "Why do we still have to expend so much of *our* manpower to destroy so much of *your* product in seizures for filth?"

The situation has not improved. A recent quarterly FDA report noted "a serious regression in sanitary standards in the food industry," and complained that food inspectors were having to work overtime to cope with increased consumer complaints. Salmonellosis and other types of food poisoning continue to fell an estimated 2 million people a year, and that number is quite apart from the thousands of more dangerous or even fatal food- and water-borne illnesses such as botulism, infectious hepatitis and bacillary dysentery. While part of the trouble is bad handling, rather more is due to food contaminated at the source, particularly processed fish and meat, sausage and some egg and dried milk products.

Breakdowns in refrigeration may occur at any stage of the production-distribution chain. Some of this is caught by the FDA, which condemns any food it thinks may be unsafe. One instance was reported to Mr. Farbstein by a shopper from Milwaukee, who noted that a two-and-a-half-hour power failure turned the frozen foods in her local A&P to slush. Told by the clerk that they were going to remove the food and refreeze it, she reported the incident to her local health department. But she still wondered "how many stores with the power failure did the same thing with no one reporting it?"

Even delivery men can add to the stores' problems of spoilage and inventory control. Sometimes milkmen skip a delivery, particularly to small stores, gambling, not always rightly, that the existing stock won't spoil. Quite of ten, bakery men, engaged in "slugging" their competitors, deliberately load customers' shelves with more bread than they think will sell.

Obviously, open dating will not solve all these problems. It will not prevent the sale of some contaminated food or, necessarily, improve the level of food handling throughout the industry. Here, more drastic measures are needed—the setting and application of microbiological standards of contamination for highly perishable foods, starting with meat, which the U.S. Department of Agriculture has begun but not completed. Higher and more uniform standards for the lower temperature at which foods should be stored would help, notably an adherence to the AFDOUS (Association of Food & Drug Officials of the United States) frozen food code, stating that frozen food must be kept at 0°F. Now this code is voluntary, and adopted by only six states, though it is used as a guideline by some twenty others. More money for federal and local food inspection is also needed, combined with a reversal of the present FDA policy of self-certification by food manufacturers, and the diversion of inspection manpower away from food and into more pressing areas such as drugs.

Open dating should not be applied without some federal-industry standards to make sure that food manufacturers cannot gain a competitive advantage by bragging about the extra freshness of their particular product. In this context, much more customer education is needed. The customer must be told how long perishable foods will keep in her home, and to be reassured that food bought on or just before the pull date will not spoil the very next day. Unless she is convinced that a safety margin exists, the food industry's prediction of an increase in rejected merchandise may well come true.

Despite its limitations and problems, open dating would certainly be a boon to careful shoppers. Since we are already paying, one way or another, for stale and spoiled food, let us at least be sure that we know what we are getting, and that the food we actually buy is as fresh as possible. In the long run, this may also benefit the food industry, by starting a process whereby stores improve their handling and inventory control, and lean on suppliers to do the same. But will we *get* open dating?

Representative Farbstein modestly hopes to get HR 14816 out of the House Commerce Committee for general hearings this session. So far, nothing has come from his second line of approach, to petition the Federal Trade Commission to include an open-dating requirement under Section 5 of the Federal Trade Commission Act. Next year, unfortunately, Mr. Farbstein will have left Congress. (He failed to win his New York Democratic primary.) His "baby" will be in other hands, possibly some of his fifty-eight co-sponsors who may reintroduce the bill. In the end, it will be up to Consumers Union, the Consumer Federation of America and other citizens' groups throughout the country to try a little harder to convince the food industry and Capitol Hill that fresh food can be good politics *and* good business.

GROCERIES, GAS AND GAMES

Jennifer Cross

Anyone who has ever accumulated a pile of useless "Bonus Bingo" slips or "Wiki Wiki Dollars," and wondered who was playing games with his food and gas money, can find most of the answers in the Federal Trade Commission's recent "Economic Report on the Use of Games of Chance in Food and Gasoline Retailing." Started during the housewives' boycotts at the end of 1966, this long-incubated study summarizes both the commission's findings and the hearings on gas station games, held last summer by Rep. John D. Dingell, chairman of a subcommittee of the House Select Committee on Small Business.

Evidence from both sources strongly suggests that the games constitute a triple-layered hoodwink. The public is fooled about its chances of winning, the oil companies and food chains are misled about the sales increases the games will provide, and the gasoline dealers are completely sold up the river as to their costs and returns. These consumer games are also peculiarly vulnerable to rigging. In the end, the ones who make out best are the successful game promoters.

Obviously some members of the public benefit, theoretically, at least. Someone has to win all those Mustangs and $1,000 jackpots. But many people do not realize how thin the goodies are spread.

From *The Nation,* 24 March 1969. Reprinted with permission.

According to the FTC, the chances of winning *any* cash prize on one random visit to your friendly game-playing supermarket are 0.34 per cent, while the chances of taking home $1,000 are 1.2 in a million. According to the Glendinning Co., as one of the four largest games promoters who submitted its own report to the FTC, odds on the $1,000 jackpot are even more microscopic—a mere one in 287 million, or one in 11,512 for a regular shopper over the whole game period.

Motorists' hopes for a lucky strike are no better. A Georgia survey submitted to the Dingell hearings showed that it would take two years of weekly visits to the gas station to get a $1 prize, and 96 years of similar fidelity to win $10. Snorted Frank Weikel, a reporter from the *Cincinnati Enquirer* who had amused himself by going through boxes of game pieces in search of the miserably few winners, the odds are worse "than a guy swimming the English Channel in a storm with an anchor round his neck."

Nevertheless, food chain and oil company advertising carries the strong implication that *you* personally will win, dangling the carrot of luscious jackpot prizes, even though these may have been won early in the game, and even though the whole lottery may have been fixed, to award prizes for strategic reasons.

The FTC found enough evidence of rigging to conclude that certain chains and oil companies occasionally distribute big prizes to favored outlets, generally where sales are large and/or competition unusually tough. In fact, a sales letter from General Marketing Corporation, creator of "Pick-A-President," which happened to stray onto Congressman Dingell's desk, stated: "We will program a pre-pack of cards to give you automatic distribution of the winners you specify to the exact locations of your choice."

Another trick is to hand out a jackpot early in the game to insure peak interest. One Los Angeles supermarket was even advised by a game promoter to take the first $1,000 prize and plant it on the most talkative woman in the neighborhood. Some advertised prizes are never awarded at all, either because the winning tickets were not redeemed, or because the sponsoring company became disappointed in the response and decided not to throw good prizes after bad money. Such was the case with American Oil's "Super Pro," where only 398 Mustangs were won out of a publicized 1,000.

A few jackpots have gone straight into the pockets of enterprising dealers or their friends. Dealers in Oregon, Maryland and Virginia bragged to Congressman Dingell about their ingenuity in spotting the winning tickets. Also, a law student, Barry Tumpson, turned Humble's face red by presenting $20,000 in winning tickets for "Heads and

Tails," which he gleaned from the "commons" by shining a slide projector light on the whole batch (he is said to have settled out of court for a respectable $5,000).

Part of the bill for the whole shenanigans gets passed directly onto the public, depending on how successful the particular game turns out to be. After studying the experience of nine games-playing food chains, the FTC found that all of them suffered a slight increase in the cost of doing business. Between 1964–66, when games were at their peak, they spent $40 million more on advertising, three-quarters of which was directly attributable to games. A few shoppers complained to the FTC that food prices were increased by as much as 10¢ on selected items. More commonly, the chains cut back on their "specials"—a tactic which was not reflected in the Consumer Price Index, but which certainly penalized many shoppers. Gas prices have also gone up by 1¢ or more since the oil company gambling mania started early in 1966. It is hard to say exactly how far games are responsible, but the FTC evidence shows that many motorists and some dealers believe them to be the villain.

Many sponsoring companies have been oversold on games as sales promotion. For example, a Walter Schwimmer brochure, advertising "Let's Go to the Races," states that grocery shoppers may come back "as often as twenty-five times a week. They hope that one of their cards will prove to be a winner. All of which adds up to a whale of a lot of extra traffic." What Schwimmer did not mention was that consumers gradually get smart, and either split their usual purchases, or stop by merely to collect their game card—leaving the chains with less sales increase than they expected, and the bill for 30 per cent more game pieces to cope with the rush.

Gas dealers have found the same thing. One of them grumbled: "Customers that I had for years, who normally filled up, would now come in several times a week and spend $1, $1.50, $2, and it takes just as much time to service that car, to gas it, to check his hood and service the windshield, as it does to fill his tank."

In theory, said the games companies, chains should enjoy an 8 to 35 per cent sales jump; averaging 20 per cent for the course of the game; gas dealers should increase their gallonage by 40 to 50 per cent.

In practice, such a bonanza is forthcoming only when the company is first, maybe second, in the market with a popular game. Hence Safeway was able to make a killing out of the first round of "Bonus Bingo," and Tidewater with "Win-A-Check." "Bonus Bingo" and "Let's Go to the Races" have also built up what promoters call a good "track record," meaning that people like to play them, and the sponsoring company can normally count on a solid sales increase.

Many firms, alas, get stuck with real bombs, and either lose money, barely recover their costs, or only manage to hold their existing sales position. Such a situation arises when competitors retaliate with stamps, giveaways and discount prices, or start games of their own. This happened to supermarkets during 1966, when game saturation was at its peak, with fifty-two varieties in play; and to many gas dealers during 1967–68. Even successful games rarely do anything more than produce a temporary windfall for their croupiers. Over the year, there is little difference in the profit picture of sponsors and nonsponsors.

Another depressant is healthy disillusion on the part of the public. Last year, the Burgoyne Index, one of the food industry's main customer thermometers, recorded that 57 per cent of its sample would like games eliminated, up from 35 per cent in 1966; 36 per cent tolerated them (down from 46 per cent) and only 7 per cent still liked them.

Even in 1966 the FTC and leading food chains received 354 consumer complaints on the subject—a relative barrage, given the public's customary apathy. "Anyone desiring to gamble can go to the race track; this is not honest advertising," said one typical letter. "Stamps, card and bingo games are the forced gimmicks responsible in great part for the extra cost of food," said a second. "We will welcome the day when stores can go back to selling quality merchandise on its own merit and provide courteous, efficient services, instead of stamps, etc., in bidding for the customer's trade."

This resentment has lately been affecting the industries concerned, producing, as the February issue of *Fortune* points out, "a curious degree of schizophrenia in corporate policy," whereby "top executives of many of the same corporations have felt perfectly free to criticize the games that their subordinates were busily buying." Said Michael Haider, chairman and chief executive of Standard Oil of New Jersey, about his firm's use of games: "I think it is a damned poor way to market gas," a sentiment endorsed on other occasions by such companies as Citgo and American.

If the brass is cynical, many gas dealers have become downright rebellious. Dealer associations in Florida, Georgia and Oregon moaned to Congressman Dingell that they were forced to participate, either by massive advertising to create consumer demand, or by occasional threats to cancel their leases. They paid through the nose for their game pieces: a typical cost was $15 for a box of 1,000 tickets containing $11 worth of winners. Often their sales increases were disappointing, particularly as the market became saturated. Their service started to go to pieces. And to cap it all, customers became hostile when they failed to win. Dealer pressure was in fact responsible for the Dingell hearings. It has also persuaded state legislatures in Massachusetts, Ohio and Wisconsin to ban games on the ground that they violate the lottery laws.

It is clear that the only winners are the games companies. In just seven years since 1961 the market has grown from nothing to an estimated $200 million, and games promoters have proliferated from one, the redoubtable Harry Reichman, to somewhere between seventy-five and 120. Today, 70 per cent of the business is held by four companies, Glendinning, Kayden Industries, Strategic Merchandising and Walter Schwimmer. Few of their financial results are published; however, it may be significant that Glendinning has enjoyed annual sales increases ranging from 221 to 37 per cent since 1962, two years after the company was founded. It is little wonder that several of the golden geese have been gobbled up by professional marketing and sales promotion companies.

Since the whole scene is so depressing, why are the games still played? Why not cut out all the hoopla and lower prices or improve service? The reason given by the sad sponsors is "competition": other firms have games, so they must play or go under.

Getting down to the unpleasant truth—which business dislikes doing outside its own trade and financial press—both the food and oil industries are overbuilt: there are more gas stations and supermarkets than the market can sustain with reasonable profits. Gas stations squat on the corner of almost every busy intersection (how do they all make a living?), while some supermarkets which had clienteles of 11,000 to 12,000 in 1954 can now count on only some 3,400.

Since both food and gas are basic, undifferentiated products, the market is relatively inelastic. People will stuff neither themselves nor their cars simply because the prices of the nourishments fall. In any case, cost pressures are such that no firm can offer more than mouse-size price cuts and hope to stay in business. Hence the value of games: they may not permanently enlarge anyone's market, but they can do wonders as temporary traffic stealers.

To the despair of the intelligent consumer, many people really enjoy games, preferring them to genuine, if limited, price competition. Howard Brown, a vice president of the Plaza Group (a successful games company), offers the following theory in a book he has written on games psychology: "When we were children we always got something for nothing. But now that we're older, it's different—you get nothing for nothing. In games, there's an opportunity to re-experience that early developmental level of getting something free. You match something, and you get a reward."

All a game has to do is attract a small number of these submerged children. A 5 per cent sales increase is enough to meet the break-even cost; above 10 per cent, the company is laughing, and at 15 per cent, it is practically drowning in gravy. Meanwhile, *everyone* gets a game card poked at him, whether he wants it or no. Many, out of sheer inertia, will play.

It is difficult to see what can be done about these deep-rooted competitive and psychological pressures. The FTC has been holding hearings with a view to passing a kind of "truth in games," which would cut down the blah about winning, and require the public to be told how many prizes will be awarded in a specified area during the game period. The commission also proposes to stop rigging, and to protect gasoline dealers from being coerced to participate. The games companies, at least, will go along with these regulations; in fact they have already been bending over backward to clean house and see that games are rig- and tamper-proof.

The food industry is currently pursuing a slightly different tack, both in defense of games as a promotion and, more important, of its right to sponsor them without too much whistle blowing by the government referee. The National Association of Food Chains hired two prestigious Harvard professors, Jesse W. Markham and Robert D. Buzzell, to review the same evidence collected by the FTC. Not surprisingly, they concluded that games "had no measurable effect upon costs, margins, prices or market shares in any of the markets analyzed." However, no mention was made about rigging, or the FTC finding that consumers were offered fewer food "specials" while the games were in progress.

We shall probably continue to be stuck with "Wiki Wiki Dollars," or similar offerings, though not in such profusion, until industry is able to produce another seductive type of promotion. Neither the FTC regulations nor the theoretical possibility of outlawing games altogether by including them in states' lottery laws quite gets to the root of the problem. Mr. R. A. Hunter, a Gulf vice president, put his finger on it when he said that games "are really more or less persuasive forms of price-competition. . . . The variety of competitive practices must be, in large part, considered inherent in our free competitive economic system. However, it does seem that we sometimes carry this freedom to extremes."

OUR DELICATE
COSTLY CARS

William Haddon, Jr., M.D.

Mr. Chairman and members of the Subcommittee: I appeared before these hearings on October 6, 1969, and presented evidence compelling the conclusion that designed-in eggshell delicateness of the cosmetic exteriors on contemporary automobiles is costing the American public billions of dollars in avoidable repair costs.

Specifically, I showed you the filmed and tabulated results of research carried out last year by the Insurance Institute for Highway Safety showing, first, that very low-speed crashes of four 1969 standard sedans produced exceedingly high-cost damage to their fragile and defenseless fenders, trunk lids, hoods, and other components, and second, that the magnitudes of repair costs thus necessitated were accounting for an immense share of insurance claims for auto-related property losses.

Stated differently, the research results presented to you at that time, as well as those I subsequently gave you in January of this year involving intervehicular low-speed crashes, indicated that current automobile exterior designs, while aimed at the eye of the consumer in the showroom, are pointed directly at his wallet on the road in the low-speed bumps and scrapes so common—and so predictable—in driving and parking today.

Our Delicate Costly Cars by William Haddon, Jr., is a testimony that was given before the Senate Subcommittee on Antitrust and Monopoly, 17 March 1970.

One may conclude on the basis of those presentations that the automobile purchaser today is paying twice for the privilege of owning a car whose front and rear ends are designed to look like French pastries in the ads and showrooms, and to act like antique porcelain or aluminum foil in minor collisions.

First, he pays when he buys the car for the privilege of owning expensive-to-shape, ostensibly sales-promoting (and, incidentally, environmentally inappropriate) exterior designs in whose rendering the stylist's hand, rather than the engineer's, is wastefully dominant. Next, when his vehicle experiences what is euphemistically called a "fender bender," he pays again—this time, the many hundreds of dollars required as the cost of replacing such inappropriate parts to undo the damage caused or aggravated by the cosmetic design and manufacture of his vehicle's exterior in the first place.

As we indicated to you in our January presentation, Mr. Chairman, we have now undertaken to test a number of 1970 model year automobiles in the same manner that we tested the 1969 sedans discussed in our earlier presentations to you. Included in our 1970 tests are four small cars—the Volkswagen 1600, the Toyota Corona, the American Hornet, and the Ford Maverick; the four standard sedans in the 1970 version that we tested last year in their 1969 model versions—the Chevrolet Impala, the Plymouth Fury, the Ford Galaxy 500, and the American Ambassador SST; and four so-called "pony cars" of the type that have been steadily increasing their share of the market over recent sales years—the Chevrolet Camaro, the Ford Mustang, the American Javelin, and the Plymouth Barracuda.

We have completed our entire series of tests for the four small cars that I just named, and we are prepared today to offer you, in film version, the results of those tests. Later in this year we will have completed all of our tests on the other automobiles I have named, and we will make the results public as they are available. Should the record of these hearings be open at that time we will, of course, make that material available to you.

The films of our small car crash tests that you are about to see follow a format similar to the films I showed you in October, 1969, and January. Each test is shown first at regular speed, then in very slow motion. Estimated repair costs, determined by a team of three qualified insurance evaluators, are shown at the conclusion of the slow motion sequences. A table summarizing the estimates is attached to my testimony.

Five sets of tests are covered in the film—three involving crashes into a standard SAE barrier at five and ten miles per hour, and two involving two-vehicle crashes. (In the latter, the striking car and the struck car are of identical make and model.) The very low speeds at which these tests were run are comparable to ordinary human walking and jogging speeds, as I pointed out in earlier testimony, and are well below those speeds at which contact sports participants often collide into one another or fixed objects. They are speeds, in other words, at which humans—but not their cars—regularly crash without such extensive, expensive damage.

Because the film is made up of many short sequences, may I ask that you reserve questions until its showing is completed. We will be happy, of course, to run it again if you desire.

FIVE MILE PER HOUR FRONT END INTO BARRIER

1. Volkswagen 1600—total estimated repair cost, $120.25.
2. Toyota Corona—total estimated repair cost, $133.70.
3. Ford Maverick—total estimated repair cost, $153.10.
4. American Hornet—total estimated repair cost, $204.50.

FIVE MILE PER HOUR REAR END INTO BARRIER

1. Volkswagen 1600—total estimated repair cost, $64.45.
2. Toyota Corona—total estimated repair cost, $69.30.
3. Ford Maverick—total estimated repair cost, $204.75.
4. American Hornet—total estimated repair cost, $193.85.

TEN MILE PER HOUR FRONT END INTO BARRIER

1. Volkswagen 1600—total estimated repair cost, $322.35.
2. Toyota Corona—total estimated repair cost, $410.94.
3. Ford Maverick—total estimated repair cost, $427.35.
4. American Hornet—total estimated repair cost, $508.40.
   (Note: In the following inter-vehicular crashes, the total estimated repair cost is for both cars. In each test, the struck car and the striking car were of identical make and model. In the front-into-rear tests, both cars were in neutral, with engines running.)

TEN MILE PER HOUR FRONT INTO REAR

1. Volkswagen 1600—total estimated repair cost, both cars, $228.20.
2. Toyota Corona—total estimated repair cost, both cars, $305.57.
3. Ford Maverick—total estimated repair cost, both cars, $449.80.
4. American Hornet—total estimated repair cost, both cars, $590.20.

TEN MILE PER HOUR FRONT INTO SIDE

1. Volkswagen 1600—total estimated repair cost, both cars, $381.55.
2. Toyota Corona—total estimated repair cost, both cars, $316.34.
3. Ford Maverick—total estimated repair cost, both cars, $423.30.
4. American Hornet—total estimated repair cost, both cars, $591.75.

As in the research results we showed you in October, 1969, and in January, these are striking not only in the dollar amounts of damage they indicate are routinely occurring in very low-speed crashes, but also in the differences that are apparent between estimated repair costs of individual cars within each test series a point of considerable relevance to consumer choice as well as to setting of insurance premiums to cover the necessary losses. Variations in estimated damage costs sustained in the crashes you have just seen ranged to recapitulate from:

A low of $120.25 to a high of $204.50 in the five mile per hour front-into-barrier test;

A low of $64.45 to a high of $204.75 in the five mile per hour rear-into-barrier test;

A low of $322.35 to a high of $508.40 in the ten mile per hour front-into-barrier test;

A low of $228.20 to a high of $590.20 in the front-into-rear two-car test, and

A low of $316.34 to a high of $591.75 in the front-into-side two-car test.

Mr. Chairman, your Subcommittee is to be commended for bringing to the attention of the consuming public the nature and sweep or repair cost burdens being borne by car owners and the economy as a whole. Technological solutions are available which would virtually eliminate damage to vehicle exterior in the very low-speed crashes so common on our highways and streets today—certainly common enough to be anticipated in the design laboratories of automobile manufacturers—and these solutions can, at the same time, dramatically reduce the likelihood of human damage at higher speeds.

If your hearings spark the beginnings of design improvements, however belated, to make automobiles crashworthy in these very low-speed ranges, they will have performed an immense service that can save this country many billions of dollars.

The chart below gives the test results of each crash test:

Crash speed	1970 Volkswagen 1600	1970 Toyota Corona	1970 Ford Maverick	1970 American Hornet	Averages
5 miles per hour, front	$120.25	$133.70	$153.10	$204.50	$152.89
5 miles per hour, rear	64.45	69.30	204.75	193.85	133.09
10 miles per hour, front	322.35	410.94	427.35	508.40	417.26
10 miles per hour, front into rear:					
Front	156.75	129.51	235.60	328.75	212.65
Rear	71.45	176.06	214.20	261.45	180.79
Total	228.20	305.57	449.80	590.20	393.44
10 miles per hour, front into side:					
Front	194.75	150.26	220.75	191.70	189.37
Side	186.80	166.08	202.55	400.05	238.87
Total	381.55	316.34	423.30	591.75	428.24
. . . .	1,116.80	1,235.85	1,658.30	2,088.70	1,524.92

Dr. Haddon's testimony before the Senate Commerce Committee, March 10, 1971, showed that the damage was even greater to the 1971 cars tested. (See following page.)

1971 LOW SPEED CRASH TEST RESULTS
Insurance Institute for Highway Safety

		5 MPH FRONT	5 MPH REAR	10 MPH FRONT/REAR*	10 MPH FRONT/SIDE**
SEDANS	Chevrolet Impala	367.90	447.00	280.50 / 221.05	328.85 / 375.30
	Ford Galaxie	341.20	318.55	248.15 / 469.60	241.00 / 439.35
	Plymouth Fury	202.25	266.35	201.85 / 246.80	247.10 / 306.55
	AMC Ambassador	415.40	285.20	256.30 / 141.35	233.25 / 379.65
SMALL CARS	Volkswagen	130.75	59.05	81.10 / 181.75	126.35 / 227.45
	Chevrolet Vega	181.30	228.45	276.55 / 244.60	191.05 / 195.90
	Ford Pinto	164.20	210.00	183.35 / 196.10	151.90 / 244.15
	AMC Gremlin	121.30	286.90	253.95 / 137.65	172.00 / 329.65
INTERMEDIATES	Pontiac Firebird	229.00	262.60	77.00 / 385.60	55.40 / 458.70
	Buick Skylark	427.10	226.85	305.75 / 190.70	354.00 / 174.50
	Mercury Montego	402.11	267.35	171.50 / 469.13	98.85 / 729.50
	Plymouth Satellite	98.45	256.35	161.35 / 241.65	120.95 / 523.25

*In the front-to-rear crashes, the price listed first for each car model is the estimated repair cost for the striking car (front-end damage); listed second is the estimated repair cost for the struck car (rear-end damage).

**In the front-to-side crashes, the price listed first for each model is the estimated repair cost for the striking car (front-end damage); listed second is the estimated repair cost for the struck car (side damage).

THE DOSSIER INVADES THE HOME

Ralph Nader

Invasion of privacy used to carry an almost luxurious connotation, a concept reserved for special public figures whose private lives were invaded by scandalmongers or seekers of vicarious thrills. It is no longer an elitist term. Hundreds of bits of information filed in dossiers on millions of individual Americans today constitute a massive assault on privacy whose ramifications are just beginning to be realized.

Most adults have at some time sought credit (or a credit card) and bought insurance. If you have done these things, there are probably at least two dossiers with your name on them.

When you seek to borrow money, your creditor receives a file from the credit bureau to establish your "credit rating." This dossier contains all the personal facts the credit bureau can assemble—your job, salary, length of time on the present job, marital status, a list of present and past debts and their payment history, any criminal record, any lawsuits of any kind, and any real estate you may own. The dossier may include your employer's opinion of your job performance or even your IQ rating from a high school test. By the time the creditor has finished talking to the credit bureau, he is likely to know more about your personal life than your mother-in-law does.

From *Saturday Review*, 17 April 1971. Reprinted by permission of the author.

When you try to buy life insurance, a file of even more intimate information about you is compiled by the "inspection agency." The insurance company finds out not only about your health but also about your drinking habits (how often, how much, with others or alone, and even what beverage), your net worth, salary, debts, domestic troubles, reputation, associates, manner of living, and standing in the community. The investigator is also asked to inquire of your neighbors and associates whether there is "any criticism of character or morals," and he must state whether he recommends that the insurance be declined.

Credit bureaus and inspection agencies are the major sources of information about individuals. But government, schools, employers, and banks are also collectors, and sometimes suppliers, of information. Employers frequently make information on their employees available to a credit bureau or inspection agency. They may also exchange information among themselves. *The Wall Street Journal* has reported that department stores in many cities have formed "mutual protection associations" that trade the names of former workers who were fired for suspected theft. This information-trading means that an individual may be denied a job on the basis of a former employer's untested—and unrefuted—suspicions.

Anyone possessing an individual's bank records—now extensively recorded on computers—can reconstruct his associations, movements, habits, and life-style. The recently enacted Foreign Bank Secrecy Act can be used to require every FDIC-insured bank to make a reproduction of each check you draw on it and keep those reproductions for up to six years. The purpose is to ensure records of large quantities of money going out of the country so as to prevent tax evasions through use of secret Swiss bank accounts. But the act contains no protection for the depositor by limiting in any way the banks' use of these records. Conceivably, a bank could sell them to a credit bureau or investigation agency.

It is the rare American who does not live in the shadow of his dossier. The "dossier industry" is a huge and growing business. There are 105 million files kept by the Association of Credit Bureaus of America (ACBA). Retail Credit Company of Atlanta, Georgia, the giant of the industry, has forty-five million files and makes thirty-five million reports each year. Credit Data Corporation, the second largest firm, has twenty-seven million files and adds seven million new dossiers each year.

These economic interests have almost total control over the information they collect and sell. They are not accountable to anyone except those who seek to purchase information. Further, for reasons of profit, these companies place a premium on the derogatory information they assemble. Except in three states, citizens do not have the right even to see these dossiers in order to correct inaccuracies. They will have that right for the first time when a federal law, the Fair Credit Reporting Act, goes into effect April 25, 1971. But they still will not have the right to control access to the information, on which there are in effect no legal restrictions, or the right to control the kinds of information that can go into their dossiers.

Until there are adequate protective measures—an "information bill of rights" that protects him against invasion of privacy through information dissemination—the citizen's major recourse is to understand how these agencies operate and what are his limited rights under present and pending law.

The first problem of the dossier is accuracy. There is no doubt that inaccurate information comes into the files of credit bureaus and insurance inspection agencies. In fact, credit bureaus disclaim accuracy in their forms, because most of the material is obtained from others (merchants, employers) and not verified by them. The information "has been obtained from sources deemed reliable, the accuracy of which [the credit bureau] does not guarantee."

Illustrations of errors are legion. New York State Assemblyman Chester P. Straub was refused a credit card because his dossier revealed an outstanding judgment. The judgment actually was against another person with a similar name, but the bureau had erroneously put it against Straub's name. Testimony before a U.S. Senate committee has accused credit bureaus of using a "shotgun" approach to recording judgments against consumers—entering any judgment on all the records bearing the same name as the defendant's, or a similar name, without checking to see which individual was actually involved.

In addition to errors of identification, there are errors due to incomplete information. A woman ordered a rug, but the seller delivered one of the wrong color. He refused to take it back and sued for payment. Although his case was thrown out of court, her credit record showed only that she had been sued for non-payment, and she was unable to get credit elsewhere thereafter. Arrests and the filing of lawsuits are systematically collected by credit bureaus and rushed into dossiers, but the dismissal of charges or a suit is not reported in the newspaper and so the credit bureau never learns of, or records, the affirmative data.

Also, there is the problem of obsolescence of information, as shown by the man whose bureau dossier in the Sixties listed a lawsuit from the Thirties. It was a $5 scare suit for a magazine subscription he had never ordered, and "nothing had come of it"—except in regard to his credit rating.

The introduction of computers can create its own set of problems. Although mechanical errors in the handling of information by people may be reduced, the probability of machine error is increased. In addition, credit data are taken directly from a creditor's computer to a credit bureau's computer without discretion. Your payments may have been excused for two months, due to illness, but the computer does not know this, and it will only report that you missed two payments. Storage problems alone will prevent the explanation from being made. Your rating with that creditor may not be affected, but with all others it will be.

These credit bureau inaccuracies generally relate to "hard data," which are subject to verification or contradiction. The insurance inspection agency, on the other hand, reports "soft data," or gossip, and they are not subject to verification at all. This creates new sources of inaccuracies. Where the information is inherently uncheckable, the biased employee or the biased informant can easily introduce inaccuracies. Even where bias is not present, innuendo or misunderstanding can create error, while a vindictive inspector can abuse his power for personal reasons.

Why don't inspectors check the accusations made by informants with the accused? One reason is they don't have the time. If they must make ten or fifteen reports a day, they can spend only forty minutes on an average report, including transportation and typing it up. This allows no time for checking accusations, or even facts.

A more vicious reason is the agency's penchant for derogatory information and the fact that it records on both a weekly and a monthly basis the percentage of cases in which an inspector recommends declines. He must file a certain percentage of derogatory reports (at one time 8 percent for life and 10 percent for auto reports) if he is to be known as a "good digger." If he has not met his "quota," the temptation to use any rumor, without confirmation, may be overwhelming. These quotas may be regarded by the agency as a necessary control device to prevent inspectors from filing fake reports without investigation, but they show a reckless disregard for the safety of the investigated public.

Gossip-mongering with a quota on unfavorable comments can lead the harried inspector to rely on innuendo. A vivid illustration of the problems in insurance reporting is the case of two successful young businesswomen who applied for a life insurance policy required for a particular business transaction. On completion of a routine report, Retail Credit Company advised the insurance company not to issue the policy. It reported "severe criticism of the morals of both women, particularly regarding habits, and Lesbian activities." The investigator's information came from neighbors. None of these neighbors actually stated they had seen any illicit activity, but innuendo accomplished the same result. "Informants [unidentified] will not come out and state that applicant is Lesbian, but hint and hedge around and do everything but state it." The insurance company followed Retail Credit's advice and denied the policy.

Until passage of the Fair Credit Reporting Act, the law offered no protection against an inaccurate report, except in three states. There was no way one could even see a report to correct it. However, this new act offers some solutions to problems of accuracy.

1) It requires users of reports to notify consumers of the name and address of the consumer reporting agency whenever the user (e.g., creditor, insurer, or employer) takes adverse action on the basis of the agency's report.

2) It gives the consumer the right to know the "nature and substance of all information" on him in the agency's files, except medical information and the sources of "investigative information" (i.e., gossip). The limitation on sources of gossip is a serious weakness. Such sources can be discovered in litigation, however, and a suit is made easy to bring. Thus, *the agency can no longer guarantee the confidentiality of its sources.*

3) If a dispute arises between the consumer and the agency about the accuracy of an item, the agency must reinvestigate and *reverify* or delete the information. This will usually mean going back to the same neighbors and obtaining the same gossip. If the dispute is not settled by reinvestigation, the item must be noted as disputed. This leaves the user free to believe the agency.

These provisions are the strongest in the bill. They are weak from the consumer's point of view in two areas: The consumer should be allowed to learn the sources of gossip before litigation so that he can effectively rebut inaccurate gossip; further, he should be provided a quick, simple procedure for obtaining a declaratory judgment on the truth of any item.

4) The act also provides for enforcement through private actions if the agency is negligent. Negligence is easy to allege, but may be difficult to prove. Only time will tell what standards the courts will set.

Even though the agency's secrecy is now partially broken, relief may still not be available because most agencies are granted immunity for agency libel. Under the law of most states, the agencies are given a "conditional privilege" to publish false statements; so the libel action will not succeed. The privilege is granted on the grounds that they are fulfilling a private duty by providing businessmen with information they need in the conduct of their affairs. Georgia and Idaho (and England) do not grant the agencies such a privilege on the grounds that the privilege itself does not benefit the general public, but only a profit-oriented enterprise, and that individual rights take precedence over the self-interest of the enterprise.

In the states granting the privilege, it is conditioned on the agency's 1) disclosing the information only to those with the requisite commercial interest, and 2) acting in good faith and without malice. However, proof of malice requires more than just the falsity of the report. In the past this has conferred an effective immunity on false reports. Malice, however, may be shown by the quota systems of the agencies or by their secrecy. Arguably, these company policies show a "wanton and reckless disregard of the rights of another, as is an ill will equivalent." Such theories, however, have not yet been tested in court.

There is no regulation on sale of the extensive personal information collected by credit bureaus, insurance agencies, and employers. The dossiers are considered their "property," and they may do what they wish with it. The only influence to limit availability is an economic one, arising from the condition on the privilege for publishing libel—the report can be given only to subscribers of the service or others claiming a legitimate interest in its subject matter. However, claims of interest are easy to make and are not often scrutinized.

Furthermore, the citizen never knows when these dossiers are opened to someone. His consent is not sought before release of the information. He is not warned when someone new obtains the information, or told who they are—unless, under the new law they take adverse action. There are no pressures on the information agencies to account to the subject of the dossier, nor have these agencies shown any willingness to assume such responsibility.

Credit bureaus may follow the Associated Credit Bureau guidelines and release information only to those who certify that they will use it in a "legitimate business transaction." This, of course, includes not only credit granters but also employers, landlords, insurers, and dozens of others. But even these weak guidelines are unenforceable by the association, and a CBS study found that half the bureaus they contacted furnished information to CBS without checking the legitimacy of their business purpose. Announced policies of inspection agencies also require a showing of a business purpose. But this includes anyone who has $5 and announces himself as a "prospective employer."

In April, the Fair Credit Reporting Act will impose a restriction on the release of information, but it is no better than those presently available. An agency will be able to sell information to anyone having "a legitimate business need" for the information. There are no economic or legal restrictions preventing any credit bureau or inspection agency from giving out their dossiers indiscriminately to anyone who can pay.

The consequences of making highly personal information easily available have only begun to be recognized. Credit reporting agencies may serve as private detectives for corporations that want to intimidate a critic. Recently the press reported that American Home Products, a drug manufacturer with more than $1 billion in sales, hired Retail Credit Company to investigate the personal affairs of Jay B. Constantine, an aide to the Senate Finance Committee who had helped draft legislation opposed by the drug industry. The investigation was stopped only "after their stupidity was uncovered," according to Senator Russell Long, Finance Committee chairman, who also said that the company had tendered "a complete letter of apology."

The introduction of computers furnishes other possibilities for use and misuse of personal information. Arthur R. Miller, in his new book, *The Assault on Privacy*, reports that MIT students in Project MAC (Machine Aided Cognition) were able to tap into computers handling classified Strategic Air Command data. If they can do this, any time-sharing user can tap into a computer data bank. There is no way at present that computer people can guarantee their control over access. They cannot even guarantee that they can prevent rewriting of the information in the computer by outsiders.

What can be done to control the availability of these dossiers? Primarily, anyone obtaining information on you should be required to obtain your express consent to the release before receiving the information. This would recognize your interest in preserving the privacy of your own personality. It would allow you to decide whether any particular transaction was worth the invasion of your privacy by the other party.

Even if the information in the dossier is completely accurate and available only to creditors, insurers, and employers, there may be personal or private details—perhaps irrelevant to the demands of the credit-insurance industries—that people want kept to themselves.

Some kinds of information may be so personal that their storage and sale are offensive. For example, it is possible to assemble a list of the books a person reads by observing his bookshelves, talking to his neighbors, or obtaining the records of the public library. An employer or insurer could manufacture a "business purpose" for obtaining such information—to determine the subject's knowledge or intelligence, generally, or in a specific field. There is little doubt that such an effort would be offensive to most people, violating their privilege of private thoughts and opinions. It would be offensive even if accurate.

Currently, the information gathered in most dossiers includes a subject's past educational, marital, employment, and bill-paying records. His "club life," drinking habits, and associates are recorded. Also included are an employer's opinion of his work habits and his neighbors' opinion of his reputation, character, and morals, which probably includes gossip about old neighborhood feuds.

Insurance company underwriters indicate that many do not use some questions (e.g., "What social clubs does he belong to?"). Some questions are overdrafted (e.g., the query "Who are his associates?" is useful to them only as "Does he have any criminal associates?"—a quite different version). The reason for asking what *kind* of alcoholic beverage an applicant drank was incomprehensible to at least two underwriters.

When asked whether they ever sought to have unnecessary questions struck from the form, the response was "Why should we? It's just as easy to skip over them when reading." There was no indication that they had any scruples about, or even any understanding of, the problem as an invasion of privacy.

Credit bureaus and investigation agencies do not generally gather such information as test scores or personality traits. Nor are lists of books assembled—yet. But there is nothing to prevent these investigators from adding this information to the standard items in their dossiers. The FBI has tried a similar form of investigation. Common law doctrines seem not to cover these problems, and, until recently, legislatures and relevant administrative bodies have shown no interest. Most information agencies have no announced policies that would preclude them from including any type of question. Thus, the only reason such information is not gathered is an economic one: No one is sufficiently interested to request and pay for it.

New technology is also tipping the balance against the individual's right of privacy as far as kinds of information are concerned. With problems of storage and transmittal solved, the technological tendency is to collect more data on individuals, inevitably more sensitive data.

The way information is gathered also has ominous implications for the individual's privacy. Credit bureaus gather their information from employers, newspapers, and credit-granters who are members of the bureau. They also collect data from the "welcome wagon" woman who visits homes and notes what buying "needs" you have so that you can be dunned by the right merchant. American Airlines' computer can give anyone information about what trips you have taken in the last two or three months. Further, it can give your seat number and be used to determine who sat next to you, perhaps inferentially describing your associates. In addition, it can tell your telephone contact number and, from this, determine where you stayed or your associates in each city of departure. Credit card accounts can do much the same thing, telling what you have bought recently (to establish standard of living and life-style) and where you shop.

Each of these methods of inquiry constitutes a serious invasion of privacy, but the most serious invasion is the neighborhood investigation by the inspection agency. Here information is gathered by questioning your neighbors, building superintendent, grocer, or postmaster about what you do while you are in your own home. There is the threat not only of gossip-mongering and slander, but of the creation of a kind of surveillance on your home. For most people, the only available private place is "home." Here, even though observed by neighbors perhaps, the individual can feel free to discard his social role and be more expressive of his own personality. It is here that the "neighborhood check" of the inspection agency is most frightening.

How does an inspector go about obtaining information from your neighbors? Frederick King of Hooper-Holmes candidly described the procedures used when a married man is suspected of an extramarital affair. "You go to a neighbor and establish rapport. Then you ask, 'What's your opinion of him as a family man?' This will usually elicit some hint—through the expression on his face or the way he answers. Then you start digging. You press him as far as he will go, and if he becomes recalcitrant you go somewhere else. If you go to enough people, you get it."

Do present laws give you any protection from these invasions of your privacy in regard to either the types of information stored and sold or the manner in which they are gathered? Probably not.

There is a tort cause of action for invasion of privacy, but instead of furnishing a broad protection device, the courts have established four subcategories of the right. Two of these subcategories related to the gathering and publication of personal material are "public disclosures of private facts" and "intrusion."

Public disclosure of private facts has not been actionable without a finding of "unreasonable publication," and publication to a "small group" would include the subscribers of a credit bureau or investigation agency, in much the same way that publication of defamation to such groups has been held privileged. The exemption is based on the same reasoning that sustains the conditional privilege to defamation and has the same dangers to the subject, who may not be able to correct falsehoods or defend himself against the consequences of having intimate details of his life revealed to the business community in his town.

Intrusion has been found most often in cases involving physical intrusion. Peering through windows, wiretapping and eavesdropping seem to strike a more responsive chord in courts than does interviewing your neighbors or acquaintances. This tort is usually held to require an "extreme" or "shocking" violation of your privacy, and physical trespasses are most easily perceived as shocking.

In a New York Court of Appeals decision involving the author and General Motors, the court went beyond physical intrusions to include surveillance for an unreasonable time. However, even this decision makes actionable only those intrusions that are for the purpose of gathering confidential information. The question whether this doctrine covers investigations seeking to discover marital relationships, sexual habits, or housekeeping abilities has not been presented to the courts since the New York decision. However, three of the court's judges specifically stated that the four recognized subcategories of the right to privacy are neither frozen nor exhaustive.

If judicial protection against the collection and sale of overly personal information is limited, legislative protection is still nonexistent, even after passage of the Fair Credit Reporting Act. That statute may provide accuracy protection, but the Senate conferees refused to accept any provisions that would limit the types of data about you that can be gathered and sold.

The invasion of privacy should more accurately be called the invasion of self. The right to protect himself against an informational assault is basic to the inviolability of the individual. On the one hand we recognize that an arrest record may haunt an individual, and there is precedent for a wrong arrest that is thrown out of court to be expunged from the record. But we have not yet recognized that the bits of information contained in dossiers kept on 105 million Americans may be just as decisive and just as damaging to their lives.

The individual's right to privacy of self is crucial to the functioning of our society. Suppose you walked into a courtroom and picked up a pamphlet relating everything the judge had ever done in his personal life. What would that information do to your interaction with that court? To some extent it is absolutely necessary to preserve barriers of privacy and protection about people's lives in order to permit ordinary interaction between people, an interaction that is to a significant degree based on trust.

Our Founding Fathers developed Constitutional safeguards in the Bill of Rights against the arbitrary authority of government. The rights against unreasonable search and seizure and against self-incrimination were examples of basic rights of privacy deemed critical for a free people. Generations passed and the country developed private organizations possessed of a potential for arbitrary authority not foreseen by the early Constitutional draftsmen. Most pervasive and embracing of these organizations is the modern corporation. Aggressive by its motivational nature, the corporation, in a credit-insurance economy spurred by computer gathering and retrieval efficiency, has created new dimensions to information as the currency of power over individuals. The secret gathering and use of such true or false information by any bank, finance company, insurance firm, other business concern, or employer place the individual in a world of unknowns. He is inhibited, has less power to speak out, is less free, and develops his own elaborate self-censorship.

What this costs in individual freedom and social justice cannot be measured. It can only be felt by the daily contacts with human beings in invisible chains reluctant to challenge or question what they believe to be wrong since, from some secret corporate dossier, irrelevant but damaging information may be brought to bear on them. The law and technology have provided the "dossier industry" with powerful tools to obtain and use information against people in an unjust way—whether knowingly or negligently. The defenseless citizen now requires specific rights to defend against and deter such invasions of privacy.

The Fair Credit Reporting Act will take steps toward solving some of the problems of accuracy in individual dossiers. For the first time, people may find out what credit bureaus and inspection agencies are saying about them, and they now have some means of correcting inaccuracies. But there are still no restraints on availability of this information or on the kinds of information gathered. Unless citizens are provided with an "information bill of rights" enabling them to see, correct, and know the uses of these dossiers, and to impose liability on wrongdoers, they can be reduced to a new form of computer-indentured slavery. The law must begin to teach the corporation about the inviolability of the individual as it has striven to teach the state.

5

COMPULSORY CONSUMPTION

There is a widespread impression that consumer abuses are restricted to the marketplace, but we are also exposed to involuntary or compulsory consumption about which we have little choice. We are forced to breathe polluted air, drink polluted water, and ingest food adulterated with dangerous chemicals. Such consumption is the more insidious because it is often unnoticed. It is a form of silent violence, with effects that are hard to trace but that are often long-lasting and irreversible. Scientists still have incomplete knowledge of the scope of potential harm from the reckless use of chemicals such as pesticides and deliberately used additives that end up in our food. But the more they learn, the more concerned they become. Joshua Lederberg, Nobel prize-winning geneticist, believes that many chemicals which enter our bodies are capable of causing mutations in future generations, resulting in such damage to the entire human race as a lowering of general intelligence, a lessening of vitality, a shorter life span, and increased sterility. Such effects, according to Lederberg, might not appear for several generations, perhaps a hundred years or more, and then go generally undetected. Birth defects are another hazard which have been caused in laboratory animals by a variety of chemicals in common use. So much lead has been released into the air from the gasoline-burning engine that some scientists now claim that auto exhaust is the primary source of lead poisoning, a horrible disease that affects the brain. Mercury, another metal which causes brain damage, has been found in frightening quantities in fish. Cancer is a common threat from additives and from such pollutants as asbestos, hydrocarbons from incomplete combustion, and airborne particles. Emphysema and bronchitis have been linked to air pollution.

Pollutants make persons more susceptible to diseases, especially respiratory infections. And chemicals may combine in the body, in unknown ways, to produce more harm than they could alone. Ecologist Barry Commoner has said: "We have been massively intervening in the environment without being aware of many of the harmful consequences of our acts until they have been performed and the effects—which are difficult to understand and sometimes irreversible—are upon us. Like the sorcerer's apprentice, we are acting upon dangerously incomplete knowledge. We are, in effect, conducting a huge experiment *on ourselves.*" In addition, the earth is being transformed into a garbage heap with dead rivers and lakes, dying wildlife, and foul-smelling air.

One of the first reports to come out of the Center for the Study of Responsive Law was on air pollution. Called *Vanishing Air,* it was written by attorney John Esposito and a group of graduate students in law, medicine, science, and engineering. The chapter reprinted here, "Progress and Poverty: The Major Manufacturing Sources of Air Pollution," documents the extent of manufacturing pollution, and the underground war which polluters wage against legal controls and the citizenry's need for knowledge. Throughout industry, the task force encountered cover-ups and sometimes outright refusals to supply any information whatever. Occasionally they were answered with wisecracks too true to be funny. When one student commented on the unpleasant odor of oil refineries, an industry representative shot back: "Some of us like the smell; it smells like money." This selection illustrates not only the problem of pollution, but also the problem of secrecy which permeates the entire corporate structure of America and thwarts public action. Such secrecy has its counterpart in government agencies and was experienced by another student task force investigating the Federal Trade Commission. (See "The Regulatory-Industrial Complex.")

My article, "Baby Foods: Can You (and Your Baby) Afford Them?" gives insight into the problem of food additives by exploring the particularly shocking situation in commercial baby foods. Such foods, like those for adults, are recklessly adulterated with flavorings and untested additives. Salt and sugar are added to baby foods to make them taste good—not to baby, who has little discriminating taste until seven months, but to mother. The harm is inestimable. Monosodium glutamate (MSG), which has caused brain damage in young test animals, was finally removed from baby foods by alarmed manufacturers but the fact remains that it was added without sufficient testing and used for years. Such is the case with thousands of additives used in a variety of foods which we eat daily. No additives should be permitted in foods until they have been thoroughly tested, particularly if their use is largely cosmetic.

Industry wants to ask the question: What will it cost to clean up air pollution? The question rather should be: What will it cost if we don't? In lives? In medical bills? In property damage? In aesthetics? The economic loss from air pollution is an estimated $16 billion yearly. In 1970 the industry spent about $3.5 billion on investments in all pollution control equipment while making $78 billion in profits. There are two essential ways to deal with air pollution: one is to build more hospitals for the victims, the other is to redesign autos and plants at the source. Obviously the latter approach is cheaper and more humane. Polluters, however, should not be allowed to push the bill for pollution control onto consumers through higher prices. The money should come from corporate profits which have grown fat from the exploitation and destruction of our environment.

My article, "The Toilet Training of Industry: Strategies for the Prevention of Pollution," details the changes that must be effected in policies towards corporate polluters if we are to make the earth again a safe and pleasant place to live.

PROGRESS AND POVERTY: THE MAJOR MANUFACTURING SOURCES OF AIR POLLUTION

John Esposito

"It's cheaper to pay claims than it is to control fluorides." These are the words of an executive of the Reynolds Metals Company, quoted in an opinion written by a federal appeals court judge. But they could have been uttered by almost any industrial manager. The fact that such egregious corporate calculus is possible bears witness to society's failure to make the pollution of our environment unprofitable. Industry will not end or significantly reduce its emissions until air pollution contaminates corporate income statements as well as human beings.

In an unconscious but quite revealing way, a steel company executive told the Task Force, "We *use* a lot of air . . . in our business." This was a tacit recognition that the nation has been providing American industry with a public subsidy by permitting the unpenalized use—and contamination—of our air. Some would argue that this is the public's investment in progress. Manufacturing, for instance, contributes more than 450 billion dollars to the annual Gross National Product. But looking beyond the 450 billion dollars, we see that these same sources also "manufacture" more than fifty-eight billion pounds of air contaminants each year. This amounts to almost 300 pounds of air pollution for every person in the United States—a poor return on society's subsidy. The air we breathe is our most basic natural resource, and it is not a limitless commodity. Only a thin blanket of air surrounds the earth. While we are making "progress" economically, we are quickly becoming impoverished with regard to the most basic requirement for sustaining life, the air around us.

Major contributors to the fifty-eight billion pounds of industrial excretions—carbon monoxide, sulfur oxides, nitrogen oxides, hydrocarbons, particulate matter, fluorides, and more exotic substances—include the following:

cement manufacture: 1.7 billion pounds (particulates)

coal cleaning and refuse: 4.7 billion pounds (particulates, sulfur oxides, carbon monoxide)

coke (used in steel manufacture): 4.4 billion pounds (particulates, sulfur oxides, carbon monoxide)

grain mills and handling: 2.2 billion pounds (particulates)

iron foundries: 7.4 billion pounds (particulates and carbon monoxide)

iron and steel mills: 3.6 billion pounds (particulates and carbon monoxide)

kraft pulp and paper mills: 6.6 billion pounds (particulates, carbon monoxide, sulfur oxides)

petroleum refining: 8.4 billion pounds (particulates, sulfur oxides, hydrocarbons, carbon monoxide)

phosphate fertilizer plants: 624 million pounds (particulates and fluorides)

smelters (aluminum, copper, lead, zinc): 8.3 billion pounds (particulates and sulfur oxides)

While the aggregate figures of factory pollution are formidable, their impact can be truly appreciated only by surveying some of the communities which suffer from the emissions generated by their manufacturing neighbors. The communities described below are strikingly different from each other in almost every respect—geographical characteristics, climate, population density. But they share one common characteristic. They all lie below dark clouds of industrial wastes.

HERCULANEUM, MISSOURI

Herculaneum, Missouri (1960 population: 1767) is the home of a smelting plant operated by the St. Joseph Lead Company. Each year, 90,300 tons of lead roll through the plant's doors, while 38,500 tons of sulfur oxides spew out of its smokestacks into the otherwise relatively pristine air of Jefferson County. This is one-third of a pound of pollutant for each pound of lead produced. This single plant accounts for 90 per cent of the total sulfur oxide emissions in the county. Under the circumstances, one might wonder whether the name should be St. Joseph Lead & Sulfur Oxides Company.

NIAGARA FRONTIER

Niagara Falls may still be a popular honeymoon haven, but living there is no picnic. The Niagara Frontier, which stretches across New York State's Erie and Niagara Counties, is one of the most highly industrialized, and filthy, regions of the nation. There are scores of major plants, concentrated primarily in a band of cities beginning with Lackawanna to the south, north through Buffalo, ending at the city of Niagara Falls. Industrial activity includes almost every conceivable manufacturing pursuit, from the production of steel and automotive parts to the milling of flour.

The city of Niagara Falls has a particularly heavy concentration of chemical industries. The mayor of the city, a gentleman named Lackey, rebuffs environmental critics by pointing out that local plants are "spending millions of dollars" to deal with pollution, and admonishes that the companies make "an enormous contribution to our lives in the area" by providing jobs and revenue. This is a defense more befitting a company executive than a public official, but it is common enough. Pollution control and economic security are pitted as disjunctives: "Don't push them too far, or they'll dismantle their factories and go to Ohio."

In February, 1969, the National Air Pollution Control Administration reported that the honeymoon city and its immediate surroundings are clouded every day by an average emission of 150 tons (300,000 pounds) of sulfur dioxides, particulates, and carbon monoxide. A conservative estimate (assuming this level for an average five-day work week) would indicate that seventy-eight million pounds of garbage floats over—and on—the city of Niagara Falls each year. On a 365-day basis, the total would be over one billion pounds annually, or 11,000 pounds per resident. Notwithstanding Mayor Lackey's staunch defense, it would appear that local industry will have to spend many more "millions of dollars" if the situation is to improve.

The situation to the south, in Buffalo, is much worse. The same NAPCA report just cited indicated that the annual average for measured suspended particulates is, for the southern portion of the city, greater than 200 $\mu g/m^3$ (micrograms per cubic meter of air). NAPCA's data on the health effects of high concentrations of particulate matter indicate that at levels above 100 $\mu g/m^3$ (one-half the measured level in south Buffalo), increased respiratory diseases among children may occur and increased death rates for persons over fifty are likely.

Research conducted in Buffalo has established a positive correlation between the high particulate levels and increased mortality. Dr. Warren Winklestein, Jr., of the University of California at Berkeley, has shown that the death rate for white males between the ages of fifty and sixty-nine was twice as high in areas of the city where the particulate levels exceeded 135 $\mu g/m^3$ than in areas where the level is less than 80 $\mu g/m^3$. The correlation between the high particulate level and deaths specifically caused by chronic respiratory disease was even more striking. In the most polluted part of the city, the number of white males between the ages of fifty and sixty-nine who died from respiratory disease was three times higher than in the least polluted area. These deaths and illnesses were not the result of so-called emergency episodes (as described in Chapter 1), but simply part of the continuing emergency which confronts the residents of the Niagara Frontier every day of their lives.

ANMOORE, WEST VIRGINIA

Anmoore, West Virginia (1960 population: 1050), is the site of Union Carbide's Carbon Products Division. Union Carbide may be the only corporation in the United States to have a newsletter devoted exclusively to the company's activities that it neither publishes nor sponsors. But Carbide would just as soon do without the free advertising. Its Carbon Products Division plant in Anmoore covers the tiny town with a perpetual black film whose consistency ranges from a dark silky soot to large flakes of fly ash. Mr. and Mrs. O. D. Hagedorn became incensed over the failure of public control officials and the company to act in response to their numerous complaints. The couple took to issuing a newsletter which appears whenever "we've got something to tell people about the company," says Mrs. Hagedorn. The newsletter is distributed to citizens by local merchants, and the Hagedorns send copies to the West Virginia Air Pollution Control Department, the local plant manager, the company's offices in Charleston, and to the Chairman of the Board of Union Carbide in his office in New York City.

The Hagedorns specialize in piercing Carbide's corporate veil. They keep a keen eye out for the company's promotional materials in the local press, and they are quick to note every public relations excess. There is usually a great deal for the Hagedorns to write about.

For instance, one of their newsletters reprinted a letter sent by the couple to Carbide's Public Relations Department in New York City:

Dear Sirs:

In your advertisement in the Clarksburg, W. Va. Sunday-Exponent Telegram, January 28, 1968, you state: "There is probably a bit of W. Va. in every room in your home . . . and in your garage, your office, or in the plant where you work." Going on from there, you indicate that Union Carbide is largely responsible for putting this "bit of W. Va." in these areas. Congratulations! A little public relations self-back-slapping is in order; and as a proud citizen of our state, I appreciate your efforts and contributions in its behalf. But . . .

As a citizen of Anmoore (where your Clarksburg plant is located) I protest your modesty in claiming only "a bit of W. Va." in every room of our home every day of the year . . . all thanks to Union Carbide. These "bits" are stubborn, black, clinging bits of soot, fly ash, or whatever which literally inundate an entire town.

If you are as interested in the welfare of the state of W. Va. and its citizens as your back-slapping public relations ad so proudly boasts, I would submit that you lend credence to your slogan "The Discovery Company" by discovering a way of relieving the people of Anmoore of this unsightly, depressing, and unhealthy black fog under which we exist.

Despite their several-year struggle with the company, the situation in Anmoore has not changed—"not for the better at least," says Mrs. Hagedorn, "but they do send out a lot more promotional material about how much they're doing about air pollution. They haven't responded to our newsletter. They think the Hagedorns will go away if they ignore us." The Hagedorns are still in Anmoore, but so is the air pollution from Union Carbide. The fact that this couple has made local residents aware that things don't have to be the way they are is a tribute to the Hagedorns' effort. The failure of the West Virginia Air Pollution Control Department and the federal authorities to respond to citizen outcries for help is a tribute to nonresponsive government everywhere.

Union Carbide's advertising response to citizen complaints is the all too frequent industrial reaction to criticism. The corporate executive faced with a rash of complaints is more likely to call his public relations office or trade association than the vice president for pollution control. It is easier and cheaper to launch a new public relations cover-up than it is to deal directly with the environmental problem.

Some corporations, like the American Asphalt Paving Company of Chicago, cover up quite literally. American Asphalt's neighbors, sickened by the stench emanating from the plant, launched a concerted drive against the company and the city's Air Pollution Control Department. The city finally sued, after two years of picketing and complaints, and collected a grand sum of 400 dollars in fines from the company. American Asphalt then installed what is euphemistically known in the trade as an "odor-masking device." As the name would imply, this gadget is nothing more than a chemical attempt to cover up a stench with a more pleasant fragrance. Quite obviously, this is cheaper than installing basic odor-control devices. But the economy move didn't quite work. Unfortunately for American Asphalt, a city pollution control inspector ventured to south Chicago and became nauseated by the perfumed "aroma" which had replaced the older, more familiar foul odor. The company was ordered to make more fundamental changes designed to eliminate the problem. But residents are not satisfied. They still complain about frequent odor problems and have again begun to fight for higher standards at the plant.

Most industries are not quite so clumsy about their cover-ups. Trade associations are masters at suppressing government attempts to gather information concerning industrial sources of air pollution. This is the most rudimentary intelligence needed by public officials to make policy judgments and to carry out legally assigned tasks, which is precisely why industry is so anxious to withhold this information.

In 1967, virtually every industry witness who testified concerning the pending Air Quality Act urged Congress to drop an Administration proposal which, among other things, would have given the Secretary of Health, Education, and Welfare (HEW) authority to require that polluters disclose what they were putting into the atmosphere. While not all testified specifically on the disclosure provision, trade associations representing almost every one of the giant industries unanimously registered opposition to the general proposal. Among these associations were the Manufacturing Chemists Association, American Paper Institute, American Petroleum Institute, National Coal Association, American Mining Congress, Edison Electric Institute, the U.S. Chamber of Commerce and the National Association of Manufacturers. As a consequence, the Air Quality Act of 1967 contained no provision for compulsory disclosure. The federal government must gather this information by securing the "cooperation" of industry.

Three and a half months after the passage of the Air Quality Act, the voluntary scheme was put to its first test. On March 4, 1968, NAPCA submitted a proposed "Air Contaminant Emissions Survey" to the Bureau of the Budget (BOB) for clearance. Under the Federal Reports Act of 1942, federal agencies may not issue questionnaires to the public without first clearing the form with BOB. Since cooperation was voluntary, it was assumed without question that the government would have to assure respondents that the information received would be kept confidential. Therefore, the questionnaire submitted to BOB on March 24, 1968, contained the standard confidentiality regulations of the Public Health Service. The regulations indicated that information collected would be given secret status but would "be disclosed at such times and to such extent as the Surgeon General or his designee may determine to be in the public interest."

NAPCA's proposed questionnaire, like all other clearance requests, was noted on BOB's "Daily List of Reporting Forms and Plans Received for Approval." Known to insiders as the "Yellow Sheet," the list is distributed daily to a variety of carefully selected recipients. Among those most interested is the Advisory Council on Federal Reports, which was set up to act as liaison between business and BOB. In theory, the Council concerns itself only with technical questions, not policy issues. In practice, as Russell Schneider, Executive Director of the Council, observed, "It is not easy to observe the policy line. Sometimes the two overlap." The confidentiality provision of the proposed questionnaire was one of those areas of "overlap."

The Council distributes the Yellow Sheets to a group of about forty businessmen, quaintly known as the "Birdwatchers." The proposed Air Contaminant Emissions Survey was spotted almost immediately and the Birdwatchers notified Schneider of their concern. He wrote to BOB asking for an Advisory Committee meeting.

According to the official minutes of the meeting, held on May 23, 1968, "Industry asked if company data could be and should be released to the press. . . . Industry did not object to aggregate figures but objected to scare headlines pinpointing a particular plant as the cause of air pollution." The issue of "scare headlines" was nothing more than a red herring. What industry was really driving for was an absolute ban against public release of the information. This, of course, would severely hamper NAPCA in carrying out its legitimate functions, some of which require public disclosure of pollution sources.

Since the issue was too important and the group too large to reach an accord at one meeting, a negotiating team was appointed. Its industry roster read like "Who's Who in Pollution and Special Access to Government":

J. S. Whitaker, National Association of Manufacturers
Kenneth P. Johnson, Manufacturing Chemists Association
William F. Claire, American Paper Institute
Harold F. Elkin, American Petroleum Institute
John Coffey, U.S. Chamber of Commerce
James M. Claban, Legal Counsel to American Institute
Joseph W. Mullan, National Coal Association

The negotiators met that same afternoon, and NAPCA agreed to specify the conditions of public disclosure in greater detail. One week later, NAPCA submitted a revised draft to the BOB. The draft prohibited public disclosure of data relating to specific plants "except as may be found necessary in connection with administrative or judicial proceedings." In other words, the information would be kept confidential except during any proceedings which NAPCA must, by law, initiate. The draft also stated that the information would be given to appropriate state and interstate control officials in order to assist them in fulfilling their responsibilities. Finally, the draft pointed out that Section 211 of the Air Quality Act required HEW to submit a report to Congress evaluating the need for national emission controls. According to Congressional mandate, the report must include "examples of specific plants, their location, and the contaminant or contaminants which, due to the amount or nature of emissions from such facilities, constitute a danger to public health and welfare." NAPCA hoped to use the data from the Air Contaminant Emissions Survey to satisfy this requirement. But the NAPCA draft made it clear that disclosure of the data would be made to Congress "only with the specific written consent of any plant involved." These were enormous concessions by the agency, but it had little choice except to plead for cooperation, since it had no mandatory authority to find out who was polluting the air and in what quantities. Yet the captains of industry were still displeased.

Messrs. Whitaker and Trussell of the National Association of Manufacturers wrote to BOB, complaining that the draft contained too many exceptions to the rule of confidentiality. They proposed language which would have effectively banned any public disclosure. Coffey, of the Chamber of Commerce, registered his opposition and closed his letter with a warning: "Unacceptable confidentiality provisions . . . will seriously curtail response to this survey, and will impede . . . [NAPCA] in its efforts to meet its responsibility under the Clean Air Act.

During the next several months (five months had passed since the survey had been submitted to BOB for approval), NAPCA was to offer several more revised drafts. Both sides had by this time been given a full opportunity to make their cases, and the decision was now nominally in the hands of Edward T. Crowder, BOB's Clearance Officer. Although it is easy to lose perspective on this point, it is important to remember that the decisions on forms clearance are governmental, made by BOB. Industry input is supposed to be completely advisory; the law gives industry no veto power over questionnaires. Yet, in the face of adamant industry resistance, Crowder decided not to decide. Although BOB had promised an answer by the end of 1968, the new year came without a decision.

In January, 1969, before any decision had been reached, a new wrinkle developed. The Texas Air Control Board sent its own emissions questionnaire to local industry. The cover letter indicated that the information had been requested by the Secretary of HEW. Texas businessmen were outraged, and letters of complaint were forwarded to the Advisory Committee on Federal Reports. The Advisory Committee, in turn, passed the correspondence on to BOB and NAPCA, but not before the authors' names and companies had been expunged. One "anonymous" executive wrote: "I surmise that HEW has been denied the *privilege* of sending out a questionnaire [directly] by the Bureau of the Budget, so that [it is] now making an end run by asking the state agencies to get this information." [Emphasis added.] Another nameless corporate official was quite candid in his protest:

> We have been at peace with our neighbors as regards nuisance [lawsuits] . . . and what pollution we have is almost nil as compared with local industry in general. It is regretful that we must at this time "kick the sleeping dog" or open "Pandora's Box," as the case may be. To give the Texas Air Control Board the factual information they request means a frank, full appraisal of the air pollution characteristics of our operation. [Emphasis added.]

Heaven forbid that someone outside of industry should have a frank, full appraisal of industrial air pollution. It might lead to nasty lawsuits or even a public outcry for intensified enforcement of the laws.

These complaints were forwarded to NAPCA, which apologized for the zealousness of the Texas Air Control Board. NAPCA explained that it had been hampered by the lack of information resulting from the delay of the questionnaire and had asked the states to supply whatever information was available. But it had never suggested, NAPCA hastened to add, that the states make an "end run" around BOB and the Advisory Committee by sending out their own questionnaires. BOB accepted NAPCA's humble explanation, but continued to do nothing.

On February 19, 1969, NAPCA submitted its final proposal. The agency promised to write the national emissions standards report by culling the specific examples required by law from public records, totally ignoring the information contained in the Air Contaminant Survey. In the face of this major concession, BOB cleared the form five days later.

In all, BOB and industry held up clearance of the form for eleven months. Forms which industry favors generally slide through in a fraction of that time. The application form used by industry to obtain investment tax credits on air pollution control equipment took only ten weeks to process.

The Task Force encountered firsthand opportunities to learn the depth of corporate determination to keep specific facts about air pollution a dark secret. Trade associations were particularly happy to supply armloads of slick-paper brochures containing aggregate figures on the extent of a pollution problem within an industry and the amount of money the entire industry claimed to be spending for air pollution abatement. But nothing causes a corporate executive to reach for his Miltowns more quickly than questions concerning his company's air pollution problem and what he's doing about it.

By the end of the summer of 1969 the Task Force was hardened by experience to expect this attitude in every corporate office. But nothing that occurred then quite prepared one Task Force member for his confrontation with the Public Relations Office of the Lubrizol Corporation, a Cleveland-based chemical additives manufacturer. That fall, the Task Force received a letter from a housewife in Wycliffe, Ohio, a suburb of Cleveland. The writer complained of the noxious odors from the local Lubrizol plant. A breakdown in the plant's equipment had caused an odor problem in August, 1968, which everyone, including the company, agreed was serious. However, company spokesmen and state authorities assured residents that the incident was a singular one and would not occur again. The writer of the letter insisted that her nose told her differently, that the problem was a continuing one. It was serious enough for 1000 residents to sign a petition complaining about the constant fumes. A Task Force member, back at school in Cleveland, spoke with Harry Jackson, Public Relations Officer for Lubrizol. The first curious incident occurred when the student called to make an appointment with Jackson:

TASK FORCE MEMBER: *I'd like to talk with you about Lubrizol's problem and program for air pollution control.*

MR. JACKSON: *What are you going to do with the information?*

TASK FORCE MEMBER: *Well, I worked for Ralph Nader last summer on air pollution. We've heard a lot about Lubrizol and its pollution.*

MR. JACKSON: *Do you work for Nader now?*

TASK FORCE MEMBER: *No, I'm in medical school at Case Western Reserve.*

MR. JACKSON: *Oh, we give a lot of money to that school.*

Unimpressed by Lubrizol's beneficence toward his school and thinking it irrelevant to his inquiry, the Task Force member pushed on and was able to secure an appointment with Jackson. At the interview, Mr. Jackson was (in his own way) quite helpful:

TASK FORCE MEMBER: *Do you mind if I take notes?*

MR. JACKSON: *No, I don't mind because I'm not going to tell you anything.*

TASK FORCE MEMBER: *[Taking notes] Why is that?*

MR. JACKSON: *That doesn't make any difference.*

TASK FORCE MEMBER: *Of course, I have no legal authority, but you are the public relations man, aren't you?*

MR. JACKSON: *Because you have no authority to ask these questions.*

TASK FORCE MEMBER: *Why won't you answer any questions? Is this the company's official policy?*

MR. JACKSON: *Yes, I've talked this over with our officials and our legal counsel, and we've decided that we don't have to answer your questions. You don't have the right to ask us these questions.*

TASK FORCE MEMBER: *Well, I wanted to talk to you about the episode in August, 1968, which resulted in a breakdown of your plant's equipment.*

MR. JACKSON: *Lubrizol made an official statement to the press. Have you seen it?*

TASK FORCE MEMBER: *No, could you tell me what it said?*

MR. JACKSON: *I'm not at liberty to say.*

TASK FORCE MEMBER: *But if it's a press release, it's obviously public information.*

MR. JACKSON: *You'll have to find it yourself. I'm not at liberty to tell you anything.*

Undaunted by the Lubrizol experience, the Task Force attempted to cut through the curtain of aggregate statistics by writing to about 200 major corporations. Each was sent a detailed questionnaire asking for information concerning the kinds and quantities of pollutants emitted, the amount of money spent for pollution control and research, and other questions directly relevant to an assessment of the individual corporation's efforts. Frankly, the Task Force expected a poor response and it was not surprised. With few exceptions, most of the companies either failed to acknowledge receipt of the questionnaire or sent terse notes explaining that they would not cooperate. Some responses were evasive:

This will advise you that our management is unwilling to incur the expense of responding to detailed questionnaires from well-meaning individuals or groups who act independently or in an unofficial capacity.

The Task Force takes the position that it has an absolute right to the information it requested by virtue of its special status—every member of the Task Force is a breathing citizen of the United States.

By far the most common response was a referral to the industry trade association. Trade associations specialize in compiling aggregate data to cover up the misdeeds of individual corporate members. Typically, the trade association compiles industrywide data of emissions, research and control expenditures, and releases this information for use by the public relations departments of the member companies. Data on individual companies or plants are kept in strictest confidence. "The thing you want to avoid," the Task Force was told by L. P. Haxby, environmental coordinator for Shell Oil Company, "is getting involved in a numbers game. You see, if we were to release that kind of information [on individual plants], someone might say that the fellow down the street is doing better than us. But the other fellow's problems might be completely different." The numbers game to which Haxby referred might, in a happier time, have been called competition. Haxby and his counterparts in other polluting industries call it "comparing apples and oranges," a favorite image of the lobbyists' community. The purpose of that characterization is to avoid the public pressures that might be engendered by comparing one company's performance with that of another. Such pressures would tend inevitably to drive an entire industry in the direction of its most responsible member, and could lead to uniform pollution control standards, the *bête noire* of American industry.

Subtle, behind the scenes pressure sometimes gives way to outright prevarication as a ploy to forestall governmental control of pollution. Two Chicago companies—the giant United States Steel Company and Republic Steel Company—have used this method to great advantage, keeping city officials at bay for the last seven years.

IN 1963, Chicago's air pollution ordinance was amended to cover the operations of the steel companies. The original law had been enacted in 1958, but the steel makers were conveniently exempted at that time. Steel making is, after all, Chicago's largest single industry, and way back in 1958 no one was very anxious to disturb the industry. Exemption from the law was justified in part on the ground that control technology was not available, even though devices for controlling smoke and particulates (the pollutants covered by the ordinance) had been around for at least fifty years. The companies promised to work on the problem.

By 1963 it became clear that nothing had been done voluntarily to reduce emissions, and Chicago's city fathers decided it was time to bring the steel companies within the provisions of the law. However, the companies (at least U.S. Steel and Republic Steel) were not quite ready to be brought in.

Hearings were held before the City Department of Air Pollution within a few months after the law became effective. The maximum emissions permitted by the ordinance were such that the companies were in violation on the day the law became applicable to them. U.S. Steel, Republic Steel, Wisconsin Steel, and Interlake Steel (representing 90 per cent of the iron and steel-making capacity of Chicago) pleaded for more time. It would take eight years, they told authorities, before their plants could comply with the law. Consequently, they sought a variance until they could install the necessary control equipment. As evidence of their good faith, the companies proposed a year by year timetable which promised regular progress until 1971, when 100 per cent of the smoke- and dust-producing facilities would be fitted with proper control equipment. To sew it up, there was talk that the companies would spend as much as fifty million dollars to bring their facilities into compliance with the law.

The steel makers got their way, and an eight-year variance from the law was granted. The Department of Air Pollution's order, as is characteristic in such cases, recited the economic importance of the steel industry to the city—"Over 100,000 persons are directly dependent upon these companies for their livelihood . . . [s]teel operations . . . add nearly three billion dollars to the Chicagoland economy" —as though the alternative was that the scores of furnaces, hearths, and sintering machines would have to be shut down, disassembled, and moved out of "Chicagoland." The order incorporated the companies' eight-year timetable and predicted that between 1963 and 1971 potential emissions would be reduced by over 58,000 tons of dust per year.

The companies dutifully submitted joint reports to the Department each year. The reports glowed with optimism and inevitably assured the Department that the timetable was being complied with to the letter. By January, 1969, emissions were to have been reduced by 85 per cent of the 1963 figure. But in March, 1969, Peter J. Loquercio, assistant director in charge of engineering services, told the *Chicago Daily News*: "I can't tell a woman on the South Side who hangs her wash that they have controlled 85 per cent of their smoke pollution. . . . It looks and smells like an outhouse out there."

How could South Chicago's ambient air be compared to an outhouse when the companies had reported inexorable progress toward clean air, year after year? The Department's engineers had an involved and circumspect way of explaining the contradiction. But what they said, in so many words, was that U.S. Steel and Republic Steel had lied. The companies had lied when they calculated potential emissions back in 1963, and they had lied during the intervening years when they reported progress in reducing emissions. In fact, the engineers determined that by 1969, rather than having reduced their emissions, "U.S. Steel and Republic Steel increased their total dust output by approximately 2000 tons per year each, while Wisconsin and Interlake companies have met their commitment as dictated by the agreements. . . ."

We are accustomed to hearing corporate apologists underestimate the magnitude of a company's air pollution problem. But the Chicago steel companies took a cynical new tack in 1963. They predicted their planned progress on *potential* emissions, *i.e.*, the quantity of pollution the steelmaking facilities would contribute if all equipment were in full operation. The sham lay in the fact that not all existing equipment was fully operative in 1963. The companies did not mention this crucial fact to the Department when they sought and received an eight-year variance from the law. Consequently, they took credit during the subsequent years for the reduction of emissions from facilities which were, in the words of Department engineers, "never in operation, disabled or not on stream at the outset of the program." While reporting a steady decrease based on emissions that had been eliminated before 1963 when the equipment became inoperative, U.S. Steel and Republic Steel were free to operate the remaining equipment at even higher levels and thus increase their actual emissions after 1963.

Edgar B. Speer, President of U.S. Steel, showed no embarrassment over his company's shoddy performance when, on August 3, 1969, he accepted what is billed as "the coveted Heddon Hall of Honor Award for excellence in air and water pollution abatement." The sponsors—who curiously insist that the award coincide with the apparently prestigious Fishing Tackle Manufacturers Association show—made the presentation at Chicago's Sherman Hotel, far from U.S. Steel's South Works. Speer appeared to be genuinely moved by the day's events: "Today is a 'red letter' day for my company—and for me. In accepting this award, I pledge to you that U.S. Steel will continue to do its full share in conserving our life-giving air and water resources and will continue to pioneer in finding more efficient ways of accomplishing this goal."

Speer and his counterparts in the steel industry, it would seem, have certainly found the most economical way of dealing with pollution problems. The method is uncomplicated: simply cut back on pollution control expenditures. A February, 1970, report by the National Industrial Conference Board indicates that the industry's 1969 capital appropriations for air and water pollution control dropped 56.9 per cent below the 1968 appropriation. This reduction from eighty-eight million dollars in 1968 to approximately thirty-eight million in 1969, represents a drop in pollution control investments from less than four-tenths of 1 per cent of 1968 gross revenues to something less than two-tenths of 1 per cent for 1969.

All of this raises the question why it took the city of Chicago until 1969 to realize that the steel companies were cheating on the terms of their variance. The report of the Department's engineers explains that the city had been accepting joint annual reports from the companies, and that it was not until 1969 that Departmental personnel were able to unravel the mass of aggregate figures. Thus, another standard deviance for polluters: submit to control officials aggregate data, thereby covering up inadequacies of individual performance and avoiding "harmful" competition among the conspirators in the reluctant race to clean up.

The most recent chapter of this story can be summarized from two Chicago newspaper reports:

Many have complained to the CHICAGO TRIBUNE *that when they protest against steel industry air pollution on the south side, air pollution officials say they are powerless to act against the company because they have an exemption.*

Four steel companies in the Chicago area reported to the City of Chicago yesterday that their air pollution plans are ahead of schedule.

The report, released jointly *by the four firms, said they had completed 86 per cent of an air pollution control program which began in 1963 and is expected to be finished by the end of this year. [Emphasis added.*]

The Chicago Conspiracy is another aspect of a pattern among industrial polluters. Trade associations specialize in releasing aggregate data which are designed to suggest in dollars how much an industry cares about environmental cleanup. The figures are invariably impressive. Fifty, sixty or seventy million dollars is a great deal of money—except when measured against the total resources available to the industry. For example, the February, 1970, report of the National Industrial Conference Board indicates that when air pollution control expenditures are compared to other (*i.e.,* profit making) capital expenditures, there is nothing short of contempt for the public and its environment.

RATIO OF AIR POLLUTION CONTROL EXPENDITURES TO TOTAL CAPITAL EXPENDITURES, 1968	Ratio in Per Cent
All Manufacturing	1.65
Primary iron and steel	3.02
Primary nonferrous metals	2.18
Electrical machinery and equipment	0.32
Machinery, except electrical	0.83
Motor vehicles and equipment	1.92
Transportation equipment, excluding motor vehicles	0.98
Stone, clay, and glass	1.42
Fabricated metal products	0.73
Instruments and photographic equipment	0.56
Other durable goods	0.77
Food and beverages	0.65
Textile mill products	0.85
Paper and allied products	2.73
Chemical and allied products	1.41
Petroleum and coal products	2.16
Rubber products	0.31

The large numbers game is even more clearly fraudulent when air and water capital appropriations from an entire industry are compared with its gross revenues:

Industry Group	I Gross Revenue* (billions of dollars)	II 1969 Air and Water Pollution Control Ap- propria- tions** (billions of dollars)	Column II as Per Cent of Column I
Primary iron and steel	$27.7	$.038	.14
Primary nonferrous metals	21.4	.015	.017
Electrical machinery and equipment	67.0	.010	.01
Motor vehicles and equipment	59.9	.018	.03
Transportation equipment, excluding motor vehicles	32.5	.003	.009
Stone, clay, and glass products	17.4	.014	.08
Fabricated metal products	35.2	.005	.01
Textile mill products	21.8	.004	.02
Paper and allied products	20.6	.051	.25
Chemical and allied products	55.5	.047	.08
Petroleum refining	58.8	.012	.02
Rubber products	16.9	.023	.14

*Quarterly Financial Report For Manufacturing Corporations, *Federal Trade Commission—Securities Exchange Commission.*

**Conference Board RECORD, *February, 1970, National Industrial Conference Board.*

In the light of such niggardly investments, industry complaints that control technology is unavailable seem less than plausible. The fact is that industry is unwilling to spend the relatively modest amounts of money which could bring effective controls. Professor Benjamin Linsky, Professor of Sanitary Engineering at West Virginia University and past president of the National Air Pollution Control Association, said in 1965: "The costs to an industry [of control equipment] rarely amount to as much as 1 percent to the cost of their products." But even such modest expenditures may reduce profits—or so industry feels—and therefore they don't get made.

Occasionally insiders will testify to the depth of industry recalcitrance against clean-up technology. On October 27, 1969, Milton Barlow, Chief Steward for the St. Joseph's Lead Company plant in Herculaneum, Missouri (discussed earlier on page 70), testified before the Senate Subcommittee on Air and Water Pollution. Barlow, shielded by the protection of his union, a luxury most engineers and scientists do not enjoy, told the Subcommittee in straightforward language:

My company will only make changes when it is forced to make changes. Health, community health plays second fiddle to increased production and bigger profits. For example, a State inspector announces the date of his inspection tour to the company, and it is very easy to cut production that day, cutting back the furnaces; there is no risk of a furnace blowhole to pollute the air. After his trip, the inspector writes a good report and then there is business as usual.

The message was clearly brought home to the Task Force when we interviewed several persons ostensibly charged with "environmental control" for the Atlantic-Richfield Oil Company. One Task Force member remarked that oil refineries are not sweet-smelling things. "Some of us like the smell," said environmental coordinator William Halladay, with a smile, "it smells like money." We got the impression that we had just heard a standard industry joke.

Pollution must stop smelling like money; it must smell like disintegrating profits before industry will act. A manufacturer of pollution control equipment told the Task Force:

They [industry] should have a conscience, but they don't. The important thing is to get the Congressmen to know the truth. Our Congress doesn't know the truth. The only way that you or anyone else will get this thing together is for the government to say clean up or close down.

Despite industry's reluctance to invest heavily in abatement equipment, manufacturers of pollution control devices see the beginning of a boom era. Many are counting on increased governmental assistance to polluters, either in the form of grants or special tax treatment, to kick off the new gold rush. Investors have come to the same conclusion and pollution control companies are the new glamor stocks on Wall Street. In view of the generally ineffectual controls throughout the nation, one wonders whether the present optimism is justified. But, in any event, if the day should come when these manufacturers have a viable market, it appears very likely that the established giants will be prepared to step in to control the market.

The irony of this possibility lies in the fact that many of the giants preparing to move into the environmental control field are themselves major polluters. This is especially true of the manufacturers of chemicals and allied products, which have a corner on a great store of the necessary knowledge and expertise. (Most pollution controls are, of course, essentially chemical processes.) Dupont and Allied Chemical, for instance, both of whom are polluters, each manufacture some pollution control equipment. But none are in the business with quite the commitment of Monsanto Chemical Company. Monsanto recently established a new division, Enviro-Chem Systems, Incorporated, to sell its new "Cat-Ox" system. Cat-Ox is promoted as a sulfur dioxide "control that works." Monsanto, like many of its smaller brethren in this new business, has complained publicly that it is unable to sell its new process. In October, 1969, Dr. Joseph G. Stites, manager of Monsanto's Air Pollution Control Department, appeared before the Senate Subcommittee on Air and Water Pollution in order to tout his company's process. Senator Thomas F. Eagleton of Missouri was unwilling to let Stites turn the hearing into a promotional campaign:

SENATOR EAGLETON: . . . *your company, Monsanto, is next only to Union Electric in terms of its use of high-sulfur coal in the St. Louis area. Is that right?*

DR. STITES: *Right.*

SENATOR EAGLETON: *I think specifically at the Queeny plant you burn 2,600 tons of coal of which the substantial large percentage thereof is a high-sulfur coal. Is that right?*

DR. STITES: *I am not familiar with those numbers, but we do burn coal at the Queeny plant.*

SENATOR EAGLETON: *2,600 tons of coal?*

DR. STITES: *Per week.*

SENATOR EAGLETON: *Have you been able to sell your Cat-Ox process to your own company?*

DR. STITES: *No, sir.*

SENATOR EAGLETON: *Well, you are refreshingly candid.*

DR. STITES: *The most important point is that the Cat-Ox unit is technologically designed for major sized units as each of the boilers at the Queeny plant is about the size of our pilot plant at Pennsylvania.*

SENATOR EAGLETON: *Do you think it would enhance your salesmanship if you were able to put a minipilot system on your company, Monsanto, thereby attesting to the company's belief in your product, thereby gathering research information on its effectiveness, thereby making its saleability to other industries more effective?*

DR. STITES: *That is a good question. Yes, sir. I am sure it would make my life a lot easier in selling a plant to my own company, but I think the likelihood of solving our problem in this manner is fairly low.*

Monsanto may pick up a little loose change by selling someone else its pollution control equipment, but the company is apparently unwilling to invest in its own control equipment (which it could presumably get at wholesale prices). The reason for this is clear. Despite the fact that it sells control devices, Monsanto has made the calculation that it is cheaper to continue to pollute than to expend money for control. The "calculation" has been aptly described by economist Kenneth Boulding as the "famous 'freeloading' problem. The individual interest is to go on polluting as long as the rest of society picks up the tab."

BABY FOODS: CAN YOU (AND YOUR BABY) AFFORD THEM?

Ralph Nader

From a casual glance at the baby-food section in the supermarket, you might conclude that we have the best-fed infants in all history. Look at the choices they have: Ham with Vegetables, Creamed Spinach, Squash in Butter Sauce, Dutch Apple Dessert. Real gourmet menus from the best tables, strained into those little jars that line the shelves.

While you are deciding which delicacy to feed your child, pick up a jar of baby food and read the label. You'll find that much of the content is water. It's also likely that it contains salt, sugar, and modified starch, substances that are acceptable in adult diets, but whose safety for infants is now being investigated by the Food and Drug Administration. And, in some grocery stores, you may still find baby food containing the officially banned monosodium glutamate (MSG).

Finally, you will find a price tag that is, on the average, twice as high as that of comparable fresh or canned foods—foods that can, with very little effort, be substituted for prepared baby foods.

The Center for Study of Responsive Law, which I operate in Washington, D.C., recently made a comparative pricing study in local super-

From *McCall's*, November 1970. Reprinted by permission of *McCall's* and the author.

markets and found, for example, that Gerber's applesauce (apples, sugar, and water) costs 2.4 cents per ounce, or one and a half times the price of Musselman's canned applesauce with the same ingredients. Gerber's strained sweet potatoes, containing salt, sell for 2.6 cents an ounce, or 1.37 times the price of Aunt Nellie's canned sweet potatoes, which contain no salt. Beech-Nut's strained bananas with tapioca, containing salt, sugar, and modified starch, cost 2.4 cents an ounce, or almost half again as much as fresh bananas, peeled and "destringed," selling for 1.7 cents an ounce.

Any of these less expensive fresh or canned foods can be easily mashed to a baby's satisfaction.

Our center's shopping study showed the same cost pattern in other products: Baby-food strained pears cost 1.33 times the price of fresh pears; strained carrots, 2.9 times the price of fresh carrots; creamed corn, 1.52 times the price of the canned vegetable; baby-food orange juice 2.45 times the price of canned or frozen orange juice.

Meats and vegetables with husks or pods are harder to compare; but here, too, the price of baby foods is significantly higher than that of fresh or canned foods. Baby-food junior meats cost 8 cents an ounce. Boneless round beef and canned boned chicken also cost 8 cents an ounce, with boned turkey and chicken livers slightly cheaper. But since baby-food meats generally contain about 50 percent water for the proper consistency, half the price of a jar of baby-food meat simply pays for something that runs out of your tap.

In fact, water was listed as the *major* ingredient of 31 out of 76 varieties of baby foods we examined during our shopping-comparison trip, and some of those foods (Ham with Vegetables and Macaroni, Tomato, Beef, and Bacon) were labeled "High Meat Dinner."

It is true that most women still buy prepared baby food because it is convenient and timesaving, but more and more mothers are beginning to make their own, using a blender when necessary. Not only do they save money, but their infants get more nutritious food.

One Kentucky mother wrote me recently: "I make my own baby food . . . and have for several years. It's done by putting meat or vegetables in a blender and adding liquid until it is the right consistency."

Another mother sent me a recipe for baby-food stew: "Cut up some steak or roast beef or stew meat, a carrot, an onion, and some potato. Or use beef or calf liver for the meat. Steam for a few minutes until soft, then purée the stew in a blender, pour into individual cube molds, and freeze. Use one cube per meal as needed—just heat and serve."

Commercial baby food goes back to the early years of the century, when a now-obscure brand sold poorly in drugstores for 35 cents a jar. Then, in 1928, Gerber Products Company began marketing baby food in grocery stores and opened up an enormously profitable market. Heinz and Beech-Nut entered the field a few years later, though Gerber remains the leading baby-food manufacturer, with about 60 percent of the American market. (It also sells strained lamb brains and macaroni in Australia and fish products in Japan.) Today baby food is a $400-million-a-year business and the second most profitable of the food industries (citrus products rate number one): about 1.5 billion pounds of baby food are consumed each year.

When the cost of vegetables and meats began to rise after World War II, baby-food producers began to reduce the amounts of these wholesome ingredients by adding increased amounts of less expensive sugar and starch. The result was an unfortunate change in flavor that was subsequently corrected by adding salt and flavor enhancers like MSG.

Such additives, however, may have adverse effects. Scientists outside the industry have pointed to evidence that:

1. Salt may increase chances of high blood pressure later in life.
2. Sugar can create cavities, increase the chance of arteriosclerosis in later life, and produce unduly fat babies (who become unduly fat adults).
3. Modified starch is not completely broken down by the baby's saliva, thus adding to the burden on the rest of the digestive tract.
4. MSG produces brain and eye damage in infant rats.

There is no reason a mother should be alarmed to learn that salt is being added to her baby's food. After all, salt makes the food taste better to her and, she imagines, to the baby. She probably doesn't know that babies have no taste discrimination between salted and unsalted food, as Dr. Samuel Foman, of the University of Iowa, demonstrated in controlled tests on infants up to seven months old.

Nor is the mother likely to know how much salt is added—that baby-food meats contain 5 to 6 times as much salt as fresh table meats and that baby-food vegetables have 6 to 60 times as much salt as fresh vegetables. These are the findings of Dr. Lewis K. Dahl, chief of staff of the Medical Research Center, Brookhaven National

Laboratory, who suggests that this high intake of salt in early life might well be a contributing factor in the development of hypertension in adults. Hypertensive diseases kill about 60,000 Americans a year.

In laboratory tests on rats, Dr. Dahl discovered that an increase in salt intake can result in a rise in blood pressure. He contends that the hypertension that appears in rats "bears a striking resemblance to the common hypertension that afflicts man and runs from benign, slowly evolving elevation in pressure to high and rapidly fatal hypertension." In people, Dr. Dahl adds, "hypertension is beginning to show up in the teens and twenties now, where it had once generally made its appearance in the thirties and forties."

In testimony before a Senate select committee on nutrition, headed by Senator George McGovern, Dr. Dahl said he has described his studies to representatives of two leading baby-food companies and that "their reaction has been essentially that their hands are tied by the sales people. They believe that if they take salt out, the mothers would stop buying their product, and that they can't afford to take this risk, for economic reasons."

I think manufacturers should consider the risk babies may be taking.

Starch that was added as a filler to baby food when manufacturers sought to cut down their costs has also turned into a potential health problem. It was found that the starch originally added to baby food could be broken down by the baby's saliva. When a jar of food was not completely used during one feeding, the saliva that had found its way into the jar "digested" the food as it sat in the refrigerator. This caused mothers to think the food had spoiled, and they tended not to buy food that appeared to spoil easily. So the baby-food companies met this "economic risk" by coming up with a modified starch that the baby's saliva does not fully digest. The food in the jar no longer appears to spoil. But some of the modified starch may never be digested at all, passing through the baby's system without providing any nourishment.

The former chief of the Heinz Nutritional Research Laboratory, Dr. Thomas A. Anderson, tried to persuade the company to look for a better way of producing baby food—without the modified starch. He failed, and modified starch is still in many baby foods. In dismay, Dr. Anderson finally left the company.

Sugar in baby food is another problem, according to Dr. Jean Mayer, the President's consultant on nutrition, because it replaces real foods with "empty" calories, which are nutritionally inferior. It thus has the unfortunate effect of nullifying pediatricians' efforts to keep mothers from adding sugar to milk. In addition, children brought up on sugar-laden baby food tend to eat sweets excessively as they grow up.

Such warnings by scientists outside industry have not been enough to get salt, sugar, or modified starch out of baby foods. The controversy over MSG indicates that the industry will respond only when significant public pressure is brought to bear.

MSG, like salt, was added to many varieties of baby food to make them more tempting to mothers' tastes. In 1969, Dr. John Olney, of Washington University in St. Louis, reported that MSG *taken orally* in amounts comparable to those in commercial baby foods produced eye and brain damage in infant mice. The producers of MSG argued that years of study and use of the chemical since 1909 showed it to be completely safe. However, in reply to questioning by the Mc-Govern Senate Committee, company representatives admitted that they had never conducted tests on infant mice or any other infant animal. Because of this admission and Dr. Olney's findings, public and private pressure mounted, and last October, a year ago, baby-food companies announced the removal of MSG from their products.

Even now, however, shoppers may be able to buy in their local store jars of baby food containing MSG, and I urge them to read the labels carefully. As recently as late July, baby foods with MSG could still be found on supermarket shelves in Washington, D.C., where its potential dangers were most widely publicized.

In early August, *McCall's* talked to Dr. Robert A. Stewart, chief nutritionist and director of research for Gerber Products Company. Dr. Stewart explained: "We agreed not to manufacture baby food with MSG any more, but we didn't agree to take what we had made off the shelves or out of the warehouses. So there are still some jars with MSG on the shelves, and in the minor markets where the turnover is slow, it may take up to two years more to get rid of it. Our products are made to have a shelf life of three years. We agreed to take out MSG not because we think it is harmful—we don't—but because the public was upset." Dr. Stewart said he and his industrial-scientist colleagues do not agree that salt is a factor in hypertension or that sugar and modified starch in baby food may present health problems.

One hazard, unrelated to additives but even more disturbing, is the potential for food poisoning from jars of baby food opened, re-closed, and left on the shelf—a danger that could be avoided if the companies would use special caps that indicate whether a jar has been opened. Such caps have been designed and manufactured, and they were praised by the American Academy of Pediatrics Committee on Nutrition as long ago as 1963, yet are not currently used.

None of these hazards should continue to exist. But instead of eliminating them, baby-food companies are concentrating on building larger markets by selling fancier foods, some with less nutritional value per dollar, to an expanded age group. Heinz applesauce has been joined by another baby food—New Apple Pie—containing flour, shortening, salt, modified food starch, and vanilla. Beech-Nut's New Squash in Butter Sauce adds butter and light-brown sugar to the sugar, salt, and water in its "old" squash.

Fred Yeakey, Gerber's vice-president of marketing, explains the trend: "We know the young mother likes variety, and she's susceptible to new products."

Perhaps the industry has underestimated its consumers. An overwhelming number of the mothers interviewed by our center said they felt companies should *prove* a substance safe *before* adding it to baby food. Until the producers agree, the best course for mothers would be to avoid prepared baby foods that contain added salt, sugar, modified starches, or MSG, and to make sure the baby food they do buy comes in jars with unbroken vacuum seals.

Or it might be easier to do as some mothers are doing—make their own baby food. As Dr. Jean Mayer has said, "I don't see any point in experimenting with our kids."

THE TOILET TRAINING OF INDUSTRY: STRATEGIES FOR THE PREVENTION OF POLLUTION

Ralph Nader

The modern corporation's structure, impact, and public accountability are the central issues in any program designed to curb or forestall the contamination of air, water, and soil by industrial activity. While there are other sources of pollution, such as municipalities dumping untreated or inadequately treated sewage, industrial processes and products are the chief contributors to the long-term destruction of natural resources that each year increases the risks to human health and safety.

Moreover, through active corporate citizenship, industry could soon overcome many of the obstacles in the way of curbing non-corporate pollution. The mighty automobile industry, centered around and in Detroit, never thought it part of its role to press the city of Detroit to construct a modern sewage treatment plant. The automobile moguls, whose products, according to Department of Health, Education and Welfare data, account for fifty-five to sixty per cent of the nation's air pollution, remained silent as the city's obsolete and inadequate sewage facilities dumped the wastes of millions into the Detroit river. Obviously, local boosterism does not include such elementary acts of corporate citizenship.

From *The Progressive*, April 1970. Reprinted by permission of the author.

The toilet training of industry to keep it from further rupturing the ecosystem requires an overhaul of the internal and external levers which control corporations. There are eight areas in which policies must be changed to create the pressures needed to make corporate entities and the people who run them cease their destruction of the environment:

ONE—The conventional way of giving the public a share in private standards through a public agency. But pollution control standards set by governmental agencies can fall far short of their purported objectives unless they are adequately drafted, kept up to date, vigorously enforced, and supported by sanctions when violated. Behind the adoption of such standards, there is a long administrative process, tied to a political infrastructure. The scientific-engineering-legal community has a key independent role to play in this vital and complex administrative-political process. Almost invariably, however, its talents have been retained on behalf of those to be regulated. Whether in Washington or in state capitals around the country, the experts demonstrate greater loyalty to their employers than to their professional commitments in the public interest.

This has been the regular practice of specialists testifying in behalf of coal and uranium mining companies on the latters' environmental contamination in Appalachia and the Rocky Mountain regions. Perhaps the most egregious example of willing corporate servility was a paper entitled "We've Done the Job—What's Next?" delivered by Charles H. Heinen, Chrysler's vehicle emissions specialist at a meeting of the Society of Automotive Engineers last spring.

Heinen, whose paper bordered on technical pornography, said the auto industry had solved the vehicle pollution problem with an eighty per cent reduction of hydrocarbons and a seventy per cent reduction of carbon monoxide between the 1960 and 1970 model years. He avoided mentioning at least four other vehicle pollutants—nitrogen oxides, lead, asbestos, and rubber tire pollutants. He also failed to point out that the emissions control performance of new cars degrades after a few thousand miles, and that even when new they do not perform under traffic conditions as they do when finely tuned at a company test facility. The overall aggregate pollution from ever greater numbers of vehicles in more congested traffic patterns also escaped Heinen's company-indentured perceptions.

TWO—Sanctions against polluters are feeble and out of date, and, in any case, are rarely involved. For example, the Federal air quality act has no criminal penalties no matter how willful and enduring the violations. In New Jersey, New York, and Illinois, a seventy-one year old Federal anti-water pollution law was violated with total impunity by industry until the Justice Department moved against a few of the violators in recent months. Other violators in other states are yet to be subjected to the law's enforcement. To be effective, sanctions should come in various forms, such as non-reimbursable fines, suspensions, dechartering of corporations, required disclosure of violations in company promotional materials, and more severe criminal penalties. Sanctions, consequently, should be tailored to the seriousness and duration of the violation.

It is expressive of the anemic and nondeterrent quality of existing sanctions that offshore oil leaks contaminating beaches for months, as in Santa Barbara, brought no penalty to any official of any offending company. The major controversy in Santa Barbara was whether the company—Union Oil—or the Government or the residents would bear the cost of cleaning up the mess. And even if the company bore the costs initially, the tax laws would permit a considerable shifting of this cost onto the general taxpayer.

THREE—The existing requirements for disclosure of the extent of corporate pollution are weak and flagrantly flouted. The Federal Water Pollution and Control Administration (FWPCA) has been blocked since 1963 by industrial polluters (working with the Federal Bureau of the Budget) from obtaining information from these companies concerning the extent and location of discharges of pollutants into the nation's waterways. For three years, the National Industrial Waste Inventory has been held up by the Budget Bureau and its industry "advisers" who have a decisive policy role. Led by the steel, paper, and petroleum industries, corporate polluters have prevented the FWPCA from collecting specific information on what each company is putting into the water. Such information is of crucial importance to the effective administration of the water pollution law and the allocation of legal responsibility for violations.

Counties in California have been concealing from their citizens the identity of polluters and the amounts of pollution, using such weak, incredible arguments to support their cover-up as the companies' fear of revealing "trade secrets." California state agencies have refused to disclose pesticide application data to representatives of orchard workers being gradually poisoned by the chemicals. Once again the trade secret rationale was employed.

The real reason for secrecy is that disclosure of such information would raise public questions about why government agencies have not been doing their jobs—and would facilitate legal action by injured persons against the polluters. What must be made clear to both corporate and public officials is that no one has the right to a trade secret in lethality.

Massive and meticulous "fish bowl" disclosure requirements are imperative if citizens are to be alerted, at the earliest possible moment, to the flow of silent violence assaulting their health and safety, and that of unborn generations as well. This diclosure pattern, once established, must not lapse into a conspiracy between private and public officials, a conspiracy of silence against citizens and the public interest. A good place to start with such company-by-company disclosure is in the corporation's annual report, which now reveals only financial profits or losses, it should also reveal the social costs of pollution by composition and tonnage.

FOUR—Corporate investment in research and development of pollution controls is no longer a luxury to be left to the decision or initiative of a few company officers. Rather, such research and development must be required by law to include reinvestment of profits, the amount depending on the volume of pollution inflicted on the public. For example, in 1969 General Motors grossed $24 billion, yet last year spent less than $15 million on vehicle and plant pollution research and development, although its products and plants contribute some thirty-five per cent of the nation's air pollution by tonnage. A formula proportional to the size of a company and its pollution could be devised as law, with required periodic reporting of the progress of the company's research and its uses. A parallel governmental research and development program aimed at developing pollution-free product prototypes suitable for mass production, and a Federal procurement policy favoring the purchase of less-polluting products, are essential external impacts.

FIVE—Attention must be paid to the internal climate for free expression and due process within the corporate sturcture. Again and again, the internal discipline of the corporate autocracy represses the civic and professional spirit of employes who have every right to speak out or blow the whistle on their company after they have tried in vain, working from the inside, to bring about changes that will end pollution practices. Professional employes—scientists, engineers, physicians—have fewer due process safeguards than the blue collar workers in the same company protected by their union contract.

When Edward Gregory, a Fisher Body plant inspector for General Motors in St. Louis, publicly spoke out in 1966 on inadequate welding that exposed Chevrolet passengers to exhaust leakage, the company ignored him for a few years, but eventually recalled more than two million cars for correction. GM knew better than to fire Gregory, a member of the United Auto Workers.

In contrast, scientists and engineers employed by corporations privately tell me of their reluctance to speak out—within their companies or outside them—about hazardous products. This explains why the technical elites are rarely in the vanguard of public concern over corporate contamination. Demotion, ostracism, dismissal are some of the corporate sanctions against which there is little or no recourse by the professional employe. A new corporate constitutionalism is needed, guaranteeing employes' due process rights against arbitrary reprisals, but its precise forms require the collection of data and extensive study. Here is a major challenge to which college faculty and students can respond on the campus and in field work.

Six—The corporate shareholder can act, as he rarely does, as a prod and lever for jolting corporate leaders out of their lethargy. The law and the lawyers have rigged the legal system to muffle the voice of shareholders, particularly those concerned with the broader social costs of corporate enterprise. However, for socially conscious and determined stockholders there are many functions that can be performed to help protect the public (including themselves) from industrial pollution.

Shareholders must learn to take full advantage of such corporate practices as cumulative voting, which permits the "single-shot" casting of all of a shareholder's ballots for one member of the board of directors. Delegations of stockholders can give visibility to the issues by lobbying against their company's ill-advised policies in many forums apart from the annual meeting—legislative hearings, agency proceedings, town meetings, and the news media, for example. These delegations will be in a position to expose company officers to public judgment, something from which executives now seem so insulated in their daily corporate activities.

Seven—Natural, though perhaps unexercised, countervailing forces in the private sector can be highly influential incentives for change. For example, the United Auto Workers have announced that pollution will be an issue in the collective bargaining process with automobile company management this year; the union hopes to secure for workers the right not to work in polluting activities, or in a polluted environment. Insurance companies could become advocates for loss prevention in the environmental field when confronted with policyholder, shareholder, and citizen demonstrative action. Through their political influence, their rating function in evaluating risks and setting premium charges, and their research and development capability, insurance companies could exert a key countervailing stress on polluters. Whether they do or not will first depend on citizen groups to whip them into action.

EIGHT—Environmental lawsuits, long blocked by a conservative judiciary and an inflexible juidicial system, now seem to be coming into their own—a classic example of how heightened public expectations, demands, and the availability of facts shape broader applications of ancient legal principles. Environmental pollution is environmental violence—to human beings and to property. The common law has long recognized such violence against the person as actionable or enjoinable. What has been lacking is sufficient evidence of harm and avoidability to persuade judges that such hitherto invisible long-range harm outweighed the economic benefits of the particular plant activity in the community.

It now appears that such lawsuits will gain greater acceptance, especially as more evidence and more willing lawyers combine to breathe contemporary reality into long-standing legal principles. An amendment to the U.S. Constitution providing citizens with basic rights to a clean environment has been proposed; similar amendments to state constitutions are being offered. Such generic provisions can only further the judicial acceptance of environmental lawsuits. Imaginative and bold legal advocacy is needed here. The *forced consumption* of industrial pollutants by 200 million Americans must lead to a recognition of legal rights in environmental control such as that which developed with civil rights for racial minorities over the last two decades.

Three additional points deserve the attention of concerned citizens:

First, a major corporate strategy in combating antipollution measures is to engage workers on the company side by leading them to believe that such measures would threaten their livelihood. This kind of industrial extortion in a community—especially a company town—has worked before and will again unless citizens anticipate and confront it squarely.

Second, both industry spokesmen and their governmental allies (such as the President's Science Adviser, Lee DuBridge) insist that consumers will have to pay the price of pollution control. While this point of view may be an unintended manifestation of the economy's administered price structure, it cannot go unchallenged. Pollution control must not become another lever to lift up excess profits and fuel the fires of inflation. The costs of pollution control technology should come from corporate profits which have been enhanced by the use of the public's environment as industry's private sewer. The sooner industry realizes that it must bear the costs of cleanups, the more likely it will be to employ the quickest and most most efficient techniques.

Finally, those who believe deeply in a humane ecology must act in accordance with their beliefs. They must so order their consumption and disposal habits that they can, in good conscience, preach what they actually practice. In brief, they must exercise a personal discipline as they advocate the discipline of governments and corporations.

The battle of the environmentalists is to preserve the physiological integrity of people by preserving the natural integrity of land, air, and water. The planet earth is a seamless structure with a thin slice of sustaining air, water, and soil that supports almost four billion people. This thin slice belongs to all of us, and we use it and hold it in trust for future earthlings. Here we must take our stand.

THE REGULATORY- INDUSTRIAL COMPLEX

The regulatory agencies and other government bodies charged with protecting the public from corporate greed and irresponsibility—the Federal Trade Commission, the Food and Drug Administration, the Interstate Commerce Commission, the Federal Communications Commission, the Atomic Energy Commission, and others—supposedly are committed to serve the public interest. In truth, these governmental guardians are wedded to the business interests they should regulate. The Interstate Commerce Commission caters to the railroads, the bus lines, and the trucking industry. The Food and Drug Administration is a shameful handmaiden to a food industry that pollutes our food supply with thousands of dangerous and untested additives and to pharmaceutical companies which sell useless and/or harmful drugs. The Department of the Interior serves the oil and gas industries at costs to consumers of billions of dollars every year. The Department of Agriculture, as Robert Sherrill, Washington correspondent for *Nation* magazine, reports in his article "The Real Villains," has been "openly shilling for the agri-chemical industry" by failing to curtail the use of such deadly and crippling herbicides as mercury.

The question is not one of outright corruption, the under-the-table bribe (though in some cases that might not be ruled out). The problem is one of "institutional corruption," a sharing of interests which perverts the regulators' proper role—a kind of "what's good for General Motors is good for the country" philosophy. For example, in amazing candor before a Congressional committee, a former general counsel for the FDA admitted that one reason the cancer-causing additive cyclamate was allowed to remain in canned goods for several months was that the discovery of its danger had come at an inopportune time for California fruit growers: the canning season had just begun. Government regulators, many of them intending to join later the industry they regulate, tend to become identified with the economic interests of an industry, sometimes to the extent that their actions directly contradict their vows of public responsibility. This kind of corruption—of shortsightedness, weakness, and a misconception of the government's responsibility to the consumer—is more serious and more difficult to document and correct than outright payoffs. Bribery can be spotted and corrected more easily than myopia, timidity, and surrender.

Industry, with its battalions of Washington lobbyists, lawyers, and representatives, including trade associations, cultivates the feeling of mutuality of interests between itself and government in any number of ways with great success. And industry is happy with the established relationships. When the first critical studies of regulatory agencies done by the Center for the Study of Responsive Law were released, the most vitriolic replies came not from the agencies (the Federal Trade Commission, the Food and Drug Administration, and the Interstate Commerce Commission), but from the industries involved.

Industry pressures are well organized. Powerful trade associations and high-powered, well-paid Washington lawyers bring their considerable influence to bear through an assortment of quasi-legal methods to persuade officials to favor their clients. Industry, directly or indirectly, finances campaigns of elected officials, hires lawyers to circumvent or endlessly delay law enforcement, pays academic consultants who often testify before Congress in support of industry views, finances professional lobbyists to wine and dine officials and their staffs, obtains industry advisory committees to help guide official decisions and flood a tiny group of overburdened staff with their materials, arranges the appointment of industry representatives to jobs in government and offers lucrative industry jobs to officials who wish to leave government. This constant interchange of personnel between industry and government is a vexing problem as Robert Fellmeth, in charge of the Center's investigation of the FTC, discusses in the introductory article of this section. Even anticipation of a move into industry can be corrupting, in the form of "a deferred bribe."

In "The Regulatory-Industrial Complex," an excerpt of a chapter from the book *With Justice for Some,* Fellmeth explains in detail how industry builds a liaison with government officials through informal contacts, wining and dining, wheeling and dealing, and the promise of high posts in industry, and how that liaison creates fear in both upper and lower level bureaucrats. Such fears, as Fellmeth relates, led to some bizarre actions by FTC officials when confronted with a student task force investigating the agency. The students finally were locked out by former FTC chairman, Paul Rand Dixon, and denied information even about the organizational structure of the agency.

Vic Reinemer, executive secretary to Senator Lee Metcalf of Montana and coauthor with the Senator of the book *Overcharge,* expands one of Fellmeth's themes by delving into the actions of those industry "advisory committees" which are virtually "another branch of government" working behind the scenes to make policy, weaken regulations and undercut consumer interests. In the final piece of this section Robert Sherrill relates a case history of how one government guardian, the Pesticides Regulations Division of the Department of Agriculture failed to protect the public from corporate greed and carelessness. Sherrill suggests, as a useful reform, a procedure to bring criminal penalities for negligence against the hierarchy of entire government agencies which refuse to perform their duties.

Fellmeth also details twelve needed reforms for the regulatory-industrial complex. One of the most important is guaranteeing consumer advocacy to counterbalance the pressures from industry. Regulatory agencies can be reformed through such pressures. The FTC has become a much tougher agency as a result of a barrage of public criticism and constant pressures from consumer advocates: witness their recent demands for back-up data to support advertising claims as we requested in our petition. (See "Claims Without Substance." Recently FTC Commissioner Mary Gardiner Jones, when asked why the FTC seemed suddenly revived, attributed its new strength to "the criticism from consumer advocates."

THE REGULATORY-INDUSTRIAL COMPLEX

Robert C. Fellmeth

What is essentially happening to America is the collusion of the two great forces in our society: government and industry. The removal of any mutual check results in a single monolithic power bloc, behind which internal secrecy and vigorous public relations can cloak corruption and favoritism, incompetence and failure.

I. THE EMERGING REGULATORY INDUSTRIAL COMPLEX: BUILDING THE LIAISON

The existence of permanent representatives of industry in Washington, a political advantage the general public does not possess, has helped cause the corporate acculturation of Washington agencies by the industries they supposedly regulate. Most important decisions are made in the middle levels of the bureaucracy; it is at this stage that policy is the most malleable, and it is at this stage that industry has both formal and informal input.

A. INFORMAL CONTACT

Most agencies stay in constant informal contact with industry leaders and lobbyists. Thousands of letters of complaint from consumers alleging fraud or pollution lead agencies into secret conference with industry executives, who then help draft new rules which invariably meet only the agency's public relations needs. The consumer has the opportunity to propose amendments—but only at the public hearing stage, when policy is fairly hardened. Very few, if any, agencies contact consumers, small businessmen, or workers on any ad hoc basis when policy is in the formative stage.

An important part of informal influence is the entertaining of agency personnel by their regulated industries. File cards are kept by industry on most key officials, noting birthdays of sons and daughters, anniversaries, hobbies, favorite foods, and more. Consequently, officials are subject to a constant barrage of soft-sell gifts and favors. With most of these practices, it is not the monetary value that is designed or expected to influence the recipient; it is their cumulative impact—that people in a particular industry care about and like that official.

The extent of this process is documented in the Nader Reports from the summer of 1969. For example, the eleven Interstate Commerce commissioners have taken approximately 220 *trips* during the past 2½ years. One commissioner has publicly estimated that 25 percent of the expenses are borne by industry with the rest being borne by government. The chance to visit the home state at government expense because of industry invitation is an example of this process. The recent chairman of the ICC, for example, has visited West Virginia (her home state) some nineteen times in the past 2½ years, at government and industry expense, due mostly to industry "invitations." More recently, a high ICC official, Neil Garson, was obliged to resign after admitting that he had falsified some records, collecting government expense money and actually traveling at industry expense. Ironically, Mr. Garson was widely acknowledged as the most honest official in that agency.

B. FORMAL ADVISORY GROUPS

Industry contact directly or through the thousands of highly paid lobbyists is given formal status at the malleable stage of agency policy-making through a second aspect of the government—the "advisory committee." Most agencies have many such "committees," unknown to the public, which meet and express opinions about prospective decisions. The ICC, for example, has *seventeen* such bodies. Agencies rarely if ever include consumers or consumer representatives (e.g., from Consumer's Union), or small businessmen, workers, or academicians. They are universally dominated by large corporate and trade association officers.

C. PUBLIC LOBBYING

Apart from these expenditures for trade association financing and for theoretically illegal campaign contributions to elected officials, the public is forced to pay for yet a third aspect of the liaison—its own persuasion through public lobbying. We are treated to astronaut Wally Schirra arguing at great expense over nationwide television and radio for "equitable regulation" for America's "great" railroads. These expenses are not clearly separated from the "increased costs" the railroads have claimed as the basis for some five general and massive rate increases in the past three years. Despite their monopoly power, a complete lack of regulatory review guarantees railroad success.

D. JOB INTERCHANGE

A fourth and critical aspect of the regulatory-industrial liaison is job interchange. Many agencies and departments are substantially comprised of former employees of the industry regulated, with close ties resulting. Conversely, attorneys view agency employment as little more than an opportunity to learn the trade for later industry practice. In fact, high officials who are often otherwise unqualified for executive positions with industry are admittedly offered such employment with industry while still in government. And indeed, over one-half of the former commissioners of the Federal Communications Commission who have left in recent years are now high executives in the communications industry. Over fifty Food and Drug Administration officials have left the agency for high posts in the food industry in recent years.

This process of the "deferred bribe" has become the normal and accepted way of maximizing the other mechanisms of influence. All but two of the commissioners leaving the Interstate Commerce Commission in the past decade (ten of twelve) have gone into the transportation industry directly, or have become "ICC Practitioners," lawyering for the industry. This job interchange process reinforces the informal influence effect in two ways: those who have served with agency or industry usually maintain close personal ties with old friends; and those still in the agency have their present views shaped by anticipated, future interests.

E. APPOINTMENTS AND HIRING

The fifth aspect is the appointment and hiring process. Any potential congressional action to control or break into the regulatory-industrial combination is negated by both pork-barreling and campaign contributions. Industry, through a variety of devices, invests millions into the campaigns of those key congressmen able to influence agency appropriations or appointments. The result, unsurprisingly, is the appointment of political and corporate hacks who are completely unqualified and can be easily overwhelmed by industry domination of technical information flow. Only four of the current eleven Interstate Commerce commissioners have had any experience with law, economics, antitrust, rate regulation, or transportation. Two of these four are from the regulated industry. All eleven had political "sponsors" and most have a long record of party work.

All of these processes cause a convergence of regulatory and corporate views. Lobbyists spend man-years convincing their agencies of the need for implementation of industry determined policy. The natural competition between specific firms is obviated by an increasingly concentrated oligopolistic structure of American industry and by the existence of hundreds of "trade associations," which lobby on behalf of firms, often on a collusive basis. Since these lobbying expenses are deductible, and since they are trivial compared to the millions of dollars at issue in governmental decision-making, industry spends lavishly in such efforts. Countervailing arguments from the diffuse public concerning indirect economic or environmental effects are lacking. The consumer is unorganized, unfinanced, and unrepresented. And agency personnel, even if they do not come from industry or expect to go to it, come to adopt the views which are daily put before them. The result is both a bias toward corporate rather than public interest policies—as a few thousand industrialists control our national politics and priorities.

II. SECRECY AND PUBLIC RELATIONS: HIDING THE LIAISON

Early in the summer of 1968, a citizen researcher working for Ralph Nader walked into the director of personnel's office at the Federal Trade Commission (FTC) and asked for the agency's organization chart. He was told that no such chart existed. Later, when a chart called the "Budget Control Records" was discovered, which contained the nonexistent information, the director nevertheless refused to release or disclose it on the grounds that the document was an "internal memoranda" and hence exempt from disclosure under the Freedom of Information Act. When asked for the legal basis for this extraordinary interpretation of the act, the citizen was told that names and positions were (of course) public information, but the *salaries* of the employees, which were listed on the far right-hand column of the records, were confidential. Puzzled that the amounts of public money paid public employees could be regarded as privileged information, the student nevertheless suggested that the salaries be simply covered in the copying process or scissored off. His request was denied by the director of personnel and subsequently by the executive director of the agency.

Only by a direct appeal to the entire commission, with the implicit threat of adverse publicity and of a lawsuit under the Freedom of Information Act, were the records made available. Even then, however, the FTC sought to charge a prohibitive price of $.60 per page for duplication. Since the chart was in a thirty-page report format, and since the student had eight reports going back to 1959, the cost of a single copy of the 240 pages was $144. Finally, the agency agreed to make an office copy of the records available for his perusal. Ironically, this copy *contained the salaries* of all the employees, the supposed basis for the original denial of the records. Almost two months had elapsed for the student's original request to see what is perhaps an agency's most fundamental document.

As graduate students and young professionals in the Ralph Nader summer study groups of 1968, and then later in 1969 and 1970, engaged in the investigation of the responsiveness and effectiveness of the Washington bureaucracy, they were totally unprepared for the receptions they received—denials of the most elementary pieces of information, constant lying about events and the existence of documents, harassment of those who were discovered talking with them out of their offices, surveillance of those they were "allowed" to see, and, always, enormous delays.

Preventing an "open" government, at least as far as relations with the general public are concerned, became an early necessity for industry corruptors. They succeeded beyond their wildest aims. They have created a government which, on its own, will suppress details of industry collusion in order to project its necessary "public interest" image. The actual atmosphere of the bureaucracy is shrouded in secrecy that is buttressed by an effective enforcement mechanism.

The notion of an "open American government" is a myth. Fear of public disclosure of everything from already public reports to the most basic and innocent personal opinions pervades the entire bureaucracy like a poisonous fog. The Freedom of Information Act has failed. The only groups with easy access to details of government operation, those accorded preferential access, are large corporations and their representatives.

A. UPPER ECHELON FEAR: THE IMAGE AND THE REALITY

At the outset of the student investigations, two fundamentally different categories of fear were encountered. There was the fear of appointed officials and upper staffs that the students would embarrass them by disclosing information they preferred to keep confidential. Secondly, there was the fear felt by lower to middle level staff, who were often eager to discuss the workings of their agencies but feared for their job security and longterm career possibilities.

The fear of upper staff was manifest when Paul Rand Dixon, then chairman of the Federal Trade Commission, physically forced investigator John Schulz out of his office when the latter asked about the basis for an information denial. Mr. Dixon then proceeded to call up his upper staff to instruct them that the "FTC investigators" were to be locked out, that no one was to communicate with them. Perhaps one reason for the banishment was that they had already learned too much about the agency. Yet Chairman Dixon went beyond this approach—he institutionalized his lockout. One year later the investigators were told by Dr. George Dobbs of the agency that *all* personnel had been instructed not to speak with them without the written permission of the Commission. At the same time, trade association representatives lobbyists, industrialists and their legal representatives came and went as they pleased.

Another example is provided by Richard McLaren, head of the Antitrust Division of the Department of Justice. Mr. Nader was refused access to information in his quest to understand why the Justice Department had "consented" to a settlement of an indictment against the Automobile Manufacturers Association of America for "product-fixing." The indictment charged that the automobile corporations, through their association, had conspired to delay or prevent the implementation of pollution control devices over a sixteen-year period. The Justice Department settled the matter, without sanction, in a way that hampered consumers and cities from using the voluminous grand jury records in later, treble-damage antitrust suits against the auto companies and their trade association. A former high level attorney in the Antitrust Division interpreted the situation: "Listen, McLaren was appointed because of Bar Association politics, not Republican politics. And he'd be unhappy if damaging information were revealed which could hurt *both* the legal fraternity and his present bosses."

Why do these officials fear exposure of their agency's activities? It is because image is the reality of Washington. Officials and upper staff will keep their jobs only so long as they can accommodate the vector theory of politics, responding to those forces which threaten them. This end can usually be accomplished through private accommodation; but if there is a major threat to the favorable image of the agency through the action of an individual, officials and upper staff realize that they might be compelled publicly to investigate an issue. Thus, while there are thousands of potential "scandals" in Washington every week—from the outright influence-peddling of Speaker McCormack's office to the FDA malfeasance on cyclamates—only those events which are likely to be publicized with the proper tone of outrageous surprise will force the matter into the public eye and will compel Congress or other officials to take some kind of scapegoat, retributive, and self-purging action.

In order to understand fully the nature of this image threat to upper staff and appointed officials, it is necessary to consider two aspects of the source of their fear. First, the agencies project themselves as active, aggressive, independent, honest, effective, increasingly productive, and dedicated champions of the diffuse and general public interest. It is a view they seek to retain. Second, there is the fact that industry, the special interest "constituency" of the agency, does not present a threat to that image. They are not going to complain of agency inaction in the prosecution of corporation violations of law. They are not going to expose political maneuverings or ask embarrassing questions. As a result, there is no need to erect a barrier to information acquisition and personal relations by these groups. But the very activities by industry groups which do not themselves pose a threat to the agency's image itself, do pose a threat if exposed. The revelation of private dealings between industry and special interests to the detriment of the public would do great harm to the agency's image, its lifeblood. Since there has been no previous substantial threat of disclosure of these activities, there has been no deterrent to these practices. Agencies consider it necessary to maintain this low-visibility situation in order to protect this regulatory-industry collusion. This goal also requires the enforcement of secrecy down to the lower levels of bureaucracy.

B. LOWER ECHELON FEAR: WEAVING THE SHROUD

The fear at the lower to middle level is different than at the upper levels. It is not the fear of an embarrassing disclosure *per se*, but of retaliation from superiors for relating something which might conflict with the official agency version. This is the fear that enabled Chairman Dixon to enforce successfully his illegal edict. Very few employees of the Federal Trade Cosmmission would in fact talk with the student investigators after the order. For example, a young attorney at the Federal Trade Commission who had spoken with a student in the hall of the FTC office building in Washington, D.C., was subsequently warned by his division chief to "be careful of his conduct" because the FTC was "back on its heels under criticism." Fearing unfavorable job recommendations from the agency upon departure, he canceled a prospective interview and would not talk with the investigators in public further—although he did so in private.

The fear at the lower level is also manifested in a myriad of subtle ways. It is an official who refuses to be interviewed alone, but insists on having another attorney or his superior present. It is requiring that a stenographer be present to record verbatim what is said, or writing copious "memos to the files" after an interview. It is lower and middle staff refusing to reveal even the most innocuous information, afraid to express even their most basic opinions about their responsibilities. It can be seen in sweaty palms and nervousness during an interview.

The institutionalization of this lower staff fear is accomplished through sophisticated enforcement mechanisms.

1. *The Agency Line.* Most agencies carefully construct an official or unofficial "agency line" concerning controversial issues. Rarely do these responses have any relation to reality, but they are repeated with such uniformity, within and by the agency, that mere repetition imbues them with a kind of sanctity. Thus, the Federal Trade Commission cannot investigate ghetto frauds because of the "interstate commerce clause of the Constitution." The Interstate Commerce Commission can do nothing about homemoving frauds because it lacks "jurisdiction." And the Food and Drug Administration cannot move "too fast" against the marketing of dangerous drugs. Of course, outside the agencies these answers are derided by those familiar with the law or issues involved. But they all have a kind of magic circularity which prevents inquiry from progressing further. The reality, however, differs from the asserted assumptions. The relevant statutory and constitutional clauses allegedly restraining the FTC and the ICC in the examples above have been liberally interpreted for the past decade, but the agencies themselves have yet to utilize them. And the FDA *can* move quickly against an unsafe drug as it did against the antibiotic combination Panalba—after years of inaction. Thus, most of these bureaucratic positions are self-fulfilling prophecies.

The agency line is generally expressed through form letters in response to complaints from consumers and through news releases and testimony to Congress. It is often codified, however, in the agency's annual report. The categories now and then change, but the tone and purpose of the annual report remain constant. It is designed to project an aura of careful progress toward the solution of current problems. They are difficult problems, yes, but the department has made great strides, as the increasing numbers of enforcement actions from year to year in all quantitative categories prove. And although the problem is not quite yet solved, solution is imminent. For instance, one can go back to the initial case before the Interstate Commerce Commission, the first large regulatory agency created back in 1887, and read about a group of small farmers complaining that the railroad refused to supply them with boxcars because they claimed a shortage. One can then follow this matter from annual report to annual report, through the 1920s and all the way to 1970. Each year one learns that the "boxcar shortage" problem, which once again forced many of America's small farmers to dump their harvest, will be solved in a very short time. There is never an indication that the ICC, in reality, has done virtually nothing in the area except protect big business, refusing to prosecute cases of massive violation of the law submitted by the agency's own special agents in the field. Thus, the only way to increase numbers year after year is to prosecute more trivial, less important violations, a mis-emphasis not reflected by annual report tables. Therefore, agency personnel in the field are directly told to meet a certain quota—and told that it does not matter what kind of case it is, as long as they do *more* than was done last year. The agency line thus becomes not only the philosophy of the agency but its goal.

Consequently, the lower to middle level employee soon learns that it is hands off big business, hands off innovative prosecutions to counter innovative violations of law, and hands off offending those who might threaten political pressure—i.e., major campaign contributors to key congressmen, industries dominated by former upper staff personnel or by the company the employee's superior just joined.

2. *Structure.* Although not set up for this express purpose, agencies are structurally arranged to aid in the enforcement of secrecy. First, most are highly compartmentalized. Departments are divided into bureaus, sections, offices, and desks. A veteran of twenty years or more in one office is likely to have no idea what is transpiring in the office down the hall. These natural lines of communication permit the isolation of a given report, meeting, or incident among a limited group. Those who would most likely reveal it are among the younger employees at the GS-9 to GS-12 levels, those who have less to lose by exposure of complicity with industry. But because of the compartmentalization, together with a policy of letting only a few of the younger staff participate in any one decision or matter, it is relatively easy for the entrenched upper staff to trace down leaks. For example, a report produced by the ICC's relatively small cost-finding section will not be widely known in detail outside that section. The official ordering suppression of a given event or document (usual-

ly by discontinuing it just short of final publication) will usually consist of a small group of from one to five upper level officials.

3. *Surveillance.* Complementing agency structure is a pervasive fear and anticipation of surveillance, including electronic surveillance.* The student investigators were frequently told by employees at lunch or at their homes that they feared an electronic bug in their office. Most of them suspected other agencies or their superiors, and some pointed to the disturbingly lucrative business conducted by electronic device manufacturers with large industrial concerns. Many of these surveillance gadget companies have large and busy offices in Washington, and agency officials feel that any criticisms about policy expressed by them may be relayed to the industry's friends and to their contacts higher up in the agency. Since offensive surveillance development is advanced over antisurveillance detection and jamming, there is little these men can do to verify or alleviate their fears even if they have the resources to do so.

Non-electronic surveillance is just as prevalent and intimidating. A high official in the Nixon administration asked two departments the students were studying to submit detailed memos on their activities, including a list of all personnel interviewed. The ICC circulated a memorandum requesting staff to record how much time the students spent talking with them and to summarize the contents of the conversations. Other agencies went even further. The Assistant Secretary of the Department of the Interior (DOI), Carl Klein, first agreed to cooperate with our study of the Federal Water Pollution Control Agency (FWPCA), which is within DOI's jurisdiction. Later, however, he refused to permit the students to interview any of the public employees in the agency or department. Mr. Klein persisted in his lockout, until rising pressures of adverse publicity compelled him to rescind his illegal bar.

Mr. Klein then attempted to regroup, however, requiring the students to schedule centrally all interviews and appointing two subordinates to "monitor" all interviews. Although the sixteen investigators working on this study, as well as the employees interviewed, were painfully aware of this policy, Mr. Klein was nevertheless brazen enough to deny it publicly to the *Washington Post.* He stated that "as far as I know" there are "no monitors." However, Mr. Klein's own staff assistant, Jeffrey Stern, and the FWPCA director of the

---

*Robert Kennedy, while Attorney General, was discussing a serious policy matter with one of his staff, when he commented that he wanted to convey the problem to FBI Director J. Edgar Hoover. His aide said, ominously, "He already knows by now," at which point Kennedy, understanding his meaning, began shouting, "Do you hear me, Edgar, do you hear me, Edgar?"
Also, Tom Wicker has recently reported that a major Democratic contender for the presidency would only be interviewed outside his normal office because he feared that his office was bugged.

Program Analysis, Richard Nalesnik, were specifically assigned to monitor our interviews. They openly acknowledged their role as such on several occasions. Further, they were told to report to Mr. Klein himself, and to his deputy, Robert L. McCormick, who also admitted the existence of the policy. Not only Mr. Klein's misuse of power in his "monitoring" but also his willingness to lie—no matter how obvious the lie might be to personnel within the agency—must impress agency employees who might be tempted to speak their minds. Of course, it must be understood that this kind of monitoring is rarely, if ever, required of the daily deluge of visitors from trade associations, corporations, and other special interest groups.

4. Sanctions. The critical element necessary to enforce secrecy and strict adherence to the agency line is the power of effective sanctions. The obvious sanctions are the denial of sought-after rewards, such as grade level advances. In addition, there are other sanctions, ranging from a sudden surge of undesirable assignments to the more extreme measure of dismissal. Even if matters do not progress to this point, their potential use is a sufficient deterrent to older, security-conscious bureaucrats.

5. Natural Selection. These sanctions of advancement denial, undesirable assignments, and dismissal are rendered most effective by a complementary system of natural selection. Agencies to some extent recruit and to a greater extent promote personnel who will be most affected by these sanctions. Those who question assumptions or who demonstrate aggressiveness or imagination are generally discouraged. The turnover rate at the lower professional levels (GS-9 to 12) of most agencies is staggering, partly because only those lacking in creativity and critical capacity are made welcome; the Peter Principle prevails. Many agencies rotate out, usually by the voluntary resignation of the discouraged or disgusted, one-third or more of the new recruits at these levels each year. Those that remain acquire an increasing interest in job security as they rise to more powerful positions. Their opportunity for new careers, especially without favorable job recommendations from the government, declines as the years pass. They become adjusted to passive acceptance of pre-set explanations. Eventual complicity with the interest group domination of agency officials provides yet greater incentive for obedience to the agency line. Often, the men most susceptible to control move from complicity to a role of active suppression enforcement themselves.

The intensity of the process can be imputed from the longevity of those who have survived the selection process to reach positions of power at upper staff levels. At the ICC, for example, the average tenure in the agency of the present bureau directors is thirty-one years. And a tangential aspect to the lack of new blood infusion is the development of cronyism, illustrated by the FTC, where *every* attorney bureau director in 1968 came from a small Southern town, as did Chairman Dixon, who promoted them.

The interaction of some of these forces: structure, surveillance, sanctions, and natural selection, is illustrated in one particularly salient example: the case of ICC special agent Frank Lawrence. During the summer of 1969, the investigators had learned that there were numerous improprieties regarding the relationship between one specific freight forwarder, regulated by the ICC, and high ICC officials. The freight forwarder, U.S. Freight, is a large company which, together with two other firms, dominates the freight forwarding industry. It was learned that the ICC's managing director was especially intimate with the company. There was evidence that he attended the company's cocktail parties, that he called U.S. Freight executives to report on the activities of rival freight forwarders within the ICC, that he vacationed on the U.S. Freight Company yacht, and that he had been offered a lucrative job by the Freight Forwarders Institute (located at the same address as the Washington office of the U.S. Freight Company).

To this extent, his activities are not unlike the agency's relationship with industry generally. Then, in 1967, special agent Lawrence, attached to the ICC's Chicago office, submitted a "Compliance Survey" (a preliminary investigative report), which documented evidence of the systematic and massive bribing of traffic managers by U.S. Freight. Agent Lawrence received no reply and no further instructions from Washington, despite numerous inquiries. Finally, Washington instructed Lawrence not to file the usual follow-up investigative report, but instead to submit an informal memorandum to his superior. Although upset by this extraordinary request, given the substantial evidence he had compiled and the seriousness of the violation, he complied with the request. Nothing happened. Agent Lawrence inquired further and was explicitly told to drop the matter. During this time and to the present day, the Bureau of Enforcement, the agency's prosecutorial arm, had never even seen the report to evaluate it for the desirability of prosecution. The bribing did not cease.

Agent Lawrence's unwillingness to let the matter drop quietly was rewarded with a denial of his "within grade step increase" (normal pay raise based on years of service). He discovered that his submissions to Washington were returned to him with hypercritical comments. Much of the commentary was clearly absurd, such as "this is not a violation of the Interstate Commerce Act," when in fact identical cases abounded in agency records and with Court affirmation. Nearly every submission, although identical in nature and quality to his previous surveys and reports submitted during his nine years as an ICC investigator, was suddenly unsatisfactory. These tactics were designed to harass Mr. Lawrence into more obeisant acceptance of the Washington upper staff desire not to offend U.S. Freight. Other special agents were affected by what they knew was happening; most were afraid it could happen to them, and all of them got the message.

Since sanctions might not be enough to keep him in line, it was determined that more extreme measures would be taken to protect the natural selection processes from contamination by prosecution-minded investigators. Mr. Lawrence was told that he should resign. If he failed to resign, the year of bogus criticism would be used against him in a dismissal action. This "documentation," even though self-created, would require that he defend himself with a major effort and thousands of dollars—which he could not easily afford. Further, a successful dismissal would mean bad job recommendations; he would have to start all over again, although near forty.

In an unusual but happy turn of events, Mr. Lawrence refused to resign, choosing instead to contest the issue. At this point, his behavior deviates from the normal reaction of quietly resigning. Attorneys researched the supposed evidence of his "incompetence" and documented in detail its falsity. They demanded a full hearing and requested as witnesses a substantial portion of the agency's upper staff. At first, the agency, contrary to elementary principles of due process, attempted to hold a "kangaroo" hearing. The same man bringing charges against agent Lawrence chose three ICC employees from whom Mr. Lawrence was to choose one as his hearing examiner. And this same official bringing the charges also partially controlled the promotion of the employees chosen as possible hearing examiners. Meanwhile, the ICC expressed its intention to hold a "closed door hearing." Mr. Lawrence's attorneys expressed the intention of obtaining a court order to compel an open hearing (a closed hearing can be waived by a defendant since *he* is the supposed benefactor of the privacy); when they requested an open hearing with press and public, and included as witnesses much of the agency's upper staff, the ICC suddenly backed down. In an unprecedented move, the letter of dismissal "was rescinded." Shortly thereafter the managing director resigned on four days' notice.

The student investigators were later told through sources in the General Counsel's office that the matter was dropped only after the commission was told that if Lawrence were to take the matter to court, he could compel the public release of his personal file, including the collection of bogus criticisms and returned, unacted upon, reports of genuine violations of the Interstate Commerce Act. The evidence could not be destroyed, since agent Lawrence had wisely Xeroxed everything he had sent or received. He could release it publicly in his defense. More recently, the agency has shifted to a tactic which would retain the prohibition on release, harassing Lawrence until he resigns on his own.

There are occasional cases making national news, such as efficiency expert Fitzgerald, fired for reporting inefficiency in the construction of the C-5A airplane. There are hundreds of less visible Frank Lawrences in our federal bureaucracy. There are thousands who are so emasculated or intimidated at an early stage, that they become willing accomplices; eventually, many become corrupt enforcers themselves.

III. TRYING TO CHANGE THE COMPLEX

The reinvigoration of this regulatory-industrial complex, not only in terms of solutions to substantive problems, but more importantly in terms of a defensible legal and governmental process, requires radical change. But there are certain interim reforms which could feasibly be attempted first. These should be attempted before the complete restructuring of the state is compelled.

1. The appointment process must be changed. Officials must be appointed on the basis of qualification. This seems to be a simple truism, but it will require public attention to appointments previously made before an audience of industry enthusiasts. Appointments must not be "cleared" with industry, as is presently the norm. Legislation should be passed prohibiting appointment of anyone with a substantial interest in the industry to be regulated.

2. Job interchange, at least the "deferred bribes" of upper level appointees, must be ended. This can be done by requiring, as a condition of appointment, that anyone taking a position may not accept employment for or compensation from an industry regulated by that government body for at least five years after leaving the government post.

3. There must be an adversary process in agency process in agency proceedings, with someone representing the counter-corporate side. There must be independent consumer counsel, with a full staff within each agency, as well as strong consumer representation on all formal advisory groups.

4. The Freedom of Information Act must be given some teeth. A summary judicial procedure must be established for easy and quick public appeal. Time limits should be set out to prevent agency refusals even to deny information (without which legal recourse is impossible). Exemptions should be statutorily limited to make more difficult current abuse. A time limit should be placed on the applicability of many of the exemptions justifying suppression—particularly the investigatory file exemption. Disclosure requirements should be set out, with maximum reproduction charges set at no more than $.05 per sheet, plus minimal labor cost. Each agency should be required to collect specified minimal information about agency operations and required to make available to the public the document identification or labeling schemes of the department. Finally, the deliberate or repeated failure to disclose information which is clearly not within one of the exemptions should be grounds for contempt of court, with criminal sanctions applied.

5. The nation's regulatory agencies must be restructured for greater accountability and effectiveness. First, their adjudicatory functions should be separated from the prosecutorial, either along the lines of present agency jurisdiction or combined in one large Commerce Court. This will remove much present unfairness, particularly for the small businessman unable to play the very expensive agency-legal game. The judges will no longer be directing the prosecutors. Second, the agencies must confine themselves to policy-making, rule-making, and prosecutorial activity under the leadership of a single, visible, and accountable leader. The notion of "independence" fostered through "group decisions" and multilayered agency authority has simply not worked as has been pointed out in the recent Ash report.

6. There must be tight policing of campaign contributions from industry, with prohibition and contribution disclosure requirements actively enforced. In addition, there should be a change in tax laws permitting deductions for contributions to candidates by private individuals, thus broadening the contributive base of officials. Further, free television time should be required and provided for candidates to minimize the importance and necessity of heavy financial aid for this purpose.

7. Tax law enforcement relating to lobbying must be changed. At present, corporations are in fact deducting their lobbying costs as business expenses. Individuals who are attempting to counter special interest bias, however, and who are not attempting to influence for eccnomically selfish advantage are denied the same privilege. In

fact, organizations formed to represent a general interest threaten their entire tax-exempt status to the extent they try to influence electors and legislative acts. If possible, this should be reversed. Lawful attempts to influence election outcome and legislation should not result in exeption removal from "charitable" or "public interest" organizations. On the other hand, these activities, if connected directly or indirectly with enterprise based on economic gain, should *not* be deductible, no matter how cloaked.

8. Congressional oversight committees must be given adequate staff to scrutinize their respective agencies and departments. Staffs are presently so small that it would require a ten-fold increase to achieve the scrutiny necessary for even elementary congressional control of the bureaucracy.

9. The seniority system must be ended to give Congress the opportunity to select its own representatives to oversee America's economy and to lessen the effectiveness of perpetual corporate control of a few identifiable congressmen—whose power position, following a corporate-financed campaign, is presently assured.

10. There must be active trust-busting of corporations, trade associations, and unions. Most, if not all, of America's top 500 corporations should be split into more competitive entities. In few corporations of this size are there appreciable economies of scale. The largest, General Motors, could just as easily be Buick, Pontiac, Chevrolet, etc., with no loss in efficiency, but great benefit to the consumer and the public. Any industry-wide research or agreement necessary for the public interest should be accomplished by or through the government.

11. Corporations must be opened up for greater direct public scrutiny. The notion of "protecting" corporate violators of the law from public exposure (a privilege individuals are not allowed) must end. Hesitancy to statistically compare individually named corporations according to public issues—whether they be cleanliness or accuracy or safety—must be overcome. To facilitate this, a comprehensive corporate disclosure law should be passed requiring more detailed breakdowns of corporate expenditures and holdings. Government should compile and publicize numbers of complaints received from consumers by type of complaint for individual firms, with number of sales or size of firm included so meaningful comparison is possible.

12. There should be legal redress under federal and state laws for parties as a class. This is the only way general public interests can be directly heard within our judicial system. The law should leniently define representation requirements and establish a clear cause of action on a class basis for consumer grievances.

CORPORATE GOVERNMENT IN ACTION

Vic Reinemer

In today's Washington the most expansive and least visible branch of government is the advisory committee. There are two to three thousand of them; no one has more than fragmentary data on their number, membership, meetings, and activities. The most influential are composed exclusively of top officials of large corporations. They meet regularly with Administration leaders, cruise the polluted Potomac in the Presidential yacht, watch from the White House rose garden as a new environmental device is displayed, assign company personnel to prepare governmental reports, listen to the decision-makers and help them decide things.

Press and public interest groups are often barred from the committees' formal meetings, which are held in such places as the Pentagon, the Department of Commerce, the big red Executive Office building on 17th Street, and the Chase Manhattan Bank in New York City. An increasingly popular meeting place is the new State Department Building—you can't get in there anymore without a pass or special permit. The restriction hampers environmental and consumer groups which would like to watch the advisory system work even though they are not permitted to be part of it.

Industry advisory committees are no Nixon phenomenon. The Business Advisory Council on Federal Reports, which operates through the Office of Management and Budget (formerly Budget Bureau) and keeps bureaucrats from asking questions which industry does not want to answer, was set up during President Franklin D.

From *The Progressive*, November 1971. Reprinted with permission.

Roosevelt's third term. President Harry Truman's Secretary of the Interior Julius Krug established the National Petroleum Council, which supplies information and personnel for the Division of Oil and Gas. President John F. Kennedy's Defense Secretary Robert McNamara established the Pentagon's Industry Advisory Council, through which the nation's top defense contractors tone down General Accounting Office reports on excess profits and urge the FBI to share with industry its files on restive students.

Congress has contributed to the growth and power of advisory committees by authorizing another one almost every time it sets up a new program. The Department of Health, Education and Welfare has so many advisory committees that this summer it computerized its 5,700 advisers, by agency, into two thick books.

Many of these professional advisory committees are inactive, useful only as a notation in the resumes of advisers as seeming evidence of their prestigious national service. More than half of the twenty-one Office of Education advisory committees established since 1965 did not meet last year. There is a compelling reason why many do not meet. Advisory committees which include modestly-paid persons such as teachers must provide at least expense money to get a quorum. Travel funds from the Federal Government are in extremely short supply.

It is different with the industry advisory committees. A corporation or trade association is more than willing to underwrite cozy conversations with top Government people. The professional advisory committees, when they do meet, often deal with acting deputy assistants. Industry advisers, on the other hand, can confide at the club what they learned from John (Nassikas, chairman of the Federal Power Commission), Maurice (Stans, Secretary of Commerce), or Dick (Himself).

There are two new elements in the industry advisory committee apparatus today. One is, at long last, an awareness of their existence and the growing realization that they constitute a fourth branch of the Federal Government. Working from a vantage point well within whatever Administration is in power, they frustrate agency and citizen attempts to obtain the information needed to enforce the laws.

Information is "the currency of power" in Washington, as Ralph Nader put it last year when testifying in support of legislation to broaden the membership of the Office of Management and Budget's sixteen all-industry advisory committees by including consumer, small business, and labor representation. Only seven persons were listening to Nader—Senator Lee Metcalf, Montana Democrat, author of the bill, who was presiding; three staff members; two correspondents for industry news services; and the busily scribbling secretary to the chairman of OMB's Business Advisory Council on Federal Reports, Charles Stewart, who declined repeated invitations to testify. Nader noted that "it is very hard, basically, to even interest people who should be interested" in Government information policy, although "the enforcement of the laws, in an Administration that shouts about law and order, depends in the economic regulatory area on the critical obtaining of information about business and industrial practices . . . [which is] by far the most single important information problem in all of Government."

This year Senator Metcalf broadened his bill to require that all Government advisory committees (rather than just OMB's) meet openly, with prior public notice, and, in the case of industry committees, include public representatives with no direct or indirect economic or financial interest in the industry involved. Republican Senators Charles Percy of Illinois and William Roth of Delaware have introduced somewhat similar legislation. The Senate Subcommittee on Intergovernmental Relations, headed by Senator Edmund S. Muskie, Maine Democrat, has conducted eight days of hearings this year on advisory committees, and more are planned for this fall.

On the House side, Representative John S. Monagan, Connecticut Democrat, has also introduced legislation to establish ground rules for advisory committees. OMB has promised—as it did last year, without fulfillment—to come up speedily with its own proposals. OMB, which speaks for the Administration, wants to set forth the ground rules by executive order, rather than have Congress do it. So the advisory committee issue is, as they say in Washington, "under active consideration" by two branches of the Government. But it is not really on the priority list of either the executive or legislative.

Until recently, political scientists have shunned advisory committees as studiously as they have avoided regulatory commissions. There is no academic library on the subject of advisory committees, unless you include among these bodies the Presidential commissions. (The latter are quite different, usually set up to restore national confidence after a traumatic assassination or riot, or to relegate to a back burner a politically insoluble problem.)

This lack of literature tends to keep the interested graduate student out of the field. Even if he were ambitious enough to attempt the original research in fragmented files, his advisers would be reluctant to approve study of a subject about which they themselves are so uninformed. And as one doctoral candidate said, he would like to do his thesis on industry advisory committees, but he would also like to consult for industry. A candid thesis would probably deprive him of side income from industry consultancies.

Two political scientists who have studied the issue emerged at this summer's Senate hearings. Their—and other—testimony illustrates the second new element in government by industry advisory committee, the overkill syndrome so evident when an industry is under attack. Wave after wave of high-powered advisers, drawn from a small and repetitive roster of the corporate elite, fire off self-serving salvos which silence the snipers. The Nixon Administration, while cutting back executive branch employment and bypassing the legislative, seems determined to proliferate the advisory branch, excluding from it potential critics and supporting it with a massive public relations program which transforms industry wishes into government writ.

Professor Robert Engler of City University of New York (and author of *The Politics of Oil*) cited the twenty-five-year-old National Petroleum Council (NPC) as a case study of how an advisory committee takes advantage of its quasi-governmental privilege to concentrate its economic power and use it for political purposes. The 119-member Council, he said, interlocks individually and corporately with the American Petroleum Institute, the Military Petroleum Advisory Board, the Emergency Advisory Committee for Natural Gas, the Emergency Petroleum Supply Committees, and advisory committees within the Federal Power Commission, the Defense Department, and the Office of Management and Budget.

On July 15, two days after Engler testified, the National Petroleum Council unveiled its *Energy Outlook,* a publication comprising findings and projections of energy industries working under Council coordination, which complained about Federal restraints on the price of natural gas. Later in the month, Secretary of Interior Rogers Morton complimented his Advisory Committee on Energy, which had just voiced the same complaint, and growled about the delay in opening up Government oil shale reserves and Alaska's North Slope, and about safety and environmental hurdles, and those "added taxes on petroleum imposed by the Tax Reform Act of 1969."

Atlantic Richfield—which had a vice president on Secretary Morton's advisory committee—and Gulf and Shell combined paid only $13.8 million in Federal income taxes in 1969, but they spent $23 million on national advertising. Tax loopholes for oil companies are so big that, as *The Progressive*'s Washington Editor, Erwin Knoll, reported last year, Atlantic Richfield paid no Federal taxes on the $465 million profit it made from 1964 through 1967, and actually obtained during those four years tax credits totaling $629,000.

None of these industry advisory committees will divulge the details of the alleged gas shortage on which they base their claim for more lenient rate, tax, and administrative treatment. This is true, too, of the American Gas Association (a trade association of investor-owned distribution and pipeline companies), whose estimates FPC Chairman Nassikas prefers to those of his own staff, which reckons reserves at forty per cent more than the AGA does.

This year Congress appropriated money for a gas supply and demand study by the FPC, which promptly set up three technical advisory committees and a forty-five-member executive advisory committee. One member of the latter, Mayor Dale Helmerich of Hunting-burg, Indiana, who is president of the American Public Gas Association (a trade association of 225 municipal distribution systems), testified that "the consumer is represented by me and Mrs. Virginia Knauer, assistant to the President for Consumer Affairs, who agreed with me in conversation during the first advisory committee meetings that consumer representatives were somewhat outnumbered." "Their committee," he said, "is still considerably more democratic in structure than the technical advisory committees."

Mayor Helmerich noted that funding for the study had not been cleared by the Office of Management and Budget. "One can speculate," he said, "about the possible impact of an OMB industry advisory council on the nonclearance decision."

And well one might. OMB's sixteen industry advisory committees—five of them composed of oil, gas, or utility executives—have strayed far afield many times.

The OMB committees have no statutory basis. They established themselves early in World War II in response to the Budget Director's request for industry help in administering the Federal Reports Act of 1942. That law was passed to help *small* businesses, plagued by wartime questionnaires; it directed the Budget Director to coordinate the collection of information from ten or more persons of firms to the end that "all unnecessary duplication of efforts in obtaining . . . information [from businesses] . . . should be eliminated as rapidly as practicable."

Large corporations and trade associations set up the advisory committee apparatus immediately and have used it continuously to quash questions which the Government should ask and does not otherwise get answered. The minutes of these advisory committees, which are stored at OMB, show that they weakened FPC regulations on reporting political, advertising, and public relations expenditures. They delayed and watered down industry reports on air pollution. This year they cut the heart out of a Federal Communications Commission (FCC) study of the effects of conglomerate ownership on broadcast stations by convincing OMB that the FCC should not be allowed to look at more than one year's correspondence between broadcasting companies and their conglomerate parents.

OMB committees kept the Federal Power Commission from ascertaining more than ten of the principal stockholders in electric and gas corporations. Even so, many utilities decline to name their ten largest security holders in their annual reports to the FPC. Instead, they list "nominees"—dummy corporations. Actual ownership or control of stock can be ascertained to a degree through use of the "Nominee List" published by the American Society of Corporate Secretaries and closely held by it until Senator Metcalf put it in the *Congressional Record* (June 24, 1971, Part II). And the members of an OMB advisory committee stopped a corporate ownership and interlock study by the Federal Trade Commission by taking their inside knowledge of the proposed study to Capitol Hill and arranging for a cut off of the funds which the FTC needed for the study.

The OMB industry advisory committees have kept bottled up, for eight years now, the crucially necessary national inventory of industrial water waste. There will not be any real law and order in the environmental field until the Government knows who is polluting what, where, and how much. And there will not be any such inventory until one of the constitutional arms of Government asserts its power over the advisory branch.

The executive branch in this Administration is not likely to order the inventory, which was recently referred to the National Industrial Pollution Control Council, created by the President in April, 1970. This advisory group, appointed by Secretary of Commerce Stans, is composed exclusively of the heads of some sixty major polluting corporations—oil, auto, utility, mining, timber, coal, airline, and manufacturing—plus presidents of the U.S. Chamber of Commerce, the National Association of Manufacturers, and the National Industrial Conference Board. This Council, said the President, would help businessmen "communicate regularly with the President, the Council on Environmental Quality, and other Government officials and private organizations"—as if they did not already have multiple channels, including political campaign finance clubs.

The Council promptly set up some thirty subcouncils embracing various fields of industrial activity. At its meeting last October, Council members squeezed out of their limousines and ascended to the Department of Commerce meeting room only to find waiting at the door representatives of the National Wildlife Federation, Friends of the Earth, Nader's Raiders, and the press. News of the unpublicized meeting had leaked from civil servents forever honored and nameless.

Council and Administration leaders were surprised and indignant. No, they said, these non-members could not attend the Council meeting, even as mute observers. No, they would not be provided with a transcript. No, there would be no press conference afterward.

The nature of the October meeting, and of the Council itself, were set forth in a memorandum sent later that month by Tom Cunning, then the Council's Director of Communications and Public Affairs although a Commerce Department official. He sent it to the designated "public relations contacts" of the corporations whose presidents and board chairmen sit on the Council. It is worth quoting:

> *At the October 14, 1970 meeting of the National Industrial Pollution Control Council the need for industry and NIPCC to get going on a 'communications-p.r.' program was mentioned time and time again . . . One logical answer is a 'case history' series. With this letter is a group of ten sample sheets. The sheets in this series will be loose leaf so they can be assembled by industry, by pollution area, geographically etc.* Each case history sheet will show results—*facts—show that industry is doing something.*
>
> *Some material has come in as a result of a request to Council members, but not enough of the right kind of stuff. The 'case history' sheets should be reprints, not re-written, of actual stories from house organs, employe magazines, annual reports, newspapers and magazines like the ten sample sheets.*
>
> *I have in my hand a volume . . . entitled 'Pollution Cleanup Actions' and these are the kind of things that were put out . . . the sample sheets.*
>
> *My bosses are calling for 200 to 250 of these, covering all the areas I mentioned, by January 1, 1971. And that is a large order for a one man shop.* I need your help.

Cunning went on to ask the sixty-three public relations officials to pass the word to their counterparts in subcouncil operations. Corporate America heard and responded to the Federal plea. The self-serving materials rolled in. One thick *Casebook of Pollution Clean-up Actions* has already been published—and probably placed in your local library. More casebooks are planned.

Concurrently the Council has worked up twenty-five attractive blue and white booklets dealing with various environmental matters. These booklets are printed and distributed by the Government Printing Office. One, entitled *Detergents,* published late in 1970, spoke glowingly of a new material, NTA, as a replacement for phosphates in laundry detergents.

Extensive human and environmental safety tests indicate, it reads, "that at the levels currently being used and contemplated for the near future, NTA is safe for people and the environment.

Months earlier Dr. Samuel Epstein, a renowned cancer researcher, had warned against use of NTA pending further study. By last December the Surgeon General and Environmental Protection Agency announced their concurrence and concern. The Council accordingly issued a sharply revised *Detergents* pamphlet in March.

Yet in May of this year, Procter & Gamble—whose president heads the Detergents Subcouncil—was sending members of Congress the old, erroneous pamphlet, referring to it as "a new Commerce pamphlet which gives the full story" on detergents.

At the Senate hearings this summer a commerce spokesman admitted that no effort had been made to remove the misleading pamphlet from the GPO list or even insert in it notification of the sharply revised medical advice regarding NTA. The matter, said Commerce, "is out of our control."

The other political scientist who emerged at this year's hearings, Professor Henry Steck of the College of Cortland, New York, testified that there was considerable overlap between the members of the National Industrial Pollution Control Council and the top twenty or twenty-five contractors from the Defense Department, Atomic Energy Commission, and National Aeronautics and Space Administration.

I am apprehensive that just as we are now speaking of a military industrial complex we may be witnessing the initial stages in the growth of what might be called an industrial-environmental complex. It is not a happy phrase, but I hope its meaning is clear. . . .[Council members] have access, they control knowledge, they control advice. . . Above all, it is virtually impossible for outsiders to challenge the thinking and the findings of the Council.

Steck questioned whether other advisory committees, which do include diverse interests, could counter the high-powered, all-industry committees. The answer seems clear enough:

The Nelson-Brademas Environmental Education Act, on the books almost a year now, provides for appointment of an environmental education advisory committee including environmental and youth representation. As of this writing, the committee has not been appointed by Secretary of Health, Education and Welfare Elliot Richardson. If the committee when appointed will include, as rumored, independent experts, it will not have the money and muscle which sustains the National Industrial Pollution Control Council.

When Congress passed the Rail Passenger Service Act last year it authorized a fifteen-man financial advisory panel, including seven persons representing the public. But the executive branch names the advisers, and it filled the panel with financiers and railroad officials, except for the two Federal employes designated by statute.

Just before Congress recesssed in August the Interstate Commerce Commission created a Tariff Users Advisory Committee, to "provide the user with a forceful and structured voice" in tariff simplification and also "provide the Commission with the nucleus of a specialized tariff advisory group which could be split or expanded as required into numerous subgroups or task forces in many areas concerning tariff users." The new advisory committee consists of seven industry and four carrier representatives, without even a nod toward the ultimate tariff payer.

On the eve of the Congressional recess the President established a 110-member National Business Council for Consumer Affairs. It met secretly in the Department of Commerce. Procter & Gamble was there, Atlantic Richfield, AT&T, Ford, Chrysler, and General Motors, General Electric and Westinghouse, numerous banking and loan institutions, four advertising agencies, three tobacco firms, Sun Oil and Deering Milliken (whoe chief executives helped get the John Birch Society started), and several drug, food, and rubber companies that are in trouble with the Federal Trade Commission. Most companies were represented by their president or board chairman, including hefty contributors to the President's 1968 campaign. And of course the group included the president of press agentry's ultimate weapon, the *Reader's Digest*, which paid out less than half what it promised in sweepstakes promotions; a publication which excludes dissenters as industry advisory committees do, and which carried eleven of Mr. Nixon's articles and sponsored some of his travels abroad as its contribution to his election.

This new "consumer" advisory committee held its secret meeting with the President in the Indian Treaty Room, there, in the words of his press release, to "identify and examine current and potential consumer problems." The Committee should have met in the Hall of Mirrors.

The advisory committee system invites conflicts of interest. This is obvious from the foregoing descriptions of the make-up of the committees. But to zero in on one, consider how Chase Manhattan Bank (Rockefeller) associates dominate the Civil Aeronautics Board's Finance Advisory Committee, appointed last year. At its first meeting (in the Board's method of compiling the chairmanship of one of Chase's 298 vice presidents) this "Government" committee decided to exclude the press and public, to make recommendations to the CAB on its "procedural and philosophical conduct," and to begin by recommending changes in the Board's method of compiling financial reports. And who is the major creditor for five of the nine local service air carriers, as well as the principal stockholder in both the Eastern and Northwest Orient airlines? By coincidence, Chase Manhattan Bank.

CAB Chairman Secor Browne, to his credit, did not ask large corporations to man his consumer advisory committee. But advisory committees composed of consumers or representatives of consumer organizations are rare indeed.

Consumer representation in government is still in gestation. We are far from fulfillment of the consumer rights enunciated by our last three Presidents—the rights to be informed, to be heard, to choose. We do not know who owns America, or who pollutes it. The public pays for costly rate increase presentations before regulatory commissions by giant energy, communications, and transportation companies. But in most states no provision is made, through either the rate or tax structure, to fund the public's countercase against utility overcharges. Government does not provide the fundamental precursor of justice and equity—adversary proceedings—be it within advisory committees, before regulatory commissions, or within key departments of the executive branch. Committees, commissions, departments, and the Congress are assiduously attended by the omnipresent lobbyists for the corporations, whose key officials provide the lion's share of the funds for political campaigns.

Thus does corporate government, which is procedurally as immune from its constituents as is the Soviet system, undergird public officialdom. And that condition will continue until public government decides to limit the pampered private corporation, logically through Federal rather than state chartering and control of corporations. (For an excellent and comprehensive account of present-day corporate abuses and the need for Federal chartering see *America, Inc.,* by Morton Mintz and Jerry Cohen, published this year by Dial Press.)

If the pending legislation regarding advisory committees results in a law requiring them to meet openly, with prior public notice, some of the committees that prize secrecy will no doubt melt away. They could probably all be abolished without public detriment. But if diversified to include the unrepresented public, at the expense of the overrepresented corporation, advisory committees could constitute a desirable avenue for public access to government decision makers.

THE REAL VILLAINS

Robert Sherrill

Beating the drum of "corporate irresponsibility" in the environmental crusade is okay if it is done with calculation, for propaganda purposes. Dow, Georgia Pacific, Olin Chemical, Wyandotte Chemical, Shell—such names are highly useful for arousing the citizenry to furious counterattacks. But only the most naive would seriously suggest that these outfits could ever be thought capable of voluntarily assuming "social responsibilities." Corporations clean up their messes and operate honestly when forced to do so. That's the American way of life.

The real villains in the environmental scandal are the government agencies which have failed to use available laws to keep the corporate poisoners and polluters in line. More penalties and taxes should be levied against industries that foul the air and water, to be sure, but a much more useful reform would be to establish a quick and effective court procedure whereby harsh penalties for negligence could be invoked against the hierarchy of entire government agencies.

Under such an arrangement, outraged citizens might wish to consider first the U.S. Department of Agriculture's Pesticides Regulations Division (PRD), a sub-arm of the Agriculture Research Service. PRD is required by law to protect the country from pesticides that could do more harm than good. Before an "economic poison"—as the pes-

From *The Nation,* 14 November 1970. Reprinted with permission.

ticides are candidly called—can be marketed, it must win the approval of the PRD.

If, as is sometimes the case, the agency finds it has registered a faulty or dangerous product, it can try to correct the situation by "canceling" a registration—a feeble procedure which allows the manufacturer to continue marketing the pesticide while a series of hearings and appeals are held (the process can take as long as two years), after which the pesticide may still be sold with only minor changes in its labeling.

Or the PRD can "suspend" the registration, on the ground that continued sale would constitute an "imminent hazard" to the public. By this method distribution of the pesticide can be stopped immediately. The PRD can recall or seize pesticides that are mislabeled, unregistered, or adulterated. And it can ask the Justice Department to prosecute for criminal violations.

Those are the ground rules by which the agency operates. See, therefore, how it has used those powers since 1947, the year the PRD went into operation.

In the past twenty-three years the PRD has registered about 60,000 pesticides, of which about 40,000 are still on the books. Each year it registers about 5,000 new economic poisons. But in all that time, and although hundreds of these poisons proved to be mislabeled or dangerous either to wildlife or plants or human beings, only twice has the PRD used its suspension powers to remove an imminent hazard from the market immediately. A third suspension—ordering Aeroseal Company's vaporizing pest-strip off the market—was not motivated by danger, but simply to protect Shell Chemical Co. from competition (Aeroseal's product contained exactly the same ingredients as Shell's No-Pest Strip, which is still being sold). Shell and PRD have been suspiciously friendly.

One of the two authentic uses of its suspension power was against the herbicide 2,4,5-T, after this poison received pages of thoroughly documented bad publicity in *The New Yorker* and other magazines, and after the National Cancer Institute found that 2,4,5-T produced cancer in laboratory mice. However, the suspension was only against household use of the poison; its primary use has always been as an agricultural weed killer, and it is still permitted for that. You'll be eating it, willy-nilly. The other use of suspension was against products containing mercury, an effort which the PRD bungled critically. More on this in a moment.

For the first thirteen years of its existence, the PRD did not ask the Justice Department to prosecute any violators. Then "about ten years ago, I think we brought charges against somebody, but I can't remember the name," Dr. Harry W. Hays told *The Nation*. Hays is former director of the PRD and now chief adviser on pesticides to the director of the Agriculture Research Service. Although hundreds of companies violated provisions of the pesticides registration law, some of them flooding the market with hazardous products, only one other prosecution was instituted—in 1967, against Hysan Co., which was tried and convicted for selling a popular disinfectant that Dr. Hays says was neither registered nor effective. The company was fined $10,500 and the president, vice president and general manager were each fined $400, after pleading guilty.

When faulty or dangerously labeled pesticides are discovered and seized in one area, the PRD does not go to the manufacturer's files to see where else the pesticide is being sold so that it can be seized everywhere. For example: Rodent poisons containing thallium were killing children so abundantly that in 1960 the PRD ordered manufacturers to lessen the amount of thallium in their formulas, to see if that would make the massacre of children a little less noticeable. It didn't do the job; in 1962 and 1963, the Public Health Service reported 400 cases of thallium poisoning among children, and predicted that probably ten times that many instances went unreported. So on August 1, 1965, the registration for thallium products was canceled. However, because the PRD made no effort to withdraw these products from the market, or by using company records, sent its investigators out to find and seize the product, rat poisons containing thallium were still on the market three years later—and may still be on the market today. The PRD doesn't know.

Although the law establishing the PRD has allowed the agency to recall dangerous products since 1947, the PRD ignored this useful power entirely until 1967, and did not set up a formal procedure for the recall of faulty products until May 5, 1969—two days before the House Intergovernmental Operations Subcommittee was to begin hearings into the misconduct and non-conduct of the PRD.

The PRD has an arrangement by which it forwards to the Department of Health and to the Interior Department all registration applications, to see if the other agencies might have any objections. If other agencies do complain, the PRD usually ignores them. In 1969 alone, the PRD registered 185 pesticides over the protests of the Department of Health (that is, either over the objections of the Food and Drug Administration or of the Public Health Service). Three examples of the PRD's defense of industrial poisoning despite health objections:

In 1963 PRD registered lindane, a continuous vaporizer, although the Food and Drug Administration and the Public Health Service both said it was dangerous. For that matter, even the Consumer and Marketing Service of the USDA banned the use of lindane around food-processing plants. For sixteen years these protests were ignored; then, last year, when the Government Accounting Office issued its report blasting the misconduct of the PRD, the agency discovered after only five days of testing that, sure enough, lindane was dangerous.

Another example is the Shell No-Pest Strip, which the Public Health Service had been denouncing since 1963 as dangerous to have around food or around infants or old people. Six years passed without action. Then in 1969 a Congressional investigation disclosed that PRD had been influenced by three of its employees who were also on the payroll of Shell Chemical Co. Embarrassed, PRD took the first step requiring new warnings on No-Pest Strip's label, but the final order on this was not sent out until this summer.

At least since 1962, when Rachel Carson's *Silent Spring* caught the attention of people who were wondering where all the wild birds had gone, conservationists and many medical scientists have been urging sharp restrictions on the use of DDT, the residue from which has covered the earth from pole to pole and has even been found in the breast milk of human mothers. But because two-thirds of the DDT is used to protect cotton crops, and since a great majority of the members of Congressional farm committees are from cotton states, the USDA has been slow to curtail the marketing of this economic poison.

The PRD employs thirty-one inspectors and five supervisors in its enforcement program; they go out collecting samples of produce on which pesticides have been used. The samples are sent to one of the PRD's five analytic laboratories, to see if the poison contains the compounds, and in the strengths, the manufacturer claims. The pesticides are also tested at one of the six PRD biological laboratories for efficacy; for example, if the manufacturer says the poison will kill weeds, then it is tested as a weed killer.

That is all that initially interests the PRD: whether or not the pesticide contains and will do what the manufacturer claims. Testimony given before Congress indicates that *the PRD does not test for safety to human beings until after somebody is killed by the pesticide or until there are enough serious injuries or enough adverse publicity to force them to make the test.*

In the USDA, hogs are treated better than human beings. The Veterinary Biological Division of the Agriculture Research Service pretests all commercial vaccines to be used on livestock, but the PRD registers economic poisons without any pretesting as to the human safety factor. It takes the word of the manufacturer. Dr. Hays feels very defensive about this. He says: "The attitude of the press and the attitude of some members of Congress is that there is something very wrong in the data you get from an industry or a commercial laboratory. Most people think the petition for registration is just a piece of paper. Let me tell you something: these petitions run now in linear feet. They may be five volumes, a stack about 2 feet high. And the data is not usually put together by the industry itself but by a commercial toxicological laboratory with which the industry contracts to do the study. They spend as much as $200,000 to $5 million to get the data. Now, why anybody should look down their nose at industry's data, I don't know. Anybody who knows the subject knows that it hasn't been padded or fixed in any way. I think we've got a pretty respectable group of economic poisons."

But no indictment of the PRD is quite so damning as its sluggish reception of evidence, coming in from around the world, that fungicides and pesticides containing mercury are highly dangerous.

Last December, three children in the family of Ernest Lee Huckleby, a school janitor in Alamogordo, N.M., became critically ill; one is still in a coma, a second is apparently permanently blind and crippled, and the other has the muscular responses of a severe spastic. Eventually the cause of their troubles was traced to the eating of a hog that had been fed the sweepings from a granary. The sweepings were apparently of seed that had been treated with a mercury compound commonly used to protect seed from fungus. Martin Waldron of *The New York Times* reports that Panogen, a commercial fungicide manufactured by Nor-Am Agricultural Products, Inc., of Chicago, was seen at the granary. Nor-Am, with DuPont, provides the needs of more than half the nation's fungicide market.

The PRD did not respond immediately to this disaster. The agency knew about the poisonings for "two or three weeks," by Dr. Hays's recollections, before he sent a telegram, on February 18, 1970, to Nor-Am invoking the imminent hazard powers and ordering the company to stop selling the fungicide immediately and recall it from the market. This action was taken the day after a National Broadcasting Company news program featured the Huckleby tragedy. In March, the PRD issued an industry-wide order for an end to the marketing of mercury-laden products.

Department of Agriculture officials must have known that the multimillion-dollar mercury pesticide industry would not take this without a fight. Mercury has been used since 1929 to prevent rusts and slime and mold, and to eradicate soil-borne fungi which choke off germination. It is commonly used to treat seeds of wheat, barley, peas, rice, other grain seed, and even cotton before planting.

So Nor-Am took the USDA to court, seeking an order overturning the suspension, and won. A three-man appellate court ruled that PRD had not established evidence of an imminent hazard and that its actions were "arbitrary and capricious."

Why did it turn out that way? Because the USDA officials fumbled the whole incident. Indeed, they were so inept that one is permitted to wonder if they really wanted to win.

The opinion of the majority of the appellate court noted that "Dr. Hays, on cross-examination, stated that so far as he was aware at the time the telegram was sent, he knew of no permanent injury resulting from the use of Panogen per se. With regard to Alamogordo, Dr. Hays testified that he 'visited the area and discussed the entire investigation going on during the latter part of December and early January.' Hays admitted that as of February 18, the date of suspension, he assumed that the case involved accidental misuse rather than intentional misuse. He was sure tests were available to identify Panogen but admitted that no such test had been conducted."

In cross-examining Dr. Hays, the attorneys for Nor-Am had asked if he knew of any other accidents to human beings involving mercury pesticides on this continent. He said no. Recently he told me, "The lawyer asked me about human accidents on this continent, so I had to say no. He hadn't asked me about accidents in other countries."

It seems an incredible excuse for not voluntarily disclosing the accident data that he had available for other countries, particularly Sweden. The rest of Dr. Hays's excuse goes like this: "We went to Chicago for the hearings with the firm belief—it was the feeling of the USDA counsel and of the Justice Department—that the court had no right to intervene, because the decisions of the Secretary of Agriculture are not subject to judicial review until the manufacturer has first been processed through an administrative review. We were pretty confident that that judge would agree with us. So we didn't go prepared to debate the facts of the case. So there I was, just me against about five from Nor-Am. They put on their testimony, did a beautiful job, then I testified and then got tied up in cross-examination."

Just why such an experienced toxicologist as Dr. Hays, a former official of the National Academy of Science, should feel so helplessly ignorant in presenting a case against mercury is hard to understand.

For years he has been following with keen interest, he says, the widening circle of new mysteries and new knowledge relating to mercury poisonings. Long before the seed case came to Dr. Hays, he was aware of the trickiness of using mercury in slimicides, algaecides, fungicides and pesticides. An algaecide used in swimming pools was registered "under protest" in 1963. He said, "This is a nasty one. We got an awful lot of protest from the Public Health Service. I went to the Surgeon General and said, 'I don't like it either. I don't like using mercury in swimming pools, but we've got to have data before we can cancel the registration.' " Finally, about a year ago, Dr. Hays did cancel the registration but, because it is grinding through the appeals process, the mercury laden product is still being used in swimming pools.

As with all toxicologists, Dr. Hays was also fascinated by the famous outbreak of 111 mercury poisonings among people who had eaten fish caught in the bay at Minamata, Japan, between 1958 and 1963. This episode and others were summarized in a book published in 1964: *Toxicity of Mercury and Its Compounds*, by P. Lesley Bidstrup. Forty-three died; there were nineteen brain-damaged births among women who had eaten the fish. Dr. Hays remembers reading all the scientific papers at the time and participating in the excitement of the unraveling mystery: "You just couldn't account for these effects from inorganic mercury. You would expect a lot of kidney damage from inorganic mercury and you weren't getting this, and it seemed so damned odd. Suddenly somebody got the idea that this was being converted to organic mercury; in the mud in the bay, the anaerobic bacteria were converting the inorganic mercury to an alkylmercury, and this kind of mercury compound we really hadn't known much about. We found that methylmercury has a high affinity for the brain, for the nervous tissue, whereas the inorganic, no. This was discovered in 1964–66. It was this conversion that was the important thing." The mud-level organisms are eaten by little fish, the little fish are eaten by bigger ones, and eventually the biggest game fish—well-laden with mercury, for the concentration increases with every step—are eaten by man, who sometimes gets sick and sometimes dies. In Niigata, Japan, 120 persons were poisoned from the consumption of mercurified fish; five died.

Sweden, moving swiftly to avert accidents when it discovered that its industry, especially its paper and pulp mills, had in numerous places discharged so much mercury that the coastal waters would be polluted for another ten to 100 years, in 1966 ruled that fish could not be eaten if they contained more than one part per million, although this appears to have been a political decision, overriding the advice of many Swedish scientists that the maximum be no more than 5 parts per million. The Swedish fish also have been contaminated by the synthesizing of methylmercury in microorganisms, which passed the poison along via the chain of eat and be eaten.

Even more to the point as it relates to USDA's responsibilities, however, was the voluminous data coming out of Sweden in recent years—and widely circulated among toxicologists—on the contamination effects of mercury-treated seeds. From tainted seeds grow tainted crops. The story of this chain of poison effect was clear: seeds—grain—hen—eggs—man, or seeds—grain—livestock—man. For the most part, the Swedish seeds were treated with Panogen, the product that poisoned the seeds the hogs ate in Alamogordo.

One of the papers circulated among scientists at the USDA was "Methylmercury: A review of health hazards and side effects associated with the emission of mercury compounds into natural systems," by Goran Lofroth of the radiobiology division of the Department of Biochemistry, University of Stockholm. It was published on March 20, 1969, roughly one year before Dr. Hays went before the court unprepared.

According to Lofroth's paper, the government of Sweden was convinced as early as 1965 that "the use of methylmercury in agriculture was responsible for the poisoning and drastic decrease of wild bird populations." Also, Swedish scientists proved that eggs laid in that country contained an average of .029 parts per million mercury, whereas eggs from continental Europe (where farmers had to survive without the blessings of Panogen) contained only .007 parts per million mercury.

This and other evidence caused the Swedish National Poisons and Pesticides Board to revoke the licenses of alkylmercury compounds in agriculture as of February 1, 1966, and thereafter the mercury content of eggs dropped off until, a year later, they contained only .01 ppm—two-thirds less.

In Sweden, where hogs and cattle had eaten fodder grown from seeds treated with mercury, there were these contrasts with meat in Denmark, where mercury was not used: Swedish pork chops, 0.30 ppm, Danish .003; Swedish beef, 0.12 ppm, Danish .003; Swedish pig's liver, .060 ppm, Danish .009.

After the ban went into effect in Sweden, there was this falling off of mercury tainting: Pork chops, down to .008 ppm in 1968; beef, down to .003 in 1968; pig's liver, down to .021 ppm.

Lofroth concluded at the end of his extensive, heavily footnoted paper, "There can be no doubt that the intentional pollution with methylmercury, e.g., in agriculture, imposes hazards on living systems including man. Methylmercury dressed seeds are eaten by wild animals causing methylmercury intoxication of these animals and their predators and resulting in severe population declines. Effects on man cannot be excluded when game is consumed. Accidental poisoning in man by consumption of methylmercury dressed seeds has occurred."

In Denmark, where seeds treated in this way had been briefly used, they were immediately banned when a decline in the pheasant population was noted. Pheasants have also been a barometer in this country—and surely did not escape the notice of USDA scientists. The California Department of Fish and Game found up to 6.6 parts per million mercury in the vital organs of pheasants taken *in the spring of 1969*, a year before the Chicago hearings. That concentration can best be judged if one bears in mind that the Food and Drug Administration's uppermost tolerance is .5 parts per million for human consumption. The sampling of game birds for mercury content actually began at least as early as the spring of 1968, but the bureaucracy has done it quietly and has not broadcast its findings. In states such as South Dakota, where mercury-treated wheat seed and pheasants both abound, the contamination must be pretty impressive.

Having flubbed its appearance before the three-man court of appeals, the USDA now reportedly is attempting to obtain a rehearing of its case against mercury before the full nine-man court of appeals for the Chicago area. There is other evidence they can submit of mercury poisonings in this country, such as the seven head of cattle in Oregon that got sick in February, the bull dying of it; and in June, 100 hogs in Laveen, Arizona, got sick from eating mercury-treated safflower seeds. United States officials have finally got around to testing for mercury in eggs and have found that the content is "approaching" the high levels once found in Swedish eggs.

Meanwhile, on August 7 the USDA canceled the registration of mercury products, which begins the long appeals process but does not remove them from the market.

The really infuriating part of it is not that industry has done all this to us but that the bureaucrats who had the power to stop it were such willing suckers. Industries that have been dumping mercury into our lakes and streams claimed they hadn't the facilities and couldn't afford the facilities to stop the outflow of poison. But faced with the threat of a shutdown by the state of New York, one plant within a matter of hours managed to cut its outflow of mercury from a daily 21 pounds down to 1 pound. Federal Water Quality Administration officials say that "many companies" have, with heavy fines in the offing, "quickly cut mercury pollution from pounds down even to ounces."

USDA pesticide officials have said for years that farmers must continue to use all the economic poisons they want, or otherwise the pests will take over. Sweden didn't find it so. Lofroth reports: "In February 1964, the Plant Protection Institute of Sweden recommended a reduction of the seed dressing formula by 50 per cent . . . and also recommended that only infected seed should be treated. These recommendations were made compulsory in October 1965. In 1965 and earlier, about 80 per cent of the spring sowing was treated, whereas in 1967 only 12 per cent was treated. *This drastic reduction has had no deleterious effects on the crop yield.*" Similarly, the August 10, 1970, *Wall Street Journal* tells of an experiment among cotton growers in Arizona, Arkansas, Mississippi, Louisiana and other states, who used to spray their entire fields with antibollworm pesticides, but now do so only on a highly selective basis, and only after they have found traces of the pest. They are saving between 25 and 75 percent on pesticide expenses, and have gained a far better control of the bollworm. All evidence would indicate that the USDA has not been looking after the interests of the farmers in this matter (and certainly not after the interests of the general public), but has been openly shilling for the agri-chemical industry.

PROTECTION OF THE POOR

All too often the struggle for consumer justice has been viewed as a middle-class endeavor, but such hazards as cigarettes, air pollution, cancer-causing food additives, and ill-designed automobiles know no economic barriers. In terms of economic waste, low-income consumers are even more grossly damaged by corporate irresponsibility when their incomes are eroded for worthless, shabby products, many of them necessities. In a classic study, *The Poor Pay More* (now available in paperback), Professor David Caplovitz of Columbia University thoroughly established that lower-income persons, primarily blacks, are forced to pay more for essentially the same goods. Moreover, once the poor have been trapped into purchasing goods for which they cannot pay, they are subjected to shameful treatment usually inflicted by financial institutions and fully backed by our archaic credit laws.

In the first article of this section, "Ghetto Fraud on the Installment Plan," Craig Karpel describes the terrifying experiences of low-income consumers in New York City. As attorneys throughout the country will testify, the situation discussed by Karpel is not radically different from situations in other cities, though the circumstances and the law may vary. Maribeth Halloran, a former Neighborhood Legal Services Lawyer, reports on the turmoil that can engulf debtors caught in the collection process. After a low-income consumer is seduced by the techniques Karpel describes, he may then find himself unable to pay and constantly dunned by his creditors. The tales that attorney Halloran tells in "Threats Against Debtors" of the coercion and invasion of privacy which accompany an exploitative collection system are those she heard from clients during three and a half years of work in Washington, D.C.

Similar exploitation exists in Philadelphia, the city of brotherly love, where poor debtors are deprived of their property for inconsequential debts, although a U.S. Supreme Court Decision has since weakened use of the confession of judgment in contracts. But in Philadelphia an unusual organization, the Consumers Education and Protective Association described by free-lance writer Jean Carper in her article "Defense Against Gouging," has formed to vigorously defend its members by picketing merchants and the large, prestigious banks and finance companies that victimize them. The Association has been highly successful in obtaining refunds and the cancellation of contracts for wrongful debts. The members of this organization act upon the theory that they must resort to organized citizen power because the credit laws weigh heavily against them and in favor of the business community.

Indeed, at the heart of the gouging of the poor are the nineteenth century laws of contract which must be revised. Such agreements as installment contracts and promissory notes that incorporate hidden traps for consumers are based on the legal fiction that purchaser and buyer are equal parties in the transaction, each with equal bargaining power. This was once more or less true when contracts were largely between businessmen and businessmen, and when each usually had legal representation. Certainly it is no longer true in the era of consumer credit explosion when unsophisticated buyers are asked to sign small-print contracts drawn up by highly paid legal minds representing corporations.

Default may be followed by expensive law suits against consumers, garnishment of wages, repossession of merchandise, and forcible sale of property at public auction—many times for unjust debts. Such exploitation is made possible by unjust remedies weighted in favor of the creditor. Most insidious of these is the "holder in due course" doctrine which, in essence, grants financial institutions immunity from responsibility for the kinds of contracts and promissory notes they buy from merchants. Generally in a credit transaction the agreement a consumer signs is sold by the merchant to a finance company or bank at a discount. The finance company then proceeds to collect. Under the "holder in due course" law, financial institutions buying such paper are regarded as mere moneylenders, innocent third parties, and are not responsible for the nature of the original debt. Thus, in many instances, they can legally collect from a debtor even though the original seller did not complete a job, or the merchandise was shoddy, or, in fact, never arrived. Holder in due course has been called "the mask behind which fraud hides," and should be abolished in consumer transactions. So also should garnishment of wages for debts be abolished, the abominable "confession of judgment clause" in which debtors agree in advance to waive their right to a court hearing and to automatically pay any debt regardless of its fairness. Magnuson and Carper propose the abolition of a number of other unfair clauses and creditor processes in their selection.

Some enlightened states have outlawed holder in due course in consumer transactions, and other unjust creditor remedies, but getting such measures through state legislatures, which often are composed largely of businessmen, is difficult. It is apparent that Congress should pass a comprehensive credit reform law. The Federal Truth in Lending Law passed in 1967 was only a fractional measure. Not until credit laws have been vastly reformed will the poor be free from the extra consumer burden which is almost exclusively theirs. Only then will they be free from gross exploitation by creditors.

GHETTO FRAUD ON THE INSTALLMENT PLAN

Craig Karpel

Warren, a grown man who lives with his mother, walked into the Harlem Consumer Education Council's basement office a few months ago. Director Florence Rice gave him a leaky ball-point pen and he wrote:

> *"Bought TV from door to door salesman—Philco 19" lot of trouble with T.V. back cracked notify company to come have fix. Company claimed misplace T.V. sent repossed T.V. 1949 had to stick in hanger to get reception—two weeks after that broke down. Called to fix that removed T.V. still pay bill by garnishment—left job on account of garnishment which effect my marital relation as the garnishee took away from our expenditures food clothing and rent. Which for which my wife was forced to except welfare and I left to establish myself again T.V. paid $500 never received T.V."*

Louis-Ferdinand Céline coined the conceit that life was nothing but death on the installment plan. For poor people in New York City, this comes close to being literally true.

Six years ago sociologist David Caplovitz of Columbia's Bureau of Applied Social Research published a book called *The Poor Pay More*. The book is a landmark in the literature of consumer problems,

From *New York Magazine,* 26 May 1969. Reprinted by permission of William Morris Agency, Inc. Copyright © 1969 by Craig Karpel.

right out there with *The Jungle* and *Unsafe At Any Speed.* As a result, Caplovitz has become witness-in-residence at a host of committees and subcommittees where he talks about the lack of "scope" which keeps poor people from leaving their neighborhoods in search of better prices and terms, about the "deviant sub-economy" which springs up like weeds through the cracks in the cement of tenement courtyards, where nothing flourishes that isn't rank.

The Great White Way of the deviant sub-economy is the L-shaped strip of 54 furniture and appliance stores running from 116th Street and Third Avenue to 125th Streeet and Lexington. The strip is the home of literal *shlock.* Not figurative *shlock,* as in "that agency has nothing but *shlock* accounts." Literal *shlock:* doll furniture, one good long cut below "borax." "Borax" is junk, but it's better-quality junk. Birch? maple? dowels? glue? fabrics? veneers? Forget it—*shlock* is made of gumwood and flakeboard, knocked together with a few screws, upholstered in plastic "brocade" and varnished like a cheap coffin. The prices, however, are strictly W. & J. Sloane. *Shlock* stores do not talk about percentages of markup, like 50 per cent markup or 75 per cent markup—they talk about how many "numbers" they jack the price up over wholesale, and a "number" is 100 per cent. All *shlock* is marked up at least one number, and on a credit sale the markup can be three or four numbers.

So why buy *shlock?* Because the *shlock* emporia will give terms: "Easy credit." "Easy credit" means that as long as you are working and have wages that can be attached in the likely event that you miss one payment, you're okay. "Easy credit" means that if, as Shyleur Barrack, head of the Harlem civil branch of the Legal Aid Soceity once did, you go into a store and give a reference who says you now have two garnishees against your salary, the salesman will come back from the phone smiling and try to hustle you into $1,114.80 worth of furniture and appliances. "Easy credit" means that there is a store on 125th Street called Future Furniture that has to have a sign in its window: "WE ACCEPT CASH."

But all the places on the strip offer "easy credit," and a store can't generate much traffic by telling poor people it's going to take them to the cleaners, so it runs an ad in the *Daily News* in which two credit managers (black and white, take your pick) offer

ECONOMY APARTMENT $198
Sleeper, matching chair, 2 walnut finish step-
tables plus decor. lamps, walnut finish bachelor
chest, matching mirror, full size bed, with 1 pc.
Firestone comb. mattress, 16 pcs. dishware, 16
pcs. cutlery, 8 towels, 11 pc. salad set, 29 table
access.

But once they've spent the money to get you into the store, they can't let you out with only a miserable $198 worth of *shlock*. That is only the bait end of bait-and-switch advertising. By the time the customer leaves, he should have put his Juan Hancock on the dotted line for at least $1,000. To cause this takes more than just an old-fashioned bait-and-switch. It requires nothing less than that balletic extravaganza of salesmanship known to the trade as the "turnover" or "tossover," code name "T.O." The salesman starts by showing the customer a pile of junk for $198. One store keeps its bait furniture piled in a dark corner, lit by a naked lightbulb. It is painted battleship gray, every stick of it, down to what used to be the chrome legs on the dinette table. If you wanted to give a salesman a heart attack, all you'd have to do is say, "Okay, I'll take it." "You don't want this stuff," he says. "It'll fall apart in a couple of months. Besides, a person like you can afford something better. Let me show you something a little bit better." The salesman than takes the stiff upstairs in an elevator, but not before shaking him down for a $50 deposit for the privilege of "seeing the warehouse." The elevator gets "stuck" after the first trip up and doesn't get unstuck until the stiff has been signed up for a bill of goods. The idea of the T.O. is to show the stiff successively more expensive suites of furniture without letting him get discouraged about the price.

When he begins to look green around the gills the first time around, the salesman turns him over to another salesman who is introduced as the "assistant manager." The A.M. immediately "sandbags"—knocks 50 per cent off—whatever the first salesman quoted. The stiff is so taken aback that he lets the A.M. build him up again. Just before he begins to feel weak again, the A.M. turns him over to the "manager," who slashes the A.M.'s prices "as a special favor for you." The manager will try to build him up to, say, $800 or $1,000. If the stiff says he "wants to think about it" and tries to leave, he finds that the elevator is on the fritz. The "owner" now appears, knocks off a hundred bucks or two, and this usually convinces the stiff to sign. At which point the elevator suddenly clicks into action.

Now the fraud starts in earnest. When the furniture arrives, it's almost invariably damaged—delivery men routinely saw off legs on couches to get them in elevators and fit them back together with a special double-ended screw. The furniture turns out to be a junkier variety of *shlock* than what was ordered. The colors bear no relation to what was displayed in the "warehouse." The stereo doesn't work. The television looks used. Two chairs are missing. You were supposed to get a 9-by-12 rug with your order; the "rug" turns out to be a piece of linoleum. When the payment book arrives, the installments listed add up to much more than the amount that was agreed on.

Try to do something about it.

Say, for example, that the glass coffee table is cracked. You bring it back and the salesman tells you he'll be happy to give you your money back. He shows you that the contract simply says "three rooms furniture" for $943.17. It doesn't list the price of the table separately, and now he tells you the price was a dollar. "Would you like your dollar back?" he asks slyly. Or tell him the dinette table keeps collapsing and he says he'll send a man up, but nobody comes. Or say you want to send everything back because it isn't anything like what you ordered. If you're very lucky the salesman agrees and the store picks up your furniture, but when you go back to pick up your $50 deposit, he says the store is keeping it as a "service charge." And you let him bulldoze you because you don't know what else to do.

Some stores rise to printworthy extremes of doublethink when it comes to not returning deposits. Dorothy Mason, a counselor with the MEND consumer education project in East Harlem, tells about a guy who came to her recently because he couldn't get his deposit back:

"He had put down $150 at Eldorado Furniture and Appliances on Third Avenue. A salesman had convinced him to buy a washing machine and a 19-inch portable television for only $649. Two things happened to bring him to my office. First, the washing machine was delivered with a broken timer. He could not get any satisfaction from the store. Second, he found out that he could buy the same washer for $199 instead of the $299 he had paid.

"I went over to Eldorado with this man to discuss the matter with Samuelson, the boss. Samuelson said, 'Your man could have had it for $199 cash.' 'Then why did you ask $299?' I asked him. 'Because the man is a bad risk,' he said. 'How bad a risk could he be,' I asked, 'if you've got 150 of his dollars?' Well, I thought of him charging this man on welfare $649 for merchandise on credit that he could have purchased for $360 with cash, and I smiled, because this was almost a daily experience on Third Avenue with complaints of poor consumers. Samuelson became very upset and threw me out for smiling."

"You wouldn't believe some of these places," says Steve Press, whose New York Institute for Consumer Education is setting up a cooperative furniture store in East Harlem. "They'll stamp NO DEPOSIT RETURNED on the contract. That would never stand up in court, but poor people are impressed and don't even bother asking for their money back."

There is a certain type of used-car dealer in New York that is especially anxious to deal with poor people. Tune in to WWRL:

"Friends, have you tried to buy a car lately? Have you been turned down? Well, call Headquarters at 538-4300 . . . You have a garnishee or a judgment against you, and no one will let you forget them? Well, call Headquarters at 538-4300 . . . Your desire to pay plus a small down payment is all you need."

"Used-car dealers really do a job on poor people," says former Commissioner of Consumer Affairs Gerard M. Weisberg, recently appointed a Criminal Court judge. "Some of those lots out on Bruckner Boulevard and Queens Boulevard—they don't deliver the car that was agreed on, they inflate prices to a point you wouldn't believe, they charge a fortune for so-called 'credit investigations.' And they refuse to refund deposits if the customer's credit doesn't check out, though they lure him out there with promises that nobody's refused. Recently we revoked the license of Motorama Wholesalers on Queens Boulevard. Motorama was taking people's money and refusing to deliver the cars. The deposits ranged up to $580.

"The Department is constantly going over these dealers' books, but it's tough to police them. You put one corporation out of business, the next thing you know there's another corporation employing the same salesman, using the same shady tactics on the same lot."

The Consumer Fraud Unit set up by U.S. Attorney Robert Morgenthau under the direction of Richard A. Givens has been looking into the used-car racket.

"Our investigations have disclosed a pattern of sales of certain used cars at many times their original cost," explains Givens, "followed by a cycle of repossession, repurchase of the car at a low price at auction and further resale at many times that price to new customers, who in turn are frequently sued by finance agencies and often claim to have received no notice of suit. The inquiry indicated that in certain cases some used-car dealers know in *advance* that there will be a complaint regarding *each and every* automobile sold and that many customers will give up the car and default because they feel it can't be made to work. We're looking into possible violations of federal law by these people."

You don't have to leave the comfort of your home to be bilked. Peddlers making the rounds of slums and projects run the oldest-established permanent floating crap game in town. Encyclopedia salesmen tell welfare mothers they are officials of the Board of Education, that the books they are pushing are required reading for their children. They sell people encylopedias who already *have* encyclopedias. They sell $379.60 worth of books in English to people who only speak Spanish, to people who can't read at all, to people who are destitute. A peddler tells a woman she can have a set of pots and pans in her home for 10 days; if she doesn't like them she can return them. When the utensils arrive, she signs a receipt for them. She decides to call the company and tell them to take the stuff back because it's junk. Then she realizes she has no idea what the company's name is or where it's located. The "receipt" she signed was actually a retail installment contract for $83.75. Soon she gets a payment book in the mail with a note saying she'll be sued if she misses one payment.

Richard A. Givens prosecuted a character named Rubin Sterngass recently for running a "chain referral" swindle, a mode of fleecing that is popular in the slums. A salesman would come to the house and offer quartz broilers and color television sets for nothing if the customer would refer acquaintances to Sterngass' company. The customer would sign up for a color TV at a credit price of $1,400; commissions were supposed to be paid to him for each "successful" referral—$50 for the first, $200 for the fourth, $400 for the eighth and $1,200 on the twelfth. Givens demonstrated the scheme had its faults by presenting a table of how many new customers would be necessary at each step if the merchandise were to be paid off by referral commissions:

Step	New customers necessary
1	8
2	64
3	512
4	4096
5	32,768
6	264,144
7	2,113,152
8	16,905,216
9	135,241,728
10	1,071,933,824

Givens argued successfully that since every last human being on earth, plus everybody who had ever lived, plus a few generations yet unborn, would have to buy quartz broilers and color TVs on the eleventh go-around for the scheme to work, Sterngass ought to go to jail and think about other ways of doing business for a few years. The judge agreed.

At any given moment there is one super-fraud that sets the tone for all the other ghetto frauds in the city. Until last year the super-fraud was the "family food plan." Ray Narral, head of a legal services office of Mobilization for Youth, describes how the plan worked.

"Mr. and Mrs. Hernandez have two infant children and live in a New York City housing project. A salesman knocked on their door and said he was offering a very good food and freezer program. 'If you join,' he told them, 'you will be able to save a great deal of money feeding your children.' All of the sales literature indicated that for $12.50 a week, the family would receive a complete order of food— prime meats, fresh vegetables, everything. The freezer, the salesman announced, was theirs to store the food in, completely free of charge. The sales pitch was so inviting that the couple signed up immediately. They later discovered that the papers they signed were a retail install- ment contract for the food in the amount of $375.00 and a contract for a freezer for $1,020.76. Payments on the food were $93.75 a month for four months and 35 installments of $28.35 for the freezer."

Two years ago, a Nassau County District Court was asked to void one of these freezer contracts. It handed down a decision that, under the "unconscionability" provisions of the Uniform Commmercial Code, "the sale of the appliance at the price and terms indicated in this contract is shocking to the conscience." Attorney General Lefkowitz' Bureau of Consumer Frauds and Protection went to court against the "family food plan" operators, seeking orders restraining Serve Best Food Plan, Thrift Pak, and People's Food from "carrying on . . . their business in a persistently fraudulent manner." In 1968, the Bureau curbed the biggest food plan operator of all, Martin Schwartz of Ozone Park, whose five companies were raking in a very neat $10 million a year.

The current super-fraud is a "sweepstakes" craze that started somewhere in the Southwest and recently arrived in New York. It offers sewing machines and stereos "free" to holders of "winning numbers." Regardless of where in the U.S. the shuck is being operat- ed, the "contest" materials are the same. A chain with seven stores in New York is now being investigated by the city's Department of Consumer Affairs. The swindle starts with this letter:

> **HERE IS YOUR OPPORTUNITY TO
> PARTICIPATE IN OUR "STEREO
> SWEEPSTAKES"**
> It's fun! It's easy! Just remove the gold seal to find your serial number, and compare it with the enclosed list of lucky numbers. If you have a lucky number, it means extra savings to you! For example! If you have a number which appears in Group 3 (GRAND PRIZE) you pay nothing for a beautiful 1969 General Electric Stereo Console.

The number under the seal on this letter is 67487. 67487 is listed on the enclosed list of lucky numbers, not once, but twice, so you won't miss it and be the only person who receives such a letter who doesn't "win." A Consumer Affairs investigator visited one of the stores with this letter. He was shown a G.E. stereo model C121. The salesman explained that the investigator had won this record player, worth $150, but that it couldn't be removed unless he signed an installment contract to buy a record a week for 39 weeks at $5 each. The investigator called the Dealer Equipment Section of G.E. and found that the C121 carries a list price of $99.95. The records which must be purchased under the plan are displayed around the store. They are the sort of off-brand, off-band cha-cha albums that one ordinarily finds remaindered for $1.19.

There is cash-and-carry cheating in poor neighborhoods, but most ghetto fraud hinges on the "easy credit" retail installment contract. It invariably has some features designed to protect the consumer, which seldom work, and others designed to nail him, which always work. Under the law there has to be a "Notice to Buyer." The first point must say: "Do not sign this agreement before you read it or if it contains any blank space." In fact, nobody ever reads one of these agreements. They ordinarily run to about 2,300 words in phrases like "time is of the essence hereof." (The Everything Card chit is a retail installment contract—ever read it?) The space for a description of the merchandise is hardly ever filled in completely at the time of the sale—usually only a few words are written in at the top, like "3 Rooms Furniture" or "one 23" Color TV." What harm in that? Just a second—point number two is: "You are entitled to a completely filled in copy of this agreement," and right above where you sign, it says: "Buyer acknowledges receipt of an executed copy of this Retail Installment Contract." But the moment your pen leaves the paper the salesman whips the contract away—including your copy—and the next time you see it, if you ever do, it says "Damaged Furniture—Accepted As Is" or "Used Television Set—Customer Will

Repair" right in the blank space you were warned against. This is all assuming you read the "Notice to Buyer," of course. One reason you might not have read it is that you only read Spanish. The stores have *"muebleria"* and *"credito"* and *"se habla español"* plastered all over the outside, but there is no such thing as a contract printed in Spanish. The finance company's linguists are apparently too busy composing dunning letters to the *campesinos.*

The fine print on the back socks it to the buyer in terms only a lawyer can savor. The kicker is contained in the following hocus-pocus: "The Buyer agrees not to assert against an assignee a claim or defense arising out of the sale under this contract provided that the assignee acquires this contract in good faith and for value and has no written notice of the facts giving rise to the claim or defense within 10 days after such assignee mails to the Buyer at his address shown above notice of the assignment of this contract." What this means in practice is described by Philip G. Schrag, attorney in charge of consumer litigation for the NAACP Legal Defense Fund.

"If Greedy Merchant gets Ernest Black to sign such a contract for a 'new color television' and the set turns out to be an old, battered black-and-white instrument, or *even if Merchant never delivers any set at all,* Merchant can sell Black's contract to Ghetto Finance, Inc., for a lump sum, and Black is out of luck. Ghetto has a right to payment in full from Black, and Black has no right to tell a court that he's been robbed."

The common-law justification for this is that Ghetto Finance supposedly knows nothing about Greedy Merchant's business practices, that it is a "holder in due course" of the installment paper. In practice, finance companies often work hand-in-glove with merchants to soak the poor.

Martin Schwartz' five food freezer companies at 105-32 Cross Bay Boulevard, Ozone Park, were selling their paper to Food Financiers, Inc., Associated Budgeting Corp., and National Budgeting Systems, Inc.—each of 105-32 Cross Bay Boulevard, Ozone Park. Attorney General Lefkowitz' injunction forbids Schwartz' salesmen from stating that Schwartz' finance companies are "unassociated" with Schwartz' freezer companies. Still, the finance companies are "holders in due course" of the freezer companies' contracts and are continuing to collect on hundreds of thousands of dollars' worth of paper they "acquired" before the injunction.

Tremont-Webster Furniture Corp. is at 412 East Tremont Avenue in the Bronx. When I visited this *shlock* shop, it was locked. There was a sign on the door that said "GO NEXT DOOR." Next door, 410 East Tremont Avenue, behind a more fiduciary storefront than Tremont-Webster's, is Argent Industrial Corp. It turns out that Argent buys Tremont-Webster's paper. No doubt it is a convenience for a holder in due course to have the store about whose affairs it knows nothing right next door. This kind of hanky-panky extends from rinky-dink outfits like Argent right up to the heavyweights. Credit Department Inc. ("That's right, Madam, no finance companies are involved in this transaction—you just sign a contract with the credit department . . .") has the distinction of suing more people in New York County Civil Court than any other finance company. Erase any image you may have of ghetto shylocks cowering behind boarded windows on burned-out, glass-littered streets. Credit Department is located in the heart of Dry Dock Country at 60th Street and Third Avenue. Credit Department does not know anything about the business practices of the operations it finances. Take Associated Home Foods of 41-01 Bell Boulevard, Bayside, which used to sell freezer plans to poor people at prices equal to those which the courts have found to be unconscionable. That's none of Credit Department's business—they bought Associated's paper, are holders in due course and are suing people for not paying. Besides, Credit Department isn't buying freezer contracts any more—they know it's "garbage paper" and they don't want to get their hands dirty. Credit Department lists a few of its clients on its door—not that it knows anything about their operations, you understand—and one of them is Vigilante Protective Systems. Vigilante is in the business of selling burglar alarm systems door-to-door and is located at—you guessed it—41-01 Bell Boulevard, Bayside.

Lately, the holder-in-due-course ploy has come under attack from consumer forces. Three states have outlawed it. A bill to end it, sponsored by Attorney General Lefkowitz, was killed in the legislature in 1968 but will be re-introduced this year. Witnesses at FTC hearings last November called for federal legislation to do away with the principle that allows finance companies to remain aloof from the dirty business practices of the companies whose paper they buy. The New York State Bar Association Committee on Federal Legislation is considering a report that would recommend that holder in due course be abolished. Richard Givens has a mail fraud indictment pending against a finance company and its officers for claiming that it was a holder in due course when in fact it had an interest in the sale of the merchandise.

Coburn Credit Company first made waves in the ghetto a decade ago when it began to carve out a commanding position in the market for furniture-and-appliance installment paper in the New York area. It rapidly gained a reputation among stores as the outfit that was willing to pay top dollar for "garbage" paper—trade cant for inflated installment contracts for purchases of low-grade goods by poor credit risks.

Today the company is listed on the American Stock Exchange as "Coburn Corporation of America." In addition to its $50 million New York metropolitan area sales finance operation, it now has small loan offices throughout the South, a mortgage operation in Louisiana and a division that runs revolving credit plans for department stores. Coburn has made skillful use of the holder-in-due-course principle to protect itself against possible charges that the merchants it finances engage in fraudulent or unconscionable practices. Under the law, for example, a finance company can't be held liable for fraud in the contract if the customer doesn't complain within 10 days after he receives notice that the contract has been sold. When Coburn buys a contract, it sends three sheets of paper to the customer. One is headed "Certificate of Life Insurance Protection" another, "American Fidelity Fire Insurance Company Insureds Memorandum of Insurance." These two are of little importance to the consumer. The third sheet, half the size of the others, has no heading. Three-quarters of the way down the page are three sentences. The first of these is 125 words long. It contains an urgent warning that if the consumer does not act quickly, he will forfeit all his rights. The second and third are seven and ten words long respectively. They read, "Enclosed you will find your payment book. Payments are to be made as directed in this book."

Coburn has had brushes with the Bureau of Consumer Frauds, but according to Assistant Attorney General Barnett Levy, it has "cooperated" in giving money back to customers who claimed irregularities in the original contract.

I visited Coburn to discuss the sales finance business with President Irving L. Bernstein. His offices are in the Coburn Building, the largest structure in Rockville Centre, Long Island. One walks toward Bernstein's office past no end of teak, brass, marble, quarry tile, bronze, royal purple couches, van der Rohe chairs and recessed lighting.

The finance company's substantial physical presence would come as a shock to its thousands of poor customers, many of whom tend to personalize institutions they never see: "I got a contract with the Coburn Company, and Mr. Coburn won't wait no longer to get paid."

I tried to get Bernstein to talk about the holder-in-due-course provision. How, I asked, did Coburn make sure that the outfits whose paper it was buying were on the up-and-up? Bernstein told me that these were technical matters that I, who was "not an expert in finance," would have difficulty understanding. He preferred to tell what a bunch of deadbeats people were who lived in certain neighborhoods. I asked whether fraudulent and deceptive practices on the part of merchants might not make poor people less than willing to pay their debts.

"Listen," said Bernstein, "I have a social conscience about these things. I grew up in one of these neighborhoods—Brownsville. These people are not exactly truthful when they give credit information. And there are entirely too many of them who have no intention of paying. It was different in my day. My mother used to steal deposit bottles rather than miss weekly payments."

I suppose Bernstein saw me wince because he asked, "Do you have a social conscience?" He talked about a social conscience as if it were painful, like an ulcer. Bernstein said we ought to cut the interview short, since an important announcement was forthcoming from Coburn and he would be in a better position to discuss the sales finance business the following week. On the way out I picked up a copy of the Coburn house organ.

"Early in December," it explained, "Coburn initiated its annual 'Adopt Needy Families' program . . . five of the neediest families were selected. To each of the families chosen, Coburn employees in Rockville Centre have contributed specified sums of money to make an otherwise bleak and destitute Christmas into a happy and hopeful one." Gelusil for the social conscience.

The next day Coburn released the news that it would "discontinue its $50 million retail installment finance business." Coburn had protected its sales finance investment with a dunning staff of 250 who engaged in what are charitably referred to in "easy credit" circles as "hard collection practices"; the staff was being let go, so $5.1 million in contracts was being written off as uncollectible. But at the end of the story it turned out that "about $30 million will be allowed to run off and the borrowers asked to convert their contracts to direct loans." "The company will continue to carry about $20 million in installment receivables, but will buy such contracts only on the condition that they be converted to loans."

In the trade, the procedure of converting sales finance contracts into direct personal loans is called "flipping." It is done by offering to lend the customer more than enough cash to pay off his contract. The trick is that the maximum interest for sales finance is about 18 per cent, while the legal rate for direct cash loans is 36 per cent. The other advantage of "flipping" was best expressed by Bernstein when I spoke to him later:

"When you have an installment finance operation, you're going to be concerned with the dealers; this way, you only worry about the willingness and the ability of the individual to pay."

If holder in due course is abolished in New York, finance companies will be liable for fraud in the original contract. Even now, if there is fraud "on the face of the contract"—if, for example, the interest rate charged is in excess of the legal rate, or the merchandise being purchased is not described—the finance company is liable. But from now on, Coburn will be lending people cash to *pay off* the original contract, so it won't be liable for anything. If other sales finance companies go Coburn's route, they will have found a way of getting around policing the dealers whose contracts they buy. Until this writing, Coburn didn't know, for example, that at least one link in the chain of stores that the Department of Consumer Affairs is investigating displays a sticker that reads, "COBURN AUTHORIZED DEALER." Now Coburn knows, but with the new policy, it won't have to care.

So whether or not holder in due course bites the dust, the customer is supposed to keep on paying. But what if the couch falls apart in three months, and the store you bought it from has gone out of business and the bills continue to come? What if the color TV explodes and the repairman tells you it was a used set to begin with and the store won't exchange it? You just can't see mailing in that money order for $26.96 every month for the next 34 months? What happens if you just *ignore* the bills?

Nothing happens until one day, a year or so after you've forgotten about the whole painful affair, your boss asks you to come into his office. He looks annoyed and shows you a paper and says he's supposed to take $7 out of your paycheck each week and send it to the city marshal and it's a damned lot of paperwork and he'd just as soon fire you if it weren't illegal. Then he hands you the paper and says you'd better take care of it or he'll find some other reason to get rid of you. So you go to the address on the paper and the marshal tells you to pay him $10 every week or he'll send the paper back to your boss. You do it because you don't want to lose your job. The furniture, the television, were long since put out on the street as junk, but you have a wife and four children. The only problem is, you only make $70 a week and you've got to pay the marshal $10 out of that. The hopeless cycle of consumer abuses goes around and around.

THREATS AGAINST DEBTORS

Maribeth Halloran

I work with Neighborhood Legal Services. I represent people who are too poor to afford private lawyers. Therefore, my clientele is made up of poor people. I work with poor people in connection with their many and varied consumer problems. I have worked at Neighborhood Legal Services for some three and one-half years, and at this point I think that it is fair to say that the poor people, the poor buyers—in fact, buyers, rich and poor—are people not protected by existing law.

The traditional commercial law, of course, was designed to codify the rights of creditors. It was not designed to protect buyers. As we work through the various consumer problems that are emerging and that are receiving more and more publicity, we can see that the law now is responding to the need that is created, by what has heretofore been a free-for-all in the consumer credit market.

You have already been told, I am sure, about the market practices that abuse all consumers, but direct their most exploitative efforts against the poor, those people who have the least bargaining power and the most need for credit, and who are at the same time the least able to defend themselves against merchants, finance companies and collectors. The fraud, the overweening pressure and the bad faith of merchants who deal with the poor are now facts notorious in our time. We know that high prices, shoddy goods and overselling charac-

From *Business Lawyer Quarterly,* January 1971. Reprinted by permission of the author.

terize this segment of the market. It is against this background that we must discuss collection devices used by creditors and collectors.

The inability of consumers to defend themselves and the disturbingly high ratio of default judgments against poor consumers must also be considered in any attempt to draw a true picture of your creditor abuses.

Collectors daily bombard creditors with letters and postcards stressing real and imaginary consequences to the debtor who fails to pay an alleged debt. Where a creditor has a strong security interest, the pressure that he needs to apply is necessarily much lighter.

I have in my files the following letter that was addressed to a man who on receiving the letter was inspired to come and find a lawyer.

The letter goes as follows:

"Dear Mr. and Mrs. X: Your note has been referred to me for action. Shall I take steps which may result in our foreclosing on your property? I shall have no alternative unless you remit $19.58 at once.

> *"Yours very truly,*
> *"Creditor."*

As the creditor's ability to collect becomes more remote, the pressure that he applies escalates. Some creditors adopt the approach of casting an unavoidable net around the debtor, impressing him that no matter how much he attempts to escape debt, all of his efforts will be fruitless.

The following letter is typical, and this is an actual letter:

"Dear Sir: Re: Thrifty Vacuum, $30

"We have some very unfortunate news for you, news which may be costly and embarrassing to you. Your failure to reply to our previous notice and arrange to settle the above obligation on an amicable basis has forced us to take the following steps:

"We are preparing your file to be forwarded to our investigator in your locality with instructions to inquire as to your credit standing in your community as well as to your place of employment, if employed, amount of income and ownership of attachable assets.

"Our investigator if necessary is prepared to visit your place of business or place of employment, if employed, relative to taking whatever steps necessary to insure payment of this account.

"Upon receipt of this report from our investigator, your entire file will be given to our attorneys in your vicinity with our recom-

mendation to file immediate suit and add all additional costs to your balance, taking satisfaction of judgment by garnishing of your income, lien or levy against your automobile, property or possessions as indicated by our investigator's report.

"Completion of the above arrangements will require approximately fifteen days. You may avert this costly and embarrassing action by remitting the balance or a substantial portion thereof, together with your definite plan of payment for the remaining balance direct to this office immediately.

"Consider your position carefully. Either you act, or we will, as indicated above.

"Yours very truly,
"Creditor."

Another letter of this type was written in Pennsylvania, where by statutory "Sheriff's Sale" a creditor is permitted to unleash the sheriff against a buyer and all of his belongings. A few paltry exemptions for the buyer's belongings are reserved for the buyer, reminding the debtor to which it is addressed of the availability of this particular tool, and at the bottom it says:

"Please put aside your Bible, sewing machine and clothing."

We can laugh about these letters. I get letters like this myself in the mail. I know when a creditor cannot carry out his threats. I know when I have a defense against the claim. Also, I know I have free counsel. But poor people do not know any of this. To the poor people the actions that are described in these letters are very real. To poor people the threat that they will be taken to court is a very real threat and instills very real fear. Their fear of being taken to court and before the legal process is often so strong that it will motivate them to settle even a debt that is not owing in order to avoid being forced through this process.

Creditors understand that fear. Hence, they use what is known as the "simulated court document," the document that comes embroidered with legal-like gobbledygook, and including various Latin words, and indicates to an ordinary citizen that something important is about to happen in a court of law. This instrument makes poor people very much afraid. The document might not have the same effect on middle class people or people who have the sophistication or knowledge available to them to be able to distinguish between the real thing and the fake.

In my experience collectors save the most venal and disturbing tactics for the telephone. The telephone conversation, of course, is hard to prove in court. It is not easily traceable. There are only usually two parties to the conversation, the creditor and the debtor. In court it is one person's word against the other.

Telephone calls go to the debtor himself, to his family and to his employer. They also go to friends and neighbors if the former device turns out not to be effective. The calls are often relentless.

The threats contained in the calls escalate as the amount of the debt gets lower. The smaller the claim is, it often seems to me, the more vehement the creditor is in attempting to collect. Of course, there is a very, very good reason behind it. It is well known that a claim below a certain amount is not worth taking to court and prosecuting through it. That limit may be sixty dollars, it may be a hundred dollars in any given jurisdiction, but we see the smallest debts of all, nineteen dollars and twenty dollars being used as a basis to threaten debtors' jobs, threaten their families, threaten their neighbors, threaten to expose the debtor and all of his real or imagined vices to his neighborhood and family.

Many times because an account has been sold by the original merchant to the credit collector with no notice to the debtor, the debtor does not understand that he owed the debt at all. Many times, he does not owe it, in fact. Frequently, the debt may be owed, but the debtor simply has no money to pay it. The collector duns without regard for these circumstances, using depraved tactics that exploit the alleged debtor's worst fears.

One client of mine, a widow, earned three hundred fifty dollars a month working in a governmental agency and supported two minor children. When she was first called by a collector and told that she owed sixty-three dollars on an unsecured debt, she responded that she had no money to pay the debt.

Within a day, the collector called again, this time saying that a fine print clause in the contract permitted the creditor to put the woman in jail and to have her fined five thousand dollars if she didn't pay the debt. The frightened woman attempted to explain that she would pay when she could, but that she had no money.

The next day the collector called the woman at work. He talked to her co-worker and told the co-worker this woman would be picked up by the marshal from her job.

The creditor pursued this woman for three weeks calling her at home and at work, claiming to whoever answered the telephone, whether the co-worker or the woman's minor children or the woman herself, that the woman had defrauded the creditor, a marshal was being sent to pick up the woman, that the woman would be put in jail and fined five thousand dollars.

At one point the creditor identified himself as an employee in the personnel office of her employer and told the woman he had a letter from the collector saying that a marshal would be sent to the office to take the woman away.

The collector called her supervisor, tied up the government agency's telephone lines, cursing and abusing every employee who picked up the phone.

The collector impersonated the supervisor of the personnel office and called the woman and said her entire paycheck had been attached for this sixty-three dollar debt, and that she would have to pay off the debt before she could get any of her paycheck. He suggested at that point to the woman, that it might be worthwhile for her to call the collector and ask if she could have a loan to make up the debt.

The calls stopped to this woman only when a lawyer entered the picture.

Another woman, a mother of five children, was victimized by similar persistent calls from a credit collector. She said she was told by the collector that he had investigated the fraud that she had committed against her landlord, "You defrauded these people out of money, and, now, you are in serious trouble. If you don't come in here right at one o'clock with fifty dollars and twenty dollars next week, I will turn the papers over to a marshal. He will come out and arrest you. I don't know what will happen to your children."

Another woman was besieged for one week with continual calls from a collector who repeated over and over that if the woman failed to pay a thirty-three dollar debt, all of her furniture would be repossessed, her wages garnished, and she would lose her job. Her children were deliberately frightened by being told unless her mother paid the debt she would have no job.

A man told me that he was called once or twice almost every week for six or seven weeks demanding one hundred seventy-five dollars for a debt the man claimed he did not owe. The collector charged the man with fraud, and they threatened that he would run him out of town, "bounce him off" his next fifteen jobs and attach everything the man owned unless the debt was paid.

He further threatened to call the man's employer, to have the man fired, and call his landlord and have him "bounced out" of his apartment. He threatened to make numerous calls to the man's wife at her job and to call his mother-in-law and tell her a few things about her daughter's husband.

At one point the man was called by someone who identified himself as a neighbor who said that the collector had by some mistake come to the neighbor's apartment with a truck and a writ to attach all his belongings.

The latter device is often used as a scare tactic. One woman told me she was called by someone who said he had the same last name as she did, and the marshal had come to his apartment to repossess all of the furniture, mistaking him for the woman's husband, and the marshal's truck had just left his apartment and was rapidly progressing toward her apartment.

Others give messages that a collector is out with a truck looking for the debtor. The stories are numerous. The collectors' tactics are limited only by their own imagination. They have been known to impersonate marshals, policemen, fellow employees, attorneys—and in one case a woman collector impersonated me to my own client.

The collectors' goal is manipulation. The modus operandi is exploitation. It is exploitation of the debtor's fears and his points of personal vulnerability.

In one case the collector pursued the debtor to a mental hospital after she had committed herself and continued to dun her, the nursing staff, the doctors who were treating her over a debt which even if it was due could not possibly be paid off under the circumstances.

The woman was released from the mental hospital on convalescent leave, and, then, she was harassed with false statements from the creditor claiming that he had obtained a judgment against her. The statements were obviously calculated to increase her mental anxiety.

Children are brutally worked over by creditors. It is suggested that their mothers or fathers will be put in jail or that the job that the family depends on to support them is going to be lost for failure to pay a small debt. Neighbors are phoned. They are sent letters in which they are told their next-door neighbor is a deadbeat or that the debtor has committed fraud.

The collector's scare tactics sometimes become bizarre. One instance came to the attention of our office where a debtor had been told that his house would be bombed if he didn't pay a debt.

Last summer a woman left a message at my office after there had been some publicity about a case in which one collection agency was enjoined by our Federal District Court from engaging in large scale abuse. In her message the woman told me that she had had a girlfriend who had been dealt with by the same collection agency. She said that she thought her girlfriend had committed suicide and that the woman often thought it was because the collector persistently continued to say in the message her friend was depressed and could not get any rest because of the continuous calls, and her friend worried a lot about the debt calls and other things the collector said to her.

Calls often go to employers. That is a particularly important problem for us in Washington because so many people are employed by the Federal and District Governmental agencies which have a policy of firing employees regardless of their financial needs and no matter what the merits of the debt claim are where a collector writes a letter and claims that the employee is failing to pay a just debt. The policy requires the federal agency to go to that employee, describe to him that he may lose his job if he doesn't pay the debt and ask him to write out a schedule for repayment of the debt. The policy is in force without regard to the ability of the employee to pay. It is enforced primarily against employees at the lowest end of the wage scale, those employees who are at GS 3 or 2 or 1.

An employer who is unwilling to cooperate in this scheme, whether he is private or public often himself becomes the new focus for the creditor's wrath. One letter was written to a District governmental agency that is fairly classic. In this case the governmental agency had received not one, but a series of letters from the creditor and had refused to take action because they had talked to the debtor, and the debtor had claimed he didn't know anything about the debt, he had never made any purchases from the merchant. They were convinced that the employee's story was true, and they, therefore, refused to take any action on the creditor's request.

In return they got the following letter:

> "Dear Sir: We are returning to you a promise made by your employee who says he will make a payment on March 13, 1961. We received this letter Wednesday, March 22, 1961.

> "How stupid can you be? You let a man make a fool out of you, who says he will make a payment on March 13 and it was, then, March 22, and we have not seen him, because you are as stupid as he is."

A recent study written by the D.C. governmental agency says being called stupid is apparently mild compared with threats and profanity used by some collection officers in dealing with the District employees:

> A favorite threat used is that they are going to report them to the Board of Commissioners in the event the District employee fails to give a collection officer whatever he may be currently demanding. The collection officers appear to be of the opinion that the District government is a collection agency regardless of the Commissioner's policy to the contrary.

These are arrogant tactics. These are the tactics of things. The availability of a remedy for debtors varies from jurisdiction to jurisdiction. These problems have traditionally been dealt with as a matter of local law. There is very little law existing on books available to the debtor to get him compensation for any damage that he might have suffered in the process.

There are a few laws, and courts are also responding creatively to carve out of our traditional laws some protection for harassed debtors.

A federal law, Title 47, U. S. Code, Section 223, makes it a crime to call any person on the telephone with an intent to annoy or harass. It also prohibits concealing identity over the telephone when any harassment has taken place in that conversation, and that is particularly important for collectors.

Collectors usually use aliases in their various communications with debtors. I once in a deposition asked a woman who was a collector why this device was used, and she said, looking at me with surprise, "Why, if we didn't use it, we are afraid they would retaliate"—an unspoken admission about her tactics.

Local laws have to be looked at with two questions in mind: (1) Is there an equitable remedy available to stop abusive practices; and (2) after the practice is stopped, will the local law permit the recovery of damages for mental anguish inflicted by collection abuses or punitive damages to reflect a public policy that condemns the kinds of collection devices that are used.

In the District of Columbia we have had some success in asking courts to exercise their equitable powers to enjoin practices. In one suit brought in 1969 the Federal District Court preliminarily enjoined one collection agency from engaging in specified acts including communicating with an alleged debtor's employer, making any contact with the family or minor children in the family over the debt, and threatening to take any action that the creditor wasn't legally entitled to do. The final injunction excluded the prohibition against communications with employers is now on appeal for review of the question of the court's power to enjoin employer contact.

The injunction of course, covers not only the threat to throw somebody in jail in those jurisdictions where you cannot be jailed for failure to pay a debt, but, also, the threat to repossess when, in fact, you have no security interest.

The court also enjoined the collection agency from engaging in blackmail. The Blackmail Statute is available in many jurisdictions as a possible source for relief. In the District of Columbia, for example, the Blackmail Statute reads as follows:

> *Whoever verbally or in writing accuses or threatens to accuse any person of a crime or of any conduct which if true would tend to disgrace such a person or in any way subject him to the ridicule or contempt of society or threatens to expose or publish any of his infirmities or failings with intent to exhort from such person anything of value or any pecuniary advantage whatsoever or to compel the person accused or threatened to do any act, shall be imprisoned for not more than five years.*

We have a number of cases in our jurisdiction in D.C. applying that statute to collection practices, and the court has there ruled that the Blackmail Statute applies whether or not the debt is owed. The court is willing to consider the allegation that a man is unjustly refusing to pay a debt as something that is tantamount to libel or an accusation that will subject him to contempt of society so that that accusation comes within the perimeters of this Statute.

In a recent case the court applied the blackmail statute to the following situation. A woman had graduated from a special government training program and was supporting herself and her children with unemployment compensation while she was looking for a job. A dunning creditor during one phone conversation told her that it was illegal for her to collect unemployment compensation under her particular circumstances. The creditor threatened to make trouble for her downtown before the Unemployment Compensation Court if she did not immediately pay his bill. In fact, the woman was legally entitled to unemployment compensation, but she was terrified at the suggestion that anyone was going to make trouble for her with the agency then providing the sole source of family income.

That threat constitutes blackmail because the collector had both accused the woman of a crime and threatened to accuse her of a crime, (the crime being the illegal collection of unemployment compensation), and he had made the threat with intent to collect the debt. His act, therefore, was literally within the meaning of the Blackmail

Statute. You will find that many local Blackmail Statutes would have the same effect.

The court of equity may be available not only to protect a single debtor against the actions of a single collection agency, but a class of debtors. In the case to which I just referred, the court was convinced that the collection agency was engaged in abusive, illegal fraudulent tactics on a large scale basis, and, therefore, issued a blanket injunction protecting all present and potential victims of the company.

Civil action is more difficult. The question in all but a few enlightened jurisdiction, is whether an individual can be compensated for pure mental pain without accompanying physical injury.

Outmoded laws persist beyond their reason for being. I think this is a good example. The law that refuses to compensate pure "mental" damage evolved from a time when property rights were elevated in importance far beyond personal rights. Physical damage was accompanied by tangible measurable evidence. Courts in the past shied away from creating a law compensating, mental anguish because of the difficulties of measurement.

Also, there was and still is a reluctance on the part of not only the courts, but the rest of our society, to accept mental anguish as the full equivalent of physical injury.

But medical knowledge acknowledging the relationship between "physical" and "mental" injury and increased societal acceptance of the importance of personal and private rights have influenced a change in the law to permit compensation for pure mental anguish intentionally, not negligently, inflicted. The doctrine is often called intentional infliction of mental distress. Other theories are also increasingly applied.

Invasion of privacy is now being recognized to extend to two situations. One, the unreasonable intrusion into the debtor's seclusion, by continuous phone calls, for example, at odd hours of the night or at a time when it is very inconvenient for the debtor, would be an invasion of privacy under this rule. The second is the unreasonable publicity of a private fact. The test in all of these situations is reasonableness. Is it reasonable to publicize facts about a debtor's private life? Is it reasonable to use the method of publication? Are there other actions that are or were available to accomplish the same purpose? These are considerations increasingly balanced by courts in opening tort law to meet the needs created by collectors' abusive tactics.

Libel is available, of course, if you have a case where a false statement is made that defames the character of the debtor. This is not as useful as it might be unless you have a jurisdiction that is ready to accept the proposition that falsely accusing him of unjustly refusing to pay a debt is a libelous statement.

Where a creditor calls an employer, there is also a possibility that the debtor can be compensated under the tort theory of intentional interference with an advantageous contractual relationship for actual resulting damage. Again, the test of reasonableness is applied and most courts in this country tend to think it is reasonable to call an employer—if you have a debtor who won't pay his debts. There are some signs, though, that courts are coming to recognize the use of that tool as an unreasonable instrument of oppression.

The response that we are seeing from courts to the use of these collection devices once considered legal, is caused by an increasing concern to protect debtors from oppression. That concern underlies Supreme Court case of *Sniadach* v. *Family Finance Corp.*, where the court held that judgments and garnishments violated due process, pointing out that garnishment before judgment was a tool for unrestrained economic leverage by the creditor and was a tool for oppression. The court laid down the rule that a debtor must be accorded a full and fair hearing before he is even temporarily deprived of the use of his wages.

This ruling is now being analyzed and applied to varying devices for summary foreclosures of security interests, for example, the foreclosure of real property and chattel repossession. At this moment there is at least one decision at declaring that repossession violates due process. Authorized by statute, it takes place outside of court. Inherent in that declaration is the recognition that the creditor's tool is being used to oppress buyers who cannot protect themselves.

As poor people, especially poor people, are finding more advocates to expose the problems created by credit extenders and collectors, more case law will develop to protect them. Some legislation is already being proposed to regulate collectors in a much more substantive way than they have in the past.

The stories that I have told you today can be repeated in each of your jurisdictions, I am sure. They are not particularly unusual. They sound slightly humorous to us because we meet the situation with a certain amount of incredulousness. But the debtors involved in these and similar stories come away from these problems, not with laughter, but with fear and explosive anger.

DEFENSE AGAINST GOUGING

Jean Carper

Low-income consumers in Philadelphia—at least some of them—are tired of being cheated. Organized as the Consumers Education and Protective Association (CEPA), they have taken to defending themselves against exploitation, primarily by exercising their constitutional right to picket, a tactic which Philadelphia's Better Business Bureau vice president, William A. Peterson, terms "not the American way of doing things."

Traditionally, it is true, the "American way" has been for businessmen to organize against the thieves in their midst and to prevent "unfair" competitors from siphoning off their business. That is the essential preoccupation of the Better Business Bureau, although most people think its aim is to protect the public. At the same time, the "American way" for consumers has been to sit quietly, hopeless and unorganized, and let the unscrupulous businessmen get on with their games. Or to organize into innocuous little groups of Midwestern ladies who sip tea and grouse over the lack of information on package labels in supermarkets. Or for individual consumers one by one to bring their grievances to the courts where the laws are so rigged against consumers that not even the most sympathetic judge can grant much redress.

From *The Nation*, 3 November 1969. Reprinted with permission.

But to organize consumers into a really effective power is indeed unprecedented, and there is no denying that CEPA, formed three and a half years ago, is effective. Without CEPA many helpless ghetto residents would have had their houses and possessions sold at public auctions to satisfy fraudulent debts in the notorious "sheriff's sales" of Pennsylvania.

One such couple is Mr. and Mrs. John Gallman, elderly and black. In 1963 a fast-talking salesman persuaded them to sign a contract for $650 to have their 14-foot-wide row house painted, tuck pointed and striped, a job worth perhaps $200. They also unknowingly signed a blank note which was later filled in for $1,632. Doggedly they paid of this ridiculous debt at $33.98 per month, until Mr. Gallman became ill and unable to work. Then the finance company closed in, although the Gallmans were only $67 delinquent, having paid $1,427.16 of the debt. The company's lawyer executed a writ of judgment on their furniture; their contract had included a "confession of judgment" clause which means that foreclosure is automatic at the note holder's whim, without court review.

The Gallmans were understandably reluctant to have their furniture, accumulated during thirty years of marriage, sold at public auction. So when the sheriff's deputies arrived to conduct the sale, the Gallmans refused to let them in. The police broke down the door, at which point Mrs. Gallman, a frail woman in her 60s, became hysterical and tried to defend her property with a barbecue fork. She was hurt in an ensuing scuffle and sent to a hospital. In the meantime, the sale was conducted and the furniture, valued at $2,347, was sold for $90 to the vice president of the finance company that had ordered the auction. In addition, Mrs. Gallman was charged with assaulting a policeman.

In the past, this would have been just one more case of consumer victimization of the sort quietly recorded almost daily in the courthouse records of Philadelphia. But it was brought to CEPA's attention and the organization collected thousands of signatures on petitions protesting the furniture auction and the assault charge. CEPA delegations visited the district attorney, asking that the charge against Mrs. Gallman be dropped. It was.

CEPA then turned its attention to the contractor who had charged the Gallmans the exorbitant price for a skimpy home-repair job. Daily, for about three weeks in freezing weather, pickets walked in front of the contractor's place of business until he agreed to lower the price to $962 and give the Gallmans a refund. CEPA pickets then moved to the Mid-Penn Discount Corporation, the finance company which had ordered the sale of the furniture. After one day of picketing, its president was persuaded to return the Gallmans' furniture. "Although we had a legal right to do what we did," he said, "nevertheless as a sign of our regret over what happened to Mr. and Mrs. Gallman and to restore the good will our company has always had with the community, we will replace the furniture."

To grasp the extent of the gouging of low-income consumers in Philadelphia one must read the monthly newspaper, *Consumers Voice*, put out by CEPA. It carries a running commentary on consumer exploitation, with names and photographs of victims and accounts of CEPA's victories and occasional defeats. Similar exploitation of the poor occurs in other major cities, but Philadelphia is somewhat unusual, because of state laws. Garnishment is forbidden in Pennsylvania; thus, instead of attaching wages to satisfy debts, creditors attach property. This, coupled with the widely used "confession of judgment" clause, which prevents a debtor from having his day in court, produces a situation that almost invites exploitation. A consumer with a legitimate grievance is almost totally deprived of legal redress. It usually costs more to sue than the debt is worth, and the laws of Pennsylvania are stacked against the consumer. Thus lawyers are reluctant to take such cases on a contingency basis. Even a man with money to hire an attorney finds it difficult to get justice in consumer matters. For the poor and black, it is impossible. If they are to be assisted at all, it must be by organized pressure. Here follow some examples:

A young black man bought a new car, paid $1,313 on it and was completely current in his payments. Yet the bank repossessed it because, according to a bank official, they didn't like the new neighborhood in which the owner was working. Such repossession "at will," and in the absence of any default in payment, is perfectly legal, although it is obviously an arbitrary and discriminatory practice. CEPA picketing managed to get the man's car back.

Another man nearly lost his house and furniture over a $10 balance at a furniture store. Because he had not paid it promptly, he arrived home one night to find that the sheriff's deputies had broken in and sold $1,200 worth of furniture to satisfy the debt. Since some of the furniture was unpaid for and was being financed by the First Pennsylvania Bank, the bank, catching wind that it had been sold, then proceeded to put the man's *house* up for sale to pay them for the furniture that had already been confiscated by the sheriff. The sale was stopped after CEPA protested.

A third black family, Mr. and Mrs. Abram Simmons, who had been making mortgage payments for eleven years, fell behind when Mr.

Simmons' work became unsteady. By borrowing from friends and cutting down on food, they scraped together enough money for the payments, but were short the extra attorney's fees incurred by their tardiness. Hoping to catch up, they sent a money order for $81.60 but still owed $91.19 in attorney's fees. The bank sent the money order back with the astounding note: "The sum is neither timely nor sufficient to stay the Sheriff's Sale. Your property was sold at sale held on October 7." A few days later the Simmonses got a seventy-two-hour eviction notice, telling them that if they were not out by the deadline, they and their six children would be "forcibly ejected by the Sheriff without further notice."

CEPA set up emergency pickets in front of the savings and loan company that had ordered the sale, and news of the injustice spread so widely that the person who had purchased the house refused to keep it and offered to sell it back to the Simmonses for the price paid. Another Philadelphia resident was so indignant that, learning the Simmonses would still need $600 in costs to get the house back, he agreed to pay them.

It cannot be said that the Philadelphia business community has taken gracefully CEPA's blunt demands and direct action, but it is learning that the group must be reckoned with. When CEPA first organized in 1966, its opening move, when it heard of an injustice, was to send a delegation to the business and ask for correction. CEPA found most businessmen were unreceptive. Some refused to see the delegations; others arrogantly shrugged off their pleas and demands with comments like: "The only thing that will stop that sale is money." The officers of the downtown banks of Philadelphia, financing some of the schemes that were wracking the ghetto neighborhood, surveyed this bunch of neighborhood men and women entering their lobby with unconcealed disdain. "Legally, we're in the right you know," they argued. "Take it up with our lawyers." (Banks and finance companies under law in all but four states do enjoy a virtually impregnable status; they are protected by the "holder in due course" legal doctrine, meaning that if they finance a scheme which bilks thousands of persons, they can still collect their money.)

Finding that businessmen were determined to stick by their legal guns, whatever the moral issue or the pain inflicted, CEPA turned to picketing. The first such demonstration was on Memorial Day, 1966. Some businessmen tried to laugh off the pickets; others called the police. Two companies succeeded in getting court injunctions against CEPA's picketing in 1967, but the injunctions were subsequently lifted. Defending CEPA, John O. Honnold, professor of law at the University of Pennsylvania, argued that picketing is an exercise of free speech, fully protected by state and federal constitutional guarantees. The judge agreed and added he could see nothing wrong with using economic pressure outside the courts, and in fact, that consumers might otherwise be powerless.

Learning that CEPA does have power because it can arouse public indignation against sharp credit practices, many businesses now receive CEPA delegates with respect. According to Max Weiner, founder of and driving force behind CEPA, although he bears the modest title of educational director: "All we have to do now, for example, with the First Pennsylvania Bank is to call them and we get an immediate appointment. There was the time they didn't think much of our group. But we picketed them three times and that made it clear we meant business."

CEPA's success can be attributed largely to the thorough and orderly preparation it makes. CEPA has been called militant, but that is not an accurate term, no one has violent confrontation in mind. There is no shouting, no pushing people around, no sit-ins, no fights with the police. For the most part, the pickets are Negro men and women who, before CEPA came along, were afraid even to phone a finance company or business to complain of being cheated.

Arrangements with the police department are carefully worked out before every picketing to make sure that protection will be on hand if there should be trouble. Businessmen, new to CEPA's methods, are often taken aback to discover that a quick call to the usually dependable arm of the law does not stop the picketing. Says Weiner: "Their first reaction when they see our pickets is to come out and say 'don't bother with the picketing; we'll get the cops and chase you away.' . . . But when carloads of police do drive up, talk to us and then go away, the merchant sees his defense, his shield, crumble away. We are not seeking confrontation on the picket line. We are not doing anything to make possible police intervention, such as keeping people off the street, etc. We are simply engaging in a constitutionally protected power and it is a terrific power when exerted."

The typical procedure is to set up at the place of business a sound truck from which Weiner or another member of CEPA explains the grievance and what the pickets are asking. The pickets, of which there are often no more than five or six, hand out leaflets. CEPA has found that usually only a few pickets are needed and that pasersby often take up the cause. Many Philadelphians have stormed into the offending store or written angry letters to finance companies and banks.

Strangely enough, CEPA was founded by a man who was once on the other side of the fence. Formerly a real estate developer who lost nearly everything in a 1962 flood, Weiner then joined a real estate agency where his job was to help refinance their mortgages. He was soon struck by the fact that a lot of this refinancing had to be done because the people were being mercilessly swindled. He saw the need for a consumer organization and was able to rally a few people to the cause, mostly on the ground, which is still the core of CEPA, that "if you help your neighbor recover his money or save his property, he will help you save yours when the time comes." It is not easy to keep people permanently in CEPA; once the problem that brought them in is solved they often have a tendency to drift away. However, CEPA has a strong nucleus of regulars, a membership of 4,000, some active, some inactive (everyone who registers a complaint for which he needs help is asked to become a member if he can afford the $2 fee), and seven branches around the Philadelphia area. Activity has stepped up as the organization has grown. CEPA members now walk picket lines on the average of three times a week.

CEPA is also expanding by trying to grow from a local to a national organization, and by taking up the consumer cause on broader issues. It has established a foundation through which it hopes to get grants to establish training centers for consumer leaders in other cities. These, it is hoped, would then become permanent organizations. In addition, CEPA International, a non-profit group, grants charters to others wanting to set up CEPA chapters. (Amazingly, CEPA operated on a budget of only $18,000 during 1968, counting salaries, overhead and publication of *Consumers Voice*. The income came from membership dues, contributions and the sale of *Consumers Voice*.)*

Branching out from the redress of individual grievances, CEPA envisions consumer picketing on a mass scale against a whole spectrum of consumer injustices. For example, it plans to picket the Philadelphia auto show against higher auto prices. "Imagine what would happen if people all over the country did that!" says Weiner in support of his concept of a nationwide CEPA. "We really could have an effect." He deplores the lack of real grass-roots consumer power. "The FDA comes out and says they can't protect the purity of our food in a recent report. Consumers should be up in arms over that. They should hit the streets all over the country in protest, bringing the issue to a living reality. The only way that will happen is through a national organization."

---

*A booklet on the history of CEPA and its activities, written in response to the many inquiries for organizational advice, can be obtained from Consumers Education and Protective Association, 6048 Ogontz Ave., Philadelphia, Pa., 19141. $3.

CEPA has picketed the district attorney's office to urge stiffer action against firms engaging in fraud ("We want to make these con criminals just as guilty as those who commit crimes in the street," says Weiner) and has demanded that the city council launch an investigation of fraud and exploitation among the poor in the city. The council did pass such a resolution nearly three years ago, but no action has been taken. Finally, CEPA in 1967 launched a consumers political party and collected enough signatures to get on the ballot, running candidates for city council and mayor. They got 6,675 votes. The Consumer Party is back on the ballot this year, with candidates for city controller and district attorney. Winning seems beyond hope, but CEPA would be happy if its candidates won at least 5 per cent of the votes, which would establish the party as permanent and assure its automatic inclusion on the ballot.

But whatever the results in an election, CEPA has undeniably brought consumer issues to the fore in Philadelphia, and Weiner feels that, just by running, CEPA is accomplishing its aims. The Democratic and Republican candidates for district attorney have been vying with each other during the campaign to emphasize their support of consumers. David Berger, the Democrat, running against Arlen Specter, the incumbent Republican, announced a consumer protection legislative reform program, including abolition of the hated confession of judgment clause.

The consumer movement, if there is such a thing, has never been known for its toughness or effectiveness. But when, after hundreds of years of apathy and disorganization, shy, middle-aged ladies, Negro at that, from the ghettos of North Philadelphia, have taken it upon themselves to walk up to the vice presidents of banks and demand an end to the gouging, no one can know what is in store. Consumers everywhere just might get fed up, and start asserting themselves.

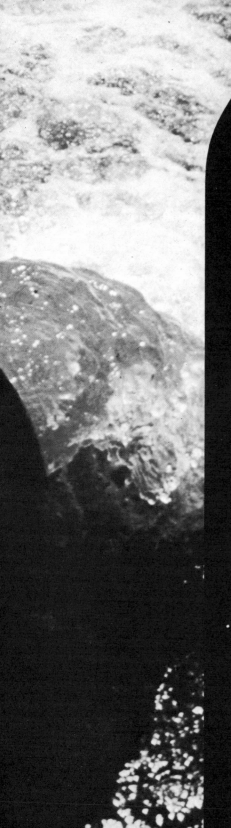

DISSENT FROM WITHIN

This nation was established by a minority of aggrieved Americans who blew the whistle on King George III. Dissent from within, or whistleblowing on corporate and bureaucratic irresponsibility, not only has a long tradition in America, it is also a highly moral activity which, because of today's unfortunately misplaced loyalties, requires considerable courage. Yet as more individuals become disillusioned with organizational decisions that have ravaged our economic and physical environment, they find they can no longer remain silent.

An allegiance to one's employer should not, as corporations would have us believe, supercede that of an individual to society, or to a higher moral authority. This does not mean that an employee should subvert or be disloyal to his corporate employer. But if an employee brings a specific safety or health hazard to the attention of his superiors and it is ignored because profit is placed above public safety, it then becomes the employee's duty to go outside the corporate structure and reveal the hazard to the authorities or private citizens who are in a position to expose and correct the situation. In cases of corporate stubbornness, it is the executive or manager who is disloyal and subversive to his organization.

There is no excuse for "following orders" if those orders harm others. Codes of professional responsibility clearly spell out this ethic. For example, the code of the National Society of Professional Engineers specifically instructs engineers to go outside the corporate structure and appeal to public authorities if management refuses to pay sufficient attention to disclosures which affect human life. The code of ethics for U.S. Government Service urges employees to "expose corruption wherever discovered," and to "put loyalty to the highest moral principles and to the country above loyalty to persons, party or Government departments."

Numerous lives could be saved, and information developed which would ward off crises before they develop and make organizations perform more justly and efficiently, if more people in internal positions of knowledge would disclose vital facts to the public, or refuse to participate in what can only be called immoral or illegal acts against society. Such courage is described by Barbara and John Ehrenreich in "Conscience of a Steelworker." One day steelworker Gilbert Pugiese "took his stand" and refused to press the button which would release oil waste into the Cuyahoga River; he caused an understandable furor among corporate employers. In another remarkable piece "Confessions of a GM Engineer" by reporter Morton Mintz, a former employee of General Motors chronicles the intrigues of that corporation's officials in their attempts to suppress technical data which demonstrated the dangerous performance of the Corvair. The engineer himself says he believed in the safety of the Corvair until he saw the hidden data which made his "stomach churn."

Since actions of the type taken by these two men are not without hazard, a potential whistleblower should ask himself the following questions prior to acting.

Is my knowledge of the matter accurate?

What are the objectionable organizational practices and what public

How far should and can I go inside the organization with my concern or objection?

Would any rules be violated if I contacted external parties?

Would any laws or ethics be violated if I did *not* contact external parties?

Once action is decided upon, what is the best way to blow the whistle: anonymously, overtly, by resignation prior to speaking out, or by some other alternative?

What can I expect to achieve by whistleblowing on the particular issue?

What will be the likely responses from various sources—inside and outside the organization—to the whistleblowing action?

Believing that citizens need a mechanism to encourage the disclosure of information about health, safety, corruption, and waste inside organizations, we have established the Clearinghouse for Professional Responsibility, P.O. Box 486, Ben Franklin Station, Washington, D.C. 20044. Organizational dissenters can contact the Clearinghouse with information of vital public interest. Where necessary, identities will be protected, but all facts will be checked. If individuals are to heed the principles of the law, their consciences, or religious ethics, there will be times when the conflict with the dictates of the organization must be resolved by appeals to more responsive authorities and to fellow human beings. If we are to regain control over our lives and shatter that corporate secrecy which reinforces corporate power, citizens must dissent from their organizational bosses to expose the waste, corruption, and hazards to health that are so abhorrent to the common conscience.

CONSCIENCE OF A STEELWORKER

Barbara and John Ehrenreich

Gilbert Pugliese's crime was a trivial one in Jones & Laughlin Steel Corporation's scale of priorities. He had not interrupted production, damaged equipment, or advocated control by the workers. It was just an irritating breach of discipline. At the beginning of the morning shift at J&L's Cleveland plant, Pugliese was ordered to press a button which would send several hundred gallons of waste oil into the Cuyahoga River. This was not an unusual order: the oil, waste from steel rolling operations, collects in sump holes under the mills and must be disposed of frequently, and pushing the button came within pugliese's line of duties as a millwright. Pugliese, J&L steelworker for twenty-eight years, knew all this, but he nevertheless refused to carry out the order. He was summarily marched to the front office and handed a five-day suspension. In normal J&L practice, a five-day suspension is an all but automatic prelude to being discharged.

J&L is a major Cleveland polluter. The emissions from its blast furnaces, coke plant, sintering plant, power house and other facilities, along with those from Republic Steel and U.S. Steel nearby, hang in a cloud over the downtown area. Its liquid wastes—oil, phenols, ammonia, etc.—have helped make the Cuyahoga River literally a fire hazard; they flow on from there to contribute to the slow poisoning of Lake Erie. Like the other steel companies, J&L is on the defensive.

From *The Nation*, 27 September 1971. Reprinted with permission.

"The quality of our environment has become an issue of critical concern throughout the country," says the 1970 annual report. "J&L is pledged to meet all government standards. Our objectives and those of the various regulatory agencies striving to achieve clean air and water are one and the same. Any misunderstanding that may exist is in regard to the time required to achieve the objectives, not the objectives themselves."

Compared to the rest of J&L's insults to the environment, oil dumping is a minor affront. It *is* a violation of the 1899 Refuse Act, but it isn't central to the plant's operation and it's relatively inexpensive to correct. When the federal government stepped up pollution abatement proceedings against J&L in 1969, the company could easily have complied on this particular form of pollution by pumping the oil into drums for proper disposal. But it was more convenient to continue dumping the oil into the river. According to several J&L millwrights, the company's major concession was to order the workers to confine oil dumping to the night shift. "During the day the coast guard patrols. But at night, the water's black, the oil's black; no one can tell," one steelworker told us. "When the inspectors come around, the company diverts the flow and puts the oil into barrels for disposal."

When we met Pugliese on the day after his suspension, the first thing he wanted to make clear to us was that he had not acted on impulse. He had a history of resistance, he told us, and the company was out to get him:

It's common practice to dump pollution into the river without any pressure from the authorities. Now you've got this serious situation and this pollution consciousness. Anyone with a conscience, who is concerned about the health and welfare of himself and his family, is concerned about this. They [the companies] just keep on stalling, polluting the waterways and air. So one day you take a stand. I took my stand on June 5, 1969. I refused to pump any more oil into the water. I suggested that they pump it into drums and throw out the drums. . . . This would mean more work for me. Dumping it into the river only involves pushing a button. Pumping it into drums is much more difficult. You have to get the drums and find a hand pump. I said I would do this, but they ordered me to pump it into the river.

Luckily for Pugliese, the company was then under considerable pressure from federal water pollution agencies. After first threatening to suspend him, the company higher-ups quietly dropped the case:

They were afraid other men would start refusing to dump the oil. So for two years they didn't ask me to do it. They got other

*men to do it. . . . The foreman or someone would do it at night,
or they'd pick on someone who wouldn't argue. . . . But they
[the foreman and the supervisor] started harassing me, they
ridiculed me, they said they'd like to fire me. They said, "Some-
time you're going to do it [dump the oil]—you've got to do it."
It turned into a personal vendetta against me.*

Other millwrights confirm Pugliese's story. One told of "the time the
foreman pointed at [Pugliese] and said, 'We don't need guys like
Pugliese around here.' "

We asked Pugliese why his bosses took his 1969 refusal so personally. Did they have a guilty conscience about pollution? Pugliese
doubted that this was the reason:

*You see, I set a precedent among the men. I showed that big
industry can be made to obey the law. . . . They think I hampered
their authority to give orders. Where it used to be ordinary procedure to pump out the floors every two hours [after the 1969
incident], the men would just let it go until they were pressured.
Consequently we would have flooding conditions with up to 48
inches of pollution in the basement. . . .*

*Like you say, I became kind of a legend. I'm a little older than
a lot of the others. Most of the older men won't do anything.
They're weary, just riding along. I feel like that, too, a lot. But
I claim that they're violating my civil rights—in the first place
by polluting the atmosphere and the waterways and causing
a condition which is detrimental to everyone, and then they are
asking—ordering—me to be a partner in violating the law. Even
if they want to break the law, they have no right to order me
to break it, too.*

For two years, the company humored Pugliese. As long as he
wasn't directly ordered to dump oil, he was all right. If he was ordered,
he knew he'd refuse. When the order came, at 7 A.M. on July 14,
it was in a tone of deliberate provocation. "Who's going to do this?"
the foreman asked. "I think *Pugliese* would be a good man to do
it." "I said, 'What are you trying to do?' " Pugliese told us. " 'We
went through this two years ago.' He told me, 'I'm telling you to pump
it into the river or go home.' I offered to get a portable pump and
pump it into drums, but he said, 'You're refusing an order to work.
Either you do it or you go home.' "

From the company's point of view, Pugliese thinks, the order was
well timed, because the local union leadership was away in Washington and a grievance on Pugliese's part could not get immediate
top-level attention. Pugliese knew this, knew he had eighteen years'

seniority behind him (ten of his years with J&L don't count toward seniority because of a technicality) and only six years to hold out for retirement with a pension. Of course, he refused.

Going to meet Pugliese, we were half prepared for some kind of oddball—a middle-aged freak, a paranoid conservationist, a sectarian holdout from the union's more turbulent days. We were not prepared for a man who, except for his single aberration, would be chiefly interesting as a prototype millwright, homeowner and father. He is an ordinary looking man; compactly built, brown-haired, wearing glasses and sports clothes, a little young looking for 59. He comes from a family of twenty-two, raised in the factory town of Ashtabula, Ohio; his wife is from Youngstown, where her four brothers still work in the steel mills. For the last thirty-seven years, the Puglieses have lived in their own home, a two-story frame house in a "mixed" (white Eastern and Southern European and Appalachian) neighborhood on Cleveland's near West Side. They put their four children through college and thence to good marriages, good jobs and homes in the suburbs. At the time of our first visit, Mrs. Pugliese's chief concern (after the job and the pension) was about the effect of the publicity on the oldest son, a successful dentist. "I don't know how he's going to explain this to his patients."

Pugliese's career as a steelworker cannot have left much time for hobbies or politics. He quit school at 16 to start work at Otis Steel (later incorporated into J&L) and, except for jobs in defense plants during World War II, has been a steelworker ever since. During the postwar readjustment, he was laid off from three consecutive steel jobs, finally settling down at J&L in 1953. After hours he likes to read—"sometimes till morning," his wife said—and this, rather than any formal education, accounts for his articulateness and wide range of information. Other than that, he likes to be as active as he can in the union.

Even in his concern about pollution, Pugliese is not stridently different from his neighbors or fellow workers. Another J&L millwright told us:

> If they had to close down the J&L plant to fix it so it wouldn't pollute, there'd be a lot of people out of jobs while they were fixing it. But if they don't fix it, then twenty years from now no one will have any jobs at all.

Like other Clevelanders of his age, Pugliese has watched the gradual destruction of the area's beaches, parks and fishing spots. "During the 1956 [steel] strike, we found fish coming back up the river because the steel mills weren't running," he told us. "Just from the steel alone stopping. The same thing again in the 1959 strike. Just think about that." And, like many other old-time steelworkers, he lives on the shallow hills overlooking the Cuyahoga Valley's industrial flatland. "You can scrub and scrub and never keep up," Mrs. Pugliese told us of the air pollution. In her immaculate rooms, she did seem to be keeping up, but the outside surface of the house, like those of the others on the block, was a corroded, peeling gray.

Pollution hounds a steelworker all day, everywhere. In the plant, Pugliese told us, "the pollution is terrible. It's dirty, greasy, full of fumes and smoke. The floors are always wet and slippery." With the outside pollution, it's as if the company were following you home, spoiling everything. Gesturing to the smoke-filled Cuyahoga Valley, Pugliese said:

> What gives them the right to monopolize the whole valley, the whole river and even the air? To take over complete control? This could be a beautiful valley for recreation. Now you can't even go down there without a badge. It's a prison camp atmosphere.

Another steelworker who had dropped in to visit the Puglieses agreed: "They [the companies] act like they own everything."

What is different about Pugliese is not how he *felt* but how he *acted*, and he seemed to take no special pride in this distinction:

> Of course, all the guys feel the same. They've been calling up and coming over. They're with me 100 per cent. . . . I guess most of the men are afraid of losing their jobs, taking a risk. The only thing different about me is I had to take a stand somewhere.

But once Pugliese had taken his stand on July 14, he found himself essentially alone. There was no immediate response from other workers; no rush to put down work and accompany Pugliese en masse to the front office. The union's initial response was no more encouraging. The only local official on hand, the assistant chief grievance man, tried to persuade Pugliese to back down, follow the order for the time being, and register his principles by filing a regular grievance. Pugliese told us:

> I said to him, "I respect your view but I'm going through with this. Are you going to represent me?" He said, "I will." I said, "O.K., represent me. Get in there. You're my attorney now. . . ." The union's on my side, of course. It's limited, though. They're taking it through channels. If I'm not satisfied with the results I'll retain an attorney and take this to the civil courts.

Pugliese said he had acted for "the health and welfare of the general public," and it was to this amorphous constituency that he appealed after he left the plant. His own calls to whatever pollution agencies, public and private, he could think of, and to the local television stations netted a series of polite but indifferent responses. It took a few calls by a sympathetic ex-*Plain Dealer* reporter to get the media interested in the story. By the afternoon of Thursday the 15th, Pugliese was being swept into the public's attention a little too fast for his own comfort. He saw his story on the front page of the *Cleveland Press*, complete with a picture of himself holding up a sample of J&L's oily wastes. He watched himself on the television news, sitting on his porch and responding gravely to the same modish young newscaster who gave the news on the phone strike and the closing of the U.S. Steel plant in Youngstown. "There's no rehearsal. They don't even tell you what they're going to ask you. Just like that—you're on the spot," he told us. By evening the Pugliese story was spreading beyond the northeast Ohio region. "If I get nothing else out of this I got my pound of flesh," he admitted. "I've got nothing personal against the company, but I don't mind seeing them squirm."

In the union and the plant, the impact of the Pugliese "story" quickly surpassed that of the event itself. Another millwright told Pugliese:

> *The guys think it's the best thing that could have happened. This puts the union on the spot and they've got to do something now after all the publicity. They got your picture out of the paper and put it up all over the plant today.*

By Friday the 16th, Pugliese's fellow workers were planning a wildcat strike if J&L tried to fire Pugliese at the end of the five-day suspension. Probably more concerned about the possibility of a wildcat than about the suspension itself, the union quickly dispatched the local's chief grievance man back from Washington. By late afternoon Friday, Pugliese could see his case moving smoothly through the regular union channels.

Meanwhile, the Pugliese case had put the pollution agencies on the spot as much as the union. The state government, it turned out, had given J&L a permit to discharge "normal sewage" into the river, on the condition that the company submit an abatement plan for treating the sewage. But the deadline for submitting the plan had already passed, with no action by the Ohio state attorney. As for the oily waste at issue, the local office of the Federal Environmental Protection Agency hastened to announce that it had noted "unusual" liquid discharges from the J&L plant on the morning of the 14th. (They were probably unusual only by virtue of having occurred in the day-time.) A few days later, the EPA confirmed that these discharges did indeed contain high concentrations of oil, and "recommended" that J&L install alternative disposal facilities.

Under fire from the union, the press and the pollution agencies, and faced with a possible wildcat, J&L had little choice but to back down on the Pugliese issue. Their only option lay in what tone to take, and they chose to be as ungracious as possible. On the 15th, at the height of the publicity, the company's Pittsburgh headquarters told the press, "J&L does not publicly discuss any disciplinary action involving an employee," and went on to refute the pollution charges as if they were a separate issue:

> In regard to the control of water discharges from the finishing mill at the Cleveland works, we have taken a number of interim measures to minimize the discharges of oil and other substances into the river pending the completion of a $2 million pollution control system which is now under construction.

On Friday afternoon, the 16th, J&L officials met with union representatives and "conceded" a two-day reduction in Pugliese's suspension. The union representatives got up and walked out. A few hours later, J&L called Pugliese to tell him he was being reinstated with full back pay. But true to its principles to the bitter end, J&L is insisting on giving Pugliese a formal reprimand.

On Saturday, June 17, Pugliese reported back for work. The company was installing drums and pumps to dispose of the oil in the sump holes. But nothing else had changed since Wednesday. Heavy smoke and filthy water still poured out of the plant. Inside, there were the same thick fumes, slippery floors and overpowering heat, the same long uncorrected safety hazards. On Wednesday, July 21, one week after taking his stand, Pugliese was helping load a roll (the cylinder which actually rolls out the steel) onto a high truck. The crane operator was inexperienced and under pressure to meet a schedule. He hoisted the crane before the roll was securely fastened and the 10-ton roll swung down on Pugliese. Jumping off the truck to avoid being crushed, he broke his leg. When we last saw Pugliese, he was at home again, facing an eight-week convalescence. "Production's the god," he said:

> That comes first. Regardless of what they say about safety, equality or anything, production is first. That's the almighty word. Machines cost money, so they spend money to repair them, to maintain them. But men are free, so who cares? If a machine overheats, they put in a fan. But we could die of heat prostration. We can't get a fan. Men are expendable.

CONFESSIONS OF A GM ENGINEER

Morton Mintz

A former General Motors engineer who played a key role in opposing lawsuits resulting from roll-over accidents involving 1960–1963 Corvairs, says that GM suppressed its own adverse test reports to prevent them from surfacing in the courts.

GM, in a denial yesterday, said in Detroit that it "has identified or produced all documents which, in the opinion of its legal counsel, it was required to identify or produce."

The engineer, Carl F. Thelin, said that a superior once produced from "a back closet" a three-inch stack of previously secret proving ground documents—but with a directive to Thelin not to copy them and to withhold them from GM's legal defense files and potential witnesses.

"Thus a witness could say he never heard of it," he told *The Washington Post* in a four-hour interview.

Thelin described the documents as "dynamite." He said that one of them, No. 17103, proved that with suspension systems such as those on later models the early Corvairs it would have been "almost impossible to roll over."

From *The Washington Post*, 27 September 1970. © The Washington Post. Reprinted by permission.

Thelin said that four years have elapsed since the documents episode. Moreover, it occurred during a long, confused period of transition from one boss to another.

For these reasons, Thelin said, he is not now certain whether the superior who produced the "dynamite" documents and ordered them suppressed was R. A. Gallant or C. D. Simmons.

Gallant was staff engineer of the "Product Analysis Group," the cover name for the "Corvair defense group" in GM's Chevrolet Division, Thelin said. Simmons succeeded Gallant.

Gallant, reached in Detroit, said, "I don't remember anything about it." Simmons could not be reached.

Thelin was among the GM employes who were "entitled to have access" to the papers "as and when required in the performance of their duties," the company said yesterday.

The papers had been "in the custody of his superiors and presumably were made available to Mr. Thelin and other employes by his superiors on that basis," GM said.

Thelin, in the interview, described in detail various methods used by the Corvair defense group to frustrate plaintiff's lawyers' interrogatories—the written questionnaires which the courts require be answered.

"We felt that some of these guys were planning to screw GM just because it had billions of dollars," he said.

The defense group never used as witnesses the "old fogies who designed this car," Thelin said. "We were told that some of these guys had to be kept off the stand because they would look like fools."

That's why GM recruited the defense group, in which he was one of about a dozen engineers, Thelin said.

"Our witnesses were very knowledgeable, very expert; more than that, they had good rapport with jurors. They would avoid engineering words; talk to the jury, not past them. They were anxious to testify and had good speaking voices."

The "most effective witness" was Frank J. Winchell, Thelin said. "He could wow that jury."

Winchell, then director of Chevrolet's research and development engineering center in Warren, Mich., and now a special assistant to GM president Cole, had recruited Thelin in September, 1965, for the Corvair defense group.

Winchell had "personal magnetism," Thelin said. "He is a good engineer and a hell of a man. He's a leader. Whatever the word 'leader' means, he's that kind."

Thelin emphasized his belief that serious design problems in the Corvair were neither inherent nor unavoidable. They resulted, rather, from engineering incompetence at middle-management levels, he said.

Young engineers, he said, could look at the car and instantly spot a needless design fault.

Thelin had first told his story to Gary B. Sellers, legal consultant to Ralph Nader. Then he told it to Frank W. Allen, a GM lawyer and, finally, to a reporter. In each case his cooperation was requested, not volunteered.

"I've got to tell the truth," he told the reporter at his home near Buffalo, N.Y.

He recalled that GM lawyers, discussing how to behave on the witness stand, had advised him, "Never attempt to lie. Just tell the truth—what you know. Then you don't have to keep track of what you've said."

"I'll always live by that," Thelin told me. "It's a good way to live. If I'm asked a question I'll go straight down the middle."

Thelin began his travels "down the middle" of the Corvair controversy when Sellers, acting for Nader, came to see him the night of Sept. 3.

This was on the eve of Nader's public charge—made in a letter to Secretary of Transportation Volpe—that GM had for about eight years suppressed adverse proving ground reports and films on the early Corvairs.

Nader had first come to prominent public attention as a Corvair critic. This was almost five years ago, when his book, "Unsafe at Any Speed," was published. Then, early in 1966, came the famed "snooping" episode. Finally, in May, 1969, with sales way down, GM stopped making the car. With that, the controversy apparently faded away.

In recent months, however, secret sources have been supplying Nader and Sellers with new information and documents in which Thelin's name repeatedly cropped up, Sellers said.

Sellers undertook a search for corroboration. It was for this purpose that he went to see Thelin, who now heads the vehicle test and design section of the Cornell Aeronautical Laboratory, Inc., in Buffalo (of which GM is a client).

Five days later—after news media had carried stories on the Nader and Cole letters to Volpe—Sellers made a second visit to the Thelin home. This time, Thelin invited him to dinner.

The next day, Sept. 10, Frank Allen, the GM lawyer with whom Thelin had worked closely in the Corvair defense group, phoned. He began with a cheerful "Hi, Carl, old buddy," and then led up to the Nader and Cole letters.

In the conversation with Allen Thelin volunteered that "Nader's people" had contacted him.

Thelin said he told Allen, in "a brief resume," that he had confirmed the authenticity of materials which Sellers had brought to him. These included copies of the "dynamite" documents.

Allen said, "Oh, boy."

He proposed to see Thelin in Buffalo. Thelin agreed.

The next day, at the same dining room table where Sellers had questioned Thelin, Allen interviewed the engineer for "a solid four hours without interruption."

"We remain friends," Thelin remarked.

Thelin, 40, is a graduate of the University of Wisconsin, a mechanical engineer, a "car buff," a Republican, an active Baptist layman and former head of the safety council of St. Clair Shores, Mich.

He came to GM in 1955 and became a front-wheel-drive, chassis and steering specialist on the engineering staff. His design innovations culminated in the experimental models of the Oldsmobile Toronado—"my claim to fame."

At the time, members of the American Trial Lawyers Association (ATLA) had filed the initial batch of what ultimately would become more than 300 lawsuits in behalf of persons injured or killed in Corvair roll-over accidents.

"We felt that ATLA was seeking to expand the product-liability business, and that they singled out the Corvair because of its uniqueness," Thelin said.

The Corvair was the first mass-produced American car with an engine in the rear—and an air-cooled engine at that. It entered the economy-car market in the fall of 1959.

And so Thelin went to work for Frank Winchell as if he were joining in a "French Foreign Legion" type of adventure, and enthusiast anxious to make "a sacrificial effort to defend the right of engineers to make design innovations."

In addition, Thelin felt he was aiding the cause of "fundamentalist" design engineers, who had been "low men on the totem pole," against the cause of the production engineers.

Thelin's assignment was engineering, liaison with GM's legal staff, especially Frank Allen, but he had certain specific primary and secondary missions.

First of all, he had to provide "engineering support for the defense of any Corvair case," such as accident investigation.

He traveled a lot to look at wrecked Corvairs and to try to figure out what had happened. Many times, at the GM proving ground in Milford, Mich., he tried to duplicate the accident site. "It was fun, man, an exciting job," Thelin said.

After a time, he also became responsible for producing 16-millimeter, wide-screen sound movies to be shown to trial juries.

Thelin would make such movies after a plaintiff, in a pre-trial deposition, had described in his own words how an accident had occurred—say, on a curve on a country road.

With the plaintiff's description as a shooting script, Thelin and his colleagues would duplicate the accident—sometimes even at the original site and with competitive economy cars of the same model year as the particular Corvair.

"Everything was entirely on the up-and-up," Thelin said.

"We would show that the Corvair went through this like all the other cars," Thelin said. "Then we would show, as a clincher, how recklessly you had to drive in order to have an accident, although our skilled test drivers could prevent one.

"Our defense was principally, almost always, that you had to drive in a very reckless manner in order to take the Corvair beyond the limit of control,' and that limit was higher for the Corvair than for competitive models of the same year," Thelin continued.

"The camera was in the back seat, viewing over the driver's shoulder, with a wide-screen lens giving close to normal vision," he said. "The movies would knock your eye out, they were so good."

EDUCATING LAWYERS

Thelin also had a couple of continuing "background" missions.

One was "to conduct seminars on vehicle dynamics for the benefit of lawyers, who had to be given a survey course in the subject so they could question witnesses intelligently." The defense lawyers were not only those on GM's staff, but also those from law firms the company retains in every state.

A second "background" job was "to acquire, index and write critiques" of materials that might be construed to be critical of the Corvair.

Some of these materials were "internally originated," such as reports on proving ground tests and Corvair shop manuals and sets of specifications. Others were "public originated," such as the Nader book and articles in car buff magazines.

In any event, Thelin's job was to process all of these materials for the legal defense files, so that GM witnesses "could study and rebut" criticisms.

Some of the "internal" materials were "freely offered" to plaintiffs' lawyers, Thelin said.

But there was a feeling, which he shared; that "we owed them no favors, and we had to give them what the law required and no more."

In a Chicago case, the decision was to "pile on the answers, snow them, bury them under material," Thelin said. The defense group shipped out a wallfull of boxes of technical materials that the plaintiff's attorney "couldn't understand" and that would leave him "glassy-eyed in two hours," he added.

GM, in its statement yesterday, said that as an engineer, Thelin "had no legal training or experience qualifying him to construe discovery questions, subpoenas and other court documents."

"DEVIL'S ADVOCATE"

As Thelin continued to search for critical material, playing the role of a self-described "devil's advocate," he said, "I eventually got to the point where I was looking for some material I couldn't find."

He came to believe, for example, that there must exist proving ground test reports that he hadn't seen. He persisted in making inquiries about this.

"Somebody—Simmons or Gallant—finally said, 'Here they are,'" Thelin said. That was when the "dynamite" documents came out of the closet and when he was told that, above all, he must not show these papers to potential witnesses. After that, he himself was "kept out of cases where he might be called," he said.

Thelin said the documents, which, oddly, included some in the public domain, consisted of proving ground reports and films on Corvair "skid path" tests and other "runs" made as early as 1961.

These materials have "purposeful attention" to handling characteristics, particularly roll-over possibilities, with various types of equipment, he said.

Thelin said he put the documents in a binder or folder. "I'm not a counter-espionage guy," he remarked.

The binder or folder was "not identified in a provocative manner," he said. He kept it in an open bookcase in his office. A few others in GM, including his office assistant, knew of it, he said.

Thelin said that one document in particular was "damning." It was "never offered to any plaintiff's attorney," at least while he was at GM, he said. Yet, in his view, GM was obligated to produce it in response to certain interrogatories.

KEY DOCUMENT

This document was No. 17103, the one which, according to Thelin, established that the early Corvairs would have been "almost impossible to roll over" had they had different—and differently positioned—suspension equipment similar to that on 1963 and later models.

All internal GM references to the document "misidentified" it, Thelin said. Therefore, "I could say there was no 17103."

The "mis-identification" was caused by an extra zero, the origin of which is unknown to him, Thelin said.

The extra digit transformed "17103" into "170103." Ultimately, Thelin said, he discovered that it had been established at GM some time earlier—in writing—that "170103 is really 17103."

GM, in its statement yesterday, said it had not produced 17103 "because in the opinion of our counsel, it has not been called for." However, GM said it has turned over this and related materials to the Department of Transportation and a Senate subcommittee.

"That's when my stomach started to churn," Thelin said. That's when I knew I was getting into deep water. Ignorance is a wonderful thing."

He said that the gung-ho feelings he had brought to his mission at Chevrolet now were sounding "a little bit hollow."

It began to seem to him that there was a possible pattern emerging from such elements as the "dynamite" documents, the exclusion of Corvair designers as GM witnesses and the odd addition of a digit to the 17103 paper.

Another important point increasingly troubled Thelin. He believed, as his own work for GM had shown, that the Corvair was not more prone to accidents than comparable cars of the same model year. Indeed, he said, a Corvair driver "had a better chance of avoiding single-car accidents, because of better brakes and handling."

What struck him, however, was more and more evidence that when there is an accident of a kind that generates "lateral acceleration, or side force" tending to overturn the vehicle, the consequences in an early Corvair are "more severe."

He put it another way: In an emergency situation in which a driver, say, seeks to avoid an accident, there may come a point at which certain maneuvers take a car out of control. Then it will no longer do what he wants it to do.

In such a situation, Thelin said, conventional cars tend to continue more or less straight ahead. The early Corvairs tended to "spin out to either side, but could also turn over," he said.

Thelin said that although he was "bothered" he continued to work.

In December, 1966, GM settled a large number of Corvair cases brought by a Los Angeles law firm. This Thelin said, "took the pressure off, or relaxed it."

At about that time, he continued GM management "perceived an oncoming recession," with the result that it ordered a 10 per cent reduction in the workforce.

THELIN QUITS

Thelin was transferred to a body drafting job at Chevrolet, "a kind of work I intensely disliked." In addition, he no longer had the use of a company car and similar perquisites. After two months of "humiliation" he quit.

Thelin went to Uniroyal, the tire company, and stayed a year and a half. Then, in March, 1969, he grabbed a chance to move to Cornell Aeronautical, where he does automotive safety work.

Thelin was himself, the owner of a Corvair, a 1962 model. He was then not yet aware of any controversy about its safety and considered it a "cute little car."

He read Nader's "Unsafe at Any Speed" early in 1966.

"My initial reaction was the straight party line," he said. "Here was a smart-aleck out to make a lot of money criticizing our good little car. We thought he was paid by ATLA."

BOOST TO ENGINEERS

He feels differently today. "Ralph Nader, through his book and other activities, has enabled 'fundamentalist' engineers to have greater design responsibility for the finished car," he said.

And because Nader "helped to elevate, to free, the design engineer," Thelin said, the cars of recent vintage are much safer vehicles than those of only a few years ago.

THE NEW ACCOUNT- ABILITY: AN AGENDA FOR ACTION

An individual is responsible for his actions. But who is responsible for the actions of General Motors? Or AT&T? Or General Electric? Or Mobil Oil? Or any of the other two hundred giant corporations that together own over two-thirds of this country's manufacturing assets? An automaker who builds a defective car that takes life is subject to no statutory criminal penalties. Drivers, on the other hand, can receive fines and even imprisonment if found guilty of gross negligence and manslaughter. Such a situation illustrates the vast corporate and managerial immunity from public accountability.

Corporate decision makers are remote in time and space from the consequences of their acts which may cause tremendous carnage and environmental destruction. Under the shelter of a sprawling corporate organization they can unleash a technology causing brutalization and injustice and still remain unaccountable to their fellow citizens. An old Roman adage says: "Whatever touches all should be decided by all." Many corporate decisions touch us all intimately: a genuine democracy should provide for some public participation in such decisions. The primary aim of corporate reform is to make the corporations respect public wishes, input, and pressures.

There are a number of ways to bring corporate power under control. This final section will treat some of the ways and provide an agenda for action.

One of the most crucial ways to bring corporate power under control is to break up monopolies as Washington attorney-economist Charles E. Mueller explains in his thought-provoking article, "Monopolies." He points out that monopolies and other collusive practices between so-called competitors are a drain on the economy, a prime cause of high prices and unemployment. Monopolies cost the consumer many billions of dollars every year. A break-up of the monopolies would lower consumer prices immediately—by as much as 25 percent according to some authorities. Ironically, as Mueller states, monopolies in theory have no friends in Washington; neither do they have adequate enemies. Anti-trust enforcement efforts are weak and often rejected by pro-business courts. Mueller and other economists propose new legislation requiring the break-up of a monopoly in any industry in which four firms share more than 50 percent of the product market. This would include the country's two hundred top corporations.

Gilbert Geis, a sociologist at the University of California, Irvine, has another approach. He calls for stiffer criminal penalties, including imprisonment, for corporate offenders. Corporate crimes are not regarded in the same manner as traditional crimes, nor will they be until the criminals who commit them are dealt with in the same manner as traditional street crime offenders. Geis believes that criminal penalties would prove a powerful deterrent to white collar criminals—more so than to other criminals—because it would subject them to unendurable public shame. One of the General Electric executives imprisoned six weeks for price fixing said after his release: "They would never get me to do it again . . . I would starve before I would do it again."

Another specific reform that could be adopted readily is suggested in a speech I gave before a Conference on Corporate Responsibility. In the text of my speech, "The Case for Federal Chartering," I show

how the states, now entrusted with chartering corporations, are cowed by the power of big business, and how they are so dependent politically and economically on resident corporations that they dare not bring the corporations under adequate regulation. As a consequence, our large corporations migrate to states with the weakest regulations. Delaware is one such state. Any attempts to strengthen state laws result in threats that the corporations will move to another state. Only the federal government has the power to promulgate a corporate chartering law that will replace the lowest common denominator practice of Delaware, a state where many of the country's largest corporations are chartered in a climate of massive permissiveness. Thus the chartering of corporations should become a federal responsibility; such action would update the law and revise the "contract" between the corporation and the government which created it, thereby effecting more responsible corporate behavior.

Corporations have proclaimed for years that they are held responsible to society through shareholders. In 1970 Campaign GM was organized to test that theory and, although the campaign met with some success, it proved that shareholder democracy is largely a myth, a contrived nonaccountability to keep citizens powerless, and not a viable method to bring about true accountability. The effects of corporate decisions reach far beyond shareholders to the public at large. Thus, instead of shareholder accountability, we must have *public* accountability. This is the subject of David P. Riley's "Taming GM, Ford, Union Carbide, U.S. Steel, Dow Chemical," where he urges a mass popular movement or "a countervailing power," as Galbraith phrased it, to confront corporate power.

Such a movement would be comprised of individuals with a commitment to what I call "initiatory democracy," or citizenship action: an *obligation* to act to expose wrongdoing, to become a "professional citizen"; to develop methods of bringing institutionalized violence, dishonesty, and waste under control; to build a new way of life in America. Students, the young, all those who have been greatly responsible for the beginnings of a corporate reform movement, those whose life choices are still unset, these are the people uniquely qualified to forge new directions, but the path is open to all who would dare before they despair.

MONOPOLY

Charles E. Mueller

The sad state of the American economy has become a partisan matter again—even for the economists, whose reputation as neutral and effective technologists has suffered somewhat in the conflicting and often erroneous pronouncements they have offered to explain our simultaneous burdens of high unemployment, stagnation, and inflation. Few people, strangely, have pointed to the one economic phenomenon that is acknowledged to increase both prices and unemployment: monopoly, which produces higher-than-competitive costs and prices, reduced output, more unemployment, reduced rates of technological progress, and high levels of advertising to differentiate (in some psychological sense) the physically identical products of rival manufacturers.

The mere *presence* of monopoly, with its centralized control and the violence it does to the reality of a free market, is supposed to raise the blood pressure of the true conservative. Yet there is little agitation in conservative circles for a full-scale antitrust campaign, although it can be shown that monopolist tendencies characterize about one-fourth of all U.S. industries numerically and a far greater portion of all corporate assets. This concentration exists not only in the well-known industrial giants like steel and automobiles but also in an enormous variety of more obscure markets: typewriters, chewing gum, razor blades, and biscuits, to name a few. The *effects* of monopoly—on the consumer, especially the poor, and the society as a

From *The Washington Monthly,* April 1971. Reprinted by permission.

whole—are supposed to be particularly offensive to liberals. Here again, however, there has been little agitation, even though monopoly is estimated to cost the country between a $16-billion rock-bottom figure and a $230-billion annual price tag espoused by a Senate subcommittee—with no offsetting economic benefits whatever.

So the economy, in all its confusion and pain, looks by its symptoms as if it suffers from monopoly. It also *is*, by the available evidence, burdened with excess concentration. Monopoly has no friends in theory nor advocates in public politics. It is not only a drain on the nation economically but a threat to individual freedom because of the monopolist organization's power over its customers and control over the security of its employees; and monopoly, given sufficient political will on the part of the nation, is relatively easy to eliminate by requiring the guilty corporations to spin off smaller competitors. Despite all this, there is no major mobilization against economic concentration, and the merger trend continues. Assistant Attorney General Richard McLaren, head of the Justice Department's Antitrust Division, has initiated a modest antitrust campaign. But even that effort is small in comparison with the task, and it is considered quite separate from the woes that beset Professors McCracken, Shultz, and Burns, the President's top economic advisers. Antitrust questions, in short, are nearly irrelevant to economic policy at a time when they should be at the forefront of the debate.

Perhaps the second most important concept in economics today—second only to the Keynesian proposition on the relationship between aggregate national expenditures and full employment—is the concept of a relationship between the structure of a product market and its social performance. In brief, it has been established beyond the point of really serious dispute that, without any necessary collusion or conspiracy, an industry becomes effectively monopolized *when the four largest firms control 50 percent of the market or more.*

More than 25 major statistical studies in the last decade have all identified the four-firm/50 percent level as the point at which marked monopolistic effects set in regarding prices, profits, and costs. This is a very conservative dividing line. In other words, many American industries with less concentration—say, with five firms having 50 percent of the market or four firms with 40 percent—also show signs of monopoly; but the evidence is so pronounced at the four-firm/50 per cent level that the significant monopolistic effects can safely be attributed to any industry which meets that test.

The Supreme Court has actually recognized a far stricter standard in one area of antitrust law—mergers. In a 1966 case, *United States v. Von's Grocery Company*, the Court disallowed a proposed merger between two California grocers who each controlled only about 4.5 per cent of the market—on the grounds that their combined market share of nine per cent would tend to restrict competition. Since then, prevailing judicial decisions have prohibited direct mergers that give two companies more than about eight or nine per cent of the market. But the Supreme Court has not handed down antitrust decisions against the multitude of *existing* companies that are already much more monopolistic than Von's Grocery. Nor has the Court barred the acquisition of monopoly power by means other than direct merger, such as advertising or market growth made possible by subsidies from a parent conglomerate.

If the Supreme Court's merger test were applied to existing American industries, the vast majority of major corporations would be held in violation of antitrust law. Far fewer industries qualify under the four-firm/50 per cent test, but the many industries that do qualify are far more concentrated than California grocers. In any case, the four-firm/50 per cent measure has been confirmed as a reliable indicator of substantial monopoly power by a host of detailed studies both in and out of the government. It is considered, in the words of Richard McLaren's economic assistant, a kind of "collusion index."

This identification of a boundary line between relatively competitive industries, on the one hand, and monopolized industries, on the other—and of the vast differences in social performance that they spawn—is of enormous practical significance. Knowing a point at which competition ceases to function in its socially desirable forms, we have for the first time some workably exact policy guidelines for a realistic industrial reform program. Thus there is no need to atomize the country's automobile industry back to the situation that existed in the second decade of the century—in the early years when there were more than 100 separate firms making automobiles. Separating General Motors into, say, five companies (Chevrolet, Pontiac, etc.) and Ford into, say, three, would produce a quite competitive automobile industry, one in which no firm would have more than about 10 percent of total industry sales, and therefore no four would have more than roughly 40 per cent. We can say with considerable confidence that this modest change in the auto industry's structure would result in a rather prompt decline in auto prices, an increase in output (more employment), safer and more pollutant-free cars (technological advancement), reduced advertising expenditures on autos, greater opportunities for smaller entrepreneurs both to manufacture and distribute automobiles and related products, and other such socially beneficial changes.

How many industries would we have to push back over the 50 per cent (four-firm) concentration line? In crude terms, the answer is about 100 industries (out of a Census Bureau total of 430) if one wants to be fairly thorough about it, or at least a dozen if one is satisfied to get the core of the job done now and leave the mopping up to the next generation. What would it get us in terms of dollars saved? Ralph Nader has estimated that monopoly in all of its various forms costs the consumer over 20 per cent of every dollar spent, or more than $100 billion per year. Senator Hart has put the figure at 35–40 per cent ($170–230 billion per year). Part of this estimate represents a loss to the entire public—a lowering of the national standard of living—and part of it represents a shifting or displacement of income: from workers to monopolists, from labor to capital, from small competitive businesses to industries of monopoly like advertising. Senator Hart's figure may turn out to be on the low side for the combined total if a program of serious reform is ever undertaken and the real extent of overpricing in these industries exposed to the light of day.

Economists working in this area offer more refined estimates of the actual public losses traceable to the absence of competition in these oligopoly industries. For example, two leading economists in the industrial organization field, William G. Shepherd and Frederic M. Scherer of the University of Michigan, have recently made separate estimates of the country's overall monopoly losses. The most conservative of these two sets of estimates, those of Shepherd, are that: a) prices tend, on the average, to be 10–30 per cent above the competitive level in the intermediate and tight-oligopoly industries; b) "market power appears to double or triple the margin of extra profitability over bedrock minimum competitive profit levels of six to eight per cent"; and c) costs tend to be increased by, on the average, some five per cent where concentration is very high." For the economy as a whole, the unnecessary costs borne by the nation as a result of its monopolies—cost being measured in the technical terms of "welfare loss" or lost output—are estimated by Shepherd at about three per cent of national income (approximately $16 billion in 1966). Scherer, applying somewhat broader criteria, puts the national welfare loss here at something on the order of 6.2 per cent of GNP, or, at current levels, roughly $60 billion per year.

The few litigated cases in which good business and statistical data have been made available indicate that the cost-effects of monopoly are almost invariably a great deal higher than those suggested here. In one case, for example, involving a price-fixing conspiracy in the sale of bleachers (folding seats used by schools and other institutions), prices rose 32 per cent during the period in which the conspirators were agreeing on them. The *profits* of the firms involved reflected only nine percentage points of that increase, however, the other 23 points having been wasted by the conspiring firms on inflated conspiracy-related *costs*. When the conspiracy was broken up by an antitrust lawsuit, prices fell by the whole amount, 32 per cent—not by just nine per cent, the amount of the residual monopoly profits.

Other cases have revealed similarly large gaps between the non-competitive and the competitive prices of goods and services. The recent breakup of a price-fixing conspiracy among a group of bakeries in the state of Washington resulted in a drop of nearly 20 per cent in the price of bread in the area. Consumers in Seattle alone, for example, realized a savings of some $3.5 million per year from that price decline, or total savings of approximately $17.5 million over the five-year period since that conspiracy was broken up in the latter part of 1964. A still more important example of this phenomenon is provided by a recent price-fixing case involving the well-known antibiotic drug, tetracycline. Its price fell by approximately 75 per cent after the conspiracy was broken up, for total savings to its purchasers of some $60 million per year. The price-fixers had charged 51 cents per capsule for a product that cost them 1.6 cents to make.

Whether one chooses the stringently conservative "welfare loss" figures suggested by Shepherd as the appropriate measure of monopoly's annual cost or the more robust $100–230 billion figure suggested by Nader and Hart, it is clear enough that the losses associated with the country's monopolized industrial sector are fairly staggering. Even that smallest of the technical estimates, $16 billion per year, is hardly insignificant alongside the cost figures associated with some of the more monumental of the country's other major problems:

- the country's total crime bill was $32 billion last year.

- the Vietnam war cost us $27 billion last year.

- removing the major sources of pollution would cost an estimated $15 billion per year.

- eliminating poverty ($3,000 minimum for all families) would cost an estimated $11 billion per year.

FROM RAZORS TO EXPLOSIVES

How much of the American economy has already been monopolized? "All in all," Shepherd estimates, "at least 35 to 45 per cent of market activity in the United States appears to take place under conditions of substantial market power." In the manufacturing sector, for example, out of a 1966 total of 420 manufacturing industries, there were 199 industries in which the four largest firms held 50 per cent or more of their respective industry's total sales. Nearly 50 per cent of all manufacturing activity in the country took place in industries in which the four-firm share was 70 per cent or more of that year. Shepherd concludes that the average American manufacturing industry is one in which the four largest sellers account for 60 per cent of the industry's total sales.

The table on p. 322 lists a sampling of the American manufacturing industries that, in Shepherd's opinion, are currently non-competitive in character—together with the share of their total sales held by the four largest firms and their estimated "value added" in 1966.

But what about "scale economies"? Aren't huge corporations and therefore concentrated industries required for efficiency? The answer is no. As Shepherd sums it up, "in the great majority of industries, efficient scale in plant production is reached at small, even minuscule, shares of the industry." Thus one industrial scholar, Thomas Saving, found that in over 70 per cent of his industries by number (86 per cent by share of employment), 'minimum optimum' plant size is less than one per cent of industry size. In automobiles, for example, estimates made in the late 1950's were that all economies were realized in plants producing at most 7.5 per cent of total industry sales (300,000 to 600,000 cars then). The larger plants are no more efficient in production.

What about the effect of such a reform program on the country's research and development effort? Aren't our big monopolies and oligopolies the ones that, via their gleaming laboratories, turn out the inventions that make us the world's leader in technological progress? Again, the answer is no. The big firms in oligopoly industries devote a great deal of effort to *suppressing* new innovations that would require them to write off as losses their heavy investments in plants rendered obsolete by the inventions and innovations of the medium- and smaller-sized firms in their industries. Summarizing Scherer's earlier findings on the conventional wisdom that the larger firms in our oligopoly industries account for the bulk of our technological progress, Shepherd notes that innovation does tend to "increase with concentration at relatively low levels of concentration," but that this phenomenon is short-lived. "When the four-firm concentration exceeds 50 or 55 per cent, additional market power is probably not conducive to more vigorous efforts and may be downright stultifying." For the leaders in a highly concentrated industry, the most profitable course is to let the smaller firms carry the risks of innovation and buy them out later if imitation fails.

Industry	4-firm share	value added (1966) $ mil.
Razor Blades & Razors	98%	145
Locomotives & Parts	98	318
Flat Glass	96	431
Aircraft Propellors & Parts	96	133
Primary Aluminum	95	725
Aircraft Engines & Parts	95	2,725
Electron Tubes, Receiving	95	244
Sewing Machines	95	97
Safes and vaults	95	64
Motor Vehicles & Parts	94	15,450
Telephone & Telegraph Appar.	94	1,432
Electric Lamps	93	495
Soaps & Other Detergents	90	1,297
Pharmaceutical Preparations	90	3,447
Metal Cans	90	1,043
Computing & Related Machines	90	2,828
Steam Engines & Turbines	90	505
Aircraft	90	4,675
Hard Surface Floor Coverings	89	135
Cathode Ray Picture Tubes	89	472
Chewing Gum	88	177
Primary Batteries	88	167
Carbon & Graphite Products	88	175
Cereal Preparations	87	443
Chocolate & Cocoa Products	85	180
Sanitary Paper Products	85	476
Pressed & Blown Glass	85	709
Engine Electrical Equipment	85	753
Glass Containers	80	763
Cement	80	839
Brick & Structural Tile	80	275
Gypsum Products	80	222
Blast Furnaces & Steel Mills	80	9,644
Primary Copper	80	363
Aluminum Rolling & Drawing	80	862
Photographic Equipment	80	2,282
Household Laundry Equipment	79	416
Typewriters	79	2,828
Household Vacuum Cleaners	78	156
Flour, Blended & Prepared	75	206
Pulp Mills	75	365
Internal Combustion Engines	75	1,075
Household Refrigerators	72	752
Industrial Gases	72	363
Explosives	72	255

IBM and General Motors are prime examples of this incentive to imitate rather than innovate. "Contrary to popular impressions carefully cultivated, IBM is not regarded professionally as a leading inventor or innovator," writes Shepherd. A series of major improvements, including both the larger 360-line computers and the time-sharing systems, "have originated with other sources, with IBM often following developments." The auto industry has succeeded in suppressing innovation in the development of automobile safety features, anti-smog technology, the small car (abandoning it, until recently, to foreign producers), and more efficient, lower-cost retailing (the industry's "exclusive dealing" arrangements with its dealers prevent the development of "chain" retailing of automobiles or discount-store operations, those handling all makes rather than just one). The principal technological contribution of the auto industry is the annual style change—which is estimated to increase the price of the average automobile by about 25 per cent, or approximately $7 billion per year.

THE TARGET PRICE

But what about the *advertising* role of the giant firms in oligopoly industries? Isn't it the more than $20 billion spent on advertising in the United States each year, the bulk of it by these major oligopolies, that keeps consumer demand high and thus prevents unemployment? On the contrary, advertising, at least in the excessive form associated with our major oligopoly industries, can actually be a cause of unemployment in some industries. High-intensity advertising creates high concentration, and concentration in turn produces higher prices and reduced levels of output—thus fewer employed people.

The rather spectacular conceit of Madison Avenue in suggesting that its labors have something to do with keeping the American economy in motion is on an intellectual par with the rooster's conviction that it is his crowing that causes the sun to rise in the morning. No reputable economist believes that America's real standard of living would waver in the slightest if the entire advertising industry closed up shop tomorrow. The fact of the matter is that Americans spend, year after year, approximately 93 per cent of their aggregate disposable income. They have done so for more than 50 years, despite the fact that advertising did not become a giant among American industries until the 1950's. The advent of television brought not only huge growth in advertising but also a qualitative change, as the emphasis shifted away from the transmission of product information toward the creation of a pleasant psychological atmosphere around the product. Television was indispensable for this shift. The function of advertising is to transfer the consumer's quite stable propensity to spend from one "brand" to another, or from one product to another. Advertising can induce the consumer to shift his money from Fords to Chevrolets, but it has always been quite powerless to induce him to raise his *total* spending from 93 per cent of his disposable income to 94 per cent.

Excessive and misleading advertising occurs in its most socially significant forms in relatively concentrated industries. In some industries—cosmetics, for example—these advertising expenditures run to as much as 40 per cent of the product's total sales volume, with price increases required to recover those costs and make a profit on the capital invested in the advertising itself. Highly-advertised products tend to be roughly 20 per cent more expensive than the identical products sold by the industry's oligopolists to their largest customers (for example, the chain food stores) under the latter's own "private" brand names. In the summer of 1970, for example, consumers generally paid 89 cents for a 14-ounce bottle of Listerine, while the same mouthwash in the same size bottle cost only 59 cents under the A&P private label, a price difference of 33.7 per cent. An 11-ounce can of Rapid Shave cost 95 cents, while the same product cost only 49 cents with an A&P label. The usual practice is for the supermarket chains (which are themselves not exactly small entrepreneurs) to purchase products from the brand producers under a contract which allows the private label. Sometimes the price differences can be enormous. A recent investigation by staff of the Federal Trade Commission showed, for example, that Washington, D.C., consumers pay 580 per cent of the price for Peoples Drug Store aspirin to get the same relief with a Bayer label.

America's great monopolies, as the critics quite accurately point out, select the level of monopoly profits they think they can get away with and then price accordingly (e.g., General Motors' "target pricing" to yield a 20 per cent after-tax return on its stockholders' equity). Styling, advertising, and the like are then "planned" to yield the level of consumer demand required to produce that pre-planned level of profits. Gosplan, the Soviet economic planning agency in Moscow, operates an automobile monopoly in the Soviet Union in precisely the same way—and with even worse results.

MONOPOLY'S HELPERS

There are two general techniques for controlling the prices of monopoly firms: the imposition of some form of regulation, such as wage and price controls, upon existing companies, and the reduction of concentration in the offending industries. Wage and price controls are neither popular nor efficient for keeping prices at a competitive level over the long haul. And price-setting by a governmental agency has been a thorough-going disaster by virtually all standards. The "big seven" regulatory agencies—the Interstate Commerce Commission, Civil Aeronautics Board, Federal Communications Commission, etc.—are consistently captured by the industry they purport to be regulating—and they end up presiding over an output-restricting price-increasing, cartel arrangement that tends to be worse, if possible, than the situation in unregulated oligopoly industries. One study shows, for example, that the airline fares fixed by the CAB are at least 30 per cent higher than the prices prevailing in the unregulated, intra-state California airline market. The unregulated Pacific Southwest Airlines charges a coach fare of $16.20 for a Los Angeles–San Francisco flight, while the CAB sets much higher fares for flights of equivalent distance on the major airlines: $33 Chicago to Minneapolis, $34 Cleveland to Philadelphia, $33 Los Angeles to Phoenix, and so on. This price inflation implies a consumer loss from the CAB's ministrations of as much as $1 billion a year. The ICC's annual cost to the consumer is estimated to be several times that figure.

Regulation is ineffective precisely because it does not remove the market power of the oligopolies which now pervade the American economy. This market power not only wears down the zeal of the most ardent regulatory crusaders but also provides the muscle for corporate acquisitions that further concentrate American industry. Monopoly power tends to snowball, spending most of its energy in the pursuit of more control and more security, which in turn makes it more difficult to turn business energy from lobbying and mergers to the competitive customer service which is supposed to make free enterprise socially useful in the first place.

Breaking up the stifling, glutinous masses which characterize many American industries is obviously the superior solution. Antitrust judgments are relatively simple to execute, and they remove the harmful effects of market control by going to the source of the problem. The hulking obstacles to this logical solution are of course the monopolies themselves, which is ample evidence of how far the snowball has rolled. General Motors, Ford, Standard Oil, U.S. Steel, and the country's other major oligopolists would hardly be enthusiastic about having their price-raising monopoly power taken away from them, and it is reasonable to suppose that they could devise a substantial amount of political unpleasantness for any administration that actually directed its antitrust agencies, the Antitrust Division of the Justice Department and the Federal Trade Commission, to make antitrust enforcement a principal tool of economic policy by breaking up the oligopolies which make our current antitrust laws almost ludicrous in a law and order era.

Part of the enforcement problem stems from the lack of economic sophistication among the attorneys and jurists charged with interpreting antitrust laws. The courts tend to view the issue as one of predatory business practices and collusion. They see market control only when there is evidence of a price-fixing scheme or other monopolistic agreements among competing corporations. Market concentration *per se* is not considered conclusive evidence of monopoly, although all the harmful economic effects of monopoly are demonstrably in operation. The courts are reluctant to stand on economic evidence, and they tend to look prudently for documents or testimony to show that an anticompetitive "deal" has been made. This judicial hesitancy could be overcome by new legislation, a law making a four-firm share of more than 50 per cent of any product market *prima facie* evidence of monopoly.

THE HIGH PRICES OF UNEMPLOYMENT

Such explosive legislation, like antitrust enforcement itself, would clearly run into a political hailstorm—virtually all major politicians depend on contributions from the representatives of American oligopolies. To a large extent, these contributions come from monopoly profits and carry, of course, an implicit understanding that the receiving candidate will not take the legal steps necessary to erase the larger pool of such profits from which he has taken his tithe. In less respectable circles, this is known as a kickback—the beauty of which is that both parties to the transaction have their needs taken care of to the unmitigated loss of the public.

Despite the long odds and the formidable opposition, these economically sophisticated legal battles must be undertaken and the necessary political coalitions must be built to remove monopoly power from the United States. For now, the issues are primarily those of economic injustice caused by the violation of every market principle on which the corporation rhetorically stands. The current unemployment only dramatizes this violence, as anti-inflationary policies that ignore monopoly have put 1.8 million people out of work in the last 18 months. In a sense, these people have taken the rap for the continuation of monopoly power among the biggest businesses. Beyond the economic issues, market power presents questions of basic freedom. Even now, it is not too difficult to imagine one's having qualms about filing an antitrust suit against an American oligopoly, for fear of losing the insurance policy, credit rating, or job that might lie within the control of the oligopoly, or in the control of its friends in high places.

TAMING GM, FORD, UNION CARBIDE, U.S. STEEL, DOW CHEMICAL

David P. Riley

The concept of "shareholder" or "corporate" democracy—namely, that shareholder votes control corporations just as citizen votes control governments—is coupled with the idea promoted by the New York Stock Exchange called "people's capitalism"—namely, that vast multitudes of Americans, not just the robber barons of old, own stock and participate in the network of corporate democracies. One corporate manager, Paul Gaddis, has described the shareholder as "the agency of legitimacy for management," and the larger the number of shareholders in the country, the stronger is "the anchor to legitimacy." Two pages later, he says that "the idea of shareholder control" is "probably always a delusion."

So was "people's capitalism." It is true that stock ownership has greatly dispersed since the early days when one or two or a handful of businessmen owned large blocks of stock through which they controlled their corporations. There are now over thirty million Americans who own stock, over one-tenth of the population; but the vast majority of them own only a few shares or only a small part of any company. You may "own" a tiny bit of something, but it doesn't mean you "control" your "property" in any way—all it means is you get a check every quarter. One study done in 1953 found that 80 percent of all personally held stock was in the hands of 1.6 percent of the adult population. The non-personally held stock is in the hands of investment institutions run by pension fund managers and others. They do not exactly represent "people's capitalism" either.

Nor does shareholder democracy exist. For one thing, all shareholders can really do is vote out one set of directors and vote in another—which they never do (except occasionally in large blocks of shares or in very small companies). The Board of Directors nominates its slate of new directors, and shareholders can only vote that slate up or down. Our "shareholder democracy" is very much like political elections in the Soviet Union: there are no opposition candidates. This state of affairs has been brought about by the diffusion of ownership of the large American corporations.* When companies used to be owned by a few people, it was different: they also controlled the companies. There was "shareholder democracy" then, but the shareholders were a few men with names like Gould and Rockefeller and Vanderbilt. With the diffusion of ownership to many people, as Berle and Means pointed out in their classic study in the thirties, there resulted a divorce of ownership from control, and it no longer meant anything in the classic capitalist sense to "own" a few shares of stock—you did not control anything through them.

A lot of people take—or used to take—the idea of shareholder democracy very seriously. One result was elaborate regulation by the SEC of shareholder voting by proxy, to try to give shareholders a fair chance to vote on company resolutions and directors. For example, management must file with the SEC its proxy statement, which it sends out every year to all shareholders, containing the resolutions to be voted on at the annual meeting. Most shareholders just send in their proxy, voting with management and never make it to the annual meeting, which Galbraith calls perhaps "our most elaborate exercise in popular illusion."** A shareholder can, with difficulty, get a proposal of his own put on the proxy statement for shareholder vote, but except for a handful of corporate democracy crusaders, almost no one bothers. As Bazelon points out, perhaps the perfect puncture of the corporate democracy myth is the fact that shareholder democracy "would hardly exist at all apart from the efforts of a handful of individuals." Then he cites figures: in 1956, out of two thousand proxy statements filed with the SEC, only 3 percent contained shareholder proposals (which was supposed to be a big reason for the SEC regula-

---

*Thus, the twin ideals of "people's capitalism," proclaimed by the New York Stock Exchange, and "shareholder democracy," proclaimed by the SEC and the corporations are antithetical. The more diffusion of ownership (or "people's capitalism") you have, the less shareholder control, and vice versa.

**Because of the danger of disruption, the GE chairman said at the 1970 meeting, as reported in the Chicago Tribune, that "management has taken the precaution of voting previously so that business will have been totally conducted."

tion). And of those 102 shareholders proposals, 78 were sponsored by the two Gilbert brothers and John Campbell Heinz, who are the major perennial meeting-going advocates of corporate democracy. The fantasy of shareholder democracy is even more widely debunked and ridiculed than the myths of antitrust enforcement and government regulation by administrative agency.

Present Obstacles. The annual corporate meeting time, Spring, 1970, was the spring of popular discontent. The new left in several cities launched attacks on a number of the country's major corporations, including AT&T, GM, Gulf Oil, GE, Honeywell, Boeing, United Aircraft, and Commonwealth Edison of Chicago. The attack consisted of conducting muckraking research projects on corporations, demonstrating and getting into annual meetings to discuss corporate policies on issues like pollution, war products, and employment discrimination. AT&T demonstrators, three thousand strong, were driven back by mounted police in Cleveland; Honeywell demonstrators, fifteen hundred of them, were maced in Minneapolis; and United Aircraft demonstrators were arrested in Hartford. It is not clear just what specific changes in corporate policies the demonstrations caused, if any; but they did make a lot of corporate executives very nervous and much more attentive to defending their corporation's practices as they affect society. They never had to do that much before; in the past it was always just profits and losses at annual meetings.

One of the spring offensives was particularly well-organized and methodical. There were no demonstrations at the GM annual meeting in Detroit; and the Campaign to Make GM Responsible worked entirely within the system—as we are forever told to do—to bring about change. It did not do any better than the demonstrators. Of course the four young lawyers who work for the Project on Corporate Responsibility, which ran Campaign GM and which controls 12 out of GM's 287 million shares, never expected to win. They hoped rather, as Ralph Nader said in announcing the Campaign, to "highlight the fiction of shareholder democracy." In 1972, a better organized Campaign GM—Round II—carried on that effort.

Campaign GM is a good example of the insurmountable obstacles to establishing shareholder democracy in our widely held major corporations today. The inflexible tenacity with which GM fought the campaign (based, to repeat, on 12 out of 287 million shares) is itself instructive. The first thing GM did was to present elaborate legal arguments to the SEC as to why none of the Campaign's proposed resolutions should even be *presented* for a vote at the annual meeting or in proxy material. The Campaign's three major resolutions were, first, to establish a special shareholder's committee chosen by management, the UAW union, and the Campaign, to do a year's study of GM's social impact and decision-making process; second, to expand the company's twenty-five–man board to include three new members representing the public interest; and third, to amend the corporate charter to include specific prohibition of any act detrimental to public health, safety, and welfare, or of any violation of federal and state law. The Campaign had six other resolutions calling for action by GM on auto safety, new car warranties, anti-pollution research, support for mass transit, plant safety, and more new car dealerships for blacks.

The SEC ruled against GM and ordered them to include the Campaign's first two resolutions in their proxy statement to all shareholders. But it still did not give them a chance to win a shareholder's vote. For one thing, GM could argue at length against the Campaign's proposals in the proxy statement, while the Campaign was limited to only one hundred words in their favor. And management can be pretty persuasive in telling you it knows best; in fact, GM has not lost a shareholder vote in a quarter century. Campaign GM sent out its own proxy statement with longer versions of its views to two thousand institutions which it *thought* owned GM stock. (Most GM shareholders are individuals with small holdings, 79 percent owning one hundred shares or less; institutions account for only 12 percent of the shareholders.) But there was no way the Campaign could reach all 1.3 million GM shareholders: first, it didn't have the list and couldn't get it from GM; second, it didn't have the money for such a mailing, and couldn't get that from GM either.

But GM was not taking any chances. It included in its proxy statement mailing a special twenty-one–page pamphlet on "GM's Record of Progress," which cost $81 thousand in additional postage alone. Then GM printed full-page ads on its anti-pollution record in 148 newspapers around the country, which a leading national newspaper ad man says cost about $300 thousand. GM also went after votes as if it were a real political campaign with the outcome hanging in the balance. It told the treasurer at Syracuse University, which holds a few thousand shares, that it was going to contact all the university's trustees, according to the Campaign. It also lobbied vigorously with banks in New York and Philadelphia, one of which showed slight signs of wavering, but then saw the light. At the annual meeting in Detroit on May 22, Campaign GM got six million votes for its resolution, or 2½ percent of the total vote; management had 237 million votes on its side.

The outcome really was never in doubt; the only interesting speculation was how much worry the Campaign would cause in Detroit.

Meanwhile, the myth goes on. In introducing the special GM progress pamphlet, Chairman James Roche wrote to the 1.3 million shareholders, "If you have any questions, I hope you will write to me." He doesn't really hope that; anyway, he won't know if they do write, unless he sees the mountain of 1.3 million letters in the warehouse. The GM chairman also writes to any shareholder who sells his stock, asking him to reply by letter if the sale of the stock has been related to "any aspect of the corporation's policies or operations." It would almost have to be so related. Does the chairman really want to hear from all the *former* shareholders as well? How would he really enjoy such a mail-in?

Future Possibilities. Even in the shareholder democracy approach to corporate accountability, there are significant possibilities for changing, or at least exposing, the system. The SEC's order of GM to include Campaign GM's resolutions in its proxy statement and the U.S. Court of Appeals for the District of Columbia's decision in the Dow Chemical case suggest that the SEC's proxy rules may be of increasing value in promoting significant shareholder challenges, at least symbolic ones, to corporate power. We may never see such a challenge actually defeat management in a shareholder vote, but you don't necessarily have to win a vote to win a victory. Management can be embarrassed into action by unfavorable publicity, while still having all the votes it needs. That has happened with the Rochester companies of Xerox and Kodak, which have taken on substantial job training programs for minorities due to the public pressure—such as the pressure at Kodak's 1967 annual meeting, brought by FIGHT, the Rochester black activist group which Saul Alinsky helped organize. GM, while denying the need for reform, has also made some changes. At respectable distances between the active phases of Round I and Round II of Campaign GM, GM appointed a black director, a "public policy committee" to advise the company on public issues, and a vice-president to run a new department on environmental problems.

Exposure of how the system actually works is a prerequisite to building the political power to change it. Thus Nader suggests that projects such as Campaign GM and Alinsky's new "Proxies for People" movement "are never going to be successful in a 51 percent manner" and should not be judged that way. The policy of Campaign GM is that it

> . . . *forced a corporation such as General Motors to look out at its support structure—the banks, colleges and others who hold large blocks of its stock—for the first time. It required General Motors to surface and use its power.*

Alinsky has a dream of one day filling Yankee Stadium with thousands of shareholders of a major corporation, having them thunderously vote "yes" on a proposal, only to have the chairman announce that management votes "no" with its 90 percent of the votes in proxy returns; the thousands in the stands therefore lose. "I'd just love to see that happen," says Alinsky; "I'd like to see him try to call 80,000 people out of order." This tactic assumes the Alinskys and Naders can get a strong enough movement organized before the corporate managers catch on and make more moderate changes to head off such dramatic exposure. Reform is always a race between the exposers and the farsighted establishment. Nothing helps reform so much as a good, obvious shortsighted enemy for an organizing target.

Exposure is contagious too. While Campaign GM was finding out and educating people about how GM works, it also revealed how other institutions worked in conjunction with GM. Campaign GM was asking GM to exercise its public responsibilities, and it was also asking shareholders to exercise their responsibilities as owners. It turned out many did not want to, showing that even many shareholders did not like shareholder democracy. At Harvard University, a majority of students, faculty, and alumni favored Campaign GM's resolutions; but the Harvard administration voted for the GM management. Harvard's noted Nobel laureate Dr. George Wald had always objected to the radical student view that Harvard was "just another part of the power structure." When the GM-Harvard relationship emerged, he called it "a slap in the eye for all of us, . . . expos[ing] an entirely unrealized degree of complicity."

There remains the question of whether shareholder democracy—or rather shareholder influence on corporate action—is a good thing even if feasible. Viewing shareholders as part of the general public, which is the real corporate constituency to which corporations must be made to answer—shareholder influence is a worthwhile approach. When viewed in the narrower sense—simply as an attempt to get shareholders to exert their powers of ownership over corporate management—the approach raises serious questions about its validity, or at least its priority compared to the major task of corporate accountability to the public. Abram Chayes points out that if corporate power, like other governing power, is to operate with the consent of the governed, the shareholder is really not the true class of the governed that we need to be most concerned about. In fact in a sense he is *least* subject to corporate power, because all he has to do to escape it, *qua* shareholder, is sell his stock. The shareholder as public citizen will remain just as subject to corporate pollution as the rest of us, but he is no longer part of the corporation's shareholder constituency.

It is the corporation's constituency of the general public that cannot escape. What we need is not shareholder accountability, but public accountability. To the extent that the shareholder democracy approach confuses that distinction, it hides the real issue and is harmful. To the extent that it understands that distinction and comes out on the public side of it, it is helpful.

CONCLUSION

In his famous 1962 Yale Commencement speech, President Kennedy pleaded for a clearing away of the old ideological rifts and devil theory myths that have dominated economic thought in the past. He said that the key problems of the economy now were not social and political, but the technical and managerial. It was a stirring speech, eloquently delivered. But today, a decade later, the opposite is true. Though there are plenty of technical and managerial problems left to solve, the key problems of our economy now are social and political.

We know the American corporate structure is technically capable of producing an unparalleled glut of goods and services; it has done precisely that and has made us the richest country in human history. The critical examination of corporations and the search for corporate accountability go on not because of technical failing, but because of the social crisis—because we now face at once a productive economy and a sick society.

To meet this crisis, we have two tasks before us, both already begun but far from finished: the tasks of questioning values and organizing for power.

QUESTIONING VALUES

An economy should be judged by what it adds to the wealth of a nation, and to the wealth of nations. Beyond that goal, judgment should measure its effect on men, on politics, and on culture of the society.

That is a good statement of the conventional view, made by Eugene Rostow in 1959. Today, the signs all about us indicate that such a view is seriously in question, particularly among the younger generation. This developing "counter-culture," as Theodore Roszak calls it, agrees with R. H. Tawney, who wrote in 1920 that we must place economic activity in "its proper place as the servant, not the master, of society." An economy can no longer be judged by its wealth, but must be measured by its effect on men, politics, and values. Such considerations are now primary, not secondary as Rostow suggests.

There are areas of the country, and many in the world, where there is little wealth, and the economy and psychology of scarcity still operate. Some parts of the counter-culture feel passionate concern for such problems, but generally in America we have an economy not of scarcity but of abundance. Many raise questions about the unhealthy passivism that our emphasis on the consumption encourages and the undue sense of power and potency which comes from material acquisitiveness.

But even assuming our American way of life is healthy for us as individuals, there is serious question whether we can afford to maintain it. Certainly if the present unequal distribution of it continues apace, the country is likely to be in shambles from internal strife. From a world view, the question is even more critical. The United States makes up 6 percent of the world's population, and every year it consumes about 60 percent of the world's consumable resources. It is not possible—either ecologically or, as more of the world awakes to such facts, politically—for such a situation to continue indefinitely, or even for very long. But if the American economy is to continue expanding, as economists thinking only of economic facts say it must, then such an imbalance will have to continue, and even increase.

Finally, assuming our economy is good for man individually and politically, there is serious doubt about whether we can afford to maintain it ecologically. The summertime city suffocations from lingering pollution air pockets bring the imminence of the ecological crisis home as well as any alarming warnings from ecologists. But changes in the economy radical enough to save the ecology of the country will require much more than technical and managerial or even political measures. Behind the economist's worship of an expanding G.N.P., demand-creating advertising, and social status through material possession lie basic cultural Western beliefs of man's dominance over nature. Theologians have pointed to the command of Genesis for man to be "fruitful and multiply, and fill the earth and subdue it, and have dominion over the fish of the sea and over the birds of the air and over every living thing that moves upon the earth."

But Christianity (as compared to Eastern religions' great respect for nature) is not the only Western belief at the root of the problem. There are many non-religious capitalists loose in the land, ravaging it like good Christians. Bethlehem Steel, through a subsidiary called Beth-Elkhorn, is strip-mining the Kentucky hills bare. Said one strip mining supporter, "I don't believe God would have put all this coal here if he hadn't intended for it to be taken out." Bethlehem has already mined millions of tons of coal, but their man in eastern Ken-

tucky gave a straight capitalist reply to the suggestion of conservationists that the company should be satisfied; he told a reporter in
amazement, "You can't just walk away from ten million tons of high-
grade metallurgical coal." In announcing the company's strip mining
plans, the Bethlehem man said, "If there's something wrong with my
company, there's something wrong with the country." It's not just
the company or the country or Christianity or capitalism; it's the whole
Western culture. When it comes to industrial irreverence for nature,
Marxism is no better. The key problems of the economy, then, are
neither technical and managerial nor political in the sense of the old
ideological quarrels that President Kennedy wanted to cast aside; the
key problem is broader still: it is cultural.

Thus, as often happens, the debate is on two levels, and those
on the superficial level cannot understand why those on the deeper
level are not satisfied. It is like the debate over Vietnam. President
Nixon says he is taking the ground troops out, but his most searching
critics want to know not just about ground troops, but also about
general military and economic support for undemocratic countries
around the world, about the dominance of military-industrial power
at home, and about domestic priorities. So, too, when the corporations
talk about anti-pollution devices and equal employment plans, that
is fine as far as it goes. But on questions of whether such headlong
consumption is psychologically healthy or politically wise or ecologically possible to continue—on such basic questions the corporations
are resoundingly silent.

ORGANIZING FOR POWER

Beyond blind rejection, the corporations are silent on another
matter too: restructuring the economy and society for public participation in running corporate America. The Harvard treasurer said that
Campaign GM, mild as it was, represented the "entering wedge" to
a complete change of American business. GM Chairman James Roche
called it a way of challenging "the entire system of corporate management in the United States." If so, the corporations have brought it
on themselves by their unresponsiveness to suggestions for change
and their silence in the face of the great issues facing our society
and, in fact, our civilization. If they will not change, will not bend,
will not even talk or listen, there is only one way to move them: organize the political power that forces change.

We have never really had the kind of sustained public consumer
movement necessary to force a restructuring of the whole system.
The Populist movement was too shallow: in the economic field, it

chased a lot of foreign Eastern devils and thought it got them, but didn't. It won more respectability than accountability for big business. The Progressive movement was more thought out, but in practical politics it resulted only in correcting the worst abuses, while leaving the general system of unaccountable corporate power intact. The New Deal was broader; it went beyond chasing devils and the most blatant abuses, but its goal was economic recovery (along with what reform was necessary for recovery), not a restructuring that would provide public corporate accountability. The New Deal was also a reform from the top brain trust down, not from a popular consumer movement up. It never cared about forming such a movement, and never did form one. FDR's political magic was enough to sustain it.

The kind of movement we need is not a new idea. The Progressive thinker Herbert Croly suggested it when he spoke of the need for the individuals who make up the public to join together in a counter-organization with enough strength to stand up to the other massive organizations that dominate modern life, those of government, business, and labor. Galbraith suggested it with his theory of countervailing power.

Ideas of how to carry out a reconstruction of the system are not lacking, and more would be forthcoming if we had the kind of political movement necessary to enact them. Without such a movement, no idea is worth trying and all are just dreams. Our past attempts in providing some corporate accountability, abortive as they have been, contain basic concepts on which to build a program of reconstruction: the concepts that at some point, somewhere, a corporation can get too big, too powerful, and too monopolistic for the public good; that government, with enough public power behind it, can and should regulate business for the public good; and that shareholders, as part of the general public, might be able to influence corporate conduct, or at least expose its current undemocratic management.

At the first level of corporate accountability, that of shareholders, Georgetown law professor Donald Schwartz, who served as counsel to Campaign GM, has suggested a variety of ways shareholders could take advantage of improved proxy rules, develop corporate monitoring procedures, nominate directors, and elect directors as representatives of the public. Campaign GM coordinator Philip Moore thinks about involving the public in corporate decision-making not just in the narrow ways that the consumer is the supposed "invisible hand" guiding corporate decisions, the labor union simply the occasional collective bargaining agent, and the shareholder the much revered and much ignored phantom "owner." Moore thinks about giving the public control, or at least very substantial influence, at every point where the corporation has contact with the public. The incisive English economist R. H. Tawney had very similar ideas when he wrote a half century ago that "proprietary rights" should be "maintained when they are accompanied by the performance of service and abolished when they are not," and that "producers" should "stand in a direct relation to the community for whom production is carried on, so that their responsibility to it may be obvious and unmistakable, not lost, as at present, through their immediate subordination to shareholders whose interest is not service but gain."

That "direct relation" can take many forms. In some cases, it might be public ownership like the Tennessee Valley Authority, only with meaningful community participation or control as well. In some cases it might be nationalization, only again not in the sterile form done elsewhere where the managerial control of the technocrats has not lessened. And we should be open about what we are doing, as Galbraith has said: "The Democratic Party must henceforth use the word socialism. It describes what is needed. If there is assumed to be something illicit or indecent about public ownership, it won't be done well." Increasingly, there is talk about experimenting with the "worker's control" model from Yugoslavia. Says the director of the Honeywell Project, "We want control of the corporate power to pass from the board to the employees and the representatives of the community."

With the existence of such an efficient movement, even the problem of corporate social responsibility could resolve itself. With corporations accountable to outside public forces concerned about the public good—concerned about, as Tawney says, service instead of gain—corporate executives can go on acting simply in their own interests, as the conservatives so desperately want them to do, only their own interests will be not to antagonize this constituency who demand more equitable corporate policies, with the sanction being loss of customers. At this point Friedman approaches Galbraith, for even the former has admitted that the corporation should engage in public service work and follow public-spirited policies *if* it is in their long run interest to do so. A militant constituency can make this so.

Perhaps it is all too good to be possible. But there have been mass popular movements in America in the past that have faced down corporate power, at least on some level. Those movements were far from complete successes, but surely we can learn from them and build on their legacy. Nor is the current racial and generational strife necessarily an unsurmountable obstacle. What this country needs is a genuine Populist, not the bogus, divisive shouters like Agnew and Wallace with their occasional Populist tinges. Perhaps before long, the black movement will understand that the government as presently formed cannot do what must be done, and that business will not do it, and that those two facts are related: because business, the dominant culture caught in its own narrow ideological prison, will not, therefore government cannot. For as the socialist Michael Harrington writes, "to take office is not to take power, particularly in a capitalist society where so much power lies beyond the reach of the electorate."

An American electorate that learns that lesson about the relative strength of corporate and electoral power will become very aroused. That is the lesson Ralph Nader's investigators, with their muckraking reports, aim to teach; it is the truth the radical black and white movements already understand, and the environmental one is moving toward; it is Justice Douglas's point when he says that the establishment today is our George III; it is the organizing point Saul Alinsky hopes to activate middle class whites around. There is a common ground that unites all these people and movements; maybe, with luck, we can find it.

DETERRING CORPORATE CRIME

Gilbert Geis

A heated debate is underway in the United States concerning the use of imprisonment to deal with crime. Enlightened opinion holds that too many persons are already incarcerated, and that we should seek to reduce prison populations. It is an understandable view. Most prisoners today come from the dispossessed segments of our society; they are the blacks and the browns who commit "street crimes" for reasons said to be closely related to the injustices they suffer. If it is assumed that imprisonment is unnecessary for many lower-class offenders it might be argued that it is also undesirable for corporation executives. In such terms, it may appear retributive and inconsistent to maintain that a law-violating corporation vice president spend time in jail, while advocating that those who work in his factory might well be treated more indulgently when they commit a criminal offense.

I do not, however, find it incompatible to favor both a reduction of the lower-class prison population and an increase in upper-class representation in prisons. Jail terms have a self-evident deterrent impact upon corporate officials who belong to a social group that is exquisitely sensitive to status deprivation and shame. The white-collar offender and his business colleagues, more than the narcotic addict or the ghetto mugger, are apt to learn well the lesson intended by a prison term. In addition, there is something to be said for *noblesse*

Speech delivered at the Conference on Corporate Responsibility, October 1971. Reprinted by permission of the author.

oblige, that those who have a larger share of what society offers carry a greater responsibility to obey its laws.

It must be appreciated, too, that white-collar crimes constitute a more serious threat to the well-being and integrity of our society than more traditional kinds of crimes. As the President's Commission on Law Enforcement and Administration of Justice put the matter: "White-collar crime affects the whole moral climate of our society. Derelictions by corporations and their managers, who usually occupy leadership positions in their communities, establish an example which tends to erode the moral base of the law. . . ."

Corporate crime kills and maims. It has been estimated, for example, that each year 200,000 to 500,000 workers are needlessly exposed to toxic agents such as radioactive materials and poisonous chemicals because of failure by corporate enterprises to obey safety laws. And many of the 2.5 million temporary and 250,000 permanent worker disabilities from industrial accidents each year are the result of managerial acts that represent culpable failure to adhere to established standards. Ralph Nader has accused the automobile industry of "criminal negligence" in building and selling potentially-lethal cars. Nader's charges against the industry before a Congressional committee drew parallels between corporate crime and traditional crime, maintaining that acts which produce similar kinds of personal and social harm were handled in very different ways:

> If there are criminal penalties for the poor and deprived when they break the law, then there must be criminal penalties for the automobile industry when its executives knowingly violate standards designed to protect citizens from injuries and systematic fraud.

Interrupted by a senator, who insisted that the witness was not giving adequate credit to American industry for its many outstanding achievements, Nader merely drove his point deeper: "Do you give credit to a burglar," he asked, "because he doesn't burglarize 99 percent of the time?"

Death was the likely result too of the following instance of apparent corporate dereliction recounted in the *Wall Street Journal* which, if the facts are as alleged, might well be regarded as negligent manslaughter:

> Beech Aircraft Corp., the nation's second-largest maker of private aircraft, has sold thousands of planes with allegedly defective fuel systems that might be responsible for numerous crash deaths—despite warnings years in advance of the crashes that the system wasn't working reliably under certain flight conditions.

Though Beech strongly denies this, it is the inescapable conclu-
sion drawn from inspection of court suits and exhibits in cases
against Beech, from internal company memoranda, from infor-
mation from the Federal Aviation Agency and the National Trans-
portation Board, and from interviews with concerned parties.

After 1970, the fuel systems in the suspect planes were corrected
by Beech at the request of federal authorities. Before that, the company had been found liable in at least two air crashes and had settled
two other cases before they went to the jury. In one case, tried in
California and now under appeal, a $21.7 million judgment was en-
tered against Beech. Of this, $17.5 million was for punitive damages,
which generally are awarded in the state only when fraud or wanton
and wilful disregard for the safety of others is believed to exist. At
the moment, suits are pending which involve the deaths of about
twenty other persons in Beech planes.

Those who cannot afford a private plane are protected against
being killed in a crash of a Beech aircraft, but nothing will help the
urban resident from being smogged. Again it is Nader who has pointed
to the parallel between corporate offenses and other kinds of crime
and the disparate manner in which the two are viewed and treated:

The efflux from motor vehicles, plants, and incinerators of sulfur
oxides, hydrocarbons, carbon monoxide, oxides of nitrogen, par-
ticulates, and many more contaminants amounts to compulsory
consumption of violence by most Americans. . . . This damage,
perpetuated increasingly in direct violation of local, state, and
federal law, shatters people's health and safety but still escapes
inclusion in the crime statistics. "Smogging" a city or town has
taken on the proportions of a massive crime wave, yet federal
and state statistical compilations of crime pay attention to "mug-
gers" and ignore "smoggers." . . .

Corporate crime also imposes an enormous financial burden on
all of us. The heavy electrical equipment price-fixing conspiracy *alone*
involved theft from the American people of more money than was
stolen in *all* of the country's robberies, burglaries, and larcenies during
the years in which the price-fixing occurred. Yet, perhaps it can be
alleged that corporate criminals deal death and deprivation not deliberately but through inadvertence, omission, and indifference, because
their overriding interest is self-interest. The social consciousness of
the corporate offender often seems to resemble that of the smalltown
thief, portrayed by W. C. Fields, who was about to rob a sleeping
cowboy. He changed his mind, however, when he discovered that
the cowboy was wearing a revolver. "It would be dishonest," he remarked virtuously as he tiptoed away. The moral is clear: Since the

public cannot be armed adequately to protect itself against corporate crime, those law enforcement agencies acting on its behalf should take measures sufficient to protect it. High on the list of such measures should be an insistence upon criminal definition and criminal prosecution for acts which seriously harm, deprive, or otherwise injure the public.

THE NEED FOR PUBLIC OUTRAGE

The first step necessary for heavier sanctions to be imposed routinely on corporate criminals involves the development of a deepening sense of moral outrage on the part of the public. The absence of intense public concern and indignation stems from a variety of circumstances. Initially, the facts of corporate crime must be impressed onto the public mind. This process requires investigation, analysis, pamphleteering, and continual use of mass media outlets. It is a formidable task, but one made easier by the fact that the ingredients for success are already present: corporate offenses are notorious and their victims—especially the young—are increasingly concerned to cope with such depredations.

That the injuries caused by most corporate violations are highly diffused, falling rather lightly upon each of a great number of widely-scattered victims is undoubtedly the greatest barrier to arousing public concern over white-collar cimre. "It is better, so the image runs," C. Wright Mills once wrote, "to take one dime from each of ten million people at the point of a corporation than $100,000 from each of ten banks at the point of a gun." Then Mills added, with wisdom: "It is also safer."

Pollution cripples in a slow, incremental fashion; automobile deaths are difficult to trace to any single malfunctioning of inadequately-designed machinery; antitrust offenses deprive many consumers of small amounts, rather than the larger sums apt to be stolen by the burglar. It is somehow less infuriating and less fear-producing to be victimized a little every day over a long period of time than to have it happen all at once. That many very small losses can add up to a devastating sum constitutes impressive mathematical evidence, but the situation lacks real kick in an age benumbed by fiscal jumboism.

Take, as an example, the case of the Caltec Citrus Company. The Food and Drug Administration staked out the Company's warehouse, finding sugar, vitamin C, and other substances not permitted in pure orange juice being brought into the plant. Estimates were that the adulteration practices of the Company cost consumers $1 million in lost value, thereby "earning" the Company an extra $1 million in profits. For the average customer, the idea of having possibly paid an extra nickel or dime for misrepresented orange juice is not the stuff from which deep outrage springs—at least not in this country at this time.

There are additional problems stemming from the class congruence between the white-collar offender and the persons who pass official judgment on him. The judge who tries and sentences the criminal corporate official was probably brought up in the same social class as the offender, and probably shares the same economic views. Indeed, a corporate official recently told a study group examining antitrust violations that "it is best to find the judge's friend or law partner to defend an antitrust client—which we have done." Also, the prosecutor, yearning for the financial support and power base that will secure his political preferment, is not apt to risk antagonizing entrenched business interests in the community. In addition, the corporate offender usually relies upon high-priced, well-trained legal talent for his defense, men skilled in exploiting procedural advantages and in fashioning new loopholes. The fees for such endeavors are often paid by the corporation itself, under the guise that such subsidies are necessary to protect the corporate image, to sustain employee morale, and to provide an adequate defense. Finally, in the unlikely event that he is sentenced to imprisonment, the corporate offender is much more apt to do time in one of the more comfortable penal institutions than in the maximum-security fortresses to which declasse offenders are often sent.

The neighbors of the corporate criminal often regard him as upright and steadfast; indeed, they will probably see him as solid and substantial a citizen as they themselves are. Witness, for example, the following item in the hometown newspaper of one of the convicted price-fixers in the 1961 heavy electrical equipment antitrust case:

> A number of telegrams from Shenango Valley residents are being sent to a federal judge in Philadelphia, protesting his sentence of Westinghouse executive John H. Chiles, Jr., to a 30-day prison term. . . .
>
> The Vestry of St. John's Episcopal Church, Sharon, adopted a resolution voicing confidence in Chiles, who is a member of the church. . . .
>
> Residents who have sent telegrams point out Chiles was an outstanding citizen in church, civic and community affairs and believe the sentence is unfair.

Finally, there is a general cynicism abroad about white-collar crime in general, a cynicism rooted in beliefs that the practices are so pervasive and endemic that reformative efforts are hopeless. "As news of higher immoralities breaks," Mills wrote, "people often say, 'Well, another one got caught today,' thereby implying that the cases disclosed are not odd events involving occasional characters, but symptoms of widespread conditions. Saturated with cynicism, citizens find that their well of moral indignation has long since run dry.

This lack of indignation can clearly benefit the white-collar criminal. The following courtroom speech, delivered by an attorney for Salvatore Bonanno, believed to be a leading figure in the network of organized crime, indicates both that white-collar crime is dealt with more leniently than other offenses and that other offenses are more readily excusable if they can be perceived as white-collar violations: "It does not speak of the sort of activity where the public screams for protection, Your Honor," the lawyer said, his voice rising. "I think that in the vernacular the defendant stands before you convicted of having committed a white-collar crime and, having been convicted of a white-collar crime, Your Honor, I most respectfully . . . suggest to the court that he should be sentenced in conformity with people who have been convicted of white-collar crimes, and not being sentenced on the basis of his being Salvatore Bonanno."

These are some of the barriers: What are the forces that need to be set in motion to surmount them?

Foremost, perhaps, is the firm assurance that justice can prevail, that apathy can be turned into enthusiasm, dishonesty into decency. History notes that corruption was rampant in English business and government circles until in the late 1800s, when an ethos of public honesty came to prevail, largely through the efforts of dedicated reformers. Similarly, at their origin the British police were a rank and renegade force; today they are respected and respectable. In fact, at least one writer believes that the decency of the English police is largely responsible for the mannerly and orderly behavior shown by the general public. Thus, change can be achieved, and such change can have eddy-like effects on other elements of social existence.

Controlling corporate crime through appeals to the public has basis for success. Fundamentally, when confronted with a problem, Americans respond by taking action to resolve the difficulty, an approach quite different from, say, that of the Chinese. As Barbara Tuchman has noted, the Chinese, at least in pre-Communist times, regarded passivity as their most effective tactic, on the assumption that the wrongdoer ultimately will wear himself out. The ideological basis of the American ethos was set out by Gunnar Myrdal in his now classic analysis of racial problems in the United States. We had to work our way out of the "dilemma" involved in the discrepancy between our articulated values and our actual behavior, Myrdal believed—and that resolution has proceeded, largely through the use of legal forces, though at a painfully slow and sometimes erratic pace.

A similar situation prevails regarding corporate crime and the imposition of effective sanctions against persons who commit such crime. The public may be relatively quiescent, but its attitudes on white-collar crime are clear. The Joint Commission on Correctional Manpower, for instance, found from a national survey a strong public disposition to sentence accountants who embezzle more harshly than either young burglars or persons caught looting during a riot. Similarly, a 1969 Louis Harris Poll reported that a manufacturer of an unsafe automobile was regarded by respondents as worse than a mugger (68% to 22%), and a businessman who illegally fixed prices was considered worse than a burglar (54% to 28%).

Corporate offenses, however, do not have biblical proscription—they lack, as an early writer noted, the "brimstone smell." But the havoc such offenses produce, the malevolence with which they are undertaken, and the disdain with which they are continued, are all antithetical to those principles we are expected to revere. It is a long step, assuredly, and sometimes an uncertain one, from lip service to cries of outrage; but at least the expressive spirit is present, needing only to be improved in decibels and fidelity, and the case to be made is quite unconvincing, since "crime in the suites" is a more serious national problem than "crime in the streets." "Without trust, a civilized society cannot endure," Marya Mannes has said. "When the people who are too smart to be good fool the people who are too good to be smart, the society begins to crumble."

It should be noted, in this regard, that Americans are perfectly willing to outlaw and to prosecute vigorously various kinds of behavior on social grounds, i.e., in the belief that the behaviors constitute a threat to the social fabric rather than a threat to any prospective individual victims. Thus, possession of narcotics, homosexuality, and a host of other "victimless" crimes are proscribed as threats to the moral integrity of our civilization. A reading of historical records indicates without question that class bias and religious intolerance were the predominant forces which gave rise to the laws against such "immoral" behaviors. It is now time that the rationale offered for prosecution of victimless crimes—that they threaten the integrity of the society—be applied to where it really belongs: to the realm of corporate offenses. The rationale will prevail here because it makes sense. It did not work with victimless crimes because there was no reasonable way by which those persons most important to the perpetrators—members of their own social group—could be convinced that what the offenders were doing was wrong. Therefore, eventually and inevitably, the logic of the perpetrators' position moved other groups either to take on their behavior (*e.g.,* the smoking of marijuana) or to take their side (*e.g.,* the performance of abortions).

With regard to corporate crime, the essential ingredient of a successful campaign for control exists backstage: there is the possibility of isolating the offender from reinforcement and rationalizations for his behavior, of making him appreciate that nobody for whom he has respect approves of corporate crime; of having him understand, as the English would put it, that "these kinds of things simply are not done by decent people." The tactics used by the corporate criminal to redefine his behavior in more benign terms is a standard defensive maneuver. "Businessmen develop rationalizations which conceal the fact of crime," Edwin H. Sutherland wrote in 1949 in his classic study, *White Collar Crime.* "Even when they violate the law, they do not conceive of themselves as criminals," he noted, adding that "businessmen fight whenever words that tend to break down this rationalization are used."

By far the best analysis of this process—and the way to combat it—is by Mary Cameron on middle-class shoplifters caught in Chicago's Marshall Field's. Store detectives advised that Field's would continue to be robbed unless some assault on the shoplifters' self-conceptions as honorable citizens was undertaken. The methods used toward this end are described by Cameron:

Again and again store people explain to pilferers that they are under arrest as thieves, that they will, in the normal course of events, be taken in a police van to jail, held in jail until bond is raised, and tried in court before a judge and sentenced. Interrogation procedures at the store are directed specifically and consciously toward breaking down any illusion that the shoplifter may possess that his behavior is merely regarded as "naughty" or "bad." . . . It becomes increasingly clear to the pilferer that he is considered a thief and is in imminent danger of being hauled into court and publicly exhibited as such. This realization is often accompanied by dramatic changes in attitudes and by severe emotional disturbance.

The most frequent question the middle-class female offenders ask is: "Will my husband have to know about this?" Men express great concern that their employers will discover what they have done. And both the men and women shoplifters, following this process, cease the criminal acts that they have heretofore been routinely and complacently committing.

344

The analogy to the corporate world is self-evident. "Criminal prosecution of a corporation is rather ineffective unless one or more of the individual officers is also proceeded against," a law professor has observed. A General Electric executive, for example, himself not involved in the price-fixing conspiracy, said that although he had remained silent about antitrust violations he knew about, he would not have hesitated to report to his superiors any conspiracy that had involved thefts of company property. Corporate crimes simply are not regarded in the same manner as traditional crimes, despite the harm they cause, and they will not be so regarded until the criminals who commit them are dealt with in the same manner as traditional offenders.

Harrison Salisbury tells of the women of Leningrad taking a captured German pilot to a devastated part of the besieged city during the second World War, trying to force him to really understand what he had been doing. Persons convicted of drunken driving sometimes are made to visit the morgue so that they might appreciate the kind of death they threaten. Corporate criminals, though, remain insulated from their crimes. The novelist Louis Auchincloss recently made the point well: "They were careless people," he writes. "They smashed up things and creatures and retreated back into their money or their vast carelessness, or whatever it was that kept them together, and let other people clean up the mess they had made."

How can this be changed? Taken together, a number of possible strategies involve widespread dissemination of the facts, incessant emphasis on the implications of such facts and the methods by which the situation can be improved. More specifically, the following tactics might prove useful:

1. Regular publication of a statistical compilation of white-collar crime, similar to the FBI's *Uniform Crime Reports*, which now cover traditional offenses. It might be recalled that in its earliest days the FBI concentrated mostly on white-collar offenses, such as false purchases and sales of securities, bankruptcy fraud, and antitrust violations; it was not until later that it assumed its "gangbuster" pose. Well publicized by the media these FBI statistical reports form the basis for a periodic temperature-taking of the criminal fever said to grip us. Numerical and case history press releases on corporate crime would publicly highlight such incidents. It is perhaps too much to expect that there will some day be a "Ten Most Wanted" white-collar crime list, but public reporting must be stressed as a prerequisite to public understanding.

2. Infiltration of criminally suspect corporations by agents of the federal government trained for such delicate undercover work. It would be rewarding both morally and fiscally to determine how the large corporations regard the criminal statutes they are supposed to obey. The cost would be minimal, since the infiltrators would likely be well paid by the corporation, and the financial yield from prosecutions and fines would undoubtedly more than offset any informer fees involved in the operation. To some this tactic may appear too obnoxious, productive of the very kind of social distrust that the corporate crimes themselves create. Perhaps, then, as a requirement of their right to incorporate, large companies should have placed in their offices a public servant who functions as an ombudsman, receiving public and employee complaints and investigating possible law violations.

There are, of course, other methods of uncovering and moving against corporate crimes, once the will to do so is effectively mobilized. Mandatory disclosure rules, rewards for information about criminal violations (in the manner that the income tax laws now operate), along with protections against retaliation for such disclosures, are among the possible detection procedures. The goal remains the arousal of public resentment to the point where the corporate offenses are clearly seen for what they are—frontal assaults on individuals and the society. Then, journals of news and opinion, such as *Time*, will no longer print stories dealing with the antitrust violations under the heading of "Business," but rather will place the stories where they belong, in the "Crime" section. And judges and prosecutors, those weathervanes of public opinion, will find it to their own advantage and self-interest to respond to public concern by moving vigorously against the corporate criminal.

ALTERNATIVE KINDS OF SANCTIONS

Sanctions against corporate criminals other than imprisonment can be suggested, milder in nature and perhaps somewhat more in accord with the spirit of rehabilitation and deterrence than the spirit of retribution. Some of these are, perhaps, less effective instrumentalities for cauterizing offending sources, but they possess the advantage of being more likely to be implemented at this time.

Corporate resources can be utilized to make corporate atonement for crimes committed. A procedure similar to that reported below for dealing in Germany with tax violators might be useful in inhibiting corporate offenses:

> In Germany, . . . they have a procedure whereby a taxpayer upon whom a fraud penalty has been imposed is required to

*make a public confession, apparently by newspaper adver-
tisement, of the nature of his fraud, that a penalty has been
imposed, that he admits the fact, and will not do it again. This
procedure is known as "tätige reue"* [*"positive repentance"*].

"The Achilles heel of the advertising profession," a former head
of the Federal Trade Commission has said, "is that you worship at
the altar of the positive image." The same is true of corporations;
thus the value of the public confession of guilt and the public promise
of reform.

There is, of course, the sanction of the heavy fine. It has been
argued that the disgorgement of illegal profits by the corporation—in
the nature of treble damages or otherwise multiplied amounts—
bear primarily upon the innocent shareholders rather than upon the
guilty officials. This is not very persuasive. The purchase of corporate
stock is always both an investment and a gamble; the gamble is that
the corporation will prosper by whatever tactics of management its
chosen officers pursue. Stockholders, usually consummately ignorant
about the details of corporate policy and procedure, presume that
their money will be used shrewdly and profitably. They probably are
not too averse to its illegal deployment, provided that such use is
not discovered or, if discovered, is not penalized too heavily. It would
seem that rousing fines against offending corporations will at least
lead to stockholder retaliations against lax or offending managerial
personnel, and will forewarn officials in other corporations that such
derelictions need to be avoided if they expect to remain in their posts.
The moral to widows dependent upon a steady income will be to avoid
companies with criminal records, just as they will be well advised to
keep their money out of the grasp of other kinds of shady entrepreneurs and enterprises.

What of corporate offenders themselves, where the penalties primarily should be aimed? The convicted violator might be barred from
employment in the industry for a stipulated period of time, just as
union leaders are barred from holding labor positions under similar
circumstances. In the heavy electrical equipment antitrust cases, for
instance, one convicted offender was fired from his $125,000 a year
job with General Electric, but was employed immediately upon release
from jail by another company at about a $70,000 annual salary. All
ex-convicts ought to be helped to achieve gainful employment, but
surely non-executive positions can be found which would still be gainful. "Business executives in general enjoy the greatest material rewards available in the world today," it has been noted. "The six-figure
salaries at the top would be called piratical in any other sphere of
activity." A brief retirement by corporate officials from what in other

forms of work is disparagingly called the "trough" does not seem to me to be an unreasonable imposition. Why put the fox immediately back in charge of the chicken coop? I recall some years ago the going joke at the Oklahoma State Penitentiary—that Nannie Doss, a woman who had a penchant for poisoning the food of her husbands, was going to be assigned duty as a mess-hall cook and then released to take a job in a short-order cafe. It was a macabre observation, except that similar things happen all the time with corporate criminals.

There have been suggestions that the penalties for corporate crime might be tailored to the nature of the offenses. Thus, the company president who insists that he had no knowledge of the crime could, if found culpable for negligent or criminal malfeasance, be sentenced to spend some time interning in the section of his organization from whence the violation arose. The difficulties in here, of course, in the possibility of creating a heroic martyr rather than a rehabilitated official, and in problems relating to the logistics of the situation. Yet, veterans on major league baseball teams are dispatched to Class C clubs because of inadequate performance; they then attempt to work their way back to the top. The analogy is not precise, but the idea is worth further exploration.

THE ISSUE OF DETERRENCE

The evidence gleaned from the heavy electrical equipment case in 1961 represents our best information on the subject of deterrence of corporate crime, since no major antitrust prosecution has been attempted since then, and very few had been undertaken earlier. Government attorneys were then convinced (I interviewed a number of them when I was gathering information on the subject for the President's Commission on Law Enforcement in 1966) that the 1961 antitrust prosecutions had been dramatically effective in breaking up price-fixing schemes by many other corporations; but by 1966 they felt that the lesson had almost worn off. Senate hearings, conducted after the heavy electrical equipment conspirators had come out of jail, shed further light on the subject of deterrence. One witness before the Senate committee—William Ginn, a former General Electric vice president—granted that the "taint of a jail sentence" had the effect of making people "start looking at moral values a little bit." Senator Philip Hart pushed the matter further, and drew the following remarks from the witness:

> HART: *This was what I was wondering about, whether, absent the introduction of this element of fear, there would have been any reexamination of the moral implications.*

GINN: *I wonder, Senator. That is a pretty tough one to answer.*

HART: *If I understand you correctly, you have already answered it. . . . After the fear, there came the moral reevaluation.*

Other witnesses, who had done jail time, stated with some certainty that they had learned their lesson well. "They would never get me to do it again. . . . I would starve before I would do it again," said another former General Electric executive. Another man, from the same organization, was asked: "Suppose your superior tells you to resume the meetings; will they be resumed?" "No, sir," he answered with feeling. "I would leave the company rather than participate in the meetings again."

These penitents were the same men who had earlier testified that price-fixing was "a way of life" in their companies. They had not appreciated, they said, that what they were doing was criminal (though they never used *that* word; they always said "illegal"); and if they had not met with competitors, they knew that more willing and "flexible" replacements were available. They were men described by one of their attorneys in a bit of uncalculated irony as not deserving of jail sentences because they were not "cut-throat competitors," but rather persons who "devote much of their time and substance to the community."* O. Henry's Gentle Grafter, speaking for himself, had put it more succinctly: "I feel as if I'd like to do something for as well as to humanity."

In the Montgomery County jail, the corporate executives were model prisoners. The warden praised them as the best workers he ever had had on a project devoted to reorganizing the jail's record-keeping system. Thus, to the extent that they conduct themselves more honestly within the walls than they had outside, corporate offenders might be able to introduce modern business skills into our old-fashioned penal facilities. Though they were allowed visitors two days a week, the imprisoned executives refused to have their families see them during the time, slightly less than a month, that they were jailed. It was shame, of course, that made them decide this, shame, a sense of guilt, and injured pride. These are not the kinds of emotions a society ought cold-bloodedly and unthinkingly try to instill in people, criminals or not, unless it is necessary to check socially destructive behavior.

The convicted saw themselves in similar roseate ways. The GE vice president, for instance, had written:
All of you know that next Monday, in Philadelphia, I will start serving a thirty-day jail term, along with six other *businessmen* for conduct which has been *interpreted* as being in conflict with the *complex* antitrust laws. [Italics added.]

What of the financial sanctions? The $437,500 fine against General Electric was equivalent to a $3 parking fine for a man with an income of $175,000 a year. That the corporations still felt the need to alibi and evade before the public, however, was noteworthy for its implication that loss of good will, more than loss of money or even an agent or two, might be the sanction feared most. Note, for instance, the following verbal sleight-of-hand by General Electric about a case that involved flagrant criminal behavior and represented, in the words of the sentencing judge, "a shocking indictment of a vast section of our economy." At its first annual meeting following the sentencing of the price-fixing conspirators, General Electric dismissed suggestions that further actions might be taken to cleanse itself. The idea, advanced by a stockholder, that the Company should retrieve sums paid to the conspirators as "incentive compensation" was said to "ignore the need for careful evaluation of a large number of factors." These factors—the expense of litigation and the morale of the organization—boiled down to a concern that "the best interests of the Company are served." The president of Westinghouse demanded that employees adhere to the antitrust laws not because failure to do so was a crime or because it damaged the public. Rather, such behavior was discouraged because it "etches away at the moral character and integrity, on which, in the long run, our program is based. Any such action is—and will be considered to be—a deliberate act of disloyalty to Westinghouse."

GE president Ralph Cordiner observed in 1961: "When all is said and done, it is impossible to legislate ethical conduct. A business enterprise must finally rely on individual character to meet the challenge of ethical responsibility." But by now the president had come to understand how the public might achieve what the Company could not: "Probably the strong example of the recent antitrust cases, and their consequences, will be the most effective deterrent against future violations," he had decided.

So the lesson had been learned—but only partly. It was much like the mother who scolds her children about stealing by saying that their behavior upsets her and might hurt the family's reputation in the neighborhood. After several such episodes, however, and a few prison terms or similarly strong sanctions against her offspring, she might suggest that a more compelling reason for not stealing is that it is a criminal offense and when you get caught you are going to suffer for it. When such an attitude comes to prevail in the corporate world, we will have taken a major step toward deterring corporate crime and protecting its innocent victims.

THE CASE FOR FEDERAL CHARTERING

Ralph Nader

Contemporary events reflect a mounting concern over corporate activities. Economic concentration and monopolistic practices, environmental pollution, product safety, occupational health, advertising and deception, employment practices, corporate secrecy, corporate crime, corporate responsibility—the list of inquiry is long, as it should be. But it is important to understand these issues in their historic context so that in focusing on behavioral effects we do not ignore the institutional causes of corporate depredations. For corporate power and the corporate form did not suddenly erupt full-blown on the American scene in the 1960s. And the causes of, and possible solutions to, problems like corporate power, size, pollution, and secrecy may all be quite related.

THE DEVELOPMENT OF STATE INCORPORATION

It was mid-millennium England when the corporate form first took shape. The Crown vested governmental authority in certain commercial groups to trade in its name. These royal charters regulated the trading company or corporation since only the Crown had the prerogative to govern trade and the right to clothe a private group with public power. This right to control the conditions of the corporation's existence, however, went largely unexercised. Monopoly power without restraint led to numerous abuses. As R. W. Boyden observed of the trading companies, "They tended to be massive, corrupt and inefficient. They grabbed power as an excuse for the failure to do business. . . . They identified themselves with ruling groups to become politically beyond challenge irrespective of their economic services." Many tended to be rapacious and imperialistic, like the East India Trade company, which even had its own flags, governors, counts, and armies.

This tradition of incorporation as a privilege rather than a right was passed on to the American colonies, which continued it through the Revolution. Special legislative charters permitted some private groups to build bridges, transport water and undertake commerce. The American Constitution, omitting any references to the power of incorporation, did not change old ways. States continued to charter corporations under special legislative acts, although the frequency of their issuance increased to 200 in the first decade after the War of Independence. But the process of petition and hearings led to delay, expense, corruption, and favoritism. As a result, and because the pace of economic growth was quickening, a movement began seeking the equal and easy granting of incorporation. North Carolina in 1795, Massachusetts in 1799, New York in 1811, and Connecticut in 1837, led the way by enacting "general incorporation laws," which allowed, without need for legislative approval, the formation of corporations "for any lawful purpose." In the early 1800s most lawyers and judges still viewed corporations as performing public functions in the public interest. But by 1870, according to Professor James Willard Hurst, this notion had all but vanished. Corporations now considered themselves private property owned and controlled by their shareholders.

The power, as distinguished from authority, to form and control corporations had thus passed from the state to the promoters and entrepreneurs of corporate ventures. Instead of granting incorporation after certain legislative minima were set, a new *enabling theory* took shape, giving private groups the flexibility to create their own conditions of existence. These groups were granted more rights than responsibilities. Enabling statutes were premised on the view that free enterprisers acting in their own interest would serve the general social interest as well, or in the words of John Locke, "private vice makes public virtue."

The state did not entirely abdicate its regulatory role. Charters, though freely available, continued to have size and scope limitations.

For example, New York had a capitalization ceiling of $100,000 and firms incorporated for one activity, say baking, could not go into another, like gravel mining. Corporations could not own the stock or assets of other corporations and were granted existence only for a specific period of years. Toward the end of the nineteenth century, fourteen states sought to control monopolies by forbidding them in corporate charters. Finally, corporations were prohibited from doing business or owning property outside the state of their existence. These restrictions reflected the historic and prevailing fear of corporate power. One recent writer saw it as the "fear . . . that a corporation was only an artificial personality and therefore did not have a soul or conscience. Lacking a conscience, it had no morals and was prima facie dangerous." So long as corporations remained local, contained by the charter's restrictions, states still maintained the control they considered necessary for the public interest to be served.

But corporations did *not* stay local. What these restrictions aimed to avoid is precisely what occurred. In an effort to attract resident corporations into their states, incorporation laws became increasingly liberalized. The winner of the race for corporate citizens went to the state of least restriction. The early victor was undoubtedly New Jersey. In 1866 it permitted the holding of property and doing of business outside of the state. In 1875 it relieved incorporators of their obligation to file their intention to incorporate, and it dispensed with the ceiling on the amount of authorized capital. During the 1880s, in a critical move, it legalized holding companies by allowing corporations to hold and dispose of the stock of other corporations. In the next decade it removed limitations on the duration of the corporate charter. The result: between 1888 and 1904, 192 of 345 companies with capitalization in excess of $1,000,000 took out New Jersey charters. New Jersey became the home of the infamous Standard Oil Trust. Trusts and holding companies declared illegal in other states simply transferred their property to corporations organized under the law of New Jersey. Partly as a consequence, the turn of the century merger movement occurred, one which changed the face of industrial America as no merger movement before or since.

But New Jersey's dominance was only temporary, for Delaware was not to be denied. As an 1899 law review article notes:

> Meanwhile the little community of truck farmers and clam diggers [Delaware] have had their cupidity excited by the spectacle of their northern neighbor, New Jersey, becoming rich and bloated through the granting of franchises to trusts which are to do business everywhere except in New Jersey, and which are to go forth panoplied by the sovereign state of New Jersey to afflict

and curse other American communities . . . In other words, little Delaware . . . is determined to get her little tiny, sweet, round, baby hand into the grab-bag of sweet things before it is too late.

To obtain the business of incorporation, all Delaware did was to be a little worse than New Jersey. Its 1899 business code, drafted by a financial reporter and three corporate lawyers, enacted most of New Jersey's liberalization and then some: any classification of stock could be issued, with or without voting powers; shareholders lost rights to preemption; there was no state transfer tax on the resale of securities; annual meetings could be held outside the state; directors need not own company stock to qualify for the directorate; state and tax rates were set slightly below those of New Jersey; and finally, charters permitted directors to issue new stock, change the terms of authorized stock previous to sale, retire preferred stock and even change the firm's by-laws—all *without* obtaining shareholder consent. Delaware thus took over the lead in the incorporation game, an advantage she has not to this day relinquished. As the local newspapers christened it, Delaware became "The Little Home of Big Business."

Worse than merely win the race, Delaware also set the pace of walking backwards into the future. Other state laws looked to the Delaware code as a model, in the process competing to the lowest common denominator. So long as there was another "Corporate Reno," it was futile for any state to reform its incorporation law. New Jersey Governor Woodrow Wilson, under a challenge from Teddy Roosevelt, did it in 1913 by passing tough, local antitrust measures. The consequence was that chartering business went elsewhere.

In a way, Delaware succeeded too well. Imitative states began to take some of its business away. To meet the competition, liberalizations of Delaware's business code occurred in 1927 and 1929; whereas in 1927, 5,424 charters had been granted generating $824,483 in fees, by 1929 the number had swollen to 7,537 charters and $3,309,698 in fees. But still Delaware wasn't satisfied. Although by 1960 one third of the top 600 industrial corporations were headquartered in Delaware, the state decided to further liberalize its business code. A Revision Commission was formed in 1964 which attempted, in its words, "To ascertain what other states have to attract corporations that we do not have." The basic redrafting was done by three private corporate lawyers working on Saturdays in their private offices. The full Commission always anticipated that the State legislature—which of course had to approve the new code since it *was* a public law—would be a rubber stamp; one member of the Commission referred to the legislature as "just a bunch of farmers." No hearings were held on the final statute and it passed the Delaware legislature unanimously on July 3, 1967. This closed process had its antecedents; a leading member of the Delaware bar assayed the system in 1932:

> Here in Delaware we have an ideal system. Our legislature would never think of passing an amendment to our corporation laws without submitting the matter to the state bar association. Proposals for change are always brought to us first. Our committee considers them, and if we approve them the legislature adopts them as a matter of course. That insures sound laws. Don't you think it is an excellent system?

The new 1967 code contained, among others, these liberalizations: only directors, not shareholders, could propose amendments to the corporate charter; plans for special compensation, stock options and bonuses were expressly permitted, but without any procedures established either to avoid abuses or to disclose the amounts involved; shareholders were denied appraisal rights; officers and directors could be indemnified by the firm for court costs and settlements of criminal and civil cases without the need for court or shareholder approval.* So that corporate buyers of this product did not miss the point, the statutory preface to it advertised, "New Law Enabling, not restrictive." These reforms achieved their purpose. While corporations were incorporating at the rate of 300 a month before the new code's enactment, it jumped to 800 registrations a month directly afterwards. By 1969, 56,000 corporations had their birth certificates filed at 10th and K Streets in Wilmington, Delaware, a number including one third of all the companies on the New York Stock Exchange and one half of the top 100 industrial corporations.**

From a time when firms were selectively chartered and controlled by the government, private corporations have grown to huge size and power without commensurate accountability. Promoters and management—not shareholders, not employees, not the community—have nearly unchecked discretion to draft and implement the governance of the corporation. How did this happen? State incorporation laws became a version of Gresham's Law, as the bad states drove out the good. Shareholders were too powerless and disinterested, and

---

*This indemnification provision was "non-exclusive," which meant that any corporation, by its by-laws, could opt for a scheme even more liberal than this one. The code itself permitted indemnification; although the law might have been broken, if the action involved was "not contrary to the best interest of the corporation." The Commission reporter, law professor Ernest Folk, explained that "an act may be contrary to the interests of the state, but it is not for that reason alone a breach of duty to the corporation or even against the best interests of the corporation." So much for the theory that private vice invariably makes public virtue.

**Despite its continued success at enticing incorporators, Delaware's continuing vigilance cannot be underestimated. A headline in the October 14, 1971 Wilmington Morning News read "Unit to lure corporate HQs named." The article said, "Formation of a committee designed to attract corporate headquarters and related business facilities to Delaware was announced by Gov. Russell W. Peterson yesterday."

legislative committees too ignorant and pliable, to challenge this accession of power. The task of drafting state laws remained firmly within the hands of corporate lawyers and business men, psychologically identifying with management. A recent *Pennsylvania Law Review* article concludes:

> The sovereign state of Delaware is in the business of selling its corporation law. This is profitable business, for corporation law is a good commodity to sell . . . The consumers of this commodity are corporations and . . . Delaware like any other good businessman, tries to give the consumer what he wants. In fact, those who will buy the product are not only consulted about their preferences, but are also allowed to design the product and run the factory.

And so long as we permit five different jurisdictions (Puerto Rico included) to compete for corporate charters, there can be no improvement. For reform, we must look elsewhere.

A HISTORY OF FEDERAL INCORPORATION

The concept of federal chartering has received support throughout our history as the government chartered, owned, or ran a corporate activity. The Federal government was a minority stockholder in the first and second banks of the United States. Nationally chartered banks were created by an Act of Congress in 1864. In 1904–1905, the American Government acquired all the shares of the Panama Railroad Company. World War I "stimulated a wide and rapid extension of the use of the government-owned corporation," such as the incorporation and take-over of the United States Shipping Board Emergency Fleet. The 1922 China Trade Act, in order to encourage trade with the envisioned bountiful Chinese market, permits federal charters for firms trading with China. In 1924, the federally run Inland Waterways Corporation was formed. In the 1930s, the Tennessee Valley authority, a Government authority, performed a function private capital had strongly refused to perform. During the Depression, numerous government-owned corporations arose. Among others, the Federal National Mortgage Association ("Fannie May" in business parlance) was a government-run corporation formed to buy and sell mortgages to provide a secondary mortgage market. (This federal corporation shifted into private control in the Nixon Administration.) More recently, hydro-electric projects are federally licensed as are interstate motor carriers. Also, government-business partnerships like Comsat, Amtrak, and the National Corporation for Housing Partnerships are examples of direct involvement by the Federal Government in the running of a corporation. Thus, there is little doubt the Federal

Government *can* and *has* chartered and created corporations; but at the same time there is little evidence to indicate it has the *resolve* to do so on a major scale.

The idea that the Federal Government should charter corporations first arose during the Articles of Confederation when, in 1781, Congress granted a national charter to the Bank of North America. During the Constitutional Convention in 1787, James Madison twice proposed, unsuccessfully, that the Constitution expressly empower Congress "To grant charters of corporation in cases where the public good may require them and the authority of a single state may be incompetent." Although no formal vote on it was ever taken, it was rejected by some delegates as unnecessary and by others as leading to monopolies.

A century later, in the 1880s, the public became concerned about the economic and political power of the huge trusts. Some reformers called for a form of federal licensing of corporations in order to control their excesses. Instead, the 1890 Sherman Antitrust Act was passed, looking to competition rather than regulation to restrain the trusts. Between 1903 and 1914, Presidents Roosevelt, Taft, and Wilson all voiced support for a federal incorporation or licensing scheme in their annual messages to Congress; President Taft had his attorney general, George Wickersham, draft a federal licensing bill and he proposed it to Congress in 1911. Mark Hanna, William Jennings Bryan, and the U.S. Industrial Commission favored it. Industrialists Judge Gary, James Dill, and John D. Rockefeller all favored versions of the idea; the *Wall Street Journal* and National Association of Manufacturers both supported it in 1908. It was endorsed by the 1904 Democratic Platform, the 1908 Republican Platform and the 1912 Democratic Platform. Twenty different bills were introduced in one or both Houses of Congress between 1903 and 1914.* Scholars and politicians favored it as a logical way of promoting the public interest, and some industrialists approved of it as a way of resolving the annoyance of conflicting legislation and jurisdictions. Despite this array of support, the Clayton and Federal Trade Commission Acts of 1914 became law instead of federal chartering.

The late thirties witnessed the most sustained drive for federal licensing to date. Senator Joseph O'Mahoney, a populist Senator from Wyoming, energetically and repeatedly promoted the idea of "National Charters for National Business." By emphasizing that "a corporation

---

*While some permitted federal charters or licenses for those who wanted them, others made the federal role compulsory. Nearly all of the versions required: (a) annual reports detailing corporate earnings and practices, (b) the public release of some of this information, (c) the end of certain unfair trade practices, and (d) penalties for violation of the reporting or charter provisions.

has no rights; it has only privileges," he sought to return to the pre-enabling act days when charters policed as well as permitted. In 1938 his Sub-Committee of Federal Licensing Corporations held four volumes of hearings on S.3072, a bill which he and Senator William Borah co-sponsored. Senator O'Mahoney later made it clear that the important choice was between a federal and a state role in the control of the corporate fiction.

In summary, at every point in our history when federal chartering was considered, an alternative remedy was chosen. The outrage against the trusts in the 1880s institutionalized itself in the 1887 Interstate Commerce Commission and the 1890 Sherman Act. Concern during the turn-of-the-century merger wave and depression of 1903 culminated in the Bureau of Corporations, which grew into the 1914 Federal Trade Commission enforcing the Clayton Act. The Depression, demanding urgent reforms, witnessed the creation of the Securities laws, industry codes, and additional regulatory agencies. During all these periods, federal chartering was prominent, topical, and finally ignored. Clearly, it is an idea whose time has come, and come, and come, almost always at moments of economic crisis. Our present economic and social ills—in the midst of corporate unaccountability and a misdirected abundance—make it topical again.

Federal incorporation is necessary because state incorporation has failed its past missions and avoided even acknowledging its future responsibilities toward a fast changing corporate society. And the reason why is clear: what good is it for forty-nine states to have tough business codes, if one is a coddler? With the states stooping to that lowest common denominator, corporations have conquered. The only remedy for this permissive structure is to have one chartering authority, not fifty.

Even *if* state business codes and authorities did not so overwhelmingly reflect management power interests, they would still be significantly incapable of following through to enforcement. Just from their limited geographic jurisdiction over world-wide companies, Delaware cannot restrain General Motors; nor can New Jersey control Standard Oil effectively. Our states are no match for the resources and size of our great corporations; in 1968, a list of the top fifty corporations, states, and cities by gross revenue found seven of the top ten, and forty-one of the top fifty to be corporations. [See Table.] (General Motors could *buy* Delaware . . . if DuPont were willing to sell it.) "The century and a half of state failure," wrote one observer in 1942, "has been the story of a battle between corporate giants and legal pygmies." To control national or multinational power requires, at the least, national authority.

TABLE
SALES OF THE 50 LARGEST U. S. INDUSTRIAL CORPORATIONS AND GENERAL REVENUES OF THE 50 STATES AND THE 10 LARGEST CITIES, 1968; AND THE NUMBER OF EMPLOYEES

	1968 sales or general revenues ($ million)	Rank	Employees (thousands)*
1. General Motors	20,026	1	728
2. Standard Oil (N.J.)	13,266	2	150
3. Ford Motor Co.	10,515	3	394
4. General Electric Co.	7,741	4	375
5. California	7,525	S1	230
6. New York State	6,462	S2	192
7. New York City	6,221		
8. Chrysler	6,213	5	216
9. Mobil Oil	5,771	6	79
10. International Business Machine	5,345	7	222
11. Texaco	5,121	8	79
12. Gulf Oil	4,202	9	58
13. U. S. Steel	4,005	10	197
14. Western Electric	3,717	11	169
15. Standard Oil of California	3,297	12	47
16. DuPont de Nemours	3,102	13	112
17. Shell Oil	3,073	14	38
18. Radio Corp. of America	3,014	15	128
19. Pennsylvania	2,970	S3	128
20. McDonnell Douglas	2,933	16	140
21. Standard Oil (Ind.)	2,918	17	45
22. Westinghouse Electric	2,900	18	132
23. Boeing	2,879	19	142
24. Michigan	2,842	S4	115
25. Swift	2,834	20	48
26. International Tel. & Tel.	2,760	21	236
27. Illinois	2,673	S5	122
28. Goodyear Tire & Rubber	2,637	22	113
29. General Telephone & Electronics	2,622	23	151
30. Bethlehem Steel	2,594	24	131
31. Texas	2,590	S6	123
32. Union Carbide	2,545	25	99
33. International Harvester	2,541	26	111
34. Proctor & Gamble	2,438	27	41
35. North American Rockwell	2,438	28	115
36. Eastman Kodak	2,391	29	105
37. Lockheed Aircraft	2,335	30	92
38. National Dairy Products	2,318	31	47
39. General Dynamics	2,253	32	103
40. Ohio	2,251	S7	104
41. United Aircraft	2,212	33	79
42. Armour	2,156	34	38
43. Continental Oil	2,082	35	53
44. Phillips Petroleum	1,981	36	36
45. Firestone Tire & Rubber	1,875	37	95
46. Ling-Temco	1,777	38	40
47. Tenneco	1,777	39	40
48. General Foods	1,651	40	32
49. Monsanto	1,632	41	59
50. Massachusetts	1,608	S8	58
51. Borden	1,588	42	39
52. Grace, W.R.	1,576	43	64
53. Litton Industries	1,561	44	95
54. New Jersey	1,560	S9	60
55. American Can	1,521	44	54

	1968 sales or general revenues ($ million)	Rank	Employees (thousands)*
56. Sperry Rand	1,487	46	102
57. Sinclair Oil	1,483	47	19
58. Wisconsin	1,477	S10	64
59. Caterpillar Tractor	1,472	48	59
60. Textron	1,445	49	62
61. Florida	1,443	S11	72
62. International Paper	1,414	50	52
63. Minnesota	1,358	S12	55
64. North Carolina	1,351	S13	65
65. Louisiana	1,349	S14	68
66. Washington	1,339	S15	65
67. Indiana	1,328	S16	67
68. Georgia	1,217	S17	53
69. Virginia	1,171	S18	75
70. Maryland	1,114	S19	47
71. Missouri	1,077	S20	63
72. Tennessee	959	S21	51
73. Alabama	955	S22	44
74. Kentucky	932	S23	42
75. Oklahoma	897	S24	47
76. Iowa	850	S25	41
77. Connecticut	809	S26	41
78. Los Angeles	703		
79. Colorado	658	S27	40
80. South Carolina	653	S28	35
81. Chicago	634		
82. Oregon	632	S29	40
83. Kansas	607	S30	39
84. Mississippi	599	S31	30
85. West Virginia	582	S32	35
86. Arizona	562	S33	26
87. Washington, D.C.	557		
88. Arkansas	519	S34	28
89. Baltimore	464		
90. New Mexico	458	S35	23
91. Philadelphia	458		
92. San Francisco	415		
93. Hawaii	402	S36	30
94. Detroit	400		
95. Boston	393		
96. Utah	379	S37	23
97. Nebraska	367	S38	25
98. Rhode Island	289	S39	16
99. Maine	250	S40	16
100. North Dakota	250	S41	14
101. Alaska	246	S42	9
102. Delaware	233	S43	11
103. Idaho	230	S44	13
104. Montana	229	S45	16
105. South Dakota	206	S46	13
106. Nevada	175	S47	7
107. Vermont	175	S48	9
108. Wyoming	168	S49	8
109. New Hampshire	155	S50	12
110. St. Louis	138		

*Corporation employment for 1968; State government employment for 1969. Sources: Corporate sales and employees from "The 500 largest industrial corporations." Fortune, June 15, 1968, pp. 188—9; State general revenues from Statistical abstract of the United States–1970, Table 620, p. 418; State employment from Statistical abstract of the United States–1970, Table 633, p. 429.

At a time when the Federal Government becomes increasingly prominent in salvaging our ailing economy, it is an anachronism for the states to create corporations which market nationally and internationally. Quite simply, state borders are not relevant boundaries for corporate commerce. In the context of the evolution of industrial enterprise in the last two centuries, state incorporation makes as much sense as fifty state currencies, or fifty state units of measurements. If a criminal crosses state borders, the FBI is called in; if a person crosses a state line with an intent to riot, and does, the Interstate Riot Act has jurisdiction; if a commodity or a service travels interstate, so too should the jurisdiction of the Federal Government be called into play. In other federal systems—German, Mexican, Brazilian—firms which do business between the states or provinces must be formed under federal law.

While no one solution can cure all the ills of our corporate economy, federal chartering can make a big advance in providing a framework for shaping and monitoring corporate power. An array of substantive reforms, discussed subsequently, can be implemented. There are procedural benefits as well. Presently, a charter is a blank check which the corporation signs and then deposits in ignored files. States do not monitor the firms they have created for violation of their birthright, nor do they impose sanctions for charter violations. Recently in Indiana, AT&T, Penn-Central, and De Paul University all lost their corporate licenses to do intrastate business for their failure to file annual reports. But there were no hearings held and no fines assessed. Until the firms filed their forms, it was business as usual, although they had legally ceased to exist in Indiana. It is quixotic to expect State boards to have either the resources or will to impose adequate sanctions. An up-to-date federal chartering authority with more comprehensive authority would be far more likely to do so or be accessible to citizen power to do so. It can remind the corporation that the charter is a compact between the government and itself to assure business behavior in the public interest. It can also remind corporations that they hold their charter in trust for public benefit, and if they violate that trust they can forfeit their charter.

A federal chartering agency could help equalize the varying burdens and benefits corporations obtain due to the vagueness of different state authorities. Incorporation fees, regulatory laws, charter provisions—powerful corporations can threaten to run away to a different state if these items are not to their satisfaction. And it is easy to see why a Textron in Rhode Island and DuPont in Delaware could make its state host anxious. A single federal authority could end this corporate whipsawing of state against state.

What if, because of a federal chartering law, many American firms simply left to incorporate in Bermuda or France? What if they treated us like they treat Canada: a place to do business but not owe allegiance? Or what about companies without countries? Carl A. Gerstacker, chairman of the Dow Chemical Company, told a White House Conference in February 1972 that he looked forward to the day of the "anational corporation," one without any national ties which could, therefore, operate freely and flexibly around the world. Gerstacker revealed how Dow had been studying the possibility for a decade of locating on an island in the Caribbean. The chief obstacle, he said, would be unfavorable tax consequences to investors in the exchange of stock involved in such a corporate emigration. Any of these business runaways could claim that requirements imposed on them not required by, say, France would create legal conflicts with their foreign charters. There is only one effective reply: The corporation and foreign government in question either complies with the conditions of the federal chartering law or it cannot trade here. Period. Since the American market is such a large percentage of the world market, we would have the leverage, if we had the will, to make this demand of expatriate firms and foreign authorities. This stance is not wholly theoretical. It is similar to the one the Nixon Administration took with its Western trade partners over international and trade markets. With the same conviction, it could be utilized to make a federal incorporation law viable. There are state "foreign incorporation laws" which require out-of-state firms to meet certain local standards (e.g., stringent reporting requirements) in order to do business there. The same principle must apply to firms existing outside our borders who wish to do business here. Another restraint could be an "equalization" tax policy making it difficult for firms to move away and then sell back to the United States.

What is needed is a new agency—call it the Federal Chartering Agency (FCA)—to issue federal charters for major corporations engaged in interstate business. The charter would be mandatory, not permissive, and it would contain "policing" as well as "enabling" provisions. What is needed now is not a new Corporate Bill of Rights—for rights they amply have—but a Corporate Bill of Obligations. A sketch of some of the possible provisions follows:

1. *Corporate democracy* would reduce the dominance of the present despotisms commandeering most corporations. The potential areas of coverage are all those which, unchallenged, have permitted management to rule free of its theoretical electorate. Such areas include: corporate loans to officers and directors should be prohibited, and other "interested" dealings must first be reported to shareholders;

all compensation schemes, as well as indemnifications for civil settlements, must be reported to shareholders for their approval; shareholders should be accorded liberalized access to "inspect" corporate records (e.g., profit and loss statements by division, shareholder lists, consumer letters of complaint) and to use the proxy machinery; the largest beneficial owners of the corporation should be routinely made public; cumulative voting, without staggered terms for directors, should be mandatory and not just permissive; shareholders must have the right to amend the by-laws and charter, as well as recall directors.

2. Strict *antitrust* standards must be a condition of the charter. Given the abundant evidence favoring competition and condemning monopoly, no corporation would be permitted to retain more than 12 percent of an oligopolistic industry, as President Johnson's antitrust task force recommended. To correct the trouble with conglomerates, they should be permitted only to acquire toe-hold acquisitions in concentrated industries and should spin-off an equal amount of assets for any they acquire.*

3. *Corporate disclosure* must replace corporate secrecy. What are the earnings of hidden subsidiaries and consolidated divisions; who are the real beneficial owners of a corporation; what is the racial composition of employees and new staff; what product and safety testing have been conducted; what plans exist to meet pollution emissions standards? Since the public is so intimately affected, answers to all these must be made public; shareholders, investors, and government officials need adequate information to act intelligently. If done extensively enough, a corporate information center could be developed, with data by firm, plant and product available for immediate use on computer tapes to respond to topical questions of significance.

4. The corporate charter should *"constitutionalize"* the corporation, in Professor Arthur Miller's phrase, applying constitutional obligations to this private aggregation of power. What underpins this proposal is that corporations are effectively like states, private governments, with vast economic, political, and social impact. A democratic society, even if it encourages such groupings for private economic purposes, should not suffer such public power without public accountability. Again, it is an old, but largely ignored, notion. Thomas Hobbes saw corporations as "chips off the block of sovereignty." The British Mon-

---

*The federal statute would have to emphatically state that the new agency and chartering scheme would in no way diminish antitrust enforcement. There will be a tendency on the part of some to assume that the regulatory and oversight functions of a new agency will substitute for competition as a controller of market power. For example, this tacit assumption kept the Justice Department for decades from suing banks under the antitrust laws. Federal incorporation seeks the rejuvenation of antitrust, not its replacement.

arch in the Middle Ages saw them as extensions of royal power. Political scientist Earl Latham calls them a "body politic," while law professor Walton Hamilton concluded in 1957:

> There has arisen, quite apart from the ordinary operations of state, a government of industry which . . . has its constitution and its statutes, its administration and judicial processes, and its own manner of dealing with those who do not abide by the law of the industry.

Our large corporations represent just the kind of concentrated power which the Constitution and its succeeding amendments aimed to diffuse. If the constitutional convention were held today, it would surely encompass *America, Inc.* It makes no public sense to apply the Constitution to Wyoming and West Tisbury (Mass.), but not to General Motors and Standard Oil (N.J.).

Unions too are private groups which have been legislated public power, but on the condition that they behave democratically, with adequate due process safeguards. The same should hold true for private corporations accorded public power via the chartering compact. Constitutionally it would involve an extension of state action and corporate restraint which is the doctrinal descendant to cases like *Marsh v. Alabama, Employees Union v. Logan Valley, Shelly v. Kraemer,* and *Griggs v. Duke Power Co.* Very simply, when a corporation deals with its employees, shareholders, and dealers, it must do so in a fair way. For example, first amendment rights to free speech means that an employee can publish material critical of the firm in a magazine or underground corporate newspaper; fourteenth amendment safeguards mean that if an employee refuses to perform an illegal task for a federally chartered firm, or blows the whistle on a corporate crime, he or she cannot be fired without a due process hearing with explicit charges and decisive evidence; the fourth amendment would forbid the firm from searching his private belongings at work without a warrant. It is inadequate to depend merely on unions to guarantee these rights since unions often ignore these rights in bargaining sessions, and since unions account for something under a quarter of all employees: the other 75 percent deserve these protections. The "Dealers Day in Court" legislation enacted in the fifties focused on arbitrary auto-management policy toward auto dealers which required remedial legislation. Various constitutional norms could have anticipated and made unnecessary such a law. For too long these private governments have enjoyed the private rights of a person (equal protection, search and seizure, denial of property without due process), but have not accepted the governmental obligations of a public body (meting out equal protection, tolerating free speech). A better balance is long overdue.

5. Rules can be devised so that consumers no longer bear the brunt of shoddy or dangerous products. The proper mix of implied warranties, breach of warranty, product liability, class actions, and informational advertising could all either make corporations pay for their full social cost or provide incentives for the production of better products. At present, due to boiler-plate contracting and legislative and judicial obstacles to class actions, firms can avoid absorbing the cost of the damage they impose.

Hovering over all these provisions, as well as any others, would be graduated penalties for violation of the charter. Depending on the nature and frequency of the violations, penalties could run from small absolute fines to fines as a percentage of sales, from management reorganization to executive suspensions, from public trusteeship to the dissolution of the charter. A scale of sanctions, then, must be developed, to guarantee compliance with the charter. And to help encourage compliance, a chartering authority would retain the ancient, equitable "visitatorial powers," which, according to Roscoe Pound, was "a power of the state . . . for investigation of the activities of, and correction of the abuses committed or suffered by, the corporate authorities . . ."

In formulating a Federal Chartering Agency, care must be taken that it does not become as unresponsive and inefficient as some of the present regulatory and enforcement agencies. Lessons should be learned from the past; but at the same time, it would be defeatist and irresponsible to urge no more federal reform measures because some have previously failed. Many corporations go bankrupt, yet the corporation is still a viable legal structure for the production and sale of goods and services. It is important to again stress the objectified nature of the FCA's standards. It would not undertake the imbroglios of rate determinations which naturally invite industry lobbying and a dependence on self-serving corporate data. By dealing with *all* industries rather than just one—like railroads, airlines or the broadcast media—there is less chance of being co-opted by a singularly organized counterattack. To an extent this explains a difference between the SEC and ICC. The FCA should also contain liberal provisions for shareholder and citizen suits—as now institutionalized in the Michigan pollution law—so that agency lethargy or inefficiency could be checked by interested citizen activity. More liberal rights of intervention into government processes could similarly permit public interest lawyers to monitor any misfeasance or nonfeasance. Mechanisms will have to be provided to help insure that a "Commissioner" of the FCA be vigorous, non-partisan and independent. Furthermore, whatever the chances a FCA could still become as inefficient as an ICC, it would have a great distance to drop before it became as supine and irrelevant as the present state chartering bodies.

While a Delaware cannot dictate terms to GM, a FCA can, but it is not inevitable that it *will*. Thus, a new federal agency is a necessary but not a sufficient remedy. If it is badly organized with weak powers, and no citizen access and participation, it will be ineffective. If the contrary, it will be effective. The form is crucial—but so are its powers.

During a 1968 liberalization of its business code, New Jersey candidly acknowledged that "It is clear that the major protections to investors, creditors, employees, customers and the general public have come, and must continue to come, from federal legislation and not from state corporation acts." Federal incorporation could relieve state chartering agencies of their impossible task of ferreting out the occasions when corporations commit antisocial acts; it would, instead, place the burden on corporations, who are granted their status by the society they so affect, to show that they *are* acting in the public interest. This is the essence of corporate accountability.

ACTION FOR
A CHANGE

Ralph Nader

This country has more problems than it should tolerate and more solutions than it uses. Few societies in the course of human history have faced such a situation: most are in the fires without the water to squelch them. Our society has the resources and the skills to keep injustice at bay and to elevate the human condition to a state of enduring compassion and creative fulfillment. How we go about using the resources and skills has consequences which extend well beyond our national borders to all the earth's people.

How do we go about this? The question has been asked and answered in many ways throughout the centuries. Somehow, the answers, even the more lasting ones, whether conforming or defiant, affect the reality of living far less than the intensity of their acceptance would seem to indicate. Take the conventional democratic creeds, for example. Many nations have adopted them, and their principles have wide popular reception. But the theories are widely separated from practice. Power and wealth remain concentrated, decisions continue to be made by the few, victims have little representation in thousands of forums which affect their rights, livelihoods, and futures. And societies like ours, which have produced much that is good, are developing new perils, stresses, and deprivations of unprecedented scope and increasing risk. As the technologies of war and economics become more powerful and pervasive, the future, to many people, becomes more uncertain and fraught with fear. Past achievements are discounted or depreciated as the quality of life drifts downward in numerous ways. General economic growth produces costs which register, like the silent violence of poverty and pollution, with quiet desperation, ignored by entrenched powers, except in their rhetoric.

But the large institutions' contrived nonaccountability, complex technologies, and blameworthy indifference have not gone unchallenged, especially by the young. The very magnitude of our problems has reminded them of old verities and taught them new values. The generation gap between parents and children is in part a difference in awareness and expectation levels. Parents remember the Depression and are thankful for jobs. The beneficiaries—their children—look for more meaningful work and wonder about those who still do not have jobs in an economy of plenty because of rebuffs beyond their control. Parents remember World War II and what the enemy could have done to America; children look on the Vietnam War and other similar wars and wonder what America has done to other people and what, consequently, she is doing to herself. To parents, the noxious plume from factory smokestacks was the smell of the payroll; children view such sights as symbols of our domestic chemical warfare that is contaminating the air, water, and soil now and for many years hence. Parents have a more narrow concept of neighborhood; children view Earth as a shaky ship requiring us all to be our brother's keeper, regardless of political boundaries.

In a sense, these themes, or many like them, have distinguished the split between fathers and sons for generations; very often the resolution is that the sons become like the fathers. The important point is not that such differences involve a statistically small number of the young—historic changes, including the American Revolution, have always come through minorities—but that conditions are indeed serious, and a new definition of work is needed to deal with them.

That new kind of work is a new kind of citizenship. The word "citizenship" has a dull connotation—which is not surprising, given its treatment by civics books and the way it has been neglected. But the role of the citizen is obviously central to democracy, and it is time to face up to the burdens and liberations of citizenship.

Democratic systems are based on the principle that all power comes from the people. The administration of governmental power begins to erode this principle in practice immediately. The inequality of wealth, talent, ambition, and fortune in the society works its way into the governmental process which is supposed to be distributing evenhanded justice, resources, and opportunities. Can the governmental process resist such pressures as the chief trustee of structured democratic power given it by the consent of the governed? Only to the degree to which the governed develop ways to apply their generic power in meticulous and practical ways on a continual basis. A citizenship of wholesale delegation and abdication to public and private power systems, such as prevails now, makes such periodic checks as elections little more than rituals. It permits tweedledum and tweedledee choices that put mostly indistinguishable candidates above meaningful issues and programs. It facilitates the overwhelming dominance of the pursuit of private or special interests, to the detriment of actions bringing the greatest good to the greatest number. It breeds despair, discouragement, resignation, cynicism, and all that is involved in the "You can't fight City Hall" syndrome. It constructs a society which has thousands of full-time manicurists and pastrymakers but less than a dozen citizen-specialists fighting full time against corporate water contamination or to get the government to provide food (from bulging warehouses) for millions of undernourished Americans.

Building a new way of life around citizenship action must be the program of the immediate future. The ethos that looks upon citizenship as an avocation or opportunity must be replaced with the commitment to citizenship as an obligation, a continual receiver of our time, energy, and skill. And that commitment must be transformed into a strategy of action that develops instruments of change while it focuses on what needs to be done. This is a critical point. Too often, people who are properly outraged over injustice concentrate so much on decrying the abuses and demanding the desired reforms that they never build the instruments to accomplish their objectives in a lasting manner.

There are three distinct roles through which effective citizenship activity can be channeled. First is the full-time professional citizen, who makes his career by applying his skills to a wide range of public problems. These citizens are not part of any governmental, corporate, or union institutions. Rather they are independently based, working *on* institutions to improve and reshape them or replace them with improved ways of achieving just missions. With their full-time base, they are able to mobilize and encourage part-time citizen activity.

With shorter workweeks heading toward the four-day week, part-time involvement can become an integral part of the good life for blue- and white-collar workers. Certainly many Americans desire to find the answers to two very recurrent questions: "What can I do to improve my community?" and "How do I go about doing it?" The development of the mechanics of taking a serious abuse, laying it bare before the public, proposing solutions, and generating the necessary coalitions to see these solutions through—these steps metabolize the latent will of people to contribute to their community and count as individuals rather than as cogs in large organizational wheels.

The emergence of capabilities and outlets for citizenship expression has profound application to the third form of citizenship activity—on-the-job citizenship. Consider the immense knowledge of waste, fraud, negligence, and other misdeeds which employees of corporations, governmental agencies, and other bureaucracies possess. Most of this country's abuses are secrets known to thousands of insiders, at times right down to the lowest paid worker. A list of Congressional exposures in the poverty, defense, consumer fraud, environmental, job safety, and regulatory areas over the past five years would substantiate that observation again and again. The complicity of silence, of getting along by going along, of just taking orders, of "mum's the word" has been a prime target of student activism and a prime factor leading students to exercise their moral concern. When large organizations dictate to their employees, and when their employees, in turn, put ethical standards aside and perform their work like minions—that is a classic prescription for institutional irresponsibility. The individual must have an opportunity and a right to blow the whistle on his organization—to make higher appeals to outside authorities, to professional societies, to citizen groups—rather than be forced to condone illegality, consumer hazards, oppression of the disadvantaged, seizure of public resources, and the like. The ethical whistle-blower may be guided by the Golden Rule, a refusal to aid and abet crimes, occupational standards of ethics, or a genuine sense of patriotism. To deny him or her the protections of the law and supportive groups is to permit the institutionalization of organizational tyranny throughout the society at the grass roots where it matters.

On-the-job citizenship, then, is a critical source of information, ideas, and suggestions for change. Everybody who has a job knows of some abuses which pertain to that industry, commerce, or agency. Many would like to do something about these abuses, and their numbers will grow to the extent that they believe their assistance will improve conditions and not just expose them to being called troublemakers or threaten them with losing their jobs. They must believe that if they are right there will be someone to defend them and protect their right to speak out. A GM Fisher Body inspector went public on defectively welded Chevrolets that allowed exhaust gases, including carbon monoxide, to seep into passenger compartments. He had previously reported the defects repeatedly to plant managers without avail. In 1969 GM recalled over two million such Chevrolets for correction. The inspector still works at the plant, because union and outside supporters made it difficult for GM to reward such job citizenship with dismissal.

The conventional theory—that change by an institution in the public interest requires external pressure—should not displace the potential for change when that pressure forges an alliance with people of conscience *within* the institution. When the managerial elite knows that it cannot command its employees' complete allegiance to its unsavory practices, it will be far less likely to engage in such actions. This is a built-in check against the manager's disloyalty to the institution. Here is seen the significant nexus between full-time and part-time citizens with on-the-job citizens. It is a remarkable reflection on the underdevelopment of citizenship strategies that virtually no effort has been directed toward ending these divisions with a unison of action. But then, every occupation has been given expertise and full-time practitioners except the most important occupation of all—citizenship. Until unstructured citizen power is given the tools for impact, structured power, no matter how democratic in form, will tend toward abuse, indifference, or sloth. Such deterioration has occurred not only in supposedly democratic governments but in unions, cooperatives, motor clubs, and other membership groups. For organizations such as corporations, which are admittedly undemocratic (even toward their shareholders), the necessity for a professional citizenship is even more compelling.

How, then, can full-time, part-time, and on-the-job citizens work together on a wide, permanent, and effective scale? A number of models around the country, where young lawyers and other specialists have formed public interest firms to promote or defend citizen-consumer rights vis-à-vis government and corporate behavior, show the way. Given their tiny numbers and resources, their early impact has been tremendous. There are now a few dozen such people, but there need to be thousands, from all walks and experiences in life. What is demanded is a major redeployment of skilled manpower to make the commanding institutions in our society respond to needs which they have repudiated or neglected. This is a life's work for many Americans, and there is no reason why students cannot begin understanding precisely what is involved and how to bring it about.

It may be asked why the burden of such pioneering has to be borne by the young. The short answer is to say that this is the way it has always been. But there is a more functional reason: no other group is possessed of such flexibility, freedom, imagination, and willingness to experiment. Moreover, many students truly desire to be of service to humanity in practical, effective ways. The focused idealism of thousands of students in recent years brings a stronger realism to the instruments of student action outlined in this book. Indeed, this action program could not have been written in the fifties or early sixties. The world—especially the student world—has changed since those years.

Basic to the change is that victims of injustice are rising to a level of recurrent visibility. They are saying in many ways that a just system would allow, if not encourage victims to attain the power of alleviating their present suffering or future concerns. No longer is it possible to ignore completely the "Other America" of poverty, hunger, discrimination, and abject slums. Nor can the economic exploitation of the consumer be camouflaged by pompous references to the accumulation of goods and services in the American household. For the lines of responsibility between unsafe automobiles, shoddy merchandise, adulterated or denutritionized foods, and rigged prices with corporate behavior and governmental abdication have become far too clear. Similarly, environmental breakdowns have reached critical masses of destruction, despoilation, ugliness, and, above all, mounting health hazards through contaminated water, soil, and air. Growing protests by the most aggrieved have made more situations visible and have increased student perception of what was observed. Observation has led to participation which in turn has led to engagement. This sequence has most expressly been true for minorities and women. The aridity and seeming irrelevance of student course work has provided a backdrop for even more forceful rebounds into analyzing the way things are. Parallel with civil rights, antiwar efforts, ecology, and other campuses causes, which have ebbed and flowed, the role of students within universities has become a stressful controversy which has matured many students and some faculty in a serious assessment of their relation to these institutions and to society at large.

This assessment illuminates two conditions. First, it takes too long to grow up in our culture. Extended adolescence, however it services commercial and political interests, deprives young people of their own fulfillment as citizens and of the chance to make valuable contributions to society. Second, contrary to the old edict that students should stay within their ivory tower before they go into the cold, cold world, there is every congruence between the roles of student and citizen. The old distinction will become even more artificial with the exercise and imaginative use of the eighteen- to twenty-year-old vote throughout the country.

For the first time, students will have decisive voting power in many local governments. One does not have to be a political science major to appreciate the depth of resourceful experience and responsibility afforded by such a role. The quality of electoral politics could be vastly improved, with direct impact on economic power blocs, if students use the vote intelligently and creatively around the country.

Such a happening is not a foregone conclusion, as those who fought successfully in the past for enfranchisement of other groups learned to their disappointment; but there are important reasons why this enfranchisement of the eighteen to twenty year old could be different. Over a third of the eleven and a half million people in this group are college students with a sense of identity and a geographical concentration for canvassing and voting leverage. Certainly, problems of communication are minimized, and a resurgent educational curriculum can be an intellectually demanding forum for treating the facts and programs which grow into issue-oriented politics in the students' voting capacities.

Full use of voting rights will induce a higher regard for students by older citizens, and elected and appointed officials. It is unlikely that legislators will rise on the floor of the legislature and utter the verbose ridicules wrapped in a smug authoritarian condescension that students are accustomed to hearing. From now on, legislators will pay serious attention to students. Therefore the student vote and the student citizen are intimately connected. Student Public Interest Research Groups (PIRGs) composed of full-time professional advocates and able organizers recruited by and representing students as citizens can have an enormous, constructive impact on society. It could be a new ball game, if the student players avoid the temptations of despair, dropping out, and cynicism.

There are other obstacles which students put in their own way that deserve candid appraisal by all those involved in establishing and directing student PIRGs. These are the shoals of personal piques, ego problems, envy, megalomania, resentment, deception, and other frailties which are distributed among students as they are among other people. On such shoals the best plan and the highest enthusiasm can run aground, or be worn to exhaustion by the attrition of pettiness. Even after the PIRGs are established, these frictions can continue to frustrate and weaken their missions. They will surface at every step—from recruitment to choice of subject matters to the relations with the PIRG professionals. They must be averted at every step with candor, firmness, anticipatory procedures, and a goal-oriented adhesion that reduces such interferences to nuisances. Such nuisances will serve to remind all how important are character, stamina, self-discipline, and consistency of behavior with the values espoused to the success of the PIRG idea and its repercussive impact.

Self-discipline must be emphasized in this student age of free-think and free-do. Many kinds of cop-outs come in the garb of various liberated styles which sweep over campuses. Clearly, there has to be, for the purposes discussed in this volume, a reversal of the dictum: "If you desire to do it, you should do it" to "If you should do it, you should desire to do it." Such an attitude makes for persistence and incisiveness. It forces the asking of the important questions and the pursuit of the pertinent inquiries. It develops an inner reserve that refuses to give up and that thinks of ways for causes to be continually strengthened for sustained breakthroughs. The drive for a firmly rooted *initiatory* democracy is basic to all democratic participations and institutions, but initiatory democracy does not rest on the firmaments of wealth or bureaucratic power. It rests on conviction, work, intellect, values, and a willingness to sacrifice normal indulgences for the opportunity to come to grips as never before with the requisites of a just society. It also rests on a communion with the people for whom this effort is directed.

More and more students today are realistic about power, and they reject merely nominal democratic forms which shield or legitimize abuses. The great debates of the past over where power should be placed—in priviate or public hands—appear sterile to them. Students are suspicious of power wherever it resides because they know how such power can corrode and corrupt regardless of what crucible—corporate, governmental, or union—contains it. Moreover, the systematic use of public power by private interests against the citizenry, including the crude manipulation of the law as an instrument of oppression, has soured many of the brightest students against the efficacy of both government and law. At the same time, however, most concerned students are averse to rigid ideological views which freeze intellects and narrow the choices of action away from adaptability and resiliency.

Such skepticism can become overextended in a form of self-paralysis. I have seen too many students downplay what other students have already accomplished in the past decade with little organization, less funds, and no support. Who began the sit-in movement in civil rights, a little over a decade ago, which led to rapid developments in the law? Four black engineering students. Who dramatized for the nation the facts and issues regarding the relentless environmental contamination in cities and rural America? Students. Who helped mobilize popular opposition to the continuance of the war in Vietnam and, at least, turned official policy toward withdrawal? Who focused attention on the need for change in university policies and obtained many of these changes? Who is enlarging the investigative tradition of the old muckrakers in the Progressive-Populist days at the turn of the century other than student teams of inquiry? Who is calling for and shaping a more relevant and empirical education that understands problems, considers solutions, and connects with people? Who poured on the pressure to get the eighteen- to twenty-year-old vote? A tiny minority of students.

Still the vast majority of their colleagues are languishing in colossal wastes of time, developing only a fraction of their potential, and woefully underpreparing themselves for the world they are entering in earnest. Student PIRGs can inspire with a large array of projects which demand the development of analytic and value training for and by students. These projects will show that knowledge and its uses are seamless webs which draw from all disciplines at a university and enrich each in a way that arranged interdisciplinary work can never do. The artificial isolations and ennui which embrace so many students will likely dissolve before the opportunity to relate education to life's quests, problems, and realities. The one imperative is for students to avoid a psychology of prejudgment in this period of their lives when most are as free to choose and act as they will ever be, given the constraints of careers and family responsibilities after graduation. The most astonishing aspect of what has to be done in this country by citizens is that it has never been tried. What students must do, in effect, is create their own careers in these undertakings.

The problems of the present and the risks of the future are deep and plain. But let it not be said that this generation refused to give up so little in order to achieve so much.

A 3
B 4
C 5
D 6
E 7
F 8
G 9
H 0
I 1
J 2